THE AFTERMATH OF REVOLUTION
SLIGO 1921–23

For Winifred, Fiona, Oisín, Sinéad and Aisling

Anam gá chéile, a Chormuic;
fada fola in otharluit
–an fhala ná déna dhuid–
do-bhéara cara ar charuid.

(Let us keep together, O Cormac;
too long does anger last
at a wound inflicted by one friend on another;
bring not such anger on thyself.)

Written by Tadhg m Giolla Brighde Meic Bruaideagha for Cormac O'Hara of
Coolaney *c.* 1581. (*The Book of O'Hara*, Lambert McKenna, SJ (ed.), Dublin, 1951)

A barricade of stone or of wood;
Some fourteen days of civil war;
Last night they trundled down the road
That dead young soldier in his blood:
Come build in the empty house of the stare.

We had fed the heart on fantasies,
The heart's grown brutal from the fare;
More substance in our enmities
Than in our love; O honey-bees
Come build in the empty house of the stare.

William Butler Yeats, Meditations in Time of Civil War (*The Tower*, 1928).

THE AFTERMATH
OF REVOLUTION

SLIGO 1921–23

Michael Farry

University College Dublin Press
Preas Choláiste Ollscoile Bhaile Átha Cliath

First published 2000 by University College Dublin Press
Newman House, St Stephen's Green, Dublin 2, Ireland
www.ucdpress.ie

ISBN 1 900621 38 X (hardback)
1 900621 39 8 (paperback)

Cataloguing in Publication data available from the British Library

Typeset in 11/13 Bembo in Ireland by Elaine Shiels, Bantry, Co. Cork
Printed in Ireland by ColourBooks, Dublin
Index by Helen Litton
Maps by Stephen Hannon

CONTENTS

ILLUSTRATIONS

BETWEEN PAGES 78 AND 79

Adjutant John Durcan, Curry, shot dead in an anti-Treaty attack on Ballymote on 13 September 1922. (Mrs Mary McGuinn)

Batt Keaney in Free State Army uniform during the early days of the Civil War. (Batt Keaney)

The three successful anti-Treaty candidates at the June 1922 election, Seamus Devins (left), Dr Francis Ferran (second from right) and Frank Carty (right). Michael Nevin, Mayor of Sligo, is second from the left. (Mrs Mary McGuinn)

Part of the funeral cortege of 22 September 1922 of the Sligo men killed on Benbulben. (Sr Elizabeth, Mercy Convent, Sligo)

William Pilkington, O/C 3rd Western Division anti-Treaty forces during the Civil War. (Mrs A. McNamara)

The former RIC barracks, Sligo, in flames on 1 July 1922 after the anti-Treaty forces evacuated and burned it. (Sr Elizabeth, Mercy Convent, Sligo)

Anti-Treaty soldiers on duty in the courthouse during Arthur Griffith's meeting in Sligo, 16 April 1921. The officer on the left is said to be Vice-Brigadier Harry Brehony. (George Morrison)

Anti-Treaty troops in a commandeered lorry during Griffith's meeting. (George Morrison)

Captain Harry Benson, anti-Treaty forces, killed on Benbulben, 20 September 1922. His body was discovered on 2 October. (Kilgannon)

Martin Roddy, pro-Treaty chairman of Sligo County Council, 1922–23. (Kilgannon)

The lying-in-state in Gilhooly Hall, Sligo, of 19-year-old Private Michael McCrann, Sligo, accidentally shot dead on 31 December 1921. (Sr Elizabeth, Mercy Convent, Sligo)

A Sligo anti-Treaty column during the Civil War (Richard Mulcahy Collection, R.24842. National Library of Ireland)

TABLES, GRAPHS AND MAPS

TABLES

GRAPHS

MAPS

FOREWORD

SINCE THE MID-1970s there has been a transformation in the historiography of the final stages of the Irish Revolution. This has been caused by
the opening up of a vast range of archival material and by the influence
of changing perspectives. Charles Townshend's *The British Campaign in
Ireland 1919–1921* and David Fitzpatrick's *Politics and Irish Life 1913–1921:
Provincial Experience of War and Revolution* in their different ways pioneered
new, scholarly assessments. These contrasted with the traditional narrative
and biographical approaches which had dominated up to that time;
concentration had been overwhelmingly on the 'high' politics of Dublin
and London, which often inflated the importance of an individual and
was preoccupied with attaching blame and responsibility for the divisions
and tragic events of the era.

A detached research-based appraisal of the Civil War took longer to
emerge, which was principally explained by the acute sensitivity of the
subject. Indeed, in the first edition of *Ireland Since the Famine*, F.S.L Lyons
wrote on the Civil War with more caution than he does on the outbreak
of violence in the six counties in the late 1960s, all too aware of the
subject's potential for stirring up old animosities. My own book, *Green
Against Green: The Irish Civil War*, published in 1988, was the first
archive-based general account of the conflict and, in attempting a non-
partisan stance, was both praised and criticised for being dispassionate. A
considerable proportion of the book was devoted to local and regional
aspects of events notable for their chaos and confusion and for the lack of
any central direction. The introduction to the book expressed the need
for more detailed regional studies in the years to come. At that time there
was no possibility that adequate consideration could be given to all
regions, let alone counties, and it was a fair criticism that social and
economic aspects were underplayed in the book. It has not taken long for
scholars to fill   in many of the gaps, taking advantage of the release of
fresh archive material. Since 1988 a host of files have been opened,

notably in the Army and National Archives in Dublin and the Public Record Offices in London and Belfast.

As a consequence, in the last decade a number of excellent regional studies have appeared following on the major stimulus of Fitzpatrick's work on Clare. Gloria Maguire, in a DPhil thesis, examines the divisions over the Anglo-Irish Treaty on a local level; Joost Augusteijn, in his *From Public Defiance to Guerilla Warfare* compares the revolutionary experience in Derry, Dublin, Mayo, Tipperary and Wexford; Marie Coleman is shortly to publish a study of County Longford in the same period and Peter Hart's *The IRA and its Enemies: Violence and Community in Cork 1916–1923* has already had a profound effect. Augusteijn and Hart were advised by David Fitzpatrick, who also supervised Michael Farry's PhD on Sligo in the Civil War.

For long the West of Ireland has been largely overlooked in studies of the Civil War: concentration in Younger's and Neeson's books was disproportionately on Dublin and Munster. The implication was that the conflict was virtually over by October 1922 in Sligo and Mayo, whereas in reality pro-Treaty forces never completely overcame Republican resistance at any stage in the War. Just as the conflict started in the Four Courts in Dublin with the West oblivious to the fact, so it ended in Dublin and the South without reference to Connacht.

Michael Farry's excellent study does much to correct this false impression. In its character and range this book represents a considerable achievement. In choosing to research Sligo, Farry has made a shrewd choice as a case study. Bordering the six counties and less remote both geographically and culturally than its neighbouring counties of Mayo and Donegal, Sligo was, and still remains, an interesting mix of small towns and rural communities. It has never had the involvement in the Northern Question which could have been reasonably expected given its proximity. Until 1921, it is noted more in Nationalist terms for the vastly different contributions of W.B. Yeats and Countess Markievicz than for involvement in anything else. Sligo is a prime example of a county, in common with Mayo and Wexford, which played only a small role in the War of Independence but a much more significant part in the Civil War. Much debate has centred recently on why areas were active or inactive during the two conflicts. Remoteness and distance from Dublin may well have been essential factors in explaining the reawakened Nationalism of many areas during the Civil War but obviously many other elements should be examined.

By consulting a massive amount of course material, public and private, Farry comes to conclusions which relate not only to Sligo but also to many different parts of Ireland. His work does much to question long-held assumptions about the War – for instance, that Treaty divisions coincided with class ones, that better-off people were more likely to support the Pro-Treaty side, and that Republican resistance represented a continuation of land grievances. Coleman's and Farry's work demonstrates that Hart's conclusions about the sectarian character of the conflict in West Cork should not apply to Ireland as a whole: moreover, Fitzpatrick's negative conclusions regarding the role of the local IRA leadership in causing localities to be active should be re-evaluated. A particularly important, novel and enjoyable part of Farry's book examines the social and economic consequences of the War. There is a strong sense of what it was like to live in that period: a wide range of social issues are studied including food prices, school attendance figures and participation in sport and leisure activities. Such vital considerations can best be studied at a local level.

Farry's work is a highly successful marriage of political, social and economic history. It is to be hoped that his scholarly, non-judgmental treatment of a still-sensitive subject will contribute towards the Civil War being generally viewed in a wider and less partisan manner than has traditionally been the case. This book should become required reading not only for students of the Revolutionary era but also for the interested general reader.

Michael Hopkinson
Stirling, December 1999

ACKNOWLEDGEMENTS

THIS STUDY WOULD never have been completed were it not for the help and encouragement of many people who encouraged my interest in the topic and helped convince me that it was possible to bring it to completion.

In the first place I wish to express my gratitude to those Sligo veterans listed in the bibliography and for their hospitality when approached, often with no prior warning. I want to thank them for sharing their experiences with me and in some cases entrusting me with valuable material. I also want to thank all those too numerous to mention who assisted me in locating veterans and those relations of activists who gave me access to statements and family papers.

I am grateful to the efficient staffs of the National Library, the National Archives, the Military Archives, UCD Archives, the Valuation Office, the Representative Church Body Library, the Grand Lodge of Freemasons Archive, the Institute of Celtic Studies and Historical Research, the Garda Museum, Sligo County Library, Sligo Town Hall and the Public Record Office, London. I wish to thank particularly the principals and Boards of Management of the Sligo primary schools who allowed me access to their records.

I wish to thank Cecil Kilpatrick, the archivist of the Orange Order, who found valuable information about that body in Sligo and Revd Ian Henderson, Sligo, who sent me detailed figures of Methodist numbers in Sligo at the relevant period. Peter Young and Victor Laing of the Military Archives, Seamus Helferty of UCD Archives and John McTernan, now retired, of Sligo County Library were especially assiduous in ensuring that I had not overlooked any relevant material. The subsequent untimely death of Peter Young has been a great loss to the numerous researchers who have benefited so greatly from his expertise and enthusiasm.

Fellow students, Fergus Campbell, Joost Augusteijn, Ferghal McGarry, Patrick Murray, Tom Crean, Jane Leonard, Peter Hart and others gave essential help at critical times. Joe Molloy helped when technical difficulties threatened to disrupt schedules. My brothers and sisters, close friends and fellow teachers all deserve thanks for their unfailing interest in my studies and encouragement to complete this work.

This book is based on a doctoral dissertation submitted for the Department of Modern History in Trinity College, Dublin. The support and interest I received from that Department over the last five years is greatly appreciated. In particular my supervisor, Dr David Fitzpatrick, was an unfailing source of support, criticism and pertinent advice. His obvious belief that I could complete the study when my own belief often wavered was the source of immense assistance and reassurance.

It has been a pleasure to work with Barbara Mennell, Executive Editor UCD Press, who expertly guided me through the process of redrafting and preparing my work for publication.

My wife Winifred, and children Fiona, Oisín, Sinéad and Aisling have been unfailing in their support and have borne stoically my preoccupation with Sligo's Civil War over the past decade. Their belief that the thesis and book could and would be completed helped me enormously.

Michael Farry
Trim, Co. Meath
December 1999

ABBREVIATIONS

Adj.	Adjutant
AD UCD	Archives Department, University College Dublin
A/G	Adjutant General
AOH	Ancient Order of Hibernians
Batt.	Battalion
Bde.	Brigade
C–in–C	Commander in Chief
CM.	*The Connachtman*
Co.C	County Councillor
C/S	Chief of Staff
DE	Dáil Éireann
D/E	Director of Engineering
DED	District Electoral Division
DELG	Dáil Éireann Local Government Department
D/I	Director of Intelligence
GHQ	General Headquarters
GSWR	Great Southern and Western Railway Company
H/A	Home Affairs
IAOS	Irish Agricultural Organisation Society
IGC	Irish Grants Committee
I.H.S.	*Irish Historical Studies*
I/O.	Intelligence Officer
IRA	Irish Republican Army
IRB	Irish Republican Brotherhood
L/G	Local Government
MA	Military Archives, Dublin
M/D	Minister for Defence
MGW	Midland Great Western Railway Company
MP	Member of Parliament
NA	National Archives, Dublin
NLI	National Library of Ireland
O/C	Officer in Command

OMN	O'Malley Notebooks
RDC	Rural District Council
R.H.	*Roscommon Herald*
RIC	Royal Irish Constabulary
S.C.	*Sligo Champion*
SCI RIC	Sligo County Inspector Royal Irish Constabulary
S.I.	*Sligo Independent*
PRO	Public Record Office, London
PRONI	Public Record Office of Northern Ireland
QM	Quartermaster
QMG	Quartermaster General
UIL	United Irish League
W.P.	*Western People*

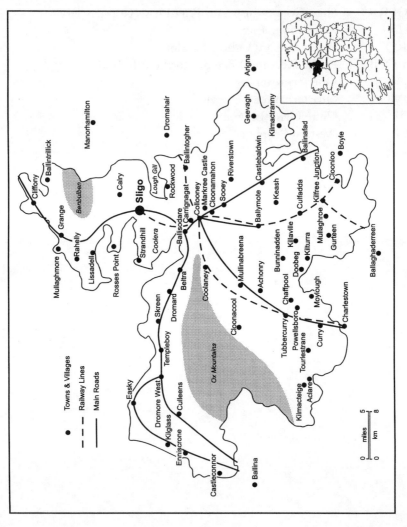

County Sligo: Places mentioned in the text

INTRODUCTION

'THE UNSAVOURY HISTORY of the renaming of those factions as Republicans and Free Staters, of the elevation of territorial jealousy into high-minded principle, and of the civil war which pitted column against column, must await examination by some other student of Chaos.'[1] Thus David Fitzpatrick ended his chapter on guerilla fighters in his pioneering study of the years 1913 to 1921 choosing, as many others had done before him, not to extend the scope of his study beyond the Truce into the 'unsavoury history' of the Civil War. The Irish Civil War has for long been a neglected area in Irish historical writing. The residual bitterness caused by the terrible split and its subsequent hardening into a lasting political manifestation have usually been given as the cause of this neglect: 'The legacy of the conflict is still so divisive that historical research remains far behind that into the Anglo-Irish War.'[2] This in spite of two general works published in the 1960s on the Civil War, each from a different viewpoint, Eoin Neeson's *The Civil War in Ireland 1922–23* (Cork, 1966), Calton Younger's *Ireland's Civil War* (London, 1968). Not until Michael Hopkinson's *Green Against Green: The Irish Civil War* (Dublin, 1988) has there been a detached and analytical study providing a systematic guide to the politics and military operations of the period. However, its concentration on these two aspects is to the detriment of any serious consideration of the war's social or economic aspects. While Hopkinson is particularly effective in analysing the military conduct of the war in the different areas, he does, however, state his belief that local studies of the period are needed to help fill out the history of those years: 'My own work on the regions is necessarily incomplete, and there is a need for detailed local studies'.[3] This work, the first systematic study of a county during the period from the Truce to the end of the Civil War, is an attempt to fill that need.

In an attempt to assess the whole period comprehensively, this book has both chronological and thematic elements. The first four chapters are arranged chronologically and cover the period from the July 1921

Truce to the end of the Civil War in the belief that this forms the smallest period that can usefully be examined as a unit. The reaction of the people and the activists to the Truce and the developments during the latter half of 1921 are vital in considering the standing and the self-image of the IRA and Sinn Féin politicians when the Treaty was signed. In turn, the reaction to the Treaty and the drift towards disagreement and faction during the post-Treaty period had a major role to play in determining the extent of the divisions, the composition of the rival sides and even the duration of the war in the county. The remaining chapters explore the period from different aspects such as the background and geographical distribution of the participants, the extent to which law and order broke down and daily life was disrupted during the period and the effect of the trouble on the Protestant community in the county.

My setting is County Sligo. Not noted for being politically to the fore, in the particular context of the War of Independence Sligo was one of the more inactive counties. Headquarters had berated the Sligo IRA for their lack of activity and Seán MacEoin later taunted the Sligo IRA for the same reason.[4] On the other hand Sligo was one of the areas which gave the Free State army most trouble during the Civil War and there were still small numbers of active guerillas operating there at the ceasefire. Why should a county, which appeared noticeably lacking in bellicosity against the foreign enemy, see so much activity when the foes were native? The answers to this question should enlighten the history of the Civil War not only in County Sligo but nationally.

In some ways Sligo was a typical Connacht county, in others atypical. Eighty five per cent of the population lived in rural districts and almost 70 per cent of its employed persons were engaged in agricultural work. Almost 50 per cent of the agricultural holdings in Sligo were 15 acres or under and only 3.5 per cent were over 100 acres. This was close to the Connacht average. However, the population density on arable and pasture land for Sligo was the highest in Connacht. The marriage rate for the ten years ending 1911 was significantly below the national rate. The proportion of those in the county who could read and write was higher than the Connacht average but lower than the national figure. One-fifth of the population could speak Irish. In terms of population drop between 1901 and 1911 Sligo county was fifth in Ireland, at 6.2 per cent. However, the population of the one large town in the county, Sligo, actually increased by 2.7 per cent during that period.

The second half of the nineteenth century was a period of improvement and prosperity for Sligo town. This improvement was helped by developments in transport by sea and by rail including the introduction of steamships which contributed much to the development of trade with

Liverpool, Glasgow and Derry. As a seaport, Sligo was the most important on the north-west coast of Ireland, exporting annually a large number of cattle and agricultural produce from the surrounding districts. The rise in the town's prosperity was reflected in the erection of new public and commercial buildings, such as the Town Hall, the courthouse and the Bank of Ireland and Ulster Bank, towards the end of the century. The growth of the Catholic middle class was reflected in new Catholic buildings, the friary, the cathedral, Summerhill College and convents and the changing of street names to honour Grattan, O'Connell and Teeling. In spite of the rise of the Catholic middle class the Protestant tradition remained strong in Sligo.

Sligo port continued to thrive until the first signs of decline came after the First World War. An unflattering *Daily Mail* article of November 1917 reprinted in the local newspapers claimed that 'Sligo has in the same time lost a third of its inhabitants, and the little industries it once possessed, of brewing, distilling, cabinet making, and shipping, have dwindled almost to extinction . . .The town wears an air of seediness, and decay, as if a blight had fallen on it. The streets are the dirtiest I have ever seen in any part of the world . . . They (the people of Sligo) have a fine sense of grievances, but none of mending them'.[5] Local businessman and photographer, Tadhg Kilgannon, writing in 1926, lamented that 'It seems a strange fact that while Sligo is advancing by leaps and bounds in elegance and comfort, its industries are almost a thing of the past . . . This writer does not remember when Sligo was an industrial town'.[6]

Sligo had not achieved a high profile in Irish politics by the beginning of the twentieth century. It could not claim to be particularly active as regards anti-government or agrarian agitation. It took no substantial part in any of the great movements of the nineteenth century, preferring to follow loyally at a distance the current national movement. It was not especially agitated at the time of the land war, ranking fourth of the counties of Connacht in the number of agrarian outrages per ten thousand persons during the period 1 January 1879 to 31 December 1882. On the other hand Sligo appeared always to the fore in its espousal of Irish nationalist orthodoxy. There had been little opposition to the Irish Party machine in the county since the North Sligo election of 1891 when the Parnellite candidate was defeated. None of the sitting Irish Party members had to face an election between 1895 and 1918 and local elections, while eagerly fought, had little of the violence associated with them as had similar events for instance in Cork.[7] The Irish Parliamentary Party through its constituency organisation, the United Irish League (UIL) was in control of all public bodies. Sligo was one of the best-organised counties in Ireland and at the end of March 1913 ranked fourth in Ireland for membership per ten thousand of the UIL. Between then and early 1916 while Connacht membership dropped ten per cent, Sligo membership dropped only three per cent, and the county was then ranked second.[8] There was no strong early radical organisation in County Sligo nor was there any record of political dissent. There is no mention, for instance, of any Sligo involvement in support of Sinn Féin in the North Leitrim by-election of 1907.[9] Even a political maverick such as John Jinks, Mayor of Sligo in 1914, operated as a faithful Irish Party supporter and a loyal follower of the North Sligo MP.[10]

The tardiness of the county in organising corps of Irish National Volunteers before that body was officially supported by the Irish Party is a measure of its degree of orthodoxy. A Sligo town branch was founded on 1 February 1914 but the rest of the county was slow to follow.[11] South Sligo was particular resistant to change and no Volunteer branch was formed there before May. Ballymote, where Alec McCabe had been attempting to organise the IRB, did not have a Volunteer branch until the end of July.[12] When the Irish Parliamentary Party did officially back the movement the number of corps increased dramatically.[13] The county quickly swung into line and by September 1914 Volunteer strength in Sligo had reached its apogee with 44 corps and 4,951 members.[14]

With the outbreak of war and the postponement of Home Rule the apparent solid phalanx of support for the Irish Parliamentary Party began to crumble. The appointment of a prominent County Sligo unionist landowner as County Inspection Officer of the Volunteers, with ideas of organising coastal defences against a possible German invasion, brought expressions of dissent from some who felt that the purpose of the Volunteers was different.[15] The landowner soon resigned. Tom Scanlan MP, returning to the town after Home Rule had received the Royal Assent, was heckled when he addressed a meeting on Ireland's duties to the Empire with special reference to the war effort and this resulted in 'a spirited bout of fisticuffs'.[16] The following day Redmond made his Woodenbridge speech which precipitated the split in the Volunteers. The majority of Volunteer branches in Sligo sided with Redmond but the movement soon lost its vitality and the County Inspector RIC reported in March 1915 that 'the Volunteer movement appears dead'. At the same time there was a decline in the activity of the UIL branches in the county. The County Inspector's report of March 1915 said that 'the UIL made no show of activity' and efforts to revive the organisation in the second half of 1915 failed.[17]

The old orthodoxy of the UIL and the Irish National Volunteers was in its death throes but it was not clear for some time what, if anything, was to replace it. During the early part of 1916 it was evident that what the authorities called 'Sinn Féin' was becoming more active. In a review of 1916 the RIC County Inspector said that 'the Sinn Féin party were very active prior to the rebellion and were gaining adherents'.[18] There were other signs, including a blistering attack on 'factionists' by South Sligo MP, John O'Dowd, in April 1916[19] and a letter from a Sligo unionist and landowner to the Irish Unionist Alliance complaining of the government's reluctance to deal with Sinn Féin, 'a movement which is directed against recruiting, and is I fear doing a great deal to stop it'.[20] W.R. Fenton, Clerk of the Peace and Crown in Sligo, told J. M. Wilson at the end of February 1916 that Sinn Féiners in the county were 'more numerous than people think'.[21] Reaction to the 1916 rising was over-shadowed by reaction to the executions. The *Sligo Champion*, a staunch supporter of Redmond, said 'a sickening thud went through the heart of Ireland with each fresh announcement [of executions]'.[22] Many of those UIL and AOH branches still functioning in the county passed resolutions of support for Redmond in conjunction with resolutions demanding the release of those interned.

When the prisoner releases came they were occasions of 'cordial welcome' with even political enemies paying tribute to the ex-prisoners and to the leaders of the rising.[23] During the rest of 1916 no public displays by Sinn Féin or the Irish Volunteers were reported in the county. However, all commentators reported a growth in membership and activity of those groups concomitant with a decline in support for Redmond and the Irish Party.[24]

It was Sligo town which first showed open dissent. In early 1917 a group on Sligo Corporation openly declared their support for Sinn Féin. Many of them campaigned for Count Plunkett in North Roscommon and their leader, merchant Dudley Hanley, was unopposed for the Sligo Mayoralty in 1917. These Sligo-town Sinn Féiners were generally Catholic shopkeepers and businessmen and were prominent in promoting the cause of Sinn Féin over the next two years.[25] Sligo Corporation granted the Freedom of Sligo to Count Plunkett and was the only public body in Sligo to send delegates to Plunkett's Mansion House Conference in April 1917. Early 1917 was a period of growth in the number of Sinn Féin clubs in the county, the County Inspector reporting two clubs in February but 15 by July. At the end of April a South Sligo Sinn Féin executive was formed at a meeting attended by delegates from eight areas. The granting of the freedom of Sligo to Countess Markievicz in July saw a large number of prominent national Sinn Féin figures spend the weekend in the county attending public meetings. A column of reports from Sinn Féin clubs began in the *Sligo Champion* in July 1917. By September the County Inspector was reporting that 'the Sinn Féin movement has spread all over the county' and at the end of December he reported 43 Sinn Féin clubs in the county. Meetings, lectures and aeraíochtaí, sometimes attended by national Sinn Féin speakers, were held throughout the county. When a vacancy arose on Sligo RDC in October 1917 the nominee of the local Sinn Féin club was unopposed.[26] The new political orthodoxy was by then in place.

The figures reported by the RIC for increase in Sinn Féin membership in County Sligo are similar to those for Mayo and Tipperary. Each reported about a tenfold increase in numbers from June 1917 to January 1918 and another rise at the conscription crisis in May 1918. In Sligo's case the highest figure represented just over ten per cent of Catholic males. The corresponding figure for Mayo was just over six per cent.[27] In January 1919 the figures for Sinn Féin membership per ten thousand people show Sligo as the fourth best organised county in Ireland.[28] Sinn Féin in Sligo achieved a membership higher than many of the counties which were to become more active in military terms.

The Sligo County Inspector reported waning interest in Sinn Féin at the end of 1917 but this decline was dramatically halted by the conacre campaign of February 1918 when Sinn Féin took advantage of the till-more-land appeal by the government to harness agrarian unrest. Conacre was commandeered in the name of the Irish Republic by large crowds led by Volunteers or Sinn Féin officials all over the county but particularly in south Sligo.[29] This part of the county had always been to the fore in agrarian agitation and this campaign marked the alliance of the new creed of Sinn Féin with the age old hunger for land. The leader of this campaign was Alec McCabe and the Sligo town Sinn Féin leaders took no part in it. Forty-eight of the 50 indictable offences in County Sligo for February 1918 were related to this conacre campaign.[30] This movement brought a large number of activists into conflict with the police in situations where there was little danger apart from arrest. Many were arrested and imprisoned and there were demonstrations to mark their trials and again to mark their release. These trials gave further chances of demonstrating opposition to the government and of making a laughing stock of the proceedings.[31]

After the conacre campaign the Sinn Féin party found almost imme-diately a new focus for action following the passing of the Conscription Bill on 16 April 1918. The county united against the threat and Sinn Féin leaders, including those from Sligo town, were to the forefront in the opposition. Neither Nationalist MP attended any anti-conscription meeting in the county. 'The Nationalist party has been completely swallowed by the Sinn Féiners', reported the Sligo County Inspector in May.[32] Sinn Féin found itself leading a campaign which was supported by the local nationalist newspapers, all the local government bodies, the trade unions and the Catholic clergy.[33]

These two campaigns, appealing as they did to two basic instincts – life and land, were a perfect platform from which to launch an election campaign. From as early as June 1918 there were reports of clubs preparing for the election which would follow the end of the war. 'The Sinn Féiners worked hard and the organisation was complete down to the last detail', the County Inspector reported.[34] The two sitting Nationalist members were defeated comprehensively as had been widely predicted. The Sinn Féin percentage of the valid poll in North Sligo was 68 per cent and in South Sligo 82 per cent.[35] In South Sligo Alec McCabe, the best known Sinn Féiner in the county, easily defeated the venerable John O'Dowd, a Fenian veteran and a founder member of the United Irish League. In North Sligo the Sinn Féin candidate, J.J. Clancy, had not been as prominent and this may account for his lower vote. The Sligo Sinn Féin candidates had almost the same percentage of the electorate (Clancy 49 per cent, McCabe 51 per cent), the difference being that more anti-Sinn Féin voters turned out in North Sligo. The fact that this constituency had a larger percentage of non-Catholics than the southern constituency may have been a factor. Of the contested constituencies in the country the Sinn Féin share of the poll in South Sligo put it at fourth highest. This with the figures for Sinn Féin membership marks Sligo as one of the most organised pro-Sinn Féin counties in Ireland in 1918.

The existence of a strong anti-Sinn Féin vote in North Sligo was again demonstrated by the results of the Sligo Corporation election held in January 1919 under Proportional Representation.[36] The percentage vote obtained by the parties was as follows: Ratepayers 37 per cent, Sinn Féin 31 per cent, Labour 19 per cent and independents 13 per cent. However, all the Labour councillors and one of the independents were Sinn Féin members or supporters and a Sinn Féin mayor was elected.[37] By the time of the next electoral test, the local elections of May 1920, the hold of Sinn Féin and the Volunteers over the electorate had strengthened. In the Sligo County Council elections Sinn Féin won every seat. Three Ratepayers candidates opposed Sinn Féin in the Sligo area but all failed to be elected. Four independents, including John Jinks, were also unsuccessful. One independent candidate and one independent Sinn Féin candidate withdrew before the election, the latter as a result of a visit by armed men.[38]

At its first meeting on 21 June 1920, the newly elected County Council acknowledged the authority of Dáil Éireann.[39] On 30 June Sligo Corporation also acknowledged the authority of the Dáil. Neither body functioned, however, to the complete satisfaction of the activists during the remainder of the War of Independence. There were times when the anti-Sinn Féin minority on Sligo Corporation became a majority owing to absences due to imprisonment and active service and there were attempts to bring the Corporation back under the wing of the British Local Government Board.[40] The same factors resulted in John Jinks defeating the Sinn Féin nominee in the Sligo Mayoral election in January 1921.[41] Dáil Éireann Local Government Department was not always happy with the way Sligo Corporation maintained its allegiance and instanced two cases of communication with the enemy Local Government Board.[42]

After the split in the Irish National Volunteers, small groups of the breakaway Irish Volunteers continued to survive in some areas of the county especially in Tubbercurry, Keash and Cliffony.[43] The County Inspector estimated their number at 252 in May 1915.[44] Volunteers in these areas were in readiness for the rising in 1916 but did not take any action owing to the confusion caused by the countermanding order.[45] Arrests following the rising were concentrated in the Cliffony area where 15 were arrested, eight of these being released by early June.[46]

It appears that in 1916 Irish Volunteer numbers in Sligo were at a comparable level to counties studied by Augusteijn but that Sligo's reported membership rose less dramatically than the others during 1918.[47] By early 1919, for instance, both Mayo and Tipperary had membership rates of 2.6 per cent of Catholic males while Sligo still languished at 1.2 per cent. It was late 1920 before there was a significant rise in the reported membership level in Sligo, up to 4.7 per cent and this had dropped again the following January. These figures indicate that Volunteer membership developed later in Sligo than in the more active counties.

The earliest actions by the Volunteers nationally were aimed at securing arms and ammunition and, in the light of the low membership of the Volunteers in Sligo, it would be expected that few arms would have been secured. This in turn would be expected to inhibit further growth in membership and preclude effective action in the later stages of the war. The RIC reported that in February 1918 18 rifles, 39 revolvers/pistols and 14 shotguns were in the possession of the Volunteers in County Sligo.[48] This would have allowed only one-third of the Sligo Volunteers at the time to be armed. Mayo Volunteers were reported as having 21 rifles and Tipperary 78 rifles at the same time.[49] Only two arms raids were reported in Sligo in early 1918, both by Volunteers in the Ballymote/Gurteen area of south Sligo resulting in the capture of 20 firearms and 2000 rounds of ammunition.[50] The main potential source of arms was the police but in Sligo the police had withdrawn from vulnerable barracks before the IRA were in a position to attack these. In a sense the

IRA in Sligo 'missed the boat' and by the time they had gained strength there were no easy targets.

Open illegal drilling became a popular way of demonstrating defiance by Volunteers in late 1917. In the last three months of the year six such cases 'without weapons or uniforms' were reported by the RIC in County Sligo. The police did not prosecute, 'No doubt they are anxious to be prosecuted in order to gain a little notoriety' a Sligo Head Constable remarked.[51] These figures for Sligo are very low compared with those for other parts of the country. In November 1917, 334 cases were reported countrywide, 272 in Munster.[52] A county like Cork had been experiencing serious conflict for some time. In March 1918 four rifles were seized from a barracks in Cork and ambushes of policemen were common there during 1918. The first assassination of a policeman occurred in Cork in December 1919 and ten people – six IRA members, two policemen, one soldier and one civilian – had been killed in that county in the period 1917–19.[53] In Sligo, activity during 1919 consisted of nothing more than futile attempts by the police to enforce bans on acraíochtaí, meetings and dramatic productions 'likely to cause disaffection'.[54] Reports of unsuccessful attempts by the RIC to prevent after-Mass meetings in support of the Dáil Loan appeared weekly in October and November in the local press and the only violent confrontation occurred when the RIC attempted but failed to halt a car in which a Dáil Loan organiser and some local Volunteers were travelling from a meeting in South Sligo. This exchange of gunfire between police and Volunteers resulted in no serious injury or loss of life.[55] In August 1919 an organiser from GHQ was sent to the county to help organise the Volunteers. He worked especially in south Sligo where, according to the Sligo Brigade O/C, 'their instincts are agrarian rather than military'.[56] This may have been true but the implied superiority of the O/C's own area seems to have had no basis in fact. Volunteers in north Sligo were neither more organised nor more active. In his December 1919 report the County Inspector said, 'the Irish Volunteers show no sign of activity'.[57]

By October 1919 the County Inspector was reporting a 'growing feeling of hostility to the police' and 'considerable political unrest' and the RIC began the evacuation of small rural police barracks in the county.[58] By September of the following year only eight barracks, including two in Sligo town, remained occupied of the original 34 in the county.[59] During the period May to September 1920 the local press reported many instances of intimidation in order to enforce the police boycott.[60] These included public warning notices, intimidation of and attacks on those who worked for the RIC, destroying houses being occupied by policemen and burning a hackney car which had been hired by policemen.

Shopkeepers were warned not to sell goods to the police and there are reports of police having to commandeer supplies. More notices warning those who were in communication with or supplying goods to the police to cease were posted in Tubbercurry in September, a sign perhaps that the boycott was not being complied with.[61] According to figures compiled by the RIC, the greatest number of 'Outrages against Police' in County Sligo occurred during June and July 1920 with ten and 13 being recorded for these months respectively. For August to November the number per month averaged six and thereafter it dropped to just over two per month.[62] 'Gradually the boycott lost strength and collapsed', the son of a Sligo policeman later wrote.[63] The ostracising of the police by the community was not completely achieved in County Sligo and so the RIC never became legitimate targets in their own right.

To fill the void in policing, the IRA began to undertake police duties and there are reports of petty thieves being apprehended by IRA 'police' in Ballymote in mid-1920. Sinn Féin arbitration courts had been mentioned as early as October 1917, but it was not until the police withdrew from rural barracks that these courts began to replace the Petty Sessions and Quarter Sessions courts in the county. In June 1920 the County Inspector reported that people were boycotting the Petty Sessions courts in favour of the Sinn Féin courts. He also reported that loyalists had gone before Sinn Féin courts and had had agrarian disputes settled there.[64] Sinn Féin District Courts for North and South Sligo began operating in September 1920 though only one sitting of the South Sligo court was actually held before the Truce.[65] According to the County Inspector no Sinn Féin court was held in the county during February or April 1921 and the *Sligo Independent* in mid-April expressed the opinion that the British courts were coming back into favour.[66] The Sligo Brigade Commandant reported in June 1921 that an effort was being made to revive enemy courts in country districts.[67]

Volunteer GHQ officially sanctioned attacks on Crown Forces in January 1920 and this resulted in a wave of attempts to capture RIC barracks all over the country.[68] In Cork, for instance, ten barracks were attacked during the first three months of 1920.[69] It was June 1920, however, before such an attack was mounted in Sligo.[70] The period of greatest activity in Sligo was the second half of 1920. The ten deaths of Crown Forces in the county for that period exceed the figures for Mayo, Wexford and Derry but lag far behind Tipperary and Dublin's figures.[71] The County Inspector said in his June 1920 report, 'Owing to the large area without police supervision they [the IRA] have full scope for drilling and organising and they are taking full advantage of the opportunity'.[72] Raids for arms, raids on postal services and on trains became common.

An attack on a police barracks by Sligo town and north Sligo IRA members in June 1920 failed, either because an officer fell off the roof at an inopportune moment or because grenades failed to explode.[73] The first successful ambush of police in the county took place in east Sligo on 26 July. After a short exchange of fire, rifles were taken from the police who were then allowed to go.[74] The coastguard station at Enniscrone was captured and destroyed in the following month.[75] Members of the Ballymote and Gurteen battalions took part in an ambush of a cycling party of police on 1 September. The extended nature of the police patrol caused confusion and what should have been a simple capture of arms became a shooting match in which one IRA member and three police-men were killed.[76]

On 26 June an impressive operation involving IRA members from Tubbercurry, Collooney and Ballymote as well as Sligo town resulted in the rescue of Frank Carty from Sligo jail.[77] After his rescue Carty gal-vanised the Tubbercurry area into action. A cycling patrol of policemen was ambushed and disarmed and a party of soldiers and police was held up and relieved of their arms. Tubbercurry police barracks was sniped at on a number of occasions during August, two policemen being wounded on one occasion. A new District Inspector, who proved more active than his predecessor, was ambushed and shot dead near Tubbercurry at the end of September. Fearing reprisals, Carty had made elaborate plans for defending the town of Tubbercurry and nearby creameries. These plans proved utterly futile as Auxiliaries came from Sligo and wreaked havoc, burning business premises and private houses and partially destroying two co-operative creameries in the neighbourhood. Significantly, no one was killed or wounded in these reprisals and there were no retaliatory actions by the IRA.[78] At Cliffony in North Sligo, in October, a police cycle patrol was ambushed and four policemen killed. Widespread reprisals by Auxiliaries took place in the area, houses belonging to known IRA activists and the Sinn Féin Hall were burned but again no civilian was killed.[79]

During this period of Sligo IRA activity, three ambushes, each by a different IRA group, had taken place which involved loss of life on the police side. All were ambushes on soft targets, small cycling patrols or single police vehicles. David Fitzpatrick mentions 'overreaction by the Volunteers to overreaction by the government to the actions of the Volunteers' as one reason for the intensification of violence during the period.[80] While the reprisals in Sligo were extensive enough to provide fodder for republican propaganda they were not extreme or extensive enough to provoke the IRA to undertake or the public to support a deadly escalation of the conflict.[81]

The Restoration of Order, Ireland, Act of August 1920 and the arrival of the Auxiliaries towards the end of 1920 altered the situation. The IRA could no longer move about as freely as before and were in greater danger of arrest and internment. Auxiliaries stationed at Boyle, County Roscommon, at Coolavin and Tubbercurry in south Sligo made frequent large-scale searches throughout the county. Towards the end of November Frank Carty was captured while recuperating after illness and the officer who replaced him was arrested in February. At the end of 1920 three officers of the Grange Battalion including the O/C were captured with a large haul of arms, including those taken at the Cliffony ambush, which were being moved to the south of the country.[82] The loss of these important officers and most of the Battalion's arms was a double blow from which the IRA in the area did not recover before the Truce. The discovery by the police of a cache of arms, including ten revolvers, in Sligo graveyard, 'as a result of secret information' was another blow to the IRA in late 1920.[83] The O/C Gurteen Battalion was captured in May 1921 as a result of an escapade in which he hijacked a train and used it as a cover from which to snipe at Ballaghaderreen police barracks.[84] To counter the mobility of the Auxiliaries the IRA began to destroy road bridges but this did not happen extensively until April/May 1921.[85]

As a result of the success of flying columns in parts of the country, GHQ issued an Organisational Memo on the setting up of flying columns on 4 October 1920.[86] The movement of arms and ammunition from north Sligo in November which resulted in the capture of the war material and north Sligo officers, was as a result of a visit by Sligo O/C to GHQ and may have been an attempt to form a Brigade Flying Column.[87] No Brigade Flying Column was in fact formed in Sligo. However, as a result of offensive actions by the IRA and greater pressure by the Crown forces, groups of active Volunteers, usually officers, went on the run in the second half of 1920. A 'flying squad' was formed in the Ballymote area in December 1920 and a 'shock squad' was formed in the Tubbercurry area in early January 1921.[88] Tom Scanlon of the Sligo battalion said that 'there were a number of men on the run but there was no organised column until we formed a small column'. This column consisted of 13 or 14 men but 'they were not as well organised as they were later on' and 'there was not much activity'.[89] By June 1921 a group of up to 25 men was operating on the northern slopes of the Ox Mountains in the vicinity of Dromore West. Apart from some sniping of police barracks the only significant operation by this group was the Culleens ambush of 1 July 1921. For this action the group was augmented by two officers from the Tubbercurry area.[90] These groups also co-operated in a limited number of larger operations. Members of the Gurteen Battalion

IRA co-operated with the East Mayo Brigade in a failed attack on Ballaghaderreen Barracks.[91] An ambush involving officers from IRA in north and south Sligo was set near Collooney in November 1920 but was fruitless. The Carty rescue in June 1920 involved men from many Sligo areas. The O/Cs, Collooney and Riverstown and Tubbercurry Battalions were rescued from Sligo jail at the end of June 1921 in a similar well planned operation which involved 20 men from the Sligo town IRA companies and one from Tubbercurry.[92]

In all there may have been in the region of 50 men involved in these Sligo flying columns.[93] The level of activity did not approach the level for the end of 1920 and the number of Crown Forces' casualties in the county fell to one in the first quarter of 1921 and six in the second quarter. This lagged far behind Mayo and Tipperary but was higher than Derry and Wexford.[94] However, it does appear that while these flying columns lacked the numbers, armament, intelligence and will to take on the enemy in large ambushes or other actions some of these men, cut off as they were from the community, moved further along the road to treating all policemen as enemies to be killed when possible. Unlike the 1920 deaths, few of the 1921 Sligo deaths occurred as a result of large-scale ambushes. In March 1921 two police constables were taken by the IRA from a train at Ballisodare and shot dead in an operation directed by the Sligo Brigade O/C. One was killed because he had directed the Auxiliaries in the carrying out of reprisals after the Cliffony ambush. The other was killed because he happened to be accompanying the marked man.[95] The Cliffony ambush of 1920 involved 38 armed ambushers but at the end of June 1921 only twelve members of the local company, using weapons borrowed from adjoining areas, could be got to lie in wait near Cliffoney Barracks for a policeman going alone to a local shop for cigarettes. He was killed.[96] At the Culleens ambush in July two policemen were taken prisoner and later shot dead when their captors were hard pressed during the retreat into the mountains.[97] In April 1921 a 72-year-old Protestant civil bill officer of Sligo County Court was shot dead by the IRA as a spy, in spite of the claim by the local IRA information officer that he was harmless.[98] This was the only incident of a 'spy' being shot dead in the county. The small number of 'spies' executed in Sligo contrasts with more active counties like Cork and Tipperary where a large number of the casualties were labelled 'spies'.

The lack of arms and ammunition continued to be a problem for the Sligo IRA. Arms in their possession were often shared. Linda Kearns was involved in transporting arms for the IRA in Sligo: 'It seemed as if a couple of flying columns were using the same material. I would bring them to Chaffpool one day and perhaps the next day back to Grange'.[99]

In the Culleens ambush in 1921 each ambusher had only 25–40 rounds of ammunition.[100] The 3rd Western Division was one of the poorest armed divisions according to a statement of munitions from late 1921. It then had 949 guns, almost 700 of which were shotguns. It had only 81 rifles, the lowest number for any division on the list. It had two Thompson machine guns. It was also low in ammunition, 22 rounds per rifle, 17 rounds per revolver.[101]

The perceived lack of activity and results in Sligo was a cause of concern at GHQ. The Sligo O/C, William Pilkington, visited GHQ in March 1921 and was reportedly given a dressing down by Collins.[102] As a result of this he organised an attempt, involving Volunteers from many Sligo battalions, to capture Collooney RIC Barracks which proved an embarrassing failure.[103] During the period from January 1921 to the Truce the Director of Information, GHQ, continually complained about the inefficiency of the O/C and of the Information Officer, Sligo Brigade claiming that dispatches were not acknowledged or replied to, queries were left unanswered and reports when submitted were difficult to read.[104] A report by the O/C for March 1921 enumerated only seven attempted actions. Four of these were attempted ambushes which failed because the enemy did not show up, one was the attack on Collooney Barracks which failed, one resulted in the disarming and release of an RIC District Inspector and one was the killing of a policeman in Ballymote.[105] The Adjutant General passed the report on to the Chief of Staff with the comment 'I consider this from Sligo is very poor indeed. Will you deal with it?'[106] As a result of these poor reports complaints were made to the O/C Sligo Brigade that his area was not active enough in the fight. He replied saying that he would not take responsibility for having his area more active 'unless it obtained better consideration in the way of stuff from GHQ'. He later explained that he thought at the time that there was plenty of 'stuff' available and since 'this area had money and willingness to fight' he thought such an attitude would help.[107] The Chief of Staff replied saying that if the O/C was unable to raise the level of activity in his area he could resign and asking if he could suggest another to take his place.[108] As a result of this communication the Battalion officers of Sligo Brigade wrote to the Chief of Staff stating their confidence in their O/C: 'Taking into consideration the small amount of war material at our disposal and the extraordinary enemy force in the area very few men would accept the responsibility [Command of the Brigade]'.[109] The reply from the Chief of Staff criticised the lack of satisfactory monthly reports from Sligo and the 'tendency to poor mouth and complain on your part, and it is because I realise the difficulties you are up against and that I know that such an attitude of mind cannot conquer or overcome these difficulties that I am dissatisfied'.[110] This letter had a chastening effect on Pilkington who replied: 'My faults, my shortcomings, my incapacities you have emphasised and depicted very vividly and admittedly correctly. When my battalion officers read your communication it will put an end to their votes of confidence in me'.[111] The complaints from the Sligo O/C do seem to have had the effect of obtaining at least the promise of some supplies from GHQ to increase the Brigade's armaments.[112]

The total number of deaths directly related to the conflict in County Sligo for the period 1920–21 was 19. Seventeen of these were Crown forces including 14 RIC. One British soldier was killed as was one marine. One person was shot dead as a spy by the IRA and only one IRA activist was killed.[113] No civilian was killed by the British forces as a reprisal or otherwise. These figures contrast sharply with figures from Mayo where 40 Crown Forces were killed and 22 IRA, Tipperary 114 and 51, Wexford ten and two, Derry 15 and eight and Dublin 163 and 35.[114] In Clare about 37 policemen, nine soldiers and six Volunteers were killed as a result of engagements and five civilians were killed as informers.[115] In Cork 190 Crown Forces, 135 IRA and 167 civilians were killed during 1920–21.[116] Thus by the time of the Truce, Sligo county fits into the general picture of Connacht counties showing a moderate level of activity and violence in the latter part of the struggle. It lagged far behind the most active counties especially in the level of deaths recorded as a result of the war. By July 1921 the military situation in the county had reached the stage where small groups of IRA were surviving on the run and at times carried out spectacular actions without ever seriously challenging the British forces.

So why did Sligo play such a minor role in the War of Independence? David Fitzpatrick and others suggest that activity in that war was positively connected with a strong early organisation.[117] County Sligo had no strong significant radical group in the county before 1914 and the Irish Volunteers were slow to spread and quick to decline in the county. The most important radical nationalist activists who did exist in the county were not arrested after the 1916 Rising. Speaking of War of Independence leaders elsewhere Augusteijn says: 'Their prison experience in 1916 radicalized them and gave them sufficient local standing to command support'.[118] Sligo leaders such as McCabe, Carty, Devins and Pilkington missed the experience of the 1916 internment camps and were always some distance behind those who had graduated from that university of rebellion. The Volunteers, inactive in arms gathering at an early stage, were subsequently deficient in armaments and this limited their potential.[119] This in turn resulted in fewer serious attacks on the Crown Forces and fewer reprisals. When attacks and deaths did take place the reprisals were limited in area and intensity. None resulted in loss of life nor was there any civilian death as a result of other Crown Forces' activity. There was therefore no escalation by tit for tat killings. The number of those actively involved in guerilla warfare was limited but some of these had progressed to the stage where they were prepared to use the most vicious type of violence against those who did not fit into their view of nationality.

How did this county which lagged behind others in its activity during the War of Independence prove such an active centre of military anti-Treaty activity? To seek an answer to that we must first consider what happened in the county in the period after the Truce was called. This is the subject of my first chapter.

ONE

THE TRUCE PERIOD

BY MID-1921 SMALL GROUPS OF IRA were surviving on the run in County Sligo and were, at best, able to carry out small-scale actions without ever seriously challenging the British forces. The Truce, which came into effect on 11 July, changed this situation dramatically. Those who had been on the run could now come into the open and those who had been passive IRA members could safely proclaim their allegiance. During the following six months the position of the IRA changed and developed to such an extent that it had become the leading force in the county by the time the Treaty was signed.

The Position of the IRA

The guerrillas who emerged from the mountains and bogs regarded themselves, and sometimes were regarded, as victors over the British. The RIC County Inspector reported in July 1921 that 'The IRA leaders believe there will be peace and take to themselves the entire credit of same'.[1] 'The murderers of yesterday were the statesmen of today. The world applauded them. They were recognised as righteous men who had made their land a nation again', said Irish teacher Pádraig O'Domhnalláin at a Sligo aeraíocht in October.[2] Sligo TD, Seamus Devins, expressed similar sentiments: 'They could not forget that it was the Irish army that brought the Irish question to what it was today and it was the army that would carry them to success in the end'.[3] Even Alec McCabe, TD, who had played a minor role in the IRA and who was to take the pro-Treaty side, said: 'they took their guns and after twelve months hard fighting they established their rights'.[4] The IRA leaders were honoured guests at public events and were often the recipients of rhapsodic addresses containing sentiments such as the following: 'Like many a brave Irishman who loved freedom dearer than life you had the minions of the oppressor ranged against you, as a result of which you were removed from home and friends and suffered the ignominy and tortures of an English convict prison'.[5] At sports meetings, special events such as football matches, tugs-of-war and relay races were confined to IRA members.[6] The local IRA played a football match against a local team at Banada aeraíocht and 'the gunmen came out of the struggle victorious', the *Sligo Champion* reported. Among the spectators at this event were 'several IRA officers in uniform all of them looking well in their dark green.'[7]

By chance immediately after the Truce, the IRA in Sligo had the opportunity to celebrate that most revered of Irish separatist occasions – the funeral of a dead hero. Michael Marren, O/C Ballymote Battalion, was drowned while swimming the day after the Truce came into effect. His funeral became a celebration of the Sligo IRA with an enormous throng of 2,000 Volunteers and those who wished to be associated with them, bearing the hero to his final resting place. The Volunteers marched four deep after the coffin and 'the steady tread of marching men' was, according to newspaper reports, the dominant sound during the ten mile journey. The local newspapers carried lengthy reports including verbal tributes from IRA companies and poetic tributes of varying quality from local versifiers. The *Sligo Champion* recorded the fact that a patrol of British troops reversed arms and stood in tribute as the funeral cortege passed them by.[8] This funeral, coming within a month of the Truce, was an opportunity for a public display of strength and solidarity by the IRA and helped establish it as a significant public presence in the county. The attendance of at least 11 priests at the Solemn Requiem Mass also lent a certain ecclesiastical acceptance to the IRA in the county.

As self-proclaimed victors in the Anglo-Irish war, it appeared as if the IRA would brook no competition in their desire to be regarded as the saviours and leaders of the Irish people. The military men on the republican side in Sligo seemed determined to belittle those on the same side who were perceived to have merely acted as politicians during the war. The glory was to be theirs and theirs alone and the idea of the supremacy of civil government seemed foreign to them. This attitude was not of course confined to County Sligo but was widespread throughout the land. Tod Andrews described how 'nearly all the members of the Dáil overnight became in my eyes 'politicians' . . . a distinction was rapidly being drawn between 'the politicians' and the Army'.[9] Many Sligo IRA leaders were also of course politicians but these left people in no doubt where their prior allegiance lay. Frank Carty, TD, 'reminded his hearers that he was not a man of words but, as perhaps others knew, a man of action (laughter and applause)'.[10] Seamus Devins, TD, speaking at an aeraíocht in Sligo, said, 'he did not profess to be a public speaker. He belonged to the section who believed deeds rather than words counted.'[11] At a similar function in October he said that 'he did not happen to belong to the side of the organisation from which the speeches came . . . He believed that he was elected because he represented what was now popularly known as 'the gunmen' (cheers). He was not offended for having being placed in that category because they would all admit it was the gunmen who had brought things to the condition they were in now'.[12] R.G. Bradshaw at the same event said: 'There were people in the country today who took the opportunity of the existing conditions to make their voices heard in everything that sounded nationalistic and patriotic but there were many of these voices which could not be heard when other conditions were prevailing.'[13] Undoubtedly the voices he referred to were those of Sligo County Council members with whom the IRA had a prolonged and bitter squabble at this period.

Local Government Divisions

To examine the causes of this dispute we need to look back at the last election to the local bodies. At the time of the May 1920 local elections Sinn Féin was the dominant republican organisation and all the successful candidates had been chosen by Sinn Féin clubs.[14] Those returned for Sinn Féin were not a homogeneous group. The growth of Sinn Féin and its political dominance meant that it encompassed many shades of nationalist opinion. This was reflected in the personnel elected, which included two who had previously been Nationalist Party councillors and only two who became senior officers in the IRA or played a prominent part in that organisation.

Elections to the four Rural District Councils in County Sligo also took place in May 1920 and Sinn Féin won all those seats.[15] The chairmen of these RDCs were entitled to become ex-officio members of the County Council and of these four chairmen three, Jim Hunt, Frank Carty and Frank O'Beirne, were to become very active IRA officers during the war.[16] Two others were to be nominated by the relevant Comhairle Ceantair to the County Council, one from North and one from South Sligo. Sligo Brigade IRA asked the North Sligo Comhairle Ceantair to nominate the Commandant of the Grange Battalion IRA, Seamus Devins, and they did this.[17] For South Sligo, Michael Marren, Commandant of the Ballymote Battalion, was nominated and it is fair to assume that this was also done at the request of the Sligo Brigade.[18] Even at this early stage the IRA assumed the right to be directly represented on elected bodies and was prepared to demand this. Thus while the election of councillors resulted in few high ranking IRA members being selected, the subsequent co-options and nominations resulted in many of the more active of the IRA commandants becoming councillors.

The fact that the Sinn Féin members elected in 1920 were not a homogeneous group is not surprising in itself nor does it necessarily follow that a split was inevitable. However, it does suggest that a division was possible and that one possible line of fraction was between those who were interested in politics per se, and those who were primarily interested in the struggle against England which was to be waged by whatever methods were available.

If the genesis of a division in the ranks of the councillors is to be traced to the members elected and co-opted in 1920, then the development of that division must have been helped by the way the struggle for independence evolved in the period between then and the Truce. Those members of the council who were active IRA members went on the run and/or were arrested and were thus unable to attend council meetings. It was impossible to function prominently as a politician and a gunman, and the politicians rather than the military men were generally the only attenders at council meetings in late 1920 and early 1921. This meant that IRA leaders like Carty, Hunt, Devins and Marren were unable to attend and influence council decisions and had either to depend on and trust those who did attend or use other means to influence decisions.

The new County Council did little to deserve distrust. In common with most local bodies throughout the twenty-six counties, at its first meeting it unanimously declared its allegiance to Dáil Éireann and cut its links with the Local Government Board. In retaliation the Board refused to pay the usual grants leaving the council in severe financial difficulties, which were exacerbated by ratepayers taking advantage of the disturbed conditions to refuse to pay rates.[19] Those councillors who regularly attended tried their best to keep the county institutions functioning in very difficult circumstances and in desperation the councillors asked the IRA for help in collecting the rates. 'There seemed no other way out', the Dáil Local Government Department inspector later reported.[20] The IRA recovered £8,000 from rate collectors who had been refusing to pay this to the council. They then demanded the sum of £1,000 as poundage for their services, but this was refused on the basis that they had not actually collected the rates. The chairman of the County Council, J.J. Clancy, met the IRA in early 1921 and on his own responsibility offered them £500. This they refused and told him to have £1,000 ready 'by a certain time or take the consequences'. Clancy paid the money, apparently to R.G. Bradshaw who acted for the IRA in the matter.[21] This affair was investigated by the Local Government Department in the post-Truce period and it appears that the IRA were ordered to refund the money.[22] Meetings on the matter between the Ministers for Defence and Local Government, the Chief of Staff and some of the Sligo officers in late

1921 resulted in the Local Government Department reducing the amount to be repaid by the IRA first to £800 and later to £250. This reduced amount had not been repaid by March 1922 and it appears never to have been paid. The Local Government Department reimbursed the balance of £750 to the council.[23]

J.J. Clancy resigned his seat on the County Council Committee of Agriculture in April 1921 'owing to circumstances over which he had no control' and the council accepted this with regret.[24] A member said 'in all the circumstances he thought the council could only accept the resignation'. Clancy was described by the Dáil inspector in late 1921 as being under a cloud 'from which he is unable to clear himself'.[25] All of this suggests that his handling of the IRA demand for payment for collection of rates landed him in trouble, both with the IRA because of his initial refusal and with other councillors since it appears that they were unaware of the reason for the missing £1,000. Clancy, the sitting TD for North Sligo, was not reselected for the 1921 election and it seems that the main reason for this was the trouble concerning the £1,000.

At the 1918 election the Sinn Féin candidates had been chosen by the Sinn Féin Comhairle Ceantair but by the general election of 1921 an active network of Sinn Féin clubs no longer existed in County Sligo and the selections were made by the IRA commandants.[26] Those selected were high-ranking IRA officers including William Pilkington, O/C Sligo Brigade, Seamus Devins, O/C Grange Battalion, and Tom O'Donnell, adjutant Gurteen Battalion. Alec McCabe, outgoing, was renominated. Pilkington withdrew and Frank Carty, O/C Tubbercurry Battalion, was nominated in his place.[27] The Sinn Féin nominees were elected without a contest. These selections indicate that the power on the republican side had passed from the Sinn Féin clubs to the IRA leadership and that that leadership considered that they themselves should be involved politically. Because there were no other local elections in the county after May 1920 the composition of the County Council reflected to a lesser degree the ascendancy of the IRA; this was a source of tension and possible conflict.

Very little dissension was reported among those councillors who could attend meetings during this period. Whatever tension existed was between those who were able to attend and those who were not. When some vacancies on Sligo County Council had to be filled by co-option, a meeting was held in the mountains near Coolaney in March 1921 for the purpose. Meetings were normally held in the council chamber in Sligo town and it seems that a remote location was chosen in this instance to allow councillors on the run ensure that the co-options would be to their satisfaction.[28] The obvious inference was that they could not trust the regular attenders in this matter. Three men were co-opted, one of whom, Michael Nevin, was to become 'the IRA spokesman' on the council.[29]

Although no clearly defined split had developed in the County Council by the time of the Truce it was already clear that tensions existed between councillors who were also active IRA members and rarely attended and those who had been able to attend council meetings regularly. To add to this, friction and bad feeling had arisen between IRA Headquarters and Sligo Brigade during the early part of 1921 as a result of criticism of the Sligo IRA for their alleged inactivity and for their infrequent and poor quality reporting. The local IRA officers were also very unhappy with the level of support from Headquarters. This was likely to increase the Sligo IRA's distrust of central authority and its determination to exercise control over county affairs both political and military.

The major divisions between the IRA and the County Councillors, which very soon became apparent, were centred on three issues; the relatively minor matter of whether a council employee should be dismissed or not, the more far-reaching question of whether the Dáil Local Government Board amalgamation scheme should be adopted as proposed, and the issue of IRA interference in and dictation to the County Council. All were issues of control, centralism and patronage. Eventually these divisions were to be reflected in the division on the question of the Treaty. These three strands of disagreement of course proceeded simultaneously in the County Council, but in the interests of clarity I shall deal separately with them.

The apparent unanimity and agreement among those on the Sinn Féin side was publicly broken by editorials in the *Connachtman* of 16 and 23 July 1921, bitterly attacking chairman James Gilligan's conduct of a special meeting of the County Council called to discuss the retention of Frank Jinks as clerk.[30] Jinks, a son of former Nationalist councillor John Jinks, had been appointed temporary clerk in the office of the County Council in 1916. Three years later he was made permanent. This was later described by the local government inspector as 'a piece of downright jobbery.'[31] In October 1920 as part of the cost-cutting exercise as a result of the stoppage of grants from the Local Government Board some officials, including Jinks, were made redundant. At the time the *Connachtman* opposed this, suggesting that it would have been better to reduce the pay of the County Secretary.[32] Jinks, however, remained in the office in place of one of the other clerks who had been arrested.[33] This clerk was released sometime in May 1921 and at a meeting in June a resolution, proposed by James Gilligan, dispensing with Jinks's service was passed. On 9 July 1921, Michael Nevin proposed that Jinks be reinstated. In an editorial on the same day the *Connachtman* suggested that the reason for

Jinks's dismissal was his father's politics. 'We dismiss as unthinkable any suggestion that the son should be saddled with responsibility for the actions or words of his father', it said, and went on to repeat the proposal that the salary of the secretary be reduced instead.[34] The chairman, James Gilligan, refused to accept Nevin's proposal on the grounds that it was not in conformity with standing orders and the next issue of the *Connachtman* ran the headline 'Chairman adopts Subterfuge to defeat Colr. Nevin's Motion', and printed editorials in this and its following issue attacking Gilligan as 'incapable of carrying out the duties of chairman with impartiality or efficiency'.[35]

When consulted, the attitude of the Dáil Local Government Department was that Jinks was needed in the office and, although not competent when first appointed, had become so in the meantime. It suggested that he be appointed on three months' probation but the Council refused to sanction this.[36] Gilligan defended himself against the attack in the *Connachtman* and he was strongly supported by other councillors including Martin Roddy.[37] A subsequent *Connachtman* editorial again attacked the chairman, claiming that 'Mr Gilligan is wholly unsuitable for the position he occupies'.[38] The majority of those who supported Jinks later took the anti-Treaty side in the Civil War while most of those who opposed him supported the Treaty. The whole business appears to have started as support for a person from Sligo town against interference from some country members. At a March 1922 meeting at which a motion to remove him from the chair was defeated, Gilligan mentioned a plot against him which, he said, had originated in Sligo.[39] Nevin in the council and the *Connachtman* outside would appear to have rallied the support of all the active IRA councillors to the Jinks cause, including some like Frank Carty and Jack Brennan who lived far from Sligo town and had no reason to support any member of the Jinks family. Gilligan, Hennigan and Roddy were most vocal on the anti-Jinks side. In the light of their many complaints about the interference of the IRA in council matters, it is ironic that in the Jinks case Gilligan and his supporters opposed the Dáil Local Government Board's recommendation and complained about its interference in local matters.

Obviously one of the key figures in the Jinks controversy was the editor of the *Connachtman*, Robert George Bradshaw, who by this time appears to have achieved a position of power within the IRA. At the time of the Truce he was the intelligence officer for Sligo Brigade and when the 3rd Western Division was formed he was appointed its intelligence officer. During the Truce he was also appointed liaison officer for the Sligo area.[40] In October 1921 he was selected as the County Council's representative on the local administrative committee which was to oversee the administration of local government in Sligo in the event of the Truce breaking down.[41] The Dáil inspector commented on Bradshaw's appointment: 'His interest on the Local Government's behalf will I'm afraid be only a secondary one and will be made subservient to that which is now of more concern to him'.[42] Bradshaw's main interest appears to have been the furthering of the power of the IRA locally. In a report of December 1921 the inspector mentioned 'the sinister influence of a man who has ever been causing trouble to the inspectors who were in this county. His influence in IRA circles is so great that he is able to swing the IRA members on the board into opposition.'[43] This man was obviously Bradshaw.

Amalgamation of Poor Law Unions

The second long-running disagreement of the period concerned the question of union amalgamation and in particular the number of representatives Sligo Corporation would have on the new County Home Committee. The Irish local government system had been regularly denounced by Sinn Féin as wasteful, extravagant and inefficient. In County Sligo each of the four electoral areas, Sligo, Tubbercurry, Dromore West and Boyle No. 2, had a Board of Guardians, a Rural District Council, its own workhouse and its own local hospital. The Boards of Guardians were charged with among other things looking after the poor and sick. Recruitment to positions within the system, including dispensary doctor positions and clerkships of Unions, was controlled at local level and patronage appointments were common. There was a desire within Sinn Féin to rid the system of corruption and the Dáil Department of Local Government saw that to achieve this, reform and centralisation were necessary. Thus was born the amalgamation scheme whereby most counties were to have only one central institution, the County Home, to replace the Workhouses and one central hospital to replace the small hospitals in each Union. Inmates of rural workhouses were to be transferred to the County Home in Sligo town or be given 'home assistance'. A single Committee of Management, which would oversee the reformed system, would replace the individual Boards of Guardians. The two great aims of economy and appointment-on-merit would thus be achieved. There was, however, widespread opposition throughout the country to the scheme.[44]

The *Connachtman* had printed a laudatory editorial on the amalgamation scheme in April 1921 saying that it 'will save many thousands of pounds per annum to the ratepayers' and suggesting that it be put in place with as little delay as possible.[45] By July of the same year it had changed its mind and led the campaign of opposition and obstruction, which continued from then until the outbreak of the Civil War. It now considered that substantial alterations would have to be made in the scheme, especially with regard to the constitution of the committee and superannuation for former officials.[46] This change of mind appears to have coincided with the paper's attacks on Gilligan and the development of the split in the council. The *Connachtman's* stand against the proposed amalgamation scheme was supported by the pro-IRA elements in the County Council and Corporation while most of the councillors who had opposed Jinks's reinstatement backed the scheme.

At a council meeting at the end of August Eamon Coogan of the Dáil Local Government Department strongly criticised the tardiness of the county in implementing amalgamation and stressed that the Boards of Guardians and their officials would cease to operate when the new scheme came into operation.[47] The inspector emphasised the savings to the county's finances – £10,000 per annum he claimed – which would result from amalgamation. Gilligan said, 'if it was going to be left to the Boards of Guardians of Sligo County the scheme would never be carried out'.[48] The scheme of amalgamation was adopted by the council at this meeting and was approved by the Department which instructed the council 'to proceed with all speed' to put it into effect.[49]

Sligo Board of Guardians quickly expressed their opposition to what they saw as County Council control of the Committee, though they did pass a resolution adopting amalgamation in principle.[50] Tubbercurry Guardians also were in favour of the scheme but thought the hospital should be in Tubbercurry, not Sligo. The inspector told a County Council meeting that Tubbercurry had deferred discussion from 8 August to 22 August and from then to 12 September, and 'he had no doubt that at the meeting of 12 September they would defer it to Christmas'. In fact Tubbercurry District Council adopted the scheme in September, recognising finally that it was a 'waste of time discussing a hospital in Tubbercurry'.[51] Despite the opposition, the transfer of inmates and patients from the outlying institutions to the County Home was not hindered and was completed by November 1921.[52]

During September all the local bodies selected their representatives for the Committee of Management.[53] The first meeting of the Committee of Management of Sligo County Home was held on 8 October 1921, the ubiquitous Frank Carty was elected chairman and Seamus Devins became vice-chairman. Three lady members were to be co-opted and the inspector explained that the idea was that the ladies should live near the County Home so that they could regularly inspect it. This was not accepted and the co-option was done on a regional basis with one from each area selected. The other criterion for selection was made clear by Carty when he proposed a number of ladies 'who had made great sacrifices and done noble work for the republican movement.'[54]

Now that the workhouses had ceased to exist the only thing left before the new regime would be fully operational was the calling by each Board of Guardians of a special meeting to abolish on one month's notice the offices of all their officials. The Department circularised the Boards of Guardians to this effect in mid-November.[55] Delay in summoning this meeting was another method by which the local Guardians could obstruct the scheme and express their discontent before they were finally consigned to history.

Dromore West Guardians were particularly upset with the failure of their clerk to obtain the position of secretary of the County Home, and they adjourned a series of meetings in November and December 1921 called for the purpose of abolishing the offices. Not only was the clerk a local official but he was also a prominent member of the IRA, the local Commandant reporting that he had 'rendered us invaluable aid in a variety of ways and has proved himself a worthy soldier of the Republic'.[56] They asked a Local Government inspector at short notice to attend a meeting to explain certain matters and used his absence to adjourn the meeting.[57] When an inspector did attend the next meeting it was also adjourned on the grounds that poor attendance rendered it 'not represen-tative'.[58] Soon afterwards, however, the Guardians recognised the inevitable and the inspector reported that 'I have heard from different sources that Dromore West have since caved in'.[59] Tubbercurry Board of Guardians also gave up the fight at this stage and abolished their offices in January.[60]

It was Sligo Board of Guardians who put up the most sustained campaign against the abolition of offices and, in spite of a number of meetings in November and December 1921, repeatedly refused to conform, demanding greater representation on the County Home committee.[61] The inspector reported that one factor behind the opposition was an attempt to keep the clerk of Sligo Union in office as Secretary to the Committee, reporting that 'the clerk I have found to be a double and an able dealer' but that there were other factors, 'the vested interests of the Guardians are at stake'.[62] The twin concerns of local patronage and local appointments were the basis of this opposition which continued well into 1922.

IRA Interference in Local Government

In addition to these two major sources of division there was a series of incidents which indicated that the IRA regarded itself as the supreme authority in the county and had no compunction about dictating to the

County Council. This was the cause of continued conflict on Sligo County Council and of unease in the Local Government Department in Dublin. On the day after the Truce came into effect the commandant of the Ballymote Battalion was drowned. At the next meeting of Sligo County Council J.J. Clancy proposed an adjournment as a mark of respect. All who spoke to the motion praised the dead IRA officer and agreed with the proposal. Councillor Connolly from Tubbercurry, attending his first council meeting, after concurring in the praise said that in his opinion an adjournment would add no respect to the dead person's memory and suggested that discussion was the best way to serve Ireland. 'This man is mad for discussion', a fellow councillor remarked. In the absence of support for his position Connolly did not pursue the matter and the motion was passed without further discussion.[63] Connolly's enthusiasm and naivety appear to have been the reason for his suggestion but the IRA did not take such a kindly view. At the August meeting of Tubbercurry RDC a letter was received from the O/C, Tubbercurry Battalion IRA, stating: 'By order received from the commandant, Sligo Brigade, I am directed to order your council to have a resolution immediately passed rescinding the appointment of Mr Patrick Connolly as substitute for Frank Carty, TD, on the County Council. You are directed to have a better qualified councillor appointed to the position.' Charles Gildea, a leading member of Tubbercurry IRA, proposed a resolution to that effect, and Connolly was replaced.[64] This clear case of IRA dictation to an elected body caused the inspector to comment: 'Sligo Brigade appears to have declared martial law for Sligo as otherwise such action is an unwarranted assumption of power'.[65] The Minister for Local Government asked William Pilkington to comment, and he replied that the action was demanded as a result of Connolly 'refusing to agree to a meeting of Sligo County Council adjourning in respect to the memory of the late Commandant Marren'.[66] The inspector reported: 'There was nothing in the way of hostility to the resolution [to adjourn] and taking the case on its merits Connolly would appear to have been harshly dealt with. His action does not appear to have been sufficiently grievous to justify his removal'. However, he went on to say that the council had not suffered a severe loss by Connolly's replacement and the Minister decided not to take any action.[67]

The next similar incident involved a letter from the IRA to the council in September 1921 asking that Miss Elizabeth McGettrick be co-opted to fill a vacancy on the council. The IRA letter was signed by the O/C Tubbercurry Battalion, Jack Brennan, himself a councillor. 'You have got your orders and it is for the council to obey', he told the meeting and the co-option was carried unanimously. The press reports of the council meeting mention no dissenting voice, though the *Sligo Independent* used the sub-heading 'Obedience to the IRA' in its report.[68] The Local Government inspector in Sligo in a report referred to this action of the IRA. 'The letter struck me as being of a rather pre-emptory nature', he said, noting that the council's procedures were not followed in this case and adding 'this incident appears to be subversive of all recognised procedure'.[69] On 14 October the Adjutant General wrote to the Minister for Local Government asking for further information. 'The question of principle must be faced', he stated, 'and the Tubbercurry IRA must confine their activities to selections and operations of a different nature.'[70] There is no record of the Minister's reply and again no action was taken.

The County Council meeting of 8 October saw open dissent and public division in the council when a number of contentious issues came up for decision.[71] The first such issue was the council's advertising contract. Tenders had been received from the three newspapers in Sligo as well as from those in Ballina and Boyle. On reading the tender from the *Connachtman* the chairman, according to the *Sligo Independent*, was heard to remark sarcastically: 'This is signed by a man called R.G. Bradshaw.' A deputation from the Sligo branch of the Typographical Association claimed that some of the papers (the non-Sligo ones) which had tendered did not comply with the Fair Wages resolution and Michael Nevin proposed a resolution that only the tenders of those which did comply be accepted. A counter proposal that the *Western People*, *Roscommon Herald* and the *Connachtman* be selected was carried. Bradshaw then made a comment about 'scab labour' and there ensued, according to the *Sligo Independent*, 'a passage of arms' between him and the chairman. Gilligan accused Bradshaw of having organised a 'ring' with the other Sligo newspapers to control the price of advertising to the detriment of the ratepayers. Bradshaw admitted that the three Sligo newspaper proprietors had met 'in their mutual business interests' and maintained that where their vital business interests were identical they were justified in taking steps to safeguard them.

The next business of the meeting was the appointment of a rate collector for the Ballintogher area. A letter was received from the O/C, 5th Battalion, IRA, 'strongly recommending' a local man whom he described as 'a most respectable young man of sterling character, an earnest and enthusiastic worker for Ireland'. This person was proposed and seconded. Martin Roddy proposed an ex-RIC man who lived outside the area but the 'respectable man' was selected on a vote of 13–7. Those who voted for him included all but one of those councillors who later took the anti-Treaty side in the Civil War.

A rate collector had also to be appointed for the Tubbercurry electoral division. Carty proposed the ex-master of Tubbercurry workhouse who was about to become unemployed because of the amalgamation scheme. He praised his work for the republican movement saying that he had the support of the officers and men of the 6th Battalion. In seconding this candidate, Brennan said that there had been many worthy candidates for the position but that it had been left to the Sligo Brigade O/C to make the choice and he had chosen the ex-master. The chairman began his reply by saying that he did not like to interfere with the affairs of the IRA. Brennan interrupting said 'Nor you won't be allowed'. This apparently angered Gilligan who replied (hotly, according to the *Sligo Independent*), 'Neither do I like the IRA interfering with the civil affairs of the county'. The temperature then rose considerably with the chairman claiming that a 'hole and corner' meeting had been held in the office of R.G. Bradshaw in Sligo that morning to select a rate collector. Bradshaw, present in his role as reporter, spoke and denied that such a meeting had taken place but admitted that the selection of rate collector, referred to the Brigadier by the 6th Battalion, had been handed over to him and that he had made the selection. 'Are you the County Council?' Gilligan asked Bradshaw, 'Do you think I would be so low as to take any dictation from you?' Bradshaw replied: 'You are only a County Councillor, sir.' Devins and Carty both referred to the fact that, as they saw it, the civil administration had fallen into the hands of the IRA during the war when it was otherwise unable to function. Gilligan took offence at this, saying that he had always been present at council meetings. After some stormy scenes the IRA nominee was confirmed as rate collector.

Less than a week after this meeting Gilligan wrote to the Minister for Local Government, William Cosgrave, complaining about the continued interference of the IRA in the council's affairs. 'From what has taken place at some recent meetings of this County Council in Sligo, it would seem that the civil powers are not masters of their own actions and have to obey the orders of the IRA', he said. He instanced the co-option of Miss McGettrick and the election of the rate collector as examples of IRA interference. This type of dictation, he said, 'raises the important question, whether the civil or military side of our Government is the supreme authority'.[72]

As a result of this the Local Government inspector visited Sligo during 20–23 October 1921 and reported back to the Minister. He remarked that neither of the two rate collectors who had been appointed on the recommendation of the IRA had taken up position by that time. He said that the affairs of the County Council were 'to put it mildly, somewhat perturbed' and that the chairman, Gilligan, had often been embarrassed:

'There is at all times a strong undercurrent of friction between him and the Bradshaw following'. He went on to elaborate on what he saw was the position of the IRA: 'From what I can learn, Mr Bradshaw and the IRA are out to run the business of the council according to their own ideas and there is a good deal of underhand work going on in this connection . . . the IRA seem to think that they can interfere when and where they like in public affairs.' He also reported that he himself was being watched and had been advised by a friendly source not to write from Sligo. In spite of Gilligan's letter and this report, the Local Government Department took no action.[73] It was unable to influence the business of the council to any great extent and relied on local councillors to conduct affairs in accordance with its wishes. The various Local Government inspectors did what they could in the way of advice, threats, letters to the newspapers and reports but their powers were limited. Sligo was not the only county causing such difficulties, 'the Local Government Department had its hands full dealing with difficult local authorities'.[74]

Those who had carried on the struggle as politicians on Sligo County Council or Corporation found themselves isolated and ignored. The cult of the heroes who had defeated the British was being furthered. These divisions in the County Council were later reflected in the divisions over the Treaty. There is in fact no evidence of any politician in County Sligo attempting to move into the limelight during the Truce period, and it appears that the actions of the IRA were based on a combination of the general idea that the people of sound republican principles were only to be found among the ranks of the IRA, and the particular local antagonism which had already developed between politicians and IRA in Sligo.

IRA Organisation

From the point of view of officers, the Sligo IRA was practically at full strength during the Truce period. Most of its officers had evaded imprisonment during the War of Independence. The Sligo Brigade O/C, later O/C of the 3rd Western Division, William Pilkington, had never been captured. Of the eight or so battalions organised in Sligo in late 1919 and early 1920, five of the O/Cs had been captured during the war. Two had been rescued from prison just before the Truce and two others, the most active Sligo IRA leaders Seamus Devins and Frank Carty, were freed with the release of the Sinn Féin TDs in early August. By then the only battalions not led by their pre-Truce O/Cs were Gurteen, where Jim Hunt was still in prison, and Ballymote, where the O/C had drowned. These were replaced but neither replacement had very much time to make his mark. Jim Hunt was the only one of the pre-Truce

O/Cs to take the Free State side in the Civil War and his absence during the July to December period of euphoria may have had a significant influence on this decision. Likewise the Ballymote–Gurteen areas were strongholds of pro-Treaty support when the split came and this may have been due at least in part to the absence of a strong IRA leader there during the Truce period.

Towards the end of August the IRA in Sligo as elsewhere began to set up training camps. In his report on the 3rd Western Division area in November Captain T. Burke mentioned the efforts made at training by the Sligo Brigade. He had attended ten of their training camps and reported that 'practically all the rank and file in addition to the officers and NCOs have been put through a course of camp training'.[75] There are references to at least 16 IRA training camps evenly distributed throughout the county.[76] Some were established in public buildings including a workhouse and a sanatorium, others were established in houses, often belonging to unionists, which were used with or without the owners' permission, food being requisitioned from the locals. The camps catered for numbers ranging from 25 trainees at the smallest to 120 at the large camp established at Cloonamahon sanatorium near Collooney. IRA officers and men attended in relays. The RIC regarded these camps as breaches of the Truce but the official IRA response was that both sides were allowed to train during the Truce.[77] The officers' camp at Coolaney was attended by 24 officers from the Collooney and Tubbercurry battalions. 'The officers appeared to be very raw and lacking in training', according to the camp O/C from Dublin. The three rifles possessed by the group were in very neglected condition and their short arms were only in fair condition. Eight of the officers were reported as being outstanding in appearance, ability and initiative, the general standard among the others was low and there were two who in the opinion of the O/C should not have held office.[78] This training had the effect of holding the IRA together and consolidating the feeling of comradeship and even professionalism. The IRA was at least behaving as a regular army as regards training.

In common with all of Connacht no divisional organisation had been established in County Sligo before the Truce. In November 1921 two officers from GHQ, T. Burke and Brian MacNeill, were sent to inspect the Sligo area as a preliminary to setting up such a divisional structure.[79] Staff Captain Burke's report on the Sligo Brigade is quite complimentary though he did find many shortcomings, reporting that the district was 'very poorly armed and prepared for war'. 'The QMG would fare badly in the hands of some of the local officers', he added, indicating resentment with the failure of GHQ to supply material during the war. He regarded William Pilkington as a 'promising type' and a 'good militarist',

Seamus Devins 'means business' though 'he might possibly need a little steadying influence', while Frank Carty interested himself 'too much in petty local politics' but would be a suitable O/C for the proposed South Sligo Brigade. The remaining officers he regarded as very promising, 'intelligent and willing to work'. Organisation was poor over the whole area, 'battalions in most cases seem to work out their own salvation or ruin independently and to receive but scant attention from the Brigade staffs'.[80] Burke recommended that the divisional staff be drawn almost exclusively from the Sligo Brigade and this advice was followed when the 3rd Western Division was formed soon afterwards. Brian MacNeill was the only outsider appointed to the staff, presumably to provide the required steadying influence. Five brigades, South Sligo, North Sligo, North Roscommon, East Mayo and North Leitrim, comprised the new Division. Pilkington became divisional O/C and Devins and Carty O/Cs of North and South Sligo Brigades respectively.[81] At the end of 1921, the IRA in Sligo had just finished a period of extensive, if not intensive, training and had just been conferred with a divisional structure which gave added prestige to those who six months previously had been hiding in dugouts or languishing in British jails. Added prestige also accrued from the fact that Sligo provided almost all the officers for the new division.

The Sligo IRA, thus boosted, seemed to be in no mood to occupy a subsidiary role or to defer to any civil power. A general levy or IRA rate was imposed in at least some parts of the county. According to the RIC, £1 per house was demanded in the Dromore West area and in the Easkey area subscriptions were being 'extorted under threats of boycott or illegal arrest'. In the Tubbercurry area a calf was taken from a farmer who refused to contribute voluntarily.[82] At the end of October the local papers carried the announcement from the Minister for Defence, Cathal Brugha, ordering that all IRA levies had to be voluntary.[83] What effect this had on collections is not known but it was surely difficult to distinguish at local level between voluntary and compulsory levies. For instance the White Cross collection in Sligo caused controversy.[84] An editorial in the *Connachtman* expressed dissatisfaction with the contributions from those of more extensive means and said that it was intended that these would be revisited 'to see that those who have suffered little or not at all should contribute in strict accordance with their means'.[85] Prominent in the published list of contributors were Sligo Protestant businesses and businessmen. Henry Lyons contributed £20, while Arthur Jackson, Harper Campbell and Pollexfens each gave £25.[86] Allegations were made by a Sligo Protestant that the local committee used unspecified 'compulsory measures' in order to secure contributions. This was denied but the committee promised to refund monies to those who claimed to have contributed under duress. The committee noted threateningly that they were glad 'to be in a position as a result of this correspondence to form an accurate judgement of the disposition of certain of their Sligo neighbours from whom they had expected better things'.[87]

There was no military or judicial opposition to the IRA. The RIC could do no more than observe and report the training of the IRA and the operation of the Sinn Féin courts, both of which activities they regarded as breaches of the Truce. In September 1921, Sligo County Inspector RIC complained that 'the constant illegal acts of the IRA who are becoming bolder and more aggressive every day show that they have no respect for the Truce'. Apart from the camps and the courts few breaches of the Truce were reported by the police or in the local newspapers. On 10 August an incident occurred at Rosses Point when local IRA officer E.J. Bofin, acting as an IRA policeman, attempted to clear a public house of customers including some Marines who were stationed nearby. Shots were fired by Bofin when the Marines attempted to disarm him.[88] A shot was fired at policemen from a party of drilling IRA at Mullaghmore in September.[89] On 19 September hay belonging to a family friendly with policemen was burned at Cliffony. Two female members of the family had had their hair cropped previously because of this friendship and had claimed compensation at Sligo Quarter Sessions.[90] In November 1921 three cars belonging to policemen were reported stolen by the IRA, all in the South Sligo area.[91] Perusal of the files of those loyalists who later claimed compensation from the British Government show few claims containing specific incidents which took place during this period.[92] Five instances of shops having been looted by masked and armed men appear in the files in the period August to December. These are presumed to have been instances of the IRA obtaining supplies, sometimes for training camps, from those who were known not to be sympathetic.[93] Five other loyalists claimed for instances of loss during this period usually for raids on houses resulting in the taking of some property.[94] There is little evidence of new agrarian outrages taking place during this period but where such agitation was already in progress it generally continued unchecked. William Fenton, Clerk of the Crown and Peace, had some of his cattle maimed on 5 and 9 November. It was strongly denied in the local paper that this was the responsibility of the IRA.[95] This lack of widespread incidents indicates that there was no general indiscipline among the IRA during this period.

The IRA seemed then to be in control in the county with no apparent opposition. However, there is a marked absence of ecclesiastical approval, either in the form of favourable public utterances or attendance at functions. No Sligo ecclesiastical figure is quoted in contemporary newspapers as eulogising the IRA. Though eleven clerics attended the Marren funeral, the Bishop did not, nor was mentioned as having been represented. Neither was there any report of a eulogy by a priest at the funeral Mass. It was left to the Catholic Bishop of Clonfert, speaking at the dedication of a new church at Strandhill in August, to comment favourably on the War of Independence when he said:

> The spirit of God has been manifestly moving over this land for the past few years. I need not refer to the troubles we have had, how they were met or how they were borne but we see that we are close to the re-birth of a nation. We see the labours of prudent yet daring men no matter what their enemies say, whose love for their nation is exceeded only by their love for God. We see the people full of piety and devotion and amid all the storm and troubles of the last six years they put their faith in Christ and in Christ's blessed mother.[96]

The Bishop of Achonry spoke at the dedication of a new organ in Collooney in the same month but did not comment on political matters, resisting the temptation to draw parallels between the rebirth of the organ and the rebirth of the nation![97] Those few priests in the county who had been strongly associated with the IRA during the War of Independence continued to be mentioned as attending aeraíochtaí, etc., during the Truce period. There were, however, some instances of public clashes between clerics and the IRA. In the two most prominent cases the perceived anti-IRA actions and utterances of the clerics involved were characterised by the IRA as pro-British and anti-national.

On Sunday 16 October 1921, a group of Volunteers from a nearby training camp marched to Gurteen Catholic church. On previous Sundays the men had occupied the front six seats in the church but this Sunday being ladies' Sodality Sunday those seats were already occupied by sodality members. The lady in charge refused to leave until the officer insisted. At the next battalion meeting it was decided to fine the lady £5 for obstructing the IRA and a notice to this effect was served on her. The Parish Priest complained to the Minister for Defence and the matter was passed via the Chief of Staff to the Adjutant General. He demanded that an apology be offered by the IRA to the lady in question and that the officer in charge of the Mass party be dismissed.[98] A long correspondence followed between Sligo Brigade O/C and the Adjutant General with the Sligo O/C claiming that the Parish Priest had been a long standing enemy of the IRA and Sinn Féin, citing six examples of this animosity dating from 1916. He also claimed that the priest, who resented the IRA attending his church in uniform, had engineered the whole affair.[99] The Parish Priest for his part claimed that the Gurteen IRA O/C had gone about the area saying that 'he would make it hot for

Fr O'Connor', that the IRA would not allow a Christmas parochial fund-raising raffle to take place and that they had picketed a fund-raising parochial dance.[100]

Another republican/clerical dispute arose in the Collooney area in November 1921 when Fr. Durkin CC was accused of being motivated by 'imperial sympathies' and a 'feeling of prejudice against the national language of Ireland' when he preached that some people in his parish were 'putting the language movement before the cause of their spiritual salvation'. His Parish Priest had already raised the ire of the Gaelic League in the area by refusing them the use of the National Schools for Irish language classes: the local Irish teacher taking the remarks as a personal attack on himself replied in the columns of the *Connachtman*.[101] When this letter appeared all but one of the teachers who had been attending the classes absented themselves. The dispute dragged on for some time with the IRA supporting the Irish teacher and imposing a boycott on two schools where the teachers taught.[102]

By December 1921 the IRA had achieved a position of dominance in the county. Almost all of its officers had been free for the whole Truce period. Its officers and men had received at least a rudimentary training and its structure had just been reorganised. Its discipline showed no sign of disintegration. The tendency of the IRA 'to domineer over civilians and to despise "politicians"', mentioned by Dorothy Macardle as developing during the Truce, was present to a large degree in County Sligo.[103] The only public criticism of the IRA had come from some civilians on Sligo County Council and these had been successfully opposed by the IRA on a number of issues. As far as the Sligo IRA was concerned, politics were dead and they were in charge. There had been no attempt to build up other nationalist organisations such as Sinn Féin. The number of Sinn Féin cumainn affiliated in 1921 in Sligo was 46, 17 in North Sligo and 29 in South Sligo but there are no indications from the local papers that any of these were active in this period. Though there were many on the nationalist side in County Sligo who had been slighted by the IRA there was as yet no cause around which they could organise. When such a cause did arise in the shape of the Treaty the IRA was to find itself outnumbered by its opponents.

During this period the IRA took charge in County Sligo, brooking no opposition, especially from mere politicians, and basked in the glory of a war won. How were they going to react when politicians in Dublin voted to accept a settlement worked out by politicians in London which appeared to give less than the IRA believed they had already won?

TWO

THE TREATY

THE 'ARTICLES OF AGREEMENT for a Treaty between Great Britain and Ireland' were signed in the early hours of Tuesday, 6 December 1921. The Irish cabinet meeting at which the Treaty was approved by four votes to three was held on the following Thursday. The editorial writers of the local Sligo newspapers had therefore little time to consider their response but could be expected to voice at least a tentative opinion by the publication date for that weekend.

Reactions to the Treaty

The *Sligo Champion* took very little time to formulate its response and reflected the generally favourable public reaction to the signing of the Treaty. In a long editorial on 10 December entitled 'Peace' it greeted the settlement in terms which stressed its historic nature: 'Thus ends the long period of misrule and oppression and bloodshed which began with the landing of Strongbow and his adventurers on the coast of Wexford in 1172'. It offered a considered assessment, stressing that Ireland would have full control over finances, trade and commerce. It mentioned possible problems with the office of Governor General but said that since he would be appointed 'in like manner as the Governor General of Canada' he would in effect be appointed by mutual consent of the Irish and British governments. The north of Ireland, it accepted, would probably opt out. It pointed to what it called 'the remarkable variation of the oath of allegiance' as evidence that England had abandoned her effort to hold Ireland and 'withdrawn from her position of overlord'.[1]

The *Sligo Independent*, under new ownership since August 1921, had traditionally seen its role as the voice of the unionists of Sligo but the new owner was making valiant efforts to widen its appeal. He had added the title 'West of Ireland Telegraph' to its masthead and announced that the principal aim of the newspaper was to be 'the advancement of agriculture, commerce and industry throughout the entire West of Ireland'. It had decided to refrain from commenting editorially on any issue, 'no sides will be taken by the editorial as the leading article has been abolished altogether'.[2] In line with this policy it offered no opinion on the Treaty only including a paragraph to the effect that 'a peace treaty was signed this week between Ireland and Great Britain and has created high hopes among the people of Ireland'.[3]

On the other hand it took some time for the anti-Treaty element to organise and publicise its opposition. This was not due to the unavailability of a suitable medium. Sligo town had in R.G. Bradshaw, the proprietor and editor of the *Connachtman* newspaper, a very active republican propagandist and later anti-Treaty activist. His newspaper was no stranger to controversy, having been involved, as we have seen, in a bitter and prolonged attack on the Sinn Féin County Council chairman during the Truce period. The *Connachtman*, in its editorial of 10 December entitled 'The Peace Treaty', mentioned the division of opinion at the cabinet meeting but stated that it did not yet intend to comment on the 'vital points at issue as raised by the draft Treaty'.[4] In its issue of the following week it stated its position clearly in a short editorial which made three points. Firstly it asserted that 'we have declared ourselves for the Republic founded by Pearse at Eastertide 1916. To the Republic we now reaffirm our allegiance'. Secondly it said that it would not be influenced in its opinions by 'whatever decision is come to by An Dáil'. Thirdly it said that while it desired peace, that peace must 'pay tribute and do honour to our living dead'.[5] It was the following week, almost three weeks after the signing of the Treaty, before this newspaper commented on the substantive issues in that document. It did so, not by words of its own, but by quoting from Sean Moylan's speech in the Dáil when he said that in place of the Republic, Ireland was offered an Oath of Allegiance (though in fact the allegiance to be sworn was to the Constitution of the Irish Free State, fidelity being pledged to the British monarch), a Governor General, an army entrenched in its flank, and only limited independence. 'It is between the Republic and this Treaty that An Dáil must decide' the editorial concluded.[6]

The response of the IRA in the country as a whole to the signing of the Treaty was, according to Michael Hopkinson, confused and undisciplined.[7] This was also true of Sligo and there were local factors which added to the confusion there. The 3rd Western Division had just been formed, the names of the newly appointed officers having been submitted to the Chief of Staff on the day after the Treaty was signed.[8] Already dealing with putting this new organisational framework into action, the IRA in Sligo was in no shape to offer a considered and coherent response to the Treaty. J.J. 'Ginger' O'Connell, former O/C of the Sligo Brigade, then with IRA headquarters, was actually in Sligo at the time to oversee the formation of the division.[9] He met Pilkington to discuss the Treaty and reportedly was dumbfounded to hear of the Sligo men's opposition. On the other hand the Sligo men were 'very annoyed with Ginger for we knew he had worked hard'.[10] It appears likely that this disagreement with O'Connell, previously a respected colleague, unsettled the Sligo officers and made them immediately less likely to assert their opinions aggressively. There was also continued disagreement between Pilkington and Carty. There is evidence, though slight, that Carty, later the foremost anti-Treaty leader in the county, was initially ambivalent about his position on the Treaty. According to Martin Brennan 'he (Carty) was going to vote for the Treaty but we told him what to do about it'.[11] This is the only evidence for Carty's original intention, which may have been influenced by the animosity between himself and Pilkington. No Sligo IRA Divisional officer or Brigade Commandant was publicly quoted on the Treaty until Jim Hunt spoke at his welcome home from prison function at the end of January saying meekly 'I will stand behind Alec McCabe and Tom O'Donnell and will do my part if necessary'.[12] The IRA leaders, Carty and Devins, were also TDs but neither spoke publicly on his attitude to the Treaty before the Dáil debates; neither spoke during the Dáil debates nor justified his vote immediately afterwards. The first anti-Treaty IRA voice to be publicly reported in Sligo was that of Carty, when he spoke at Tubbercurry on 23 February 1922.[13] It can only be inferred from this that there was a degree of confusion and disorganisation among those who were soon to be on the anti-Treaty side. They may also have been waiting for guidance from a strong anti-Treaty national leadership before revealing their stance.

There was no doubt about the position of the O/C of the 3rd Western Division, William Pilkington. He was involved in the many meetings and conferences which were held by the anti-Treaty faction, and between them and GHQ in the early months of 1922. Among the anti-Treaty group there were different shades of opinion and Pilkington seems to have been a strong voice against compromise. On 10 January, divisional officers including Pilkington met under Rory O'Connor to formulate their anti-Treaty policy.[14] Pilkington was clear on what he wanted: 'They have the money', said Billy Pilkington, 'the press, the clergy and the arms. All our areas are being sapped in one way or another. I vote we here and now form an independent headquarters.' The officers sent a communication to the Minister for Defence, Richard Mulcahy, demanding that an Army Convention meet and an Army Council be set up.[15] Mulcahy met the anti-Treaty officers on 18 January. 'During the discussion Liam Pilkington declared his desire for separation from GHQ'.[16] 'We intend to cut away from this Headquarters', said Pilkington. 'All you', pointing to the staff and to the officers on the left [pro-Treaty], 'want to build up a Free State army so that you can march in step into the British Empire. Do it openly. We stand by the Republic.'[17]

Many of those IRA leaders who later took the anti-Treaty side were members, in some cases chairmen, of public bodies in the county, and thus had ready platforms for expressing their views. These platforms were not used. There was no reported meeting of Tubbercurry District Council, whose chairman was Frank Carty, during this period to express opposition to the Treaty. This tardiness in making a definitive response to the proposed settlement on the part of what was to be the anti-Treaty side was also evident at the Sligo Corporation meeting of 7 December. A proposal was made by an independent member that a telegram of congratulations be sent to de Valera,[18] Griffith[19] and Collins on the signing of the Treaty, but this was successfully objected to by, among others, Michael Nevin, later a strong anti-Treaty voice. He did not, however, criticise the Treaty but advocated a 'wait and see' attitude.[20] This lack of a clear anti-Treaty voice was not confined to Sligo. In County Meath, for instance, Navan Urban Council and Meath County Council passed motions in favour of acceptance of the Treaty in late December 1921. Unsuccessful amendments at both meetings were not out and out condemnations of the Treaty but suggestions that the matter should not be discussed at that time.[21]

By the end of December this 'wait and see' attitude had disappeared and was replaced by a strong anti-Treaty stance. Sligo Corporation discussed the Treaty at a special meeting called by the Mayor, John Jinks, on Thursday 29 December. Jinks proposed a resolution supporting the Treaty and urging Dáil Éireann to ratify it which was carried by a vote of 14 to five. It was clear that there was a deep and fundamental split on the issue among what had been the Sinn Féin/Labour party on the Corporation. Two former Sinn Féin Mayors of Sligo, Hanley and Fitzpatrick, voted for the Treaty while Michael Nevin led the opposition. His speech dealt only with the claim that if the Treaty was rejected war would ensue. 'Let it be war', he said, 'We may go down in the fight but there is one thing that will live and that is the spirit of unconquered Ireland'.[22] The *Connachtman* in its editorial comment on this meeting said that the councillors were 'in pursuit of peace – peace regardless of principle – peace at any price' and were disregarding such fundamental matters as the Oath of Fidelity to a foreign king and the Governor General. It characterised those councillors who voted for the resolution as 'Onetime Unionists, constitutional Nationalists and supposed Republicans'.[23]

The split in the ranks of labour activists in Sligo was apparent with the Transport Union's John Lynch a strong anti-Treaty voice at the Corporation meeting: 'Speaking as a soldier of the Irish Republic he protested against the Treaty as degrading and insulting to the Irish people.' On the other hand the chairman of Sligo Trades and Labour Council, William Reilly, proposed at a meeting in early January 'That we, the members of the Sligo Trades and Labour Council, call upon our representatives in Dáil Éireann to ratify the Peace Treaty in the interests of the workers of Ireland, although we are convinced we will have to fight no matter who rules.' While many members declared their support for ratification they protested that the resolution was 'introducing politics' into the Council and the resolution was not put.[24]

Throughout the country statutory public bodies met and debated their position. By 5 January 1922 a total of 328 such bodies had declared for acceptance of the Treaty and only five had declared against.[25] There was, as we have seen, reluctance on the part of Sligo public statutory bodies to discuss the Treaty and Sligo Corporation was the only such body to do so. An attempt on the part of James Gilligan, the chairman of Sligo County Council, to have that body debate the Treaty was thwarted by an unhappy coincidence. A special meeting of the County Council was called at the end of December 1921 to discuss ratification of the Treaty. As luck would have it, a member of the IRA was accidentally shot dead in Sligo that morning and the meeting had before it a letter from the Battalion O/C asking them to adjourn as a mark of respect. Gilligan read the letter and began to explain why he thought they should not adjourn: 'The County Council is independent, there is nobody only the ratepayers who can come and give them orders'. Jack Brennan interrupted and pointed out that the letter contained a request, not an order. The gallery was filled with IRA members and sympathisers and much heckling and applause came from that quarter. Gilligan made a spirited defence of his point of view in the face of determined anti-Treaty councillors, a vociferous gallery of IRA members and was supported by only one other pro-Treaty councillor.

> *Chairman* – I say again that we are sincerely sorry that any such accident should arise, but I also say that I am not in agreement that in the present grave circumstances, so serious for the future welfare of Ireland, that this Council should adjourn without expressing its views on the national situation . . . They wanted during the past four or five years men of independence, men of backbone, grit and determination to face the common enemy –
>
> *Mr Hughes* – We don't want this b——y harangue here. Stop it (applause and interruption from the gallery)

Chairman – You will have an opportunity of expressing your views later
   on. I came here with the intention of carrying on the meeting
   (interruption).
Mr Hughes (striking the table) – You have a corpse up there in the Hall and
   you have his comrades here, and we won't have this (applause).

Finally a proposal that the meeting adjourn was put and carried with
only three dissenting voices. Many of those who voted for the adjournment
were supporters of the Treaty and there was obviously no co-ordinated
action among the pro-Treaty group with respect to the meeting. On the
other hand the anti-Treaty side was obviously well organised and well
prepared to ensure that its intentions were carried out.[26]

The funeral of the dead IRA member, 19-year-old Michael McCrann
from Sligo town, was another occasion of republican display and cere-
mony. The dead Volunteer was laid in state at the IRA headquarters for
two days with a guard of honour of armed IRA men. All businesses in
the town were closed on the morning of the funeral and twelve priests
attended the High Mass in the cathedral. Twenty-four senior Sligo IRA
officers marched behind the hearse as did IRA contingents from other
parts of the county, as well as Cumann na mBan, Fianna, GAA and
ITGWU members. The streets were lined as the cortege made its way to
the cemetery and British soldiers presented arms as their posts were
passed. The Union Jack flew at half-mast on the Courthouse. Three
volleys were fired at the graveside.[27]

The momentum of public expressions of support for the Treaty grew.
A meeting of County Sligo Farmers' Association at the end of December
unanimously supported ratification. The chairman said that the Treaty
was 'a great measure which offered them complete control of their own
house with opportunities for developing their own distinct civilisation
according to their own ideals'.[28] The Skreen branch of the Farmers'
Association also unanimously supported ratification 'since in our opinion
it is best calculated to bring about peace between the two countries and
harmony and prosperity to the people of Ireland'.[29] The Bunninadden
branch of the Irish Farmers' Union unanimously passed a resolution
thanking McCabe for his pro-Treaty stand while Killaville branch of the
same organisation congratulated him on his able speech in favour of the
Treaty.[30] A meeting of South Sligo Sinn Féin Comhairle Ceantair held on
Sunday 1 January in Ballymote, which was attended by delegates from
24 cumann, passed a resolution supporting the Treaty on a vote of 48 to
three.[31] A meeting of Tubbercurry Sinn Féin club resulted in a vote of 19
to seven for ratification and Sinn Féin clubs at Killaville, Gurteen and
Cloonloo, all in south Sligo, voted to ask their TD, Alec McCabe, to
vote for ratification.[32] Collooney club, on the other hand, was reported

as having decided to leave the matter to Dáil Éireann.[33] A meeting chaired by the Parish Priest in Castleconnor, in west Sligo, supported a resolution asking the deputies to ratify the Treaty recognising that while it 'does not give the full measure of freedom to Ireland . . . it gives the best terms that Ireland can obtain'.[34] This is apparently the only report of a County Sligo Catholic clergyman being publicly involved in a response to the Treaty, there being a noticeable silence on their part and on the part of their bishops to intervene in the debate. Sligo clergy seem to have followed the practice adhered to in the rest of the country: 'In the early months of 1922 a number of bishops made clear their support for the Treaty, but in general they relied upon the voters to elect candidates who favoured it in the coming election.'[35]

As the Treaty debates dragged on the *Sligo Champion* complained about the 'long drawn out discussion' and the divisions in the Dáil and country. It claimed that 90 per cent of Irish opinion favoured ratification.[36] The editorial in its first issue for 1922 was entitled 'Political Insanity' and criticised the 'dreary debate . . . tiresome reiteration of argument . . . the same contemptible quibbles and wrangles'. It criticised the deputies who, it claimed, were disregarding the wishes of the people who 'were powerless to enforce their will'. It speculated that the chances of ratification were fifty–fifty and deplored the tendency towards a bitter split in the Dáil and a more bitter split in the country. 'There seems little hope that reason, good sense and true patriotism will prevail' the editorial concluded. The *Connachtman* of the same date published a short editorial which referred to de Valera's 'proposed alternative Treaty of Association' and proclamation to the people which was printed elsewhere in the paper, but said that it would refrain from commenting for the moment. It did of course carry reports of the arguments in the Dáil debate on the Treaty and its headlines included 'Stand True to Ireland and to Your Own', 'Scathing criticism of proposed "Peace" Treaty'.[37]

The news of ratification, when it came, was received in the county with general relief but no public show of rejoicing. In Tubbercurry it was greeted 'with calmness mingled with relief'.[38] The news was received with 'general satisfaction' in Gurteen while in Ballymote a previous rumour that ratification was not likely to succeed caused the news to be 'more gladly welcomed'. Though 'the people were glad peace was in sight they refrained from expressing the joy in illuminations or band parades'.[39] The *Sligo Champion* editorial of 14 January celebrated the first two Saturdays of January 1922 with the ratification of the Treaty and the establishment of the Provisional Government as 'the most fateful days in Irish history'. There was no triumphalism in the editorial but it warned about the country being 'bulldozed by political leaders' and it contained a plea that all Irishmen give their support to Griffith in his task of establishing 'order out of chaos'.[40]

The *Connachtman*, on the other hand, searched desperately to find what it called 'unmistakable evidence of dissatisfaction at the acceptance of the Treaty' in Sligo town but this consisted merely of the erection of notices on two public monuments. A placard reading 'Sold again – but not for long' was hung on the 1798 memorial opposite the *Sligo Independent* office while the statue of former Nationalist MP, P. A. McHugh, was adorned with a sign reading 'I couldn't do better'.[41] The *Connachtman* editorial on the ratification of the Treaty entitled 'Forging the Chains' used the time-honoured symbolic language of chains, shackles, and seven and a half centuries of tyranny, plunder and exploitation. It attacked the idea that the Treaty ensured more freedom than Ireland had previously enjoyed without using any substantive argument. Instead it used the metaphor of chains and claimed that the newly forged chains imposed by the Treaty, though of home manufacture, were designed in England and though longer than the 'shackles now worn to the verge of breaking' were still unacceptable. It claimed that those who supported the Treaty did so under the influence of a hostile press and threats of war and it assured everyone that the Republic still lived. It also looked for omens of doom in recent events – Dublin Castle had been surrendered to Michael Collins not to the IRA, existing British officials were to be retained and law and order was still to be in the hands of enemy agents.[42] The claim that the Republic still lived was repeated in its editorial on the Sinn Féin Árd-Fheis on 4 February.[43]

The *Sligo Independent* after a long period of self-imposed editorial silence again began to divulge its deepest thoughts in its issue of 21 January hailing the 'Opening of a new era in Ireland'. 'The destiny of Ireland is now in the hands of Irishmen themselves', it said and expressed the hope that its editorials would be useful 'in helping to mould public opinion along the path of common sense and justice'.[44] The same newspaper offered some thoughts on patriotism in its editorial of 18 February: 'We need to learn that there is a patriotism of peace as well as a patriotism of war'.[45]

The anti-Treaty side in Sligo received a boost with the election of Michael Nevin as Mayor of Sligo on 30 January. His proposer expressed the hope that, like Nationalists and Unionists, Free Staters would soon be a thing of the past. John Lynch seconded Nevin. Former Sinn Féin Mayor of Sligo, Dudley Hanley, proposed Henry DePew. Nevin, in his acceptance speech, said 'The only authority we recognise is the Republican government of Ireland'. The meeting was attended by a large interested crowd, including 'young men possessing republican views' who made their support for Nevin very clear by means which the *Sligo Independent* thought 'bordering on intimidation'. 'Under a Free State or a Republic we have been promised greater freedom than ever before and why is it so difficult to permit this liberty at the election of a Mayor which should be lifted higher than mere politics?' the editorial asked concluding with the statement: 'We must have true liberty'.[46] Though many of those who voted for Nevin made it clear that they differed from him in politics, his election was an indication that there was a strong anti-Treaty voice in Sligo which would not be easily silenced. Nevin's strong anti-Treaty acceptance speech suggests that no deal or arrangement of any kind had been put together to secure his election. His election, however, was also an indication that the Treaty split was not yet irreconcilable and that compromise was possible.

Arguments For and Against the Treaty

The arguments put forward in County Sligo by both sides of the Treaty divide seem to have been merely echoes of the arguments that were voiced at great length during the Treaty debate in the Dáil and in the columns of the national newspapers.[47] There appear to have been no local issues which impinged upon the argument in Sligo. Despite the county's closeness, physically and economically, to Northern Ireland the issue of partition hardly surfaced and, apart from an acknowledgement of the likelihood of the six counties exercising their right to remain outside the Free State, it was not mentioned in Sligo newspapers of this period.[48] On the anti-Treaty side the issue of the Republic was mentioned so often as to assume paramount importance. J.R. Treacy, one of the elders of Sinn Féin in Sligo, speaking at a welcome for released prisoners claimed that the welcoming cheer which greeted them was a 'cry of allegiance . . . a profession of loyalty . . . to the still existent Irish Republic'.[49] The theme of the Republic already established was the main argument in editorials in the *Connachtman* of 17 and 24 December. The former editorial, the first in that paper to declare against the Treaty, was entitled 'The Republic' and declared that it was 'strong in the deter-mination to maintain to the end the principle which it (the Republic) symbolises'.[50] In its editorial on the ratification of the Treaty the same paper said 'The Republic still lives and shall continue to live as long as the spirit of nationality endures in our people'.[51] 'The only authority we recognise is the Republican government of Ireland', said Michael Nevin in his acceptance speech after having been elected Mayor.[52]

When details were discussed by the anti-Treaty side, the Oath of Fidelity and the Governor General were mentioned as tangible signs of the control Britain would still exercise. Frank Carty's speech at a Tubbercurry anti-Treaty meeting at the end of February dealt with both the Republic and the oath. He mentioned what he regarded as the 'real issue': 'When we were elected . . . we were elected as Republicans and not as Free Staters or Home Rulers'. Mentioning the oath of allegiance to the Republic he said: 'That oath I regard as sacred and binding and I will not swear another oath pledging fealty to the British king . . . The spirit of the Republic is unconquered and unconquerable'. He concluded by asserting that the people of Tubbercurry would stand by 'the Republic proclaimed by the men of Easter Week, sanctified by their blood and ratified and legalised by two general elections'. What the Treaty granted fell far short of a Republic and would result in less freedom for Ireland, he said, claiming that the 'so-called Treaty would give Ireland merely a mutilated dominion status and make the Irish subjects of the British crown'. For Carty, acceptance of the Treaty meant becoming 'West Britons' and 'crawling slaves in the British Empire'.[53] The *Connachtman* claimed that the Free State was 'simply the British Government masquerading in a new guise'.[54]

When the pro-Treaty side dealt with this issue of the Republic they did this in either of two ways which reflected 'two divergent and competing interpretations of the Treaty settlement'.[55] Alec McCabe appears to have been a lone Sligo voice emphasising the Treaty as a stepping stone to the Republic. During the Treaty debate he said,

> He had come to the conclusion that the Treaty could be honourably and profitably accepted, because it represented the goods delivered and not promised, goods that were never offered, or, indeed, seriously asked for before. Consequently, as a matter of expediency, it was better to take it than run the risk of war or worse. He regarded the oath as a binding obligation on him to use every endeavour to secure the realisation of the ideal. It did not, in his mind, bar any particular method of achieving it. The Treaty meant that they secured practically complete control of the army and natural resources, and these were things which no Republican in his sober moments could or should refuse to accept.[56]

Speaking at Jim Hunt's homecoming from jail, McCabe dwelt at length on the reasons for his pro-Treaty vote: 'His conscience told him he was right in voting for the Treaty because it gives Ireland the ways and means to win the Republic'. He mentioned the Republic many times saying that getting control of the army and of the entire resources of the country would bring the obtaining of the Republic nearer. 'At the first opportunity of getting a Republic he would vote for it and as in the past fight for it if necessary', he pledged.[57] Many pro-Treaty commentators on the other hand attacked the idea of a popular commitment or electoral mandate for the Republic. 'In the name of common sense does any-one seriously suggest that the Irish plenipotentiaries went to London to negotiate for the recognition of an Irish republic? . . . On the other hand what could a Republic give that the Treaty does not give?' asked the *Sligo Champion*.[58] Ballinafad Sinn Féin club unanimously passed a resolution condemning those who had voted in Dáil Éireann against the Treaty asserting that they had 'flouted the expressed wishes of their constituents'. It went on to claim that the Dáil had received a mandate for self-determination, freedom and independence but not specifically for a Republic.[59] Many stressed that Ireland had in fact obtained what had been fought for and had been granted a measure of freedom greater than any enjoyed by the country since the Norman invasion. Tom O'Donnell, TD, called it 'the dawn of a day they had not had for 750 years'.[60] The probable material benefits were often mentioned. Alderman D.M. Hanley said 'Under this Treaty the Irish people will have full control of their own monies. You can have as much green white and gold over this Town Hall as you like.'[61] The *Sligo Champion* editorial in reaction to the news of the signing of the agreement enthused that Ireland would be 'absolute mistress of her own domain with full control over finances, trade and commerce and at liberty to work out her own salvation by the energy and capability of her sons'.[62]

On the anti-Treaty side allied with the concept of the Republic went the ritualistic invocation of dead heroes, called 'the living dead' by the *Connachtman*. The same newspaper ingeniously printed the lists of those TDs for and against the Treaty adding the names of the dead signatories of the 1916 proclamation to the anti-Treaty side and declared the result a draw, 64 against 64![63] The only Sligo man to be included in the pantheon of dead heroes invoked by Sligo anti-Treaty orators or leader writers was Martin Savage, killed at the ambush of Lord French at Ashtown, Dublin. 'Is that what Martin Savage went out to fight for?' a republican councillor asked at a Sligo Corporation meeting.[64] The only Sligo man to be killed in action locally during the War of Independence, Thomas McDonagh, was not mentioned presumably because he was a native of the Gurteen area where the IRA leadership was pro-Treaty.[65]

Together with the idea of the Republic being already established went the notion that a successful War of Independence against Britain had resulted in at worst stalemate and at best a glorious victory. Michael Nevin claimed at the Corporation meeting in December that 'we had war before and we were equal to it and we will be able to continue war with equal success'.[66] Carty echoed this, 'For three years the Republic established by the people's will resisted all the might and savagery of their Godless empire . . . British politicians won at the Council Chamber in London what their army and their Black and Tans failed to accomplish on the field'.[67]

Amongst those who had not been militarily active during the war there was no glorification of the previous three years. There was instead relief that the war was over and a fear that it might resume. A speaker at the Farmers' Association meeting on 31 December mentioned 'the terrible conditions existing in the country for the past few years' and said that 'if it (the Treaty) wasn't accepted it would mean chaos, blood and murder all over Ireland'. Sir Malby Crofton, unionist and former landlord, said at the same meeting that 'their country would be destroyed, their homes, their farms and their wives and families might be wiped out altogether if the Treaty was not ratified'.[68] Tom O'Donnell, TD, said in explanation of his Dáil pro-Treaty vote that 'he did not like to risk the lives and properties of the people of Ireland'.[69] Presumably he meant to indicate that he considered that the lives and property of the people were more important than the pursuit of political goals. The *Sligo Champion* in successive editorials warned of the 'dreadful consequences' and 'dire consequences' which would follow the rejection of the Treaty.[70] The anti-Treaty side derided this attitude as accepting peace at any price, contrasting it with 'Peace with Honour' which the *Connachtman* used as the title of an editorial critical of Sligo Corporation's declared support for ratification.[71] A poem in the *Connachtman*, presumably by a local scribe, satirised this desire for an end to strife at any cost:

> Let them rest, the martyred dead,
> For the living want their bread
> And a cosy downy bed
> Free from all anxiety.[72]

It appears that the anti-Treaty side accepted that the majority of the people were indeed in favour of the Treaty settlement. The *Connachtman* editorial of 14 January said as much: 'Today the majority of the people of Ireland may believe that [the country will have a much greater measure of freedom than before] will be so, but we are convinced that as time goes on they will realise that their judgement has been badly at fault . . . But with time will come clearness of vision'.[73] This lack of clearness of vision the anti-Treaty side attributed to the influence of the press or of pro-Treaty politicians. Michael Nevin said, 'the press was trying to stampede the country to get the people to accept the Treaty'.[74] The *Connachtman* editorial on the ratification claimed that those who supported the Treaty did so 'blinded by a dust cloud of false issues, stampeded by a consistently hostile and bitter press, coerced and intimidated by threats of war'.[75] On the other hand, the Sligo pro-Treaty press during the Treaty debates complained that the wishes of the vast majority of the people were being disregarded by the deputies in the Dáil.[76] 'The country finds its expressed wishes disregarded by its elected representatives, the people who should be masters are utterly powerless to enforce their will', a January editorial said.[77]

John Lynch's speech at the Corporation meeting which elected Michael Nevin Mayor, long and rambling, elitist and vainglorious as it was, typified 'the romantic and heroic order which the IRA represented in the minds of many young men'.[78] Lynch said that he supported Nevin for Mayor because 'he [Nevin] was one of the few who had the courage to withstand the onslaught of the enemy' when that enemy 'thought it well to invade this country with fire and sword'. 'I believe my friend [Nevin] and my other friends who withstood this onslaught are in the same position. We are never easy only when we are in the thick of the fight'.[79] There is no evidence that either Nevin or Lynch played any role in the single major ambush of policemen near Sligo town or in any other significant military action during the War of Independence.[80] In Nevin's own account of his activities for the War of Independence period he does not mention taking part in any such operation. He was jailed from March to May 1921 but was released, he believed, as a result of the intercession of the Bishop of Raphoe 'who had some influence with the British authorities'.[81] Lynch's role, if any, in the war is likewise doubtful. In the month of May 1921 he was in Liverpool trying to procure arms for Sligo Brigade, much to the annoyance of GHQ in Dublin.[82]

The signing of the Treaty came as a major blow to the Sligo IRA at a time when they were being divisionalised and it took them some time to make a coherent stand against the settlement. Internal dissension and the lack of initial clear leadership at county, divisional and national level on the anti-Treaty side increased the confusion. Meanwhile the popular verdict in favour of the Treaty was clear and the leading Sligo newspaper, the *Sligo Champion*, was to the fore in expressing this. The rhetoric in County Sligo on both sides of the emerging split mirrored the national arguments to a great extent. On the pro-Treaty side the arguments were based on the desire for peace and recognition that the settlement gave a substantial measure of self-government to the country. On the anti-Treaty side the emphasis was on the historic ideal of the Republic already established to which many considered themselves oath-bound and which they considered greater than any selfish desire for peace or lesser degree of independence. The vehemence of the views expressed in Sligo by the anti-Treaty side and the degree to which they focused on the immediately unobtainable goal of the Republic suggested that it would be extremely difficult to bridge this split between idealism and pragmatism during the following months. The degree of power and independence which the

Sligo IRA had enjoyed during the Truce period also suggested that they would find it very difficult to give their allegiance to any centrally controlling body or function as a loyal branch of a national army whether that army was pro- or anti-Treaty. It would take a remarkable willingness to accept compromise if the division caused by the Treaty was not to result in an armed conflict.

THREE

====

THE DRIFT TO CIVIL WAR

A RUMOUR CURRENT IN Ballymote to the effect that Frank Carty had
been fired on while travelling through Charlestown on the Sligo–Mayo
border was reported in early March 1922. 'This rumour is so sensational
that one can scarcely credit it. The wonder is how a man so deservedly
popular as Brigadier Carty could be made a target by his own countrymen'
the local paper said.[1] The following week it reported that the rumour had
been 'entirely without foundation'.[2] Six months later Carty and his own
countrymen were exchanging gunfire to deadly effect. What happened in
the meantime to cause this? This chapter examines the events of the first
half of 1922 and discusses how these contributed to the outbreak of war
rather than to the advent of peace. It also looks at the election of June
1922, examining how the campaign was fought and the extent to which
the electoral pact agreed by Collins and de Valera was adhered to.

The period was characterised by confusion. The rapid withdrawal
by the British forces left a vacuum, which no body seemed powerful
enough to fill. There was confusion as to where power rested both
politically and militarily and there was confusion as to where loyalty
should or would be given. In Sligo most of the IRA took the anti-
Treaty side and the army split, the separation of the 3rd Western Division
from GHQ, together with the lack of any central anti-Treaty control,
increased the power of local officers. At the same time there was a
general descent into lawlessness which the IRA seemed at best powerless
to prevent, and at worst contributed to. The series of confrontations,
compromises and pacts between the opposing sides increased the uncer-
tainty. Public opinion in the county seemed to favour the pro-Treaty
side but the absence of any way of indicating this added to the confusion.
Originally it had been envisaged that a General Election would be held
in mid-April 1922 and for some this election could not come soon
enough. A *Sligo Champion* editorial said 'The time which must elapse
before a General Election can be held is fraught with the greatest danger
because until stable government backed strongly by public opinion is

established the country will continue to drift into a state that will compare unfavourably with Mexico at its worst or the least desirable of the Central American Republics'.[3]

January–May 1922

After the Dáil vote of January 1922 the next indication of the depth and form of the split was to have been the Sinn Féin Árd-Fheis in February. The *Connachtman* printed de Valera's Árd-Fheis anti-Treaty motion and speculated that 'those who believe the Republic to be dead . . . are likely to receive a severe shock when the result of the ballot [at the Árd-Fheis] is made known'.[4] At the South Sligo Comhairle Ceantair meeting six cumann voted anti-Treaty while 24 voted pro-Treaty and Tom O'Donnell was delegated to vote pro-Treaty at the Árd-Fheis.[5] A report in the *Irish Independent* claimed that the anti-Treaty decision of Tubbercurry cumann was influenced by intimidation including the firing of Verey lights outside the meeting house windows, but this was denied by the chairman of the meeting.[6] There is no record of a North Sligo Comhairle Cheantair meeting to discuss the issue but the Sligo Sinn Féin club appointed R.G. Bradshaw as one of its two anti-Treaty delegates to the Árd-Fheis.[7]

As it happened, the Sinn Féin Árd-Fheis in February decided 'to postpone awkward constitutional and political issues', avoiding a vote on the issue of the Treaty and delaying the election for three months.[8] It seems certain that if a vote had been taken the anti-Treaty side would have been in the majority. The *Connachtman* proclaimed the Árd-Fheis decision to be a 'Sweeping Republican Victory' saying that it 'dealt a severe blow to the supporters of the so-called 'Treaty' and has amply demonstrated that the claim put forward in Dáil Éireann and the general press that the Treatyites have behind them 90 per cent of the Irish people is as false as it is absurd'.[9] The *Sligo Champion* leader writer put a brave face on it: 'Those who desired a split open and unashamed have been sadly disappointed. We hope the postponement of the General Election for three months will be allowed to prove a breathing space for the Irish electorate . . . that it should be availed by either or both parties to dig themselves in and prepare for a long and bitter campaign is too awful to contemplate.'[10]

In the meantime the newly formed 3rd Western Division got a fillip when it took over barracks on the departure of British soldiers and RIC from Sligo.[11] The speedy troop evacuation meant that evacuated barracks were taken over by local IRA units regardless of their Treaty attitude and in the case of Sligo town the attitude was strongly anti-Treaty.[12] Ballymote Courthouse was also evacuated by British military and in mid-February its RIC Barracks was formally handed over to the IRA. The newspapers did not specify which faction of the IRA took possession but it seems that it was a pro-Treaty group.[13]

The 3rd Western Division saw action along the border from early 1922. In January a crisis arose when some of the Monaghan GAA team, including IRA members, were arrested in County Tyrone.[14] Some had papers on them relating to plans for rescuing three prisoners then awaiting execution in Derry jail. This crisis caused the formation of a united IRA Northern policy by Dublin and an Ulster Council Command was established. With the approval of Mulcahy and Collins this Command early in February organised the kidnapping of 42 prominent loyalists in cross-border raids who were held as hostages for the footballers and the three Derry prisoners. A Mayo IRA man, Tom Ketterick, was sent by Collins to Collooney, County Sligo, to help organise these raids.[15] In what was presumably part of this action a number of prominent Sligo Protestants were also kidnapped and held as hostages. The Sligo Protestants were released after being held for one day, the Derry prisoners having been reprieved on the day the kidnapping took place.[16] Some of those who had been kidnapped from across the border were held for much longer. The extent of the 3rd Western Division's involvement in the larger operation is unclear but they were certainly involved in raiding north Fermanagh.

During March 'a state of guerrilla warfare' existed along the border.[17] Tom Scanlon said that his Division became involved as a reaction to the activities of the B Specials: 'The specials used to come across and throw their weight around so we sent down our ASU column.' This column had several engagements with the B Specials and destroyed some outposts. It was operating on the border at the end of March when it was recalled urgently to deal with the situation in Boyle Barracks.[18] The Craig–Collins pact of 30 March resulted in a lessening of activity during April.[19] When it became clear that no worthwhile gains would accrue from this pact, Collins planned a joint IRA offensive with anti-Treaty leaders.[20] There is no direct evidence that the 3rd Western Division was involved in this offensive but it seems probable that it was. Considerable activity among the IRA forces was reported in Sligo in late May, which according to the *Roscommon Herald* was connected with the dispatch of some forces to the 'troubled border area'.[21] Part of the national plan for this offensive involved IRA units who were to take part exchanging their British supplied weapons for guns which were not supplied by the British but imported from Germany.[22] Members of the 3rd Western Division went to Birr where they got the guns – Mausers. This is mentioned by at least two interviewees of Ernie O'Malley but neither mentions any swapping of arms. Tom Scanlon said 'An arrangement had been made with GHQ that they could not give us rifles that had been given by the British but other areas were to give us 100 or 200 rifles. We went to Birr for the Mausers which had been landed in Waterford'[23] and Matt Kilcawley said 'The Mausers came in, we had about twenty of them. About 150 Mausers came into the Brigade'.[24] Whether this was connected with the northern offensive or not, it did increase the armament of the Division and meant that they were better prepared for the war when it did break out. The involvement along the border also gave members the opportunity to see action and to engage in guerrilla warfare of the type that would be commonplace in County Sligo during the second half of 1922.

Another opportunity to operate on a national stage presented itself when in early March a crisis developed in Limerick caused by rival units contesting the right to take over evacuated barracks. For a time it appeared that violence was certain to break out and reinforcements were rushed to the city from many parts including a substantial number of 3rd Western Division troops from Sligo.[25] Eventually the matter was settled without bloodshed and it was generally agreed that the anti-Treaty side came out best.[26] This involvement with a national incident must have increased the confidence of the Division and given it a feeling of comradeship with others of like mind. Both the involvement along the border and in the Limerick affair meant that the Division felt that it was now being taken seriously as part of the army and was calculated to increase the likelihood that the Division would perform strongly in a war against fellow Irishmen.

In the previous chapter I have noted the paucity of clerical pronouncements on the Treaty. This apparent reluctance of the clergy to become publicly involved in the political debate continued during early 1922. The Lenten Pastorals of late February contain the only references to the opinions of the bishops on the political situation and even here only two out of the three Bishops involved saw fit to comment. In his pastoral letter the Bishop of Killala recommended that the Provisional Government 'should get the most generous assistance and cordial co-operation from all classes and sections of the people'.[27] While he acknowledged the possibility and indeed advantage of different political views he said that 'any threats or intimidation on the part of one political party to enforce their ideas on their opponents would be against the moral law and gravely unjust'. He said that there must be 'perfect freedom of thought and liberty of action for the people in general to exercise their lawful rights'. The Elphin pastoral said:

Political freedom will be of little advantage if Irishmen of all creeds and parties are not prepared to co-operate wholeheartedly with each other in the difficult task of reconstruction. A period of national unity and peaceful activity is now essential . . . During the past six years of the nation's crucifixion the young men of Ireland displayed a unity of purpose and a chivalrous valour and discipline for which there is scarcely a parallel in the annals of history. In the days of the nation's resurrection we should endeavour to maintain the same unity of purpose, the same stern discipline, the same high souled honour in our relations with other nations, loyalty and allegiance to the government constitutionally established and controlled by Irishmen and a readiness to obey its laws.

Surprisingly the Lenten Pastoral of the Bishop of Achonry contained no mention of political or national matters.[28] Bishop Morrisroe had been regarded by Sinn Féin as antagonistic to their cause during the War of Independence and there is little doubt but that he was strongly pro-Treaty.[29] His silence may have been due to a belief that as his views were well known an intervention would have done little good and that matters were best left in the hands of the politicians.

The anti-Treaty IRA officers defied the Provisional Government ban and held an Army Convention on 26 March, the 3rd Western Division being well represented with 18 delegates.[30] William Pilkington was elected one of the temporary executive members whose task it was to frame a constitution for the anti-Treaty IRA. This constitution was presented at the next meeting and an executive of 16 was elected, Pilkington not being among them.[31] The holding of the Convention represented a clear break by the anti-Treaty section of the army from GHQ but there was a signal lack of definite decisions. It was decided to reimpose the Belfast Boycott and to collect dog licence money. Financial problems increased for anti-Treaty IRA divisions since the cabinet had decided that only officers who remained loyal and obeyed orders from GHQ would receive financial assistance. This led to an increase in bank raids and commandeering.[32] In practice local IRA units and divisions still had local autonomy for 'despite the establishment of the IRA executive, local initiative remained the dominant characteristic of anti-Treaty actions'.[33]

Elsewhere in Ireland 'during February and March, in one district after another, minor clashes occurred between pro-Treaty and Republican units; arms, munitions and lorries were taken from one side by the other; arrests and counter-arrests were made'.[34] Very few such incidents occurred in Sligo because of the strength of the anti-Treaty IRA and because only one post was held by a pro-Treaty garrison. However, one incident demonstrated how fragile was the allegiance pledged by some members of the IRA. Boyle, County Roscommon, was in the 3rd Western Division area and the Barracks there had been handed over by the British military to the North Roscommon Brigade O/C, Martin Fallon.[35] He declared for the anti-Treaty side and attended the banned Army Convention in Dublin on 25 March. The following Wednesday, however, he had a meeting in Carrick-on-Shannon with pro-Treaty officers which resulted in him and his staff going over to that side. On hearing this, Sligo anti-Treaty Divisional officers who happened to be visiting Boyle barracks took over the position after an exchange of fire and all the pro-Treaty officers left the barracks: 'The mutineers now withdrew and the Barrack is now held by forces of the Republic'. Armed men arrived from all over the 3rd Western Division area to strengthen the barracks defences and ensure that it was not retaken by the pro-Treaty side. The ASU was recalled from the border area and the headquarters of the Division was moved from Sligo to Boyle.[36]

As the break with GHQ occurred individual army members had to declare their allegiance one way or the other. Some few incidents of disciplinary action being taken against those who declared pro-Treaty were reported. In the Tubbercurry Battalion area one 2nd Lieutenant was reduced to the ranks and eight privates were court martialled and sent to Boyle IRA Barracks for 14 days' hard labour.[37] Two IRA men who had been imprisoned in Tubbercurry for having refused allegiance to the anti-Treaty side escaped and made their way towards Ballymote where they attended a dance. A party of 13 anti-Treaty IRA arrived at the dance having apparently been informed that the escapees were there. On being refused admission they sent for the Tubbercurry commandant who forced his way into the hall. The defenders claimed that 50 shots were fired but the commandant said that only half that number were fired, all deliberately aimed wide. Those inside resisted, 'delf were used against rifle and revolver'. At least one person was wounded and the IRA arrested the two escapees and two others for aiding and abetting, and lodged them in Sligo jail.[38] These incidents suggest that discipline was being strongly enforced in the Tubbercurry Brigade area under Brigadier Frank Carty.

The Convention decision as regards the Belfast Boycott resulted in a sudden upsurge in attacks and raids on railway property in March and April 1922. On the Collooney to Limerick GSWR system the company listed nine incidents which occurred in County Sligo between 26 March and 22 April 1922. These included raids for Belfast goods and attempts to stop Free State supporters travelling to rallies at Castlebar and Sligo. Thirty-five incidents were reported by the MGW Company in County Sligo between 26 March and 22 April 1922. The majority of these incidents involved the halting and raiding of trains between Boyle and Ballymote especially near Kilfree Junction. There were approximately

150 raids on the whole of MGW property and the company's reported that the Kilfree Junction area was the single most raided place on their whole system.[39]

Following the decision of the Convention regarding dog licences, a number of IRA men visited post offices in Sligo town and asked for and were given the dog licence money collected to date. The 3rd Western Division IRA issued a proclamation that all dog licences were to be paid for at the nearest IRA barracks on or before 15 April. That this was not fully obeyed is suggested by a later decision to extend the deadline to 30 April.[40]

The problem of lack of finance was partly solved by the anti-Treaty IRA raiding branches of the National Bank, the Provisional Government's bank, on 1 May 1922 by order of the executive.[41] The Quartermaster in the 3rd Western Division was Charles Gildea and he organised the raid on the Sligo branch in which close on £2,000 was taken.[42] Tom Scanlon told Ernie O'Malley that not enough money was taken in Sligo and that 'the QM had to go to Tubbercurry' and Gildea himself noted 'Carried out QMG's order re collection of monies at National Bank, Sligo and Boyle' but no report of any such raid in either Tubbercurry or Boyle appears in local newspapers or elsewhere.[43]

The split in Sligo County Council was now formalised and there was a major national issue of principle – the Treaty – on which to disagree. Between the Treaty and the Civil War (while the Jinks controversy and the amalgamation dispute rumbled on) there were many disagreements on issues relating to the split, and in all these the divisions already apparent were reinforced. In March 1921, Michael Nevin moved a motion that the Council strike a rate of 3d in the pound for the IRA. James Gilligan said he would not have military dictation on the council: 'I will not recognise the unofficial body'. 'And d...n little you recognised the official IRA', replied Brennan. In the division on the adoption of the estimate without the IRA rate, the Hennigan/Gilligan group won 8–7.[44] Comparison with the voting record on the Jinks case shows that all but one who voted for the IRA rate voted in favour of Jinks. At a County Council meeting in March a request was received asking for the use of the council chamber for the purpose of recruiting for the Civic Guard. Nevin proposed and Brennan seconded that this be referred to the proper military authority, meaning the local (anti-Treaty) IRA but an amendment that the request be acceded to was carried.[45]

The General Election Campaign

The widening of the split as a result of the Convention and the break with GHQ was intensified by the fact that an election campaign had begun in the country. Early in March preparations began to be put in place in Sligo: 'Both parties in the Free State, supporters of the Provisional Government and the Republicans, are feverishly preparing for the general election', a local newspaper reported.[46] A conference of pro-Treaty supporters, at which Alec McCabe, TD, presided, was held in Collooney on 13 March and a Director of Elections for the Sligo–Mayo East constituency was appointed as was a sub-director for south Sligo. Significantly a similar position for north Sligo, where there was no out-going pro-Treaty TD, was left vacant.[47] Three organisers were appointed, one for each part of the constituency.[48] At the same time the anti-Treaty side held a meeting in Tubbercurry attended by three outgoing TDs, Frank Carty, Seamus Devins and Francis Ferran, and they set up an executive committee for the constituency.[49]

Campaigning began immediately. Pro-Treaty meetings in south Sligo on Sundays 19 and 26 March were addressed by Tom O'Donnell, TD, and James Gilligan. According to the *Sligo Independent* 'excellent work in the way of canvassing' was done in Sligo [presumably meaning the town of Sligo] at the same time. A pro-Treaty election committee, chaired by a local merchant, was set up in Tubbercurry.[50] The anti-Treaty campaign in the constituency opened with a St. Patrick's Day meeting at Swinford in east Mayo. Speakers included the Mayor of Sligo, Michael Nevin, who assured his listeners that 'Sligo still stood staunchly by the Republic'.[51] By 1 April the *Sligo Independent* could report that 'the election campaign may now be said to be in full swing in Sligo. Free Staters and Republicans have been particularly active as regards to propaganda, handbills been [sic] distributed by both sides'.[52] In this pre-pact period 14 meetings were recorded for the pro-Treaty side and only one for the anti-Treaty side. The anti-Treaty leaders were in the main also IRA leaders and their commitment in this area may have precluded their organising an election campaign, especially at a time when the date of the election had not been definitely settled. Army matters, the campaign on the border, the Limerick affair and the various efforts at national and divisional organisation were obviously more urgent.

The question of whether Labour candidates should stand in the election was both a national and a local one. The labour movement in Sligo was badly divided as a result of the Treaty and this affected its ability to come to an effective decision. Alderman John Lynch, strongly anti-Treaty, considered that labour should not contest the election.[53] A delegation from Sligo Trades and Labour Council, which was generally pro-Treaty, attended the special Labour Congress in Dublin in February which decided to contest the election.[54] At the next Council meeting it was agreed that all affiliated Trade Unions be invited to a special meeting to discuss the matter.[55] At the subsequent meeting on 14 March it was decided that a Sligo branch of the Labour party be formed and this was done at a meeting on 25 March, delegates attending from seven unions affiliated to the Trades Council. William Reilly became president.[56] The *Connachtman*, as might be expected, did not approve of a Labour presence in the election. It noted that of the nineteen societies affiliated to the Sligo Trades Council only seven were represented at the inaugural meeting. It pointed out especially the absence of any support from the powerful Sligo TGWU. According to it 'there is ONE AND ONLY ONE [Capitals as in original] issue on which this election will be fought and it is the maintenance or disestablishment of the Republic. The question of proper labour representation must and shall have the support of every democrat when the existence of the Republic is not as now in jeopardy'.[57] A conference subsequent to the formation of the Labour branch made a tentative decision to put forward a Labour candidate pending meetings to be held in Claremorris, Tubbercurry and Ballina with a final conference of three delegates from each centre to decide the issue.[58] There is no evidence that such meetings ever took place nor was there any further mention of a Labour candidate for Sligo until late in May when it was reported at a Trades Council meeting that no progress had been made. *The Voice of Labour* made no further mention of the possibility of a Sligo candidate.[59] There is no doubt but that the split in the labour movement in Sligo prevented the selection of a candidate there.

During April and May there was a series of confrontations between rival forces throughout the country. Political meetings, especially those addressed by Collins or Griffith, some deep in enemy territory, also caused an escalation of tension.[60] The local Sligo newspapers reported these confrontations at length. Few clashes were reported in County Sligo during this time. The Ballymote RIC barracks had been held by pro-Treaty IRA but on the night of 2 April it was taken by anti-Treaty forces. No resistance was offered and it was believed that the takeover occurred when most of the garrison was attending that day's pro-Treaty meeting at Castlebar.[61] The pro-Treaty forces then took possession of the Courthouse in the town and remained there, with the anti-Treaty forces making no effort to remove them. 'Matters some time ago looked somewhat threatening between these two armed forces causing a certain amount of uneasiness to many', reported the *Sligo Champion* at the end of April, but by then the 'fears of a conflict had been reduced to a minimum'.[62]

All local newspapers devoted much space to the tempestuous Free State election meeting at Castlebar, County Mayo, on 2 April. At one stage there was an attempt by republican supporters to rush the platform while Collins was speaking, and Alec McCabe, who was on the platform, drew a revolver. For a while it appeared that an outbreak of armed hostilities was imminent but the meeting broke up peacefully, having been proclaimed by officers of the anti-Treaty 4th Western Division.[63]

The first notice of a Sligo pro-Treaty meeting to be held on Easter Sunday was a report in the *Sligo Independent* of 1 April, stating it had been officially informed that a 'monster pro-Treaty meeting' would be held in Sligo on that day, to be addressed by Arthur Griffith.[64] The Sligo local papers of the following weekend carried the announcement that William Pilkington, O/C 3rd Western Division, had issued a proclamation dated 7 April prohibiting 'the holding of public meetings and demonstrations of a political nature' in the 3rd Western Division area. According to an editorial in the *Connachtman* this was done in view of the incidents at the Castlebar meeting.[65] An anti-Treaty meeting which was to have been held at Sligo Town Hall on Sunday 9 April was cancelled in accordance with the proclamation. According to the *Roscommon Herald* the meeting was announced by poster only on Thursday evening suggesting that it had been hastily arranged and there is a suspicion that it was announced merely in order that it could be cancelled to demonstrate the republican side's willingness to adhere to their own proclamation.[66] A pro-Treaty meeting which was to have been held at Calry, near Sligo, on the same date was not held 'on the advice of a local priest'.[67]

As the day of Griffith's meeting approached, tension and anxiety rose. On Wednesday the Mayor of Sligo, anti-Treaty Michael Nevin, telegraphed Griffith: 'All public meetings proclaimed in this area by military authority to preserve peace. Is announced that you are to address public meeting at Town Hall, Sligo on Sunday. Authorised by you? Reply requested latest Thursday noon'. Griffith replied: 'Dáil Éireann has not authorised and will not authorise interference with right of public meeting or free speech. I, as President of Dáil Éireann, will go to Sligo on Sunday next'.[68] Seán MacEoin wired: 'As Competent Military Authority of mid-Western Command I know nothing of proclamation'.[69] During Thursday night a column of Provisional Government troops, led by Alec McCabe, entered Sligo under cover of darkness and took up position in the undefended jail.[70] 'I never thought of the jail for it was so far out of our way. I wanted to put them out several times but it was thought to be bad policy so I didn't,' said Tom Scanlon.[71] The Corporation held an extraordinary meeting on Friday at which the Mayor urged all citizens to avoid any political demonstration on the Sunday. Brigadier General

Devins, anti-Treaty IRA, addressed the meeting, saying that the last thing his superior officers would do would be to order their men to fire on the soldiers of Ireland: 'They would carry out the terms of the proclamation to the last man, while at the same time, protecting the civil population'.[72] When it became clear that the meeting would go ahead anti-Treaty troops were drafted into Sligo from all parts of the 3rd Western Division area and from some parts of the 4th Western Division. By Friday the town was reported to be 'almost in a state of siege'.[73] Over a hundred IRA men arrived by train from south Sligo on Saturday and the Enniskillen train was commandeered and used to carry large numbers of IRA into Sligo. Many public buildings occupying strategic positions were occupied, including the Town Hall where the meeting was to be held. Supplies were commandeered and windows were sandbagged. During Saturday, the Bishop of Elphin made unsuccessful efforts to arrange a truce. When the evening train reached Sligo it was ascertained that Griffith, together with Darrell Figgis and Sean Milroy had travelled on it as far as Carrick on Shannon and had been met there by Seán MacEoin with an armed escort of Provisional Government troops. During the night the party arrived in Sligo.

Everything seemed ready for a major outbreak of violence. It was not to be. According to Tom Scanlon, who was Director of Operations on the day, anti-Treaty GHQ told the Sligo officers 'at the last minute on Saturday' that if the banning of the meeting meant the shedding of one drop of blood the proclamation was not to be enforced: 'The Free State got to know of this and that is why they were so courageous. Officers and men did not know what had happened. Morale as a result was very bad'.[74] Liam Mellows later wrote: 'The cause was the issuing on his own responsibility of a proclamation by Commandant Pilkington declaring a meeting in favour of the Treaty to be illegal. The executive could not sustain this action as it would create a precedent it would not be able to follow up elsewhere.'[75] Tom Deignan said, 'When they [pro-Treaty forces] knew there was not going to be a fight they careered around with armoured cars'.[76] Scanlon in another interview told O'Malley that Pilkington 'had been forbidden to interfere by Liam Lynch, the Chief of Staff'.[77]

On Sunday morning a patrol of three pro-Treaty lorries, containing about 40 troops under the command of J.J. O'Connell, arrived from Dublin. It stopped outside one of the hotels, unaware that it was occupied by the IRA, and a ten minute exchange of fire took place in which some IRA were injured and three Free State soldiers were captured. Pilkington asked to meet MacEoin to parley, but the latter demanded that the IRA first vacate the Post Office. They refused and there was no more contact. Commandant Pilkington remained shut up in his own office for most of the day and 'would not see any of his officers', his Information Officer Bradshaw dealing with them instead. Eventually Pilkington met his officers and said that 'he thought this [not opposing militarily the holding of the meeting] was best for the people of Sligo'.[78] Few of his officers were happy. Tom Deignan said that 'Jim Devins was out for a fight' but that 'the discipline of our lads held that day and only under protest was it maintained'.[79] Scanlon also relates that during the day reports came to him that 'the Free Staters were being aggressive, jostling the people' and he ordered two Crossley tenders to be prepared and asked permission to patrol the town. Pilkington refused.[80] Jack Brennan also mentioned this incident, saying that 'they were stopped as they were going out the gates . . . I walked out of the Division as a result'.[81]

In the afternoon the meeting went ahead at the end of the main street opposite the Post Office. One of the pro-Treaty Crossley tenders was used as a platform and a large crowd gathered. The chairman was D.M. Hanley and speakers included Arthur Griffith, Darrell Figgis, TDs O'Donnell and McCabe, James Gilligan, William Reilly and Harry DePew. DePew said that 'he could not help but wonder how the natives of the town could be so backboneless as to allow an English bookie's clerk [Apparently a reference to Bradshaw] to walk into Sligo and set up a military dictatorship without making an effective protest'.[82] The day passed off without further incident, the Dublin party attending a banquet that night and leaving by the train the following day. The IRA evacuated the town on Monday night and Tuesday morning.[83]

In what was clearly an attempt to prevent the *Sligo Champion* gloating at the outcome, its offices and premises were raided and the following week's issue was destroyed. In its report of the raid the *Champion* said, 'The raiders did their work with a completeness which showed that at least one among them had a keen knowledge of the workings of the mechanical side of a printing office', insinuating the involvement of someone from the *Connachtman* office.[84] A full report of the meeting did appear in the other local newspapers, and the sales of the 22 April issue of the *Sligo Independent* was said to have gone up 'many thousands'.[85]

The failure of the anti-Treaty forces to prevent the holding of the meeting in spite of their huge numbers in Sligo had far reaching consequences. Several of the IRA officers resigned because of the fiasco, but Mayo anti-Treaty IRA officer, Padraig Hegarty, claimed to have gone to each individually and persuaded them to withdraw their resignations.[86] Martin Brennan said that as a result of the meeting 'Good lads of ours . . . joined up the Free State'.[87] According to Scanlon, Rory O'Connor and Sean Moylan came down the next day to heal the breach: 'It ruined us. We were powerless. We could not do a thing to stop the Free Staters from walking up and down'.[88] Frank Carty was in Sligo on the day of Griffith's meeting and was afterwards scathing in his comments on how the affair was handled, calling it a 'tragedy'. This added to the rift between himself and Pilkington and influenced his actions at the start of the Civil War when he justified his intention of going it alone without divisional sanction: 'I had strongly before my mind the way the divisional staff had mishandled the situation . . . on the occasion of Arthur Griffith's meeting in Sligo and the disastrous effect which this had on the morale of our troops'.[89] Sligo IRA, often criticised for their poor performance during the War of Independence, were once again made to appear foolish and amateurish.[90] This reinforced the already strong distrust of central authority. Most significantly, for the first time since the split, pro-Treaty forces had been able to establish a post in Sligo town itself from which they could expand.

On 1 May pro-Treaty forces occupied three more posts in Sligo town.[91] During May there appears to have been a considerable amount of sniping between the two forces in Sligo though no reports of injuries appear in the local press. On the morning of 9 May a Mills bomb exploded in the vicinity of the Bank of Ireland which was then under guard by the pro-Treaty forces but no injuries were reported. In mid-May the *Sligo Champion* reported 'not a night has passed but rifle and revolver shots have been heard in Sligo much to the terror of the citizens'.[92] The pro-Treaty forces based in Sligo town made a concerted attempt to expand the number of posts they held on 2 June. They assisted what appears to have been an attempt by local pro-Treaty sympathisers to occupy the Town Hall in Charlestown. Anti-Treaty forces rushed the building before the assistance could arrive and when the cars from Sligo did reach the town they were fired on and had to return.[93] At the same time 40 to 50 pro-Treaty forces occupied Dromore West workhouse. About 500 anti-Treaty troops, under the command of Carty, took up positions around the workhouse and an ultimatum was sent to the pro-Treaty officer in charge. He said that he was acting under the authority of Brigadier Jim Hunt and was told that Hunt had no authority in the area. The pro-Treaty troops were allowed to return to Sligo with their arms and ammunition.[94] On the same date pro-Treaty forces from Sligo Gaol occupied Sligo Courthouse and Town Hall. The Town Hall was vacated the following Monday and the troops moved on to Markree Castle near Collooney under the command of Brigadier Hunt.[95] All this activity demonstrated that the expansion of pro-Treaty forces throughout the county was not going to be easy and that strong and effective opposition from anti-Treaty forces could be expected especially in the west of the county.

Two incidents which involved exchange of gunfire took place in the Curry area. In late April Brigadier Jim Hunt with a group of five men travelled to the Curry district to organise pro-Treaty IRA.[96] While there, they were approached by a party of anti-Treaty IRA who opened fire on them. The fire was not returned. Hunt refused to surrender but agreed to go voluntarily to the anti-Treaty barracks in Tubbercurry, where he met the Commandant who had them detained overnight while awaiting instructions from the Divisional staff in Boyle. They were allowed to go the following morning but their arms and car were confiscated.[97] On 6 May shots were exchanged and some men were wounded when a group leaving a Free State election meeting at Curry were challenged by a republican patrol.[98]

Following Griffith's meeting, the pro-Treaty citizens of Sligo felt confident enough to convene a meeting at which they set up a Sligo Citizens' Association. This passed a resolution asking that the Provisional Government take steps 'to secure to the citizens of our town ample protection for life and property and we do hereby undertake to give any assistance which the Government may consider necessary for this purpose'.[99] Among the list of those attending were many of the leading businessmen of the town, a number of clergymen of different denominations and the chairman and secretary of the Trades Council. The secretary of this association wrote another reminder to the Provisional Government on 1 May stressing the importance of the resolution in view of the raids by the IRA on the bank in Sligo town on that very day. The acknowledgement merely stated that it was 'fully alive to the necessities of the situation. Within the present very difficult period of transition it is using every endeavour to restore peace and order throughout the country.' A minute on the file noted with apparent relief, 'It is not suggested that the people of Sligo intend to raise a force of their own' suggesting what the Government's limited priority at the time was.[100]

The proclamation on election meetings seems to have been quietly dropped in the wake of the Sligo meeting, and many pro-Treaty meetings were held at the end of April and early May, including four in north Sligo on Sunday 30 April.[101] This is the first mention of pro-Treaty meetings in north Sligo and may have signalled a growth in confidence as a result of Griffith's meeting. None of the local newspapers carried any news of anti-Treaty election meetings or activities during this period suggesting a corresponding low morale among the anti-Treaty camp.[102]

In spite of the deep split in Sligo labour ranks, a labour anti-militarism strike took place in the town as it did in most other towns and cities in Ireland. It was said to have been a 'magnificent demonstration' with 'the commercial and industrial life of the borough entirely stopped'.[103]

William Reilly chaired the meeting and resolutions were passed opposing military interference in civil life and demanding that both parties honour the democratic programme. John Lynch was conspicuous by his absence. In Tubbercurry, business was completely suspended even though it was market day and country people who came into town found closed shops.[104] Likewise Ballymote was reported as having 'joined in heartily'.[105]

The only reported clerical intervention of this period of electioneering was that of Revd P. A. Butler, Administrator, Sligo, who said at the AGM of Sligo Temperance Insurance Society in early May:

> We are truly a strange people. Just when we had placed in our own hand the management of our own affairs . . . dissension in our ranks must threaten seriously to shatter the very foundations of the nation which cost so much of the blood of our race. A strange doctrine seems to have got loose in Ireland – a doctrine foreign to the social and Catholic interests of the Irish people and that doctrine is the rule of the gun . . . Men in their ambition to be leaders and dictators are prepared to subvert every honest material principle, to rob the country which it has now been given to develop and to spill the blood of their brothers in the pursuit of a phantom republic.[106]

This intervention, coming as it did after the Sligo meeting when anti-Treaty morale was already low, was hardly calculated to make a significant impact on the mind of the electorate.

The pro-Treaty candidates were announced in the *Sligo Champion* of 13 May. For south Sligo Alec McCabe and Jim Hunt were put forward, for north Sligo John Hennigan and Seamus McGowan, and for east Mayo Tom O'Donnell.[107] Three of these candidates, McCabe, O'Donnell and Hunt, came from the Ballymote–Gurteen area of south Sligo. The first two were outgoing TDs but the selection of Jim Hunt is difficult to explain. He resigned as chairman of Coolavin D.C. in June 1922 saying that he was not a politician. He was, however, the only pre-Truce commandant to take the pro-Treaty side and this factor appears to have outweighed the disadvantage of his proximity to the other two candidates and his reluctance to enter the political arena. This coupled with the fact that there was no candidate in the Free State interest from east Mayo suggests that it was difficult to find suitable persons willing to offer themselves as candidates.

The Collins–de Valera Pact

On 20 May 1922, Collins and de Valera signed a pact designed to avoid an election contested on the issue of the Treaty. A national Sinn Féin coalition panel of candidates was agreed and it was expected that outgoing TDs would be returned unopposed though non-Sinn Féin candidates could be nominated.[108] Judging from editorial comment in the Sligo newspapers, the anti-Treaty side welcomed the pact much more enthusiastically than the pro-Treaty side. The *Connachtman's* comments were general, verbose and unusually restrained:

> That our people will carry out the terms of the pact in the spirit in which it has been entered into we have no doubt nor will there be neglect of the opportunity afforded to show the world no matter what internal difference may and must exist in our midst, we as a people are at all times ready to suppress our personal viewpoints and stand together when the common cause of the nation so demands.[109]

On the other hand the *Sligo Champion* did not disguise its disappointment at the news of the pact. Since January it had looked forward to the verdict of the Irish people on the Treaty and saw the pact as another stratagem to avoid this: 'It [the pact] means to an extent the muzzling of the Irish electorate . . . The coalition executive implies the complete wiping out of the Provisional Government and the abandonment of the election on the Treaty. Have Messrs Griffith and Collins signed their political death warrants?'[110] Its editorial of 3 June entitled 'The Treaty in Peril' warned that if the Treaty was broken 'the social and economic ruin of the country is accomplished'.[111]

In accordance with the general interpretation of clause 5 of the pact: 'That constituencies where an election is not held shall continue to be represented by their present deputies' – it was expected that the outgoing TDs, three anti-Treaty and two pro-Treaty, would be nominated for Sligo–Mayo East constituency. This posed no problem for the anti-Treaty side as only the three outgoing TDs had been selected. However, the other side had selected five candidates and only the outgoing TDs, Alec McCabe and Thomas O'Donnell, were re-selected at a pro-Treaty convention in late May. John Hennigan and Seamus McGowan, who were dropped, immediately announced that they were standing as independent candidates.[112] There were few public expressions of support for the independents. Indeed they were attacked from all sides. The Sligo Free State election committee issued a short statement disassociating themselves from their candidature. A joint manifesto from the panel candidates stated: 'A contested election has been forced upon us by two candidates claiming to be independent . . . Any person or party who at this moment forces personal or party issues on electors is acting against the best interests of Ireland and contrary to the spirit of the Collins–de Valera agreement'.[113] 'A Believer in the Panel' asked 'where were J. McGowan and J. Hennigan when Alec McCabe with rifle in hand and hunted like a hare took a stand on the mountain side, true to Ireland to the last and when the watchdogs of the British government were to be shot or when their strongholds were to be stormed where were the independent candidates?'[114] There is, however, no record of any subsequent attack on the independents by pro-Treaty speakers. It was from the anti-Treaty side that the bitter personal attacks came. The *Connachtman* surmised that 'A desire on their [the independents] part to gratify their personal vanity' was the reason for their candidature.[115] A meeting of Sligo Corporation unanimously endorsed the national panel and there were personal attacks on the independents from anti-Treaty councillors. Michael Nevin said that while both candidates had disagreed with his proposal to add a shilling in the pound to the rates for the IRA they were now causing unnecessary expenditure on the taxpayers by standing in the election. John Lynch said that one of the independents [He clearly meant Hennigan] 'wouldn't give Almighty God a halfpenny in the way of wages if He came down to earth again'.[116] Lynch repeated this personal abuse of Hennigan at a later public meeting but claimed McGowan had been misled into going forward: 'He would give McGowan the credit of having been one of the earliest Sinn Féiners in Sligo, with himself'.[117]

At first it had appeared that there were going to be contests in each of the five Connacht constituencies but in the event Sligo–Mayo East and Galway were the only ones contested. In each of the other constituencies pressure appears to have been exerted by pact candidates in order to prevent a contest. In Mayo South–Roscommon South the candidacy of the chairman of the County Council in the farmers interests was mentioned as early as April.[118] He withdrew at the last moment 'lest the introduction of independent candidates in the present crisis might cause any embarrassment or in any way imperil the National situation'.[119] In the Leitrim–Roscommon North constituency a farmers' meeting held on the Saturday before nomination day chose a candidate.[120] When he arrived at the courthouse on nomination day the four panel candidates held a meeting with him after which he withdrew 'in the public interests of the nation'.[121] Bernard Egan intended to contest the constituency of Mayo North and West as a Farmers' candidate but his nomination papers were not presented on the day. A claim in the national press that the person carrying his nomination papers had been kidnapped was strongly denied by both sides of the pact and by the *Connacht Telegraph*. The newspaper report also said that armed men had visited Egan the night previous to nomination day. Whatever the truth of the matter it appears that pressure of some sort prevented Egan's nomination.[122] In Galway the Labour party put up a high profile candidate, who 'successfully resisted pressure designed to force him out' and was elected.[123]

The decision of the two independents to stand in Sligo-Mayo East effectively precluded the Labour party and farmers from putting forward their own official candidates. McGowan stood as an independent labour candidate proposed by William Reilly who was chairman of both the Sligo branch of the Labour party and the Trades Council. Reilly was also election agent for both independents.[124] Hennigan, chairman of Grange branch of the Farmers' Association, stood as an independent farmers' candidate, and was proposed by Denis Leonard, the branch's secretary. The *Connachtman* claimed that 'organised labour and the majority of the farmers have already repudiated both of them' but subsequent events showed this not to be the case. A special meeting of the Sligo Branch of the Labour Party unanimously passed a resolution of support for both independents.[125] Subsequent to this being reported in the national press Labour leader Tom Johnson was quoted as saying that there was no branch of the Labour party in Sligo but William Reilly contradicted this saying that Seamus McGowan was a member.[126] John Lynch called a public labour meeting for the Wednesday prior to polling day to demonstrate labour support for the pact but none of the speakers except himself had been prominent in Sligo labour ranks.[127] The only organised farmers' group in the county was the Sligo Farmers' Association and John Hennigan was one of its officers. A meeting of the executive chaired by Hennigan held on 11 June considered their stand with regard to the election, and, while no resolution of support was reported, the secretary was ordered to instruct each branch secretary immediately to have collections taken up to defray the expenses of the two independents and to ensure that a reliable personating agent was present at each booth on election day.[128]

In a statement in the local newspapers the independents pointed out that they had been originally chosen to stand as pro-Treaty candidates: 'Since then the political situation has completely altered. While in no way desiring to cause disunity, or to hamper the National Movement, we believe that the people have a right to determine who shall represent them. We also consider that the time of the Councils of the Nation has been wasted in political vapouring and petty jealousy.'[129] The independents were considered a serious threat to the pact candidates. The Gurteen and Ballymote correspondent of the *Roscommon Herald*, J.S. O'Donnell, also the Free State organiser, reported that the general opinion was that, while McCabe would top the poll, one of the independents would also be elected.[130]

The election campaign seems to have lost whatever impetus it had on the announcement of the Pact. Ballymote Notes in the *Sligo Champion* in early June said that a 'real wholehearted canvass has not as yet been widely made for the elections'[131] and 'Hitherto the eve of parliamentary elections was a time of great activity. On this occasion scarcely a syllable has been spoken by the man in the street as to the pros and cons. No active canvassing has taken place on behalf of the panel or independent candidates'.[132] Very few public election meetings were reported in the period after the Pact though the anti-Treaty side was much more active than the pro-Treaty side. A panel meeting was held at the Town Hall, Sligo on Sunday 11 June which all panel candidates were to attend but 'whether by accident or design or merely coincidental' only anti-Treaty speakers were there.[133] The *Sligo Independent* reported that telegrams of apology were received from Tom O'Donnell, TD, and from D.M. Hanley. Reports of the meeting reflected the political bias of the newspaper, the *Sligo Champion* reporting that 'the meeting was one of the most apathetic ever seen in Sligo' while the *Connachtman* called it 'a most successful meeting'. A candidate, Seamus Devins, told the meeting that 'he had come to ask them to vote for the panel candidates. He did not ask a first preference or a second one for himself. They could give their first and second preference to any one of the panel candidates that they liked.'[134] Eamon de Valera made a tour of the constituency, which included meetings at Ballymote, Tubbercurry and Sligo, accompanied by Devins and O'Donnell. O'Donnell was a friend of de Valera's since their teaching days together in Rockwell College, Tipperary, which explains his presence on the platform with de Valera.[135] This seems to have been the only instance where pro- and anti-Treaty candidates appeared on the same election platform in Sligo.[136] The other pro-Treaty candidate, Alec McCabe, appears not to have addressed a meeting or otherwise engaged in electioneering in the period after the announcement of the pact.

On the Sunday previous to the election, anti-Treaty speakers, including Bradshaw and Devins, addressed six meetings in north Sligo on behalf of the panel candidates.[137] Prominent Treaty supporter Martin Roddy spoke at a separate pact meeting in the area. According to the *Sligo Champion*, some meetings were also held on behalf of the independents but their supporters 'mainly confined themselves to distribution of literature and the canvassing of voters'. The *Connachtman* gave two instances, both in north Sligo, where it claimed independents had to abandon meetings because of what it called 'public hostility'.[138] There were two reported instances in north Sligo of postmen being held up and election notices being taken by armed and masked men.[139] Local newspapers reprinted the following typewritten letter which they claimed was received by a number of Protestants in the Drumcliff district of the constituency: 'The bordermen expect that the unionists will kindly stay at home next Friday as they did in the 1918 election. If they do not it will mean some night duty for us next week. Please convey these instructions to your neighbours'. The *Sligo Independent* claimed that some of these Protestants had been impersonated early on election day.[140]

The editorial in the *Sligo Champion* on the day of polling was very unenthusiastic and said little to encourage people to vote: 'They [the people] know that to return the panel candidates will not result in a miraculous change in the character . . . of individuals . . . and if the national panel were returned in its entirety it is morally certain that the bear garden proceedings would be resumed exactly where they were left off and the country's drift towards disaster would be accelerated'.[141] The *Sligo Independent's* editorial in the week previous to the polling day did not explicitly advise its readers to vote for the independents but certainly suggested as much: 'On Friday next the Electors of Ireland will have an opportunity of recording their votes for men who represent Agriculture, Commerce and Industry, and who are better entitled to the control of the destinies of the Nation? . . . The Farmers, or Ratepayers, and Labour are here represented. And the workers are also justly entitled to representation. Therefore both candidates are certain to receive much support. We appeal for freedom for all, and good order.'[142] The *Connachtman* published a special edition on the Wednesday before the election containing an editorial entitled 'The Way to Peace – Vote the Panel' strongly urging people to vote pro-panel: 'Those who vote for the national panel candidates vote for unity. Unity means stable government and stable government means peace'. It also contained the following verse:

> Vote for Devins, Ferran and Carty,
> But that's not all you've got to do.
> To keep the panel alive
> You must vote the panel five
> Which includes McCabe and Tom O'Donnell too.[143]

Comments on the election day itself confirm the picture of general apathy. The election passed off very quietly in the Tubbercurry area with 'little or no excitement' and the poll was not a heavy one there.[144] According to a Ballymote correspondent, about 60 per cent from that area cast their vote and there was no impersonation.[145] However, the *Roscommon Herald's* Ballymote and Gurteen correspondent reported that the 'number of electors who exercised their franchise was not large' attributing this to the fact that 'people were more or less in the dark as to whether they should go to the polls or not. The agreement between the political leaders left the man in the street somewhat confused.'[146]

News reached Sligo early on polling day that election agents of the independent candidates had been kidnapped in the early hours of the morning. The *Sligo Champion* named one of these personating agents as John P. Jordan, grocer and publican, who was kidnapped and held in Sligo Military Barracks until late afternoon.[147] The independent candidates wired their protests to Griffith on polling day and he telegraphed a reply to the effect that an enquiry would be held.[148] When the counting of votes commenced the independent candidates withdrew 'as a protest against the gross impersonation and intimidation which was practised on and before the day of the poll and the kidnapping of impersonating agents'.[149]

There were many rumours that personation had been rife in the east Mayo and north Sligo areas of the constituency. Two correspondents to the *Irish Independent* complained about such intimidation and impersonation. 'Disgusted No 2' claimed that 'parties summoned to the great beyond months ago were amongst the first to exercise the franchise' and 'Anti-Humbug' stated that anyone who objected was intimidated into silence and said that 'some young men voted five times in Sligo–East Mayo'. A letter from a Sligo correspondent attributed such complaints to lack of sporting spirit: 'Personation probably did go on, it went on in every election that I ever remember and will go on to the end of time but with the same rules governing the candidates of all parties – the same machinery at the disposal of each of them – it is simply moonshine to suggest on one side are all saints and on the other side all sinners'.[150] This was, of course, to ignore the fact that the same machinery was not at the disposal of each party in County Sligo. The anti-Treaty side had at their disposal the majority of the IRA, while the pro-Treaty side and the independents had no similar military force either to aid or defend them. In McCabe's victory speech after the announcement of the results he alluded to the problems and allegations saying: 'Certain circumstances were not what they might have been'.[151]

Analysis of the Election Results

The percentage turnout in Sligo–Mayo East was 55 per cent, higher than the national figure of 45 per cent.[152] The result of the election in the constituency was a clear victory for the Sinn Féin panel with the five seats going to the five outgoing members. The Independents failed to make an impact, receiving only 0.84 of a quota between them. Even though the Treaty was not an issue in the election the result was claimed as a clear victory for the anti-Treaty side, this constituency being the only one in the country in which the anti-Treaty candidates got an overall majority of the vote. The percentage share achieved by each side in the constituency was as follows: Anti-Treaty Sinn Féin – 56 per cent, Pro-Treaty Sinn Féin – 30 per cent, Independents – 14 per cent. The pro-Treaty side did, however, have the satisfaction of providing the poll-topper, Alec McCabe. Because of constituency changes it is impossible to compare election results for 1922, 1923 and 1927 with any degree of accuracy,[152] although comparison suggests that the republican vote in 1922 was exceptionally high. The percentage figures for the Sligo-Leitrim constituency in the 1923 election were Republican – 36 per cent, Cumann na nGaedheal – 48 per cent, Others (Farmers, Labour and independents) – 16 per cent. The figures for 1927 were Fianna Fáil – 23 per cent, Cumann na nGaedheal – 43 per cent, Labour and Farmers – 18 per cent, Others – 15 per cent.

What were the reasons for the extraordinary high percentage of anti-Treaty vote in 1922? Because of the terms of the Collins–de Valera pact it was expected that outgoing deputies would be renominated. The three anti-Treaty TDs were strategically placed, Frank Carty in south Sligo, Seamus Devins in north Sligo while Frank Ferran came from the east Mayo part of the constituency which accounted for 40 per cent of the electorate. This geographical spread was obviously to the advantage of the anti-Treaty side. The two Sligo based candidates were also high profile candidates as a result of their activity as IRA commandants. On the other hand, the pro-Treaty side had only two deputies, both from the south of the county, within ten miles of each other. Alec McCabe was a high profile candidate having been first elected in 1918, but his running mate, Tom O'Donnell, was a lightweight and was to lose his seat at the 1923 election. Thus in two areas, north Sligo and east Mayo, the anti-Treaty candidates had no locally based opposition. We have also seen that the anti-Treaty side campaigned much more vigorously than the other side in the period after the announcement of the pact. Of the two independents, one, the independent labour candidate, had not been a prominent labour activist and the split in the labour ranks over the Treaty made his election prospects remote. In the election of the following year John Lynch, the well-known labour activist and republican supporter, obtained almost twice the number of votes as McGowan did in 1922.

The election was fought using proportional representation and this means that by examining transfers we can gauge the extent to which the pact was observed by both sides. In the single instance, that of the transfer of Devins's surplus, of anti-Treaty transfers with pro- and anti-Treaty candidates available the figures were: to anti-Treaty 92 per cent, to pro-Treaty 3.4 per cent, to independents 4.6 per cent. This shows a much higher proportion of anti-Treaty voters maintaining the party solidarity than was the case nationally. Of the remaining transfers there is no sign of pact solidarity with both independents and pro-Treaty candidates receiving a very similar small proportion. This may be a reflection of the fact that Devins, in North Sligo, was geographically far removed from the remaining pro-Treaty candidate and nearer the independents.

When we examine the distribution of the surpluses of the other anti-Treaty candidates we see a more marked adherence to the pact. In the case of Frank Carty's surplus there was no remaining anti-Treaty candidate and 13 per cent of his surplus was non-transferable. Of the surplus the vast majority, 82 per cent, went to the only remaining pro-Treaty candidate, Tom O'Donnell, and only 6 per cent to the two independent candidates. The pattern of anti-Treaty adherence to the pact and refusal to give lower preferences to independents when no anti-Treaty candidate remained is also clear when we look at the transfers from the other republican candidate, Ferran, 90 per cent of which went to pro-Treaty candidates as against 10 per cent to the independents. Taking the two cases where anti-Treaty surpluses were being distributed without anti-Treaty candidates remaining the figures are: to pro-Treaty 85 per cent, to independents 7 per cent and non-transferable 7.5 per cent. The non-transferable votes all came from Carty and reflect the fact that he was the last republican candidate. This represents a very small proportion of 'plumpers' who voted anti-Treaty only. The figure for transfers to the opposing side within the pact is significantly above the national figure.

The only pro-Treaty candidate whose surplus was distributed while there were pro- and anti-treaty candidates left in the field was Alec McCabe and his went thus: pro-Treaty 57 per cent (to Tom O'Donnell, his only running mate), anti-Treaty 14 per cent (to Frank Carty, the only remaining anti-Treaty candidate), Independents 29 per cent (12 per cent to McGowan, 18 per cent to Hennigan). There were no non-transferable votes. Firstly this shows a large proportion of pro-Treaty voters giving their lower preferences to anti-Treaty candidates or independents rather than to their own party. This is in marked contrast to the pattern observed in the distribution of anti-Treaty surplus. Secondly the destination of those transfers which went outside the pro-Treaty side shows a significantly higher proportion going to independents than to anti-Treaty candidates. This demonstrates a failure on the part of pro-Treaty voters to observe the spirit of the electoral pact.

The only other distribution of votes was that which followed the elimination of independent McGowan and decided the final seat between the other independent Hennigan and the second pro-Treaty candidate, Tom O'Donnell. The votes transferred thus: to Hennigan 52 per cent, to O'Donnell 37 per cent, non-transferable 12 per cent. It would have needed almost 100 per cent transfer rate to give Hennigan the seat and O'Donnell was elected. This pattern of transfers strengthens the indications apparent from the destination of pro-Treaty transfers that there was a fellow feeling between the independents and the pro-Treaty side in the Sligo–Mayo East constituency.

In summary then, it appears that in Sligo–Mayo East constituency anti-Treaty voters were more inclined to vote strictly for their own candidates and then adhere to the terms of the pact by voting pro-Treaty rather than independents. The pro-Treaty voters, on the other hand, were less likely to vote strictly pro-Treaty and were more likely to give lower preferences to independents than to the anti-Treaty candidates. The pact was more strictly observed by the anti-Treaty side and the figures show that while the pact patched things up for a time the basic split still remained and was not likely to be easily remedied. The slide towards confrontation during the post Treaty period had not been halted by the electoral pact and in Sligo the results gave a boost to the anti-Treaty side. The *Connachtman* in its editorial of 24 June said that the results from a republican point of view were satisfactory 'in view of the fact that the pact entered into between Mr de Valera and Mr Collins was broken by the latter and his supporters'. It coupled this with criticism of the new Free State constitution which had been published on the eve of the election: 'Such a constitution would be an unqualified surrender and abandonment of the nation's rights and would constitute a voluntary acceptance and acknowledgement of the status of slavery by the Irish people. The pact has been broken and with it has disappeared any immediate prospect of a settlement. The verdict of the polls is clearly not one of peace.'[154] Seamus Devins speaking at the declaration of the results said that he did not wish to see any differences between either side. He also asked them to remember that the fight was not over yet but only starting.[155] The truth of this statement became apparent very soon.

At the statutory meeting of Sligo County Council on 17 June 1922 the brief spirit of unity engendered by the Collins–de Valera pact was still to the fore. In spite of their political differences Frank Carty proposed Martin Roddy for chairman describing him as an 'honest, straight man' and he was seconded by McCabe. Roddy was unanimously selected, a unanimity which contrasted starkly with the dissension which had divided the council for the previous year and was to be reflected in the bitter fratricidal strife which was about to break out in the country.[156]

Table 3.1. 1922 General Election. Sligo–Mayo East Constituency.

TRANSFER OF VOTES
A. *Destiny of Pro-Treaty Transfers*

When pro-Treaty, anti-Treaty and independent candidates were available.
(Total 2,009)

	To Pro-Treaty	To Anti-Treaty	To Independents	Non Transferable
Number	1,140	276	593	0
Percentage	57%	14%	29%	0%
National %	74%	12%		

A. *Destiny of Anti-Treaty transfers*

(i) When pro-Treaty, anti-Treaty and independent candidates were available.
(Total 1,620)

	To Pro-Treaty	To Anti-Treaty	To Independents	Non Transferable
Number	55	1,491	74	0
Percentage	3%	92%	5%	0%
National %	8%	74%		

(ii) When pro-Treaty and independent candidates but not anti-Treaty
candidates were available.
(Total 2,354)

	To Pro-Treaty	To Anti-Treaty	To Independents	Non Transferable
Number	2,012	0	166	176
Percentage	85%	0%	7%	7%
National %	70%	0%		

Source: *S.C.*, 24 June 1922.

FOUR

THE COURSE OF THE CIVIL WAR

THE OUTBREAK OF THE Civil War should have caught nobody in County Sligo by surprise. The leadership of the Sligo IRA had been deeply involved in the interminable conventions and conferences in Dublin during the previous six months.[1] Members of the new national army had marched the streets of Sligo and had exchanged fire with the IRA. The new force had established a strong presence in Sligo town and in a small number of other places nearby. It might be expected that a clear strategy would have been developed by the 3rd Western Division as a response to an expected outbreak of hostilities. That this was not the case was a reflection of the national confusion among anti-Treaty forces and of the local divisions in the ranks of the anti-Treaty IRA. This initial confusion ensured that the action of the anti-Treaty IRA would be fragmented and uncertain. The 3rd Western Division had increased its armament considerably since hostilities with the British had ceased but had failed to develop clear lines of command or become a cohesive military unit. It had learned nothing new as regards tactics and it was soon clear that its preferred modus operandi was a repeat of what it had convinced itself had been a successful guerilla campaign against the British. This time, however, the enemy was native not foreign, most of the war-weary populace were hostile, and the new government and its army could claim a democratic mandate following the June 1922 election. A defensive guerilla campaign was thus not likely to achieve anything of significance.

July 1922

When the news of the attack on the Four Courts reached Sligo a meeting of the 3rd Western Divisional staff was held in the town. In the absence of any communications from the Executive in Dublin there was confusion. Frank Carty advocated immediate offensive action against Provisional Government posts in the area. This was in line with what was the first concern of the republican side nationwide, to consolidate the control of areas in which they already had a strong presence.[2] Tom Carney on the other hand wanted the division to advance towards Athlone.[3] William Pilkington and most of his divisional staff opposed both suggestions and advocated attacking British forces on the border instead. There was no agreement and Pilkington and his adjutant Brian MacNeill left the meeting to seek the advice of Michael Kilroy, O/C 4th Western Division in Castlebar. Carty and Carney returned to Tubbercurry, met the O/C of the North Mayo Brigade and decided to take independent action. In his own words: 'Immediately following the attack on the Four Courts we assumed the offensive in this area [4th Tubbercurry Brigade]. We formed an ASU of twenty four men and while awaiting further instructions we arrested prominent local Free State leaders and transferred them to Castlebar for detention.' On 2 July this joint force captured a strategically important position at Collooney which had been occupied by a Provisional Government force of less than forty at the outbreak of the war.[4] During the following week and a half republican forces operated freely in the immediate area, capturing a lorry of 14 Provisional Government soldiers, destroying the bridge at Ballisodare and attacking the government post at Gurteen which had a garrison of 13. This attack failed and one republican soldier was killed.[5] They also took the government outpost at Riverstown and made numerous sniping attacks on Markree Castle.

Carty's forces showed no inclination to move from Collooney and link up with comrades either in the Sligo town area to the north or the strategically important Boyle area to the south. Government reinforcements would be expected to arrive from the south but there was no attack on the government post at Ballymote or strengthening of the small republican post there. The 4th Brigade's activities for the week beginning 4 July consisted only of 'destroying enemy lines of communication throughout the brigade area. In all there were eleven large bridges demolished, several culverts opened and trenches cut and trees felled on all the main roads likely to be of use to the enemy'.[6] This was a repeat of the kinds of activities engaged in the latter stages of the War of Independence. Joe Baker of the 4th Western Division recalled the lack of orders or direction in the Collooney area after the taking of the post there.[7] This concentration on their own brigade area was a fatal weakness and it meant that in spite of their initial gains the republicans merely waited to be confronted by the government forces, which were always likely to be superior in numbers and armament.

In line with Pilkington's initial instinct the 1st (North Sligo) Brigade attacked and captured Ballaghameehan Barracks on the Leitrim–Fermanagh border which had been held by Provisional Government troops.[8] In

Sligo town itself the republican forces did not take the initiative and it was the government troops in the courthouse who made the first move by taking over an adjoining garage which directly faced the republican occupied ex-RIC barracks. There was to be no armed conflict at this stage. 'Our orders were to evacuate the town and burn the barracks', said Tom Scanlon and they did so early on the morning of 1 July. Later the same day the government forces again moved, commandeering the Harp and Shamrock Hotel near the Military Barracks. The following morning the Military Barracks was evacuated and burned by the republicans who then established their headquarters at Rahelly House near Lissadell in north Sligo. Some republican police based in the Wine Street ex-RIC barracks remained on and patrolled the town.[9] MacNeill reported to the O/C 4th Western Division at the time: 'The tactics in this area will have to be altered to the guerilla form as attacks on enemy posts on a large scale are impossible for the following reasons (a) too expensive on ammunition, (b) strength of enemy posts, (c) more effect can be gained by ambushing them when passing between posts'.[10] Republicans throughout the northern part of the county also abandoned and burned their posts, taking to the hills. In spite of these developments the government's hold on Sligo town was far from secure. Shooting incidents took place in the town during the following days and nights, one government soldier being killed in an ambush near the jail. Sligo Post Office was also entered and the telephone and telegraph equipment wrecked.[11] The government forces made no attempt to engage the republicans outside the town either to the north at Rahelly or to the south at Collooney. Collooney, less than ten miles away, was eventually retaken not by troops from Sligo but from Athlone.

Government reinforcements with the Ballinalee armoured car arrived in Sligo on Wednesday 5 July and on the following day the Wine Street republican police post was taken, a civilian being accidentally killed during this action.[12] The Ballinalee was then used to maintain communications by a circuitous route between the threatened Markree Castle post and Sligo town. The extent of the lack of co-ordination among the republicans is evident from the fact that both the 1st and 4th Brigades laid ambushes on this route unknown to each other on 13 July. The government army convoy – three or four lorries and the armoured car – first ran into Carty's ambush at Rockwood (actually in the 1st Brigade area) and had to surrender after a long exchange of fire, with four government troops killed. The Ballinalee's gun jammed but the car made its escape towards Sligo only to be captured when it ran into the second ambush. Carty does not record how he felt at having let such a prize slip through his fingers.[13]

On the following day the north Sligo republicans used the Ballinalee in an attack on Sligo town and the government troops were confined to their positions in the courthouse and the jail. An ultimatum was delivered to the courthouse garrison asking them to surrender or be attacked. The garrison refused to surrender. The Bishop of Elphin then arrived and when his efforts at intercession failed he took up position inside the courthouse. Tom Scanlon explained what happened: 'Not wishing to expose the Bishop to danger and realising the propaganda the enemy would make of it if the Bishop was either killed or wounded by our attack we left the town with all our men.'[14]

The ambush at Rockwood seems to have been the factor that led to the government side taking decisive action against Collooney. On the evening of 13 July Seán MacEoin took a troop train of 300 to 400 men from Athlone to Collooney. Ballymote was on the railway line to Collooney but had only a small republican post garrisoned by six men armed with shotguns which was unable to delay the troop train. The garrison defending Collooney was thus taken by surprise and, after a battle which included artillery bombardment, the town was taken and forty republican prisoners captured including Frank O'Beirne, O/C of the Collooney Battalion. There were surprisingly few casualties with only one anti-Treaty soldier reported as having died from wounds received in the battle.[15] The following is an extract from a letter written immediately after the battle by a local:

> At 4.15 the firing started. There was no rushing of motors or armoured cars as we expected but the Free Staters had quietly surrounded the village. They had a big gun at the bridge on the Knockbeg road and were firing from this to the Church steeple where one of the Kellys and other Republicans had taken a position with two Lewis guns. McKeon I think was anxious to spare this church and not until two of his best gunners were severely wounded did he give the order to bomb this tower. The explosion was terrific, it shook our house and gave us an awful fright . . . There was a machine gun on our Fort going pip pip incessantly, one in the nursery doing its duty equally well . . . so as regards noise we got our money's worth. At 10pm the Free Staters were in possession of the town and the Republicans had retreated to Sim's house. After constant firing all night they routed them out of Sim's.[16]

Carty claimed that the post at Ballymote was taken by the troops on their way to Collooney and that the Information Officer was also captured and was unable to inform him of the impending attack. This he gave as the reason why he did not come to the aid of Collooney. The diary of the 4th Brigade, however, stated that Ballymote post was taken two days after Collooney and Martin Brennan claimed that Carty

Adjutant John Durcan, Curry, shot dead in an anti–Treaty attack on Ballymote on 13 September 1922. (Mrs Mary McGuinn)

Batt Keaney in Free State Army uniform during the early days of the
Civil War. (Batt Keaney)

The three successful anti-Treaty candidates at the June 1922 election, Seamus Devins (left), Dr Francis Ferran (second from right) and Frank Carty (right). Michael Nevin, Mayor of Sligo, is second from the left. (Mrs Mary McGuinn)

Part of the funeral cortege of 22 September 1922 of the Sligo men killed on Benbulben. (Sr Elizabeth, Mercy Convent, Sligo)

William Pilkington, O/C 3rd Western Division anti-Treaty forces during the Civil War. (Mrs A. McNamara)

The former RIC barracks, Sligo, in flames on 1 July 1922 after the anti-Treaty forces evacuated and burned it. (Sr Elizabeth, Mercy Convent, Sligo)

Anti-Treaty soldiers on duty in the court-house during Arthur Griffith's meeting in Sligo, 16 April 1921. The officer on the left is said to be Vice-Brigadier Harry Brehony. (George Morrison)

Anti-Treaty troops in a commandeered lorry during Griffith's meeting. (George Morrison)

Captain Harry Benson, anti-Treaty forces, killed on Benbulben, 20 September 1922. His body was discovered on 2 October. (Kilgannon)

Martin Roddy, pro-Treaty chairman of Sligo County Council,
1922–23. (Kilgannon)

The lying-in-state in Gilhooly Hall, Sligo, of 19-year-old Private Michael McCrann, Sligo, accidentally shot dead on 31 December 1921. (Sr Elizabeth, Mercy Convent, Sligo)

A Sligo anti-Treaty column during the Civil War (Richard Mulcahy Collection, R.24842. National Library of Ireland)

deliberately did not come to the aid of Collooney: 'We heard the shooting but Frank Carty wouldn't let us go in so O'Beirne had to surrender. That was jealousy.'[17] After this Tubbercurry was soon abandoned by the republicans and was occupied by government troops on 28 July. Vice-Brigadier Harry Brehony was captured in this action. Republicans also abandoned and burned their remaining posts at Easkey and Dromore West and took to the mountains.[18] The first phase in the Civil War in County Sligo was over with the government troops in control of the main towns and the republicans adopting guerilla tactics and controlling large parts of the countryside. The mountainous nature of much of the county meant that guerilla bands had large areas of suitable terrain from which to operate. The aim of the government army had been clear: 'The general policy is to prevent enemy troops evacuating barracks in possession of rifles and ammunition and reverting to guerilla warfare.'[19] The failure of this policy in the county during this first phase ensured that a decisive victory over the republicans would be difficult.

The situation in Sligo was similar to that in areas of the country where republican resistance was strong: 'The Provisional Government army had only superficial control over large areas'.[20] In spite of initial successes, large areas of Connacht, especially in counties Sligo, Leitrim, Mayo and the Connemara area of Galway, still caused major problems for the government and hopes of a quick end to the war were soon seen to be premature.

August–October 1922

While they now controlled the main towns in County Sligo, the government forces were confined almost totally to those positions and ventured out very rarely. Sniping of government posts was a common occurrence, though such activity was said to have decreased in Sligo town when government reinforcements arrived at the end of July. Republicans from the town were said to be spending nights at home or in the Mercy Convent where they were often sheltered. On one occasion the convent bell was rung, presumably by members of the order, as a warning signal to republicans.[21] The Ballinalee was a constant threat and was liable to turn up anywhere in the county as it was passed around among the Brigades. It caused terror in Sligo on 5 August when it entered the town and was used to attack and capture a small Provisional Government post.[22]

Army intelligence officers reported in early August that the republicans were then based in three areas in the county. Most of the divisional staff, including Pilkington and Devins, were based at Rahelly House in north Sligo. Their strength was estimated at 100 men with 90 rifles, 70 revolvers and 4 machine guns. This group controlled most of north Sligo, and its headquarters, in a low-lying area between the mountains and the sea, lay on the northern edge on the army's Western Command which may explain their tardiness in dealing with it. Isolated as it was it posed little threat. To the north, Finner Camp and Bundoran were held by the army's 1st Northern Division and there was little republican activity in Donegal. To the east lay the Northern Ireland border and to the south the town of Sligo was never seriously threatened. Carty's group was based along the Ox Mountains between Coolaney and Curry and was estimated at 40–60 strong. 'He is the most relentless of all the irregular leaders', an August report stated. In the mountainous Geevagh and Arigna area on the south Sligo/Roscommon border Harold McBrien and Ned Bofin led a party, estimated in early August at 150 men, which had a plentiful supply of rifles and revolvers. A smaller group of 13 armed with rifles and revolvers was reported as operating near Ballymote. It was reported that excellent communications were maintained between the different republican columns but that there was no evidence of any co-ordinated actions or any unified command structure.[23] There had been some communications by boat between the republicans of north and west Sligo but Alec McCabe commandeered the SS Tartar which he used to patrol Sligo Bay and attack the republican-held coast of north Sligo.[24]

August and September was a time of military stalemate, neither side attempting any decisive action. Both sides seemed devoid of any strategic plans apart from maintaining control in their respective areas. For the republican side this represented the losing of a vital chance to inflict severe setbacks on the government army before it had a chance to build up its forces. The republicans' greatest military objective appeared to be the capture of an enemy post, disarming the occupants and retreat to their strongholds. They sometimes laid ambushes but these were often unsuccessful because of the timidity of the army and because of leakage of information. Lack of arms and ammunition appears not to have been a problem on the republican side. Between the outbreak of the war and the beginning of August the 3rd Western Division had captured 160 rifles, one Lewis gun and an armoured car with a Vickers gun. They lost 45 rifles at Collooney. 'From the point of view of armament we are much stronger than when we started', MacNeill reported at the beginning of August.[25] The August 1922 diary of activities of the 1st Brigade, which controlled north Sligo, details only four actions during the whole month. These included the successful attack on the Ulster Bank post in Sligo town and three attacks on army posts in Bundoran. They also sniped the Bundoran and Finner Camp posts for a week.[26] The impression created is of them waiting for an attack and being unable to undertake any offensive action on their own initiative, in spite of the availability of the Ballinalee and the obvious inaction of the government forces. The diary of the 4th Brigade for the same period confirms this impression and shows that Carty, for all his early emphasis on action, was just as devoid of offensive ideas as were his north Sligo comrades. His reported actions for the month consisted of setting three unsuccessful ambushes, one successful ambush in which one government soldier was killed, and sniping three enemy posts. As Carty himself stated 'There was a lull as far as large scale operations were concerned until near the end of August'.[27]

Some few skirmishes did take place during this period. Near Enniscrone a party of government soldiers from Ballina surprised a republican ambushing party, reportedly killing two and capturing three. On 25 August Carty lured a party of 45 troops from Tubbercurry into an ambush in which one government soldier was killed, three wounded, and arms and ammunition, including 40 rifles and a Lewis gun, captured.[28] One of the reasons for the failure of some of the ambushes was that local people were giving information to the pro-Treaty troops: 'On one occasion our efforts were foiled by the intervention of the civilian population who revealed our whereabouts to the enemy'.[29] There was some disruption of rail communications. The Collooney–Claremorris line, which ran through Carty's territory, was damaged in a number of places and no trains ran on the line during the remainder of 1922. The Sligo–Leitrim and Northern Counties line was subject to constant attacks and stoppages during July and August. The main Sligo–Dublin line operated normally for most of the period with only one attack reported during August.[30]

In early August there were rumours that some of the republicans in the Arigna and north Roscommon areas were anxious to surrender. A republican with a white flag came to the government outpost at Ballyfarnon and asked for a meeting with an officer from Boyle. Commandant Lavin came from Boyle and after a short meeting it was decided to hold a conference the following Sunday in Ballyfarnon to be attended by two army officers from Boyle, the republican column leader Bofin, his adjutant McBrien and Fr Roddy, CC Gleann, County Sligo. This conference which appears not to have been authorised by higher authority was held on 6 August 1922 without any positive result. However, hostilities in the 2nd Brigade area were postponed from the Sunday until the following Wednesday, apparently with the intention of facilitating further meetings. On Monday some of the Riverstown column members came to the barracks in Boyle under the impression that the terms of the truce also applied to them. They were disarmed and arrested. The arrival of Commandant General Farrelly, O/C 3rd Western Division, at

Boyle ended the truce. He released the republicans with a message to the effect that there would be no truce. According to the Western Command Intelligence Officer this episode 'has had the effect of hardening up those irregulars who were wavering'.[31]

The government troops still lacked the numbers, transport and confidence to undertake large-scale attacks even on those republicans who were concentrated in accessible areas like north Sligo. Reports in August, containing as they do many warnings of possible republican attacks on towns, demonstrate the defensive attitude of the Free State troops. The Intelligence Officer of the 3rd Western Division in early August warned of a possible 'coup', probably an attack on Sligo with the aid of the Ballinalee. In his 4 August report he warned that Carty 'will probably attack the town [Ballymote] very soon'. On the 11 August he warned that 'the irregulars will certainly in the very near future attack these two posts [Ballymote and Tubbercurry]' and again on 22 August 'It is evident that the irregulars are rapidly completing preparations for an attack on National forces in Sligo town'. He also listed ambushes which had been laid by republicans and added, 'In all of these operations our troops in Swinford and Tubbercurry knew of their preparations but were powerless as the garrison in each place is too small to admit of raiding parties being sent out.'[32] What the government side especially feared was co-operation among republican forces. During the early days of conflict in Sligo town and just before the battle for Collooney they reported without foundation: 'A mobile column of Irregulars under Maguire of Castlebar are [sic] moving towards Sligo.'[33] Similarly during the attack on north Sligo they assumed, again mistakenly, that Carty would assist the north Sligo republicans: 'Supposed McCarthy [sic] of Irregulars advancing from his own quarter'.[34] Even in November the dreaded scenario was mentioned: 'there is always a chance of Kilroy and Carty uniting forces'.[35] In spite of some limited co-operation such as that in the early days of the war and the sharing of the Ballinalee, there was no significant collaboration between the various republican groups within the county or between them and republicans in adjacent counties.

The government troops did have some success by their use of 'Flying Columns' of mobile troops to harass the IRA. Alec McCabe, in particular, was active in the south Sligo area from his base at Ballymote: 'Colonel Commandant McCabe has frightened a few Irregulars who were in this area by his surprise parties.' Carty was reported to have complained of the condition of his feet in August 1922 'on account of Alec McCabe's Lancia cars being on all the roads'.[36]

There were organisational and logistical problems on the government side. The Western Command was unwieldy, covering as it did an area from Longford to the west coast. An attempt was made in August to reorganise the Command, which was to include the evacuation of some of the smaller positions and the sending of 'surplus' men to the Curragh for training. About thirty posts in the area were closed including Gurteen in County Sligo. Four flying columns of 150 men each were to be organised on a regional basis. Column B was to work in the Sligo–Boyle–Foxford area. The total strength of the army in the command at the time was 2,234. This did not include the 'more than 1,000 additional men in this area that he [MacEoin] cannot at present indicate the distribution of'. MacEoin at once reported difficulties in implementing the scheme, especially opposition from traders in towns which were to lose their posts and he asked for a two weeks' delay in its implementation. This was granted but with a stern rebuke from Mulcahy: 'We are simply going to break up what we have of an army if we leave it any longer in small posts and do not give it proper military training.'[37]

On 4 September MacEoin reported that the scheme was ready to be put into operation as directed and he was waiting for promised supplies. MacEoin complained of 'serious trouble with some of the men – in fact mutiny in some places for want of pay . . . Do something about pay for regulars at once'. He reported that Dromahair, County Leitrim barracks had been surrendered to the republicans because of the garrison's dissatisfaction with pay and supplies. The terse reply pointed out that 3,000 men were being paid regularly in the Western Command.[38] A confidential report by MacEoin to the Commander in Chief in September reported that 'grave dissatisfaction exists over the command area' for a considerable time. While many of the complaints related to matters of army appointments which were made without any reference to Command or officers, all the Divisional and Command officers had also reported to MacEoin their dissatisfaction on matters of pay and supply of uniform.[39]

Early in September Frank Carty obtained the Ballinalee from north Sligo and used it to attack Tubbercurry. One government soldier was killed in a determined but unsuccessful attempt to take the two army positions but the republicans had to retreat having commandeered food, clothing and footwear.[40] An attempt by Carty's column to take the government post at Ballymote failed, one of their number being killed.[41] Meanwhile, the Ballinalee had been sent to assist in the capture of Ballina by members of the 4th Western Division, IRA. The republicans held the town for one day, retreating on the news of the advance of a government convoy under Tony Lawlor.[42] This convoy, having retaken Ballina, headed across the Ox Mountains towards Tubbercurry accompanied by the armoured car, The Big Fella. The Ballinalee had returned to Carty's column by this time. Carty's forces mounted several ambushes and inflicted two fatalities as Lawlor's men made their way to Tubbercurry. Seán MacEoin led another force from Athlone and joined forces with Lawlor at Tubbercurry on the night of 14 September before sweeping the Ox Mountains from there to Coolaney. According to Carty, he demobilised his men in the face of this sweep and had only one man captured.[43]

MacEoin and Lawlor next turned their attention to the north Sligo republicans. A carefully planned attack was launched on 19 September utilising 1st Northern Division troops from Finner Camp, 1st Midland Division troops operating from Manorhamilton and 3rd Western Division troops from Sligo and Boyle. The republicans had planned an orderly retreat towards the mountains on the Sligo–Leitrim border in the event of an attack but in fact their forces became disorganised and separated in the mountainous area and many slipped through the cordon in small groups.[44] The Ballinalee which was in the area at the time was trapped and rather than let the enemy regain useful possession of this valuable asset its occupants put it out of action. How exactly this was done is unclear but the statement by Hopkinson that it was 'wrecked by shells from an enemy armoured car' seems not to have been the case. Even MacEoin did not claim that the aim of his men had been so precise.[45] The driver of the Ballinalee, Alfie McGlynn, stated that he 'stuffed a mattress down the tower, followed by a gallon of petrol'.[46] The local newspapers said that the republicans used explosives to put the car out of action and the *Sligo Champion* said that its engine had been completely destroyed. It was still mobile enough to be triumphantly towed by the victorious government troops through the streets of Sligo to the Town Hall where it was 'inspected by the curious public'. A report from Army intelligence said that the armoured car had not been badly damaged but that the engine was 'smashed'.[47]

In an event which caused much bitterness, six republicans including Brigadier Seamus Devins and Adjutant Brian MacNeill were killed on Benbulben Mountains during this operation.[48] MacNeill was son of the Provisional Government minister Eoin MacNeill and his brother was a member of the national army. Two of the bodies were not found until almost a fortnight afterwards. An official army press statement said that the republicans had been surprised by government troops in the preparation of an ambush and that as they retreated four of their number were killed. Reports from the Intelligence Officer, 3rd Western Division Government troops, mentioned only that the four were killed in action and that 'Carroll and Banks were absolutely mangled by machine gun fire'. The IRA investigated the killings and cited evidence from unnamed Provisional Government troops that the six had been shot by soldiers after they surrendered and had been disarmed. They blamed the atrocity on a detachment of troops from the Midland Division who left the area when the big round up was over.[49] While conclusive evidence is lacking it appears likely that this version of the killings is true. The funeral of the dead in Sligo, with the exception of MacNeill who was buried in Dublin, was a large affair 'attended by all creeds and classes and political opinions'.[50] No attempts at revenge appear to have been made which are attributable to the weakness of the republicans in the area after the September round up and to the fact that the supposed perpetrators were not Sligo based.

These Sligo round ups failed to achieve their aim which was to surround and capture the republican concentrations. Intelligence reports had put the number of republicans in the north Sligo area at 120 and reports indicate that at most 40 were arrested during the round up. The remainder continued to pose a problem in the mountainous area in the north east of the county and in the area around Lough Gill. The attack did, however, break up the concentration based on Rahelly and opened up this area to the government troops. The deaths of Devins, MacNeill and Benson and the capture of the information officer and the Vice-Brigadier were serious setbacks for the republicans in the area from which they took some time to recover: 'The loss of Brigadier Devins and his companions was a very severe blow to the Brigade which had practically to be reorganised again . . . A month was spent reorganising the Brigade'. To make matters worse Pilkington had fallen and broken a limb and was also out of action: 'In fact the only member of the staff working during that time was the Quartermaster who tried to keep things as far as he was able'. The vacancies on the divisional staff were filled by the end of November.[51]

During October it would appear that the republicans were on the defensive and government reports were full of optimism. In a round up in north Sligo on 6 October, 36 republicans were captured and there were also arrests in Tubbercurry and Strandhill.[52] Apart from sporadic sniping of posts in Sligo town the only major incident there was the escape of ten prisoners from the jail which was accompanied by a general attack with rifles, machine guns and rifle grenades on all the government posts in Sligo town.[53] A Western Command report said: 'Everywhere our troops have gone they have gained the sympathy of the people. The people are coming out, building bridges and repairing roads'.[54] This reopening of roads seems to have taken place especially in the Skreen–Collooney area.

A report of 4 November said that Carty had lost men due to desertion caused by 'harrying and chasing' by government troops and claimed that most of Sligo was clear apart from some groups operating more as highwaymen than as flying columns. A weekly appreciation of the situation of 6 November reported that 'On the whole this Divisional area is fairly clear of irregulars. Carty's column is dwindling. It is reported most of his men have gone home'.[55] Some evidence from the other side seems to agree that this was a low point in the fortunes of the republicans. According to Martin Brennan, people began to be hostile to them in autumn 1922: 'It looked by their conduct that the people there thought we were beaten'.[56] 'During this time [23 September–4 November] we found it impossible to lie in ambush for any length of time especially on the Tubbercurry–Ballymote road owing to the activity of enemy spies', they reported and their activities were confined to destroying communications and sniping enemy posts.[57] Attempts to repair the Sligo–Claremorris railway line during late November proved futile. Rails were torn up at Curry and Collooney; signal boxes were destroyed at Sligo and Collooney. Repaired bridges at Curry and Drumcliff were again demolished during October. Drumcliff bridge had been repaired in September, was damaged again 14 October, repaired by locals assembled by the parish priest on 23 October and demolished again on 28 October – 'Our troops compelled the people who built it up to knock it down again'.[58]

The Provisional Government forces failed to take full advantage of this lull in enemy activity because of continuing problems with morale, organisation, supplies and equipment. Headquarters blamed administration in the Command, Command officers blamed lack of support from Headquarters, especially shortages of ammunition and transport. A Western Command meeting at the end of October reported that 'area is well in hand' but also reiterated complaints about neglect in sending arms which had been requested and said that transport in the area was also bad.[59] McCabe reported on 7 November 1922 that 'Carty is making a circuit of the Tubbercurry area leaving a trail of blood behind' and stated that it was impossible to follow him as the troops were short of ammunition, rifles and transport, instancing that at Ballymote there were only 26 rifles for a garrison of 50 men. There were also shortages of ammunition at Ballymote, Tubbercurry, Markree, Collooney, Ballisodare and Sligo.[60] A report for Commandant General Farrelly dated 17 November said, 'We cannot move from our barracks for the reason that we have neither transport or ammunition. We have plenty men of the best material possible but as we are we are helpless. During a recent raid after forces under Carty a column of ours went out with 15 rounds per man'.[61]

The official view from headquarters was that much of the problem was caused by internal difficulties. In October Mulcahy wrote to MacEoin pointing out that only 60 men had been sent from his command to the Curragh for training whereas he had expected a number in the region of

1,000. He also expressed dissatisfaction with the progress being made by
the command: 'Personally I cannot sense that there is any solid administration or organisation over the area pressing back the forces of disorder
there . . . The people of the area feel that no impression is being made on
the situation . . . A re-organisation of the area is absolutely essential.'[62] A
report of December 1922 mentioned 'the comparative inactivity of the
[government] troops' in the Western Command area and said, 'there is a
need for . . . greater discipline and efficiency'. The report went on: 'In
the 3rd Western Division there is much destructive activity on the part of
the irregulars, telegraph poles being cut down in the Sligo area. No
activity of any moment on the part of the troops is reported from this
division'.[63] A local doctor reported to the President that government
intelligence in the Sligo area was very poor and that there seemed to be
no administration done in the Command: 'Columns of 15 and 20 and
even up to 50 go on raids but apparently without any direct objective and
suggests that our intelligence there is altogether a farce'.[64]

November 1922–January 1923

By early November the anti-Treaty forces in the county appear to have
reorganised. Eight republicans had been arrested on 1 November in a
government round up near Tubbercurry, and Carty, obviously considering
that members of his column had been informed on, took drastic action. On
the night of 5 November he had two men shot dead as spies in the area.
His adjutant claimed that they had not received the General Order about
spies by that time and that the Divisional Command had approved of
the killings. In army activity as a result of these deaths a civilian was
accidentally killed and a republican shot dead while trying to escape.[65]
Liam Lynch, IRA Chief of Staff, on reading the press reports of these
killings, wrote to Pilkington demanding an investigation claiming that
'General Order No. 6 has not been complied with' and ordered that 'the
officer or officers responsible will be suspended pending further instruction after full facts are investigated'.[66] No action was, however, taken by
Pilkington or any higher authority. General Order No. 6, which had
been issued on 4 September 1922, related to spies and stated that all those
charged with espionage must be tried by military courts set up by the
Brigade Commandant and that death sentences should be passed only
where the information given to the enemy resulted in the death of a
Volunteer. All death sentences had to be confirmed by GHQ before
being carried out.[67]

The killings by Carty had an immediate effect. Eight Tubbercurry
inhabitants fled to Markree Castle post for refuge and McCabe reported

that 'there are crowds of refugees coming in from the terrorised areas to Ballymote and Tubbercurry barracks'.[68] For the remainder of the year Carty's column was very active. Sniping at Tubbercurry was a regular occurrence and a more serious attack on the post in the town took place on 22 December. A car carrying government troops was ambushed on 30 November at Powellsboro outside Tubbercurry and two soldiers killed.[69] On 14 December the column held up a train near Kilfree, disarmed some government troops on the train and sent the engine out of control towards Sligo in an unsuccessful attempt to wreck the line.[70] In the first fortnight of December, Carty's men were reported as being very active in the area, disrupting communications, raiding mail cars and commandeering transport. Attacks were made on Collooney Barracks and on Markree Castle at the end of December.[71]

By early December the north Sligo republicans also seemed to have moved back on the offensive. A small group captured and held the Town Hall government position for some hours, killing a soldier who resisted arrest. They then escaped with 21 rifles, four revolvers and 1,300 rounds of ammunition. This event caused considerable embarrassment to the authorities and an enquiry was held. It reported that a garrison of seventy-five troops was not sufficient for a town of Sligo's size.[72] The harrying of government forces in Sligo town reached its climax with the almost total destruction of Sligo Railway station on the night of 10 January 1923 in a well-planned operation carried out by forty republicans. This event attracted unfavourable national coverage and it was alleged that the troops in the town had been very slow to respond. It was pointed out in their defence that their effective strength on the night was seventy.[73]

In a survey of the north-west Sligo area by an unnamed army officer in December 1922 it was stated that the republicans controlled the entire area between Ballina and Ballisodare: 'They move about as they please and they commandeer everything they require . . . Column work from Ballina is useless as all Irregulars get timely warning and clear out'. Sentries posted on the hills could give warnings of any troop movements. 'Every day the irregulars are strengthening their position and recruiting more men', he went on. If things remained as they were, the irregulars might be worn down in two years but his opinion was that they were actually strengthening their position: 'You cannot hold the country as things are being done at present'. He blamed the methods adopted in combating the enemy, the procedure for paying the troops, and the lack of supplies and uniforms. His suggestions for a quick solution of the problems in that Sligo area included utilising a force of 5,000 men with flawless transport and equipment and ensuring the utmost secrecy.[74] The former was unlikely to be made available and the latter was impossible to guarantee.

By the end of the year republican columns continued to operate in the same areas as they had done since the outbreak of the war. A column of 20 to 30 operated in the Ballintrillick area of north Sligo, and the Calry area near Sligo town was frequented by about twenty led by Pilkington. Bofin's column of about twenty still ranged over south-east Sligo and Carty was operating in the Ox Mountains area with a column of upwards of thirty men. The government forces had posts at the following places in the county in November 1922: Sligo 211 men, Collooney 33, Markree Castle 110, Ballisodare 18, Tubbercurry 57 and Ballymote 43.[75]

A Western Command comprising the 2nd, 3rd and 4th Western Divisions IRA had been established sometime in the early months of the war but never functioned satisfactorily.[76] At a Western Command meeting on 22 November 1922 which was 'principally concerned with bringing about unification of action and complete co-operation within the Command' it was reported that there was a complete lack of communications between the Divisions. The meeting was adjourned until the following morning but an enemy round up started and it was never concluded.[77] In mid-January 1923 the Command Adjutant reported that his communications had not even been acknowledged by any of the divisions which comprised the Command. The Western Command had been without an O/C from the capture of Kilroy in November until January 1923.[78]

As had happened during the War of Independence there was great dissatisfaction at higher levels with the frequency of reporting by the 3rd Western Division. Liam Lynch wrote to Pilkington in November 1922 complaining that very few communications from his division had been received and that no communications from headquarters had been acknowledged. He was, however, gracious enough to compliment the Division on its high level of activity in the early stages of the war. Pilkington replied that communications had been sent to the Field General Headquarters at Mallow, Limerick and Clonmel but not to GHQ in Dublin 'chiefly for the reason that I was unaware of its existence'.[79]

At the end of 1922 Pilkington, again possibly reflecting what Mulcahy had called his 'tendency to poor mouth and complain', reported on the situation in his division, stressing the handicaps under which he had laboured. He reported that the division had not at any time had a full complement of officers, there had been no munitions output because of difficulty in finding a safe place for a factory and because the munitions officer had been killed in the war, intelligence had been badly hit by defections before the war and by the arrest of the Divisional Information Officer in the north Sligo round up. Engineering was a particular problem because of the death of the Engineering Officer and the failure to find a suitable replacement, Company and Battalion organisation had been neglected, and communications were unsatisfactory in the area. In spite of such a litany of misfortune he managed to find some source of optimism: 'I may mention that I find the civilian population generous and sympathetic in most of the area; there is no difficulty in finding billets and food for the Active Service Units. And it is my belief if our fight is maintained it won't be long until we have the people wholeheartedly with us in our struggle for the life of the REPUBLIC [sic]'.[80] This optimism as regards food supplies was not shared by the O/C of two columns operating on the Ox Mountains on the Sligo/ Mayo border who in January 1923 reported difficulty in obtaining food. The poor people among whom they were billeted had little food, the supplies in villages such as Enniscrone and Easkey were becoming exhausted, roads were blocked so that traders were having difficulty obtaining supplies, and large towns like Ballina which had been good sources of food and provisions were being heavily garrisoned. 'The food item is the worst item we have to face', the report said.[81]

January–June 1923

By early 1923 the situation nationally was that 'the conflict had become patchy and localised and scarcely merited the term "war"'. Sligo was one of the few areas of the south and west where activity by the anti-Treaty forces was still widespread though generally defensive in nature. While the major part of the Free State army's resources during spring 1923 were devoted to subduing the south, a reorganisation of the government army command structure in January 1923 resulted in a more efficient pursuit of the war against the republicans in Sligo.[82]

This reorganisation saw parts of County Sligo under three Command areas. North of the Ox Mountains including Sligo town was transferred to Donegal Command; the rest of the county was under Claremorris Command except for a smaller area in the south east under Athlone Command.[83] Since Donegal was almost free of republican military activity and the Command was free to concentrate on the Sligo area, these changes seem to have led to a more determined and effective policy of dealing with the republican columns. Their strongholds were repeatedly combed, often in combined Claremorris and Donegal command operations. In February and March a number of leading republican activists were captured or killed.[84] Some sniping at towns was reported during February to April but the only incident of note was an attack on Tubbercurry in which one Free State soldier was killed. The 4th Brigade reported having to lie low during the first half of February owing to activities of the Claremorris Command and six of their men were captured and one killed during this period.[85] A report from the anti-Treaty 1st Brigade at the end of January said, 'Since this area has been handed over to the Northern Command under General Sweeney the enemy has been very active. They are raiding the country constantly in large bodies'. In March 1923 a meeting arranged between 4th Brigade officers and 2nd (Collooney) Battalion staff could not be held because of enemy activity.[86]

Activities by IRA groups at this time tended to be those which involved little risk to themselves such as destruction of civilian property and communications. For instance, the diary of activities of the 1st Brigade for the fortnight ending 15 February 1923 reports only eight minor activities including five telegraph wire cutting or road trenching operations, one raid on a mail train, one sniping at an enemy post and one raid on a post office. In the period to the end of April there were 14 instances of private houses being bombed or burned in the county, all but one by anti-Treaty forces. One house was burned by Free State troops as a reprisal for a republican house burning and two were burned to prevent occupation by Free State forces. The others were houses of Free State supporters. 'This action had the desired effect especially in that area', said a republican report on a house burning.[87] Communications continued to be a target and the main Dublin to Sligo railway line was attacked a number of times. Attempts were made to damage the line badly by runaway trains during and at the end of January and at the end of March. Signal cabins were burned at Kilfree, Carrignagat and at Coolaney.[88] Free State troops began to repair bridges and clear roads as they penetrated more regularly into the republican areas and few reports of destruction occur after the end of March.[89]

Reports indicate that the 3rd Western Division IRA had continued strength in numbers and armaments; in mid-March the division was said to have had 400 men on active service and 1,300 reliable men on roll, 300 Lee Enfield rifles with 15,000 rounds of ammunition, four Lewis guns, one Vickers and one Thompson machine gun.[90] This high level of armament together with relative lack of action angered Liam Lynch who wrote: 'What is the cause of the comparative inactivity throughout area? Are all rifles in 3rd Western manned? . . . I cannot make out what they are doing . . . You must press that all rifles are manned; rifles if necessary to be sent to the 2nd Western and used.'[91] Later in the same month he said, 'Our position in this area appears to be very strong though the enemy had a good number of posts in it. You should press for more activity. The enemy garrisons in many cases only 40, 60 to 80 men. If all our forces on active service are properly organised into columns and well led they should be able to make things very hot for the enemy'.[92] In a letter in May 1923 about the poor state of armaments in the 4th Western Division, Lynch said 'You should get the 3rd Western Command to give them a little help also, as they are very well off; in fact better off than we are'.[93] His faith in the ability of the western divisions to turn the tide in the war seems to have rested on these reports of their level of manpower and armament and the hope that they would shake off their apparent lethargy and seriously engage the enemy.

Government troops continued to mount large-scale sweeps of areas frequented by the IRA. These resulted in a few arrests or deaths of the enemy rather than any large scale captures, but the cumulative effect was to limit severely any offensive activity on the part of the republicans and to hold them in constant fear of attack with few areas now being regarded as safe havens. Operations in the Arigna area commenced on 15 February and resulted in few arrests. A March round up in the area was more fruitful and resulted in the capture of the leader, E.J. Bofin.[94] Donegal command reported that they had repeatedly combed the Dromore West and Skreen areas of the Ox Mountains between Ballisodare and Ballina for the first time during the period 6–13 April 1923 in combination with Claremorris command and that while they had captured very few republicans they had deprived the guerillas of a hitherto secure base.[95] The anti-Treaty adjutant estimated that about 1,100 Free State troops took part in this operation from all the garrison towns in the area as well as some from Dublin and Athlone. About eleven anti-Treaty activists were captured.[96] There were still complaints on the Free State side about the calibre of the newer recruits: 'Most of the men in this party . . . were hopeless marchers and useless for further operations.' The establishment of three new government posts in this area by the first week in May consolidated these gains.[97]

Columns were still in existence in three areas, along the Ox Mountains where Carty's column was said to number about 20 men, in the Riverstown area where the column was now no more than five or six strong, and in the north Sligo area where numbers were estimated at ten to 15.[98] Athlone Command reports for April on the south east Sligo area claimed that the morale of the republicans there was very low and that 'their organisation is completely broken'. They were reported as moving about in very small groups, their activities being confined to looting, post office raids, road blocking and cutting of telegraph wires.[99] A report from Donegal Command confirmed the low morale among anti-Treaty forces while a Claremorris report said: 'The people are becoming very friendly to the troops and are now feeling more secure as practically every town in the area is now garrisoned'.[100]

IRA Chief of Staff, Frank Aiken, issued his call for the dumping of arms by republican forces on 24 May. According to Tom Scanlon, Pilkington was against the cease-fire.[101] Pilkington himself reported:

Although the feelings and opinions of all ranks in the Division were against the decision calling off the war and dumping the arms, still the orders enforcing this decision have been faithfully and effectively carried out . . . The prospect of getting money enough locally to meet our needs is not very encouraging as owing to all the demands of the past years on the sources at our disposal these have been bled white, dried up they are now.[102]

By the end of May Donegal Command could report that conditions in its area were practically normal with none of the republican columns showing any activity.[103] In a 26 May report, mention is made of two large-scale operations by government troops, one in the north Sligo and the other along the Ox Mountains. No arrests were made and there was no contact with the enemy. 'All their energies are concentrated in keeping out of reach of the troops', the report stated. It also stated that the attitude of the people was improving and that more information was being supplied to the Free State forces.[104] A Claremorris Command report for 2 June stated that 'all irregular arms seem to be dumped'.[105] Reports for the rest of June emphasise the deterioration of the republican columns: 'In the Sligo area especially conditions seem to be improving rapidly and in the area along the Ox Mountains which was the only important irregular stronghold in the area the irregular organisation is going to pieces completely . . . In no part of the area have irregulars given any indications of their presence'.[106] By July 1923 the Civic Guards could report that Sligo county as a whole was in a satisfactory condition and was rapidly recovering from lawlessness.[107]

Two of the principal leaders of the IRA in the county still remained at large – William Pilkington was not captured until August 1923 and Frank Carty was never arrested. In all about 54 persons lost their lives as a result of the Civil War in County Sligo. Of these, 20 were members of the government army, 23 members of the anti-Treaty forces, and 11 were civilians. A quarter of the army deaths were accidental and point to the fact that the soldiers were by and large inexperienced. Only two IRA deaths were accidental and almost half of the civilians who died did so as a result of accidents. By far the greater proportion of the deaths occurred during the first months of the war: 20 in July, six in August and 12 in September 1922. There were only eight war-related deaths during the period January to May 1923.[108]

Neither of the protagonists in the Civil War in County Sligo was at any time strong enough to inflict a decisive defeat on its opponent. Initially the republican side had the advantage of superior numbers and posts in the county, but lack of co-ordinated action and clear strategy rendered them ineffective and after some initial gains they merely waited to be attacked or threatened by government troops. When thus confronted the IRA either abandoned or were driven out of their town posts and took up the more familiar and apparently more comfortable role of guerilla fighters. The government forces were not strong enough or secure enough in their occupation of the towns and surrounding areas to threaten the IRA seriously at this time and stalemate followed. It required large sweeps by the combined forces of MacEoin and Lawlor in September to break the concentration of the IRA in north Sligo. While this offensive by the government forces achieved much, it failed to deliver a knockout blow. Both sides continued to concentrate on defensive strategies with the government side hampered by poor organisation and morale, insufficient training and difficulties with supplies. Survival rather than offensive action was the priority of the IRA and the ineffectiveness of the army meant that survival was relatively easy. When one side inflicted a severe blow to the other, as with the burning of Sligo Railway Station by the IRA or the north Sligo sweep by the Provisional Government forces, that side seemed unable to follow up the victory with a series of decisive actions. The army reorganisation of January 1923 improved the situation to some degree and from then they had greater, if still limited, success. The republicans on the other hand failed to cooperate to any significant degree and did not develop any meaningful offensive strategy. The government side were thus given as much time as they needed to build up their forces and they gradually wore down the IRA, as they captured significant leaders, encroached slowly on previous republican strongholds and allowed normality to return to most of the county. The sweep of Tireragh in May 1923 penetrated the last secure fastness of the guerillas but did not result in any significant captures. It was clear at least from early 1923 that the IRA in Sligo had no hope of victory but it was also clear that the Free State army was not capable of finishing off the enemy within a short period of time. Most of the IRA leadership in the county were against the ceasefire believing that they could survive indefinitely.

The Civil War, which had begun dramatically in County Sligo with armed confrontation in the streets of the towns and an artillery bombardment of Collooney, ended with a whimper as the few bands of surviving republicans, who sporadically carried out small-scale nuisance operations, dumped their arms and continued to evade the government troops as far as possible.

FIVE

===

THE GEOGRAPHY OF THE CIVIL WAR IN COUNTY SLIGO

THIS CHAPTER IS AN attempt to examine the Civil War in County Sligo in the light of the geography of the county, it being almost self-evident that the geography of a region influences to a lesser or greater degree any conflict which takes place therein. At the simplest level, the nature of the terrain of a particular area must influence the ability of a guerilla band to survive and the possibility of their opponents dislodging them. Did this mean that the war would be fought in the remote mountain areas of County Sligo, with opposing forces clashing in the bogs while areas of better land remained unaffected? Roads and railway lines were vital if the government forces with their superior mobile armaments were to make that superiority tell. For this reason these communication systems, difficult to protect as they were, should have been prime targets for anti-government forces. I shall in the first place examine the distribution of incidents during the war and assess its significance in relation to factors such as topography, land quality, lines of communications and poverty as evidenced by proportion of small holdings.

What about comparisons between War of Independence activity and Civil War activity? Does an examination of the respective areas of greatest activity tell us anything useful about the nature of the latter conflict? And then there is the question of agrarian unrest. Did this take place in areas which saw much conflict during the two wars? What about the geography of the participants? Did those who participated on either side come from clearly defined areas of the county and is it then possible to infer a geographical basis to the conflict in the county. Did poorer areas provide more support for the anti-Treaty side? Did better-off areas provide more personnel, soldiers and police, for the government side? To investigate this I will examine the distribution throughout the county of almost 600 known Sligo participants in the Civil War.

It is first necessary to examine the land quality and population distribution of the county. With the exception of one small area in the south of the county, all of County Sligo is in the 'limited' and 'very limited' land use capability range.[1] North of the Ox Mountains the best land is found in a strip of varying width of the north-west coastal lowlands from Ballina to Sligo. To the north of Sligo town the land is less productive though there are some pockets of better land along the coast. The central lowland area, south of the Ox Mountains around Ballymote, contains the best land in the county with the quality deteriorating towards the east, west and south. The slopes of the Ox Mountains as they widen towards the west into extensive boglands contain large areas of very poor land.[2]

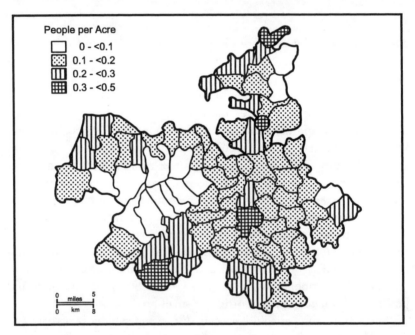

Map 5.1. County Sligo population density

Map 5.1 shows the population density of each district electoral division (DED) in the county in four categories.[3] The places of densest population coincide with the areas of better land in the coastal lowlands north of Sligo town which were classified as congested in 1891. The density lessens as the land quality declines towards the mountains on the east. The north-west coastal lowlands from Ballisodare to Ballina have a moderate density except at the western end where the population is densest. The poorer land on both northern and southern slopes of the Ox Mountains has the lowest population density in the county. The area of better land in the interior lowlands of south Sligo is only moderately dense, though there is a very densely populated area around the town of Ballymote. The south-east of the county with its poorer land is also moderately densely populated. There are only two areas, one in the extreme south around Gurteen and the other in the south-west of the county around Curry, which have a combination of poor land and dense population. These areas were also classified as congested in 1891.

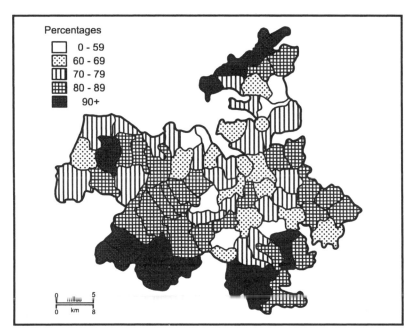

Map 5.2. Percentage of holdings under £15 valuation

An attempt to define the areas of high poverty in the county is illustrated by Map 5.2. I chose the percentage of holdings under £15 valuation in each DED as an index of poverty and calculated this from the statistics in the 1907 Report of the Royal Commission on Congestion.[4] To a large extent, these areas of high percentage of holdings of low valuation occur in the regions containing the poorer land. The slopes of the Ox Mountains in the west of the county, the mountainous area on the eastern border of the county and the poor land in the south of the county all have high percentages of such holdings. On the other hand the areas having the lowest percentages of such holdings are areas of better land including the north-west coastal lowlands, the inland areas to the north of Sligo town and the central portion of the interior lowlands south of the Ox Mountains. An exception to this pattern is the extreme north-west coastal area where there is a concentration of high percentages of these holdings on better land. This is also an area of high population density.

The two areas of dense population on poorer land have, as might be expected, a large percentage of small holdings as well. There appears to be no correlation between population density and poverty, the high population density area around Curry and the adjacent low population density area along the southern mountain slopes having similar poverty levels.

Distribution of Civil War Incidents

The natural starting point in investigating the geography of the Civil War would appear to be consideration of the distribution of war incidents in the county. I have compiled a list of 185 such incidents based on reports in local newspapers, official pro-Treaty reports and anti-Treaty diaries of activities. This list should then reflect the general pattern of war activity in the county though it cannot claim to be exhaustive. The extent to which newspapers reported events may have been influenced by the bias of the paper and by reporting restrictions. While the bias of most Sligo newspapers was pro-Treaty, the presence of the anti-Treaty *Connachtman* newspaper in the early days of the war should have ensured a balance in the reporting of actions at that time. Incidents such as intimidation of civilians occurring in areas outside the control of the government forces were presumably less likely to come to the attention of the press. However, this should be balanced by the fact that similar incidents involving the government side were likely not to be reported because of press censorship. On the other hand official records and pro-government newspapers may have sometimes exaggerated the number and gravity of IRA actions. No doubt local army officers did this at times to explain their own lack of success or their need for more manpower or war materials. It sometimes suited the government side to have such IRA actions reported, as evidence of that side's commitment to extra-democratic means at the very time when the apparatus of democratic government was being built up. It appears from comparison of newspaper reports, interviews with participants, IRA diaries and army reports that few incidents of any substance went unreported in the local press.

These 185 incidents (Map 5.3) generally involved attacks by the IRA on government posts, personnel or supporters or interference with communications and property. Incidents such as searches by government troops which did not meet with opposition are not included. Therefore large-scale operations involving great numbers of troops may not be included while the action of a single gunman, firing a few rounds at an army post in the dead of night from a safe distance, may be included as a sniping incident. This list does not differentiate as to the seriousness of the actions, which obviously vary in their intensity and in the commitment

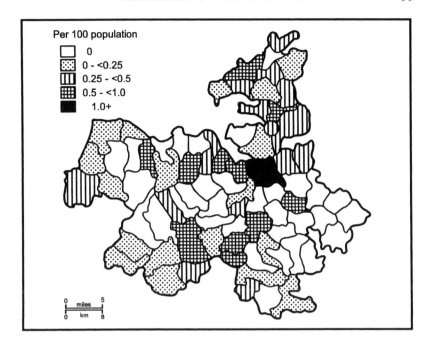

Map 5.3. Civil War incidents in County Sligo

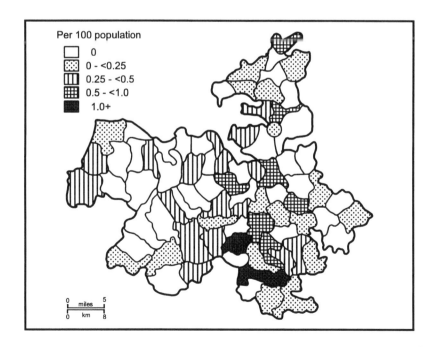

Map 5.4. War of Independence incidents in County Sligo

demanded of their perpetrators. It was presumably easy to find some one to go out and cut telegraph wires under cover of darkness. It was surely more difficult to find men to attack the Free State post in Sligo Town Hall in the twilight of a December evening in 1922.[5] Both incidents are ranked equal in my list.

I categorised these incidents by district electoral division and compared them with land quality, population density and poverty in order to assess if there was any correlation between the number of incidents and any of these three factors. The incidents were neither evenly distributed throughout the county nor concentrated on any one area. In south Sligo the poorer areas, both in terms of land quality and small holdings, to the east and west have very few incidents. In fact there was a large block of 14 divisions in the south-east of the county without a recorded incident, with the exception of the division containing the town of Riverstown. Similarly the poor land on the southern slopes of the Ox Mountains had very few recorded incidents. It is noticeable that all but one of the divisions in south Sligo with large proportions of incidents contain a town, Tubbercurry, Ballymote, Riverstown, Coolaney and Collooney being examples. The central portion of the interior lowlands in the southern part of the county, an area of better land and smaller percentage of holdings under £15, also had a large number of incident-free divisions. The south-west corner of the county had a low level of incidents. In the north-west of the county, incidents occurred in the coastal lowlands which had better land and smaller percentages of small holdings rather than on the poorer slopes of the Ox Mountains where there were some divisions with no incidents. The eastern end of this area had a concentration of incidents.

There seems therefore to be some evidence of a connection here between poorer areas and fewer incidents, better-off areas and more incidents. In the area north of Sligo town, however, there is little evidence of any such connection. The four maritime divisions here with the highest percentage of holdings under £15 valuation each had a different rate of incidents from the highest rate to none at all. This area has already been noted as being exceptional, it being an area of better land with high population density and high percentage of smaller holdings. While the evidence from this distribution does suggest that incidents were less likely to occur in areas of poorer land it also suggests that land quality or density of population were not the most important factors in determining occurrence of incidents.

There is much evidence from contemporary sources as to the areas of County Sligo in which the IRA were most active during the Civil War and an examination of this in the light of the incidents distribution may suggest a rationale for that distribution. According to Free State Army material there were three concentrations of republican groups in the county. The areas involved remained the same for the duration of the war though the numbers of IRA and the size of the areas were reported as dwindling as the conflict progressed.[6] Frank Carty commanded a group which operated in the west of the county, on both sides of the Ox Mountains. In early August 1922 he was stated as ranging between Curry and Coolaney and in an end of December report was said to control the whole area between Ballina and Ballisodare. Indeed it was not until April 1923 that Free State troops claimed to have penetrated this north-west area to any extent and Carty himself was never captured during the war.[7] The only Free State post in this area was at Tubbercurry and this was obviously a prime target for the IRA, accounting no doubt for the high rate of incidents there. Of the 16 incidents recorded for the DED containing Tubbercurry, ten involved an attack on or sniping at the army post in the town.

The second area where republicans were reported in numbers through-out the war was the south-east of the county, where a column operated on the mountainous poor quality land near and across the Roscommon and Leitrim borders. There was an absence of incidents in this area with the exception of the district around the town of Riverstown in the centre and at the northern end where there were some attacks on the Sligo–Leitrim and Northern Counties railway system. The anti-Treaty group here under Ned Bofin and Tom Deignan was either very inactive, unchallenged or careful to avoid conflict.[8] In fact it appears that a com-bination of all three contributed to the lack of action here. A Provisional Government Army report dated November 1922 states that while Bofin and his column was in the area, it was 'very difficult to get in touch with him'. Tom Scanlon told Ernie O'Malley in the early 1950s that 'there were no results from Ned Bofin's area during the Civil War' and the lack of incidents in the area seems to bear this out.[9] There was no government post in the district, Boyle being the closest, so there was no easy sniping target in the area. Of the seven incidents recorded for the Riverstown area, three occurred in July 1922 and two of the others were raids by IRA on shops for supplies towards the end of the war. The expanses of the mountains on the Roscommon and Leitrim borders were readily available refuges into which they could escape when attacked.

The area between Sligo town and the Donegal border was a troubled and contested area for the whole of the war and the widespread dis-tribution of incidents there confirms this. After the anti-Treaty forces evacuated their posts in Sligo town they exercised control over this area from headquarters within ten miles of the town.[10] The large-scale assault by the Provisional Government Army in September 1922 managed to break the hold of the anti-Treaty forces on the area and open it up to the army.[11] The IRA remained strong here, operating from the mountains to the east and south-east, and often attacked communications. The area about Grange appears to have come in for special attention and this group was also responsible for many of the incidents in Sligo town. The 25 incidents recorded in this area are distributed evenly over the period July 1922 to March 1923 illustrating the fact that, even after the penetration by the government forces of the area, the IRA were able to operate to some effect.

Comparison of this evidence with the distribution of incidents indicates an apparent contradiction, in that Civil War anti-Treaty forces remained in strength in the more remote and inaccessible mountainous areas which generally had fewer incidents. However, when it is considered that incidents are an index of conflict between the opposing sides not of strength of any one side, this apparent contradiction can be explained. Absence of incidents in an area does not necessarily denote an area of little if any IRA activity. These mountainous areas were difficult to search and afforded plentiful cover for the IRA, careful to avoid any direct confrontation, when the opposition did invest them. In February 1923, when the Free State troops made a determined search of the west Sligo area, the IRA had no great difficulty in avoiding them reporting: 'during this period our men had for the most part to lie low owing to intense enemy activity'.[12] The Free State Army, on the other hand, was not over zealous in combing these areas because of the perceived strength of the IRA there, their own inadequacies in personnel and armament and the difficulty of the terrain. Absence of incidents can therefore indicate either unchallenged IRA control or the avoidance of a challenge by the IRA.

The significance of the absence of incidents in many of the DEDs on both northern and southern slopes of the Ox Mountains is that these areas were controlled by the IRA who were generally unchallenged there. As has been stated in chapter 4, a state of equilibrium was attained in many such areas with very slow progress being made by the government troops in dealing with the IRA in their mountain hideaways. The main Sligo to Ballina road, on the northern side through the strip of better land near the coast, was often used by Free State troops and this resulted in more incidents in its vicinity. Incidents should then be expected in those areas at the periphery of IRA controlled regions where control was contested by the pro- and anti-Treaty forces, and conflict, including sniping and ambushes, was more likely. One such region marked by a high incidence of conflict extended from the eastern end of the Ox Mountains to the Mayo border. This marked the limits of Frank Carty's area of dominance. For instance, Carty's men were responsible for the attacks at Gurteen and on the railway line between Collooney and Kilfree at the eastern edge of their area.[13]

Another consideration which influenced the distribution of incidents was the situation of lines of communications. Impossible to protect completely, these roads and bridges, railway lines and buildings, together with telegraph installations and lines, were often the target of the anti-Treaty forces. An examination of the map of Civil War incidents in the light of the positions of main routes and principal towns and villages in Sligo suggests that incidents were more frequent where there was a town or a main route. The reasons for this are almost self-evident. In the early days of the war republicans held positions in all the large towns and in some of the villages. In some of these, Sligo, Collooney and Ballymote for example, pro-Treaty posts also existed and this often resulted in clashes.[14] After the anti-Treaty forces evacuated or were driven from their posts, the government posts in the larger towns commonly became targets for the IRA.[15] Efforts to penetrate republican strongholds used roads, and ambushes of their very nature generally took place on roads. The IRA also targeted railway communications and a large number of the incidents are of this nature. Of the 185 incidents used in this study, 56 were attacks on or sniping at pro-Treaty posts and 33 were attacks on or damage to communications including attacks on railway track, station premises or rolling stock, telegraphs and mail cars.

The DEDs containing the towns of Collooney and Ballisodare had the greatest number of incidents in proportion to their population in the whole county. This area, which contained the main route through the mountains between north and south Sligo, was the axle at the centre of the county communications. There, all road and rail routes from north and south Sligo converged, and three railway companies had stations and lines – the Midland Great Western, the Sligo–Leitrim and Northern Counties and the Great Southern & Western. Both towns had pro-Treaty garrisons during the Civil War. Collooney was a key town in the early days of the war in County Sligo having changed hands twice in July 1922.[16] In the division containing the town of Collooney, for instance, I have listed 18 incidents. Half of these involved attacks on or sniping at the Free State posts either in Collooney itself or in nearby Markree Castle and five were attacks on the railway lines that ran through the district. In south Sligo the areas of greatest number of incidents follow closely the lines of rail and roads as well as concentrating on towns. The railway line between Ballisodare and the Roscommon border was a common target, 14 incidents involving attacks on trains or railway buildings being reported from this area.

It does appear that the significance of the distribution of incidents lies in the fact that they occurred in general where targets were available. These targets commonly were government positions in towns together with communications lines and structures. The anti-Treaty forces did not have fixed positions susceptible to attack and so there are few incidents of this nature. The distribution of incidents then reflects the fact that most towns are in areas of better land quality and most important routes traverse similar regions. This accounts for the apparent correlation between poorer areas and lack of incidents already noted.

Civil War and War of Independence Incidents Compared

Having considered the distribution of Civil War incidents, it is of interest to compare them with the distribution of 159 incidents reported in the county during the period from January 1920 to the truce in 1921 (Map 5.4) with a view to investigating similarities and differences. The smaller number of War of Independence incidents over a longer period of time confirms the view that activity during the later conflict was more intense than during the War of Independence. The number of active County Sligo combatants on the anti-government side in each war was different. During the War of Independence a small number of full-time volunteers, probably no more than 50, were in action, while in late 1922 the number involved on the anti-Treaty side was estimated by pro-government intelligence sources at about 300. The nature of the conflict was also different in that during the early stages of the Civil War both sides occupied positions in towns.

The War of Independence incidents tended to be concentrated in the interior lowlands of the county with DEDs containing towns and lines of communications to the fore. As in the Civil War, large areas in the east and west of the county saw very little action. In the area to the north of Sligo town there were many more incidents during the Civil War and these incidents had a wider distribution. In south Sligo the opposite was the case. A large area in this region, which had a very high number of incidents during the War of Independence, saw very little action during the Civil War. This area included the main railway line and its branch at Kilfree Junction, which was a frequent target during the earlier conflict. The difference in intensity here was mainly owing to two factors. The terrain in the area was unsuitable for guerilla warfare of the type prevalent in the latter conflict and many activists in the area went strongly pro-Treaty. In the War of Independence this area had been to the fore from an early date, both politically and militarily. Almost all of the leaders here took the pro-Treaty side in the Civil War. Tom O'Donnell, TD, from the Gurteen area, told Seán MacEoin 'All the men of our battalion are on the government side.'[17] Jim Hunt of Gurteen Battalion was the only Sligo Battalion O/C to take the pro-Treaty side and most of his men followed him. He and his column had been primarily responsible for the incidents in this area during the War of Independence. In the Ballymote area Alec McCabe also took the pro-Treaty side and, according to Martin Brennan, 'more than half went with him'. A small column of republicans, stated to number only thirteen, was reported in the Ballymote area in August 1922, while at the same time both Carty's column and the north Sligo column were stated to number 100 each and the east Sligo/Arigna column 150.[18] Staff Captain Thomas Henry reported in November 1922 that there had been no irregular activity in the Ballymote area 'for a long time' and that most of the IRA actions in the Ballymote area were carried out by members of Carty's column.[19]

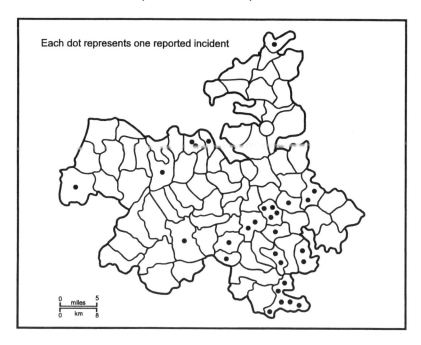

Map 5.5. Agrarian incidents 1919–21

To what extent was there a connection between agrarian agitation and incidents in the War of Independence and the Civil War? A map of the small number of reported agrarian incidents during the War of Independence (Map 5.5) shows such incidents almost totally confined to the south and south-east part of the county apart from a small pocket in the Skreen–Dromard area.[20] This agrarian agitation of mid-1920 appears to have been in many cases the opportunistic resurfacing of local agitations at a time of reduced police presence and power. It was not organised by Sinn Féin or the IRA hierarchy in the area and many of the landholders offended against took their complaints to the local Sinn Féin courts and were afforded protection by the IRA.[21] These were areas where small-scale agrarian trouble had been common in the period before the War of Independence. The Easkey area, which included Skreen, had seen almost continuous low-level agrarian trouble from early 1913 to mid 1915 and sporadic outbreaks in 1916 and 1917.[22] The RIC County Inspector reported similar sporadic agitation in the south Sligo area at intervals during 1915, 1916 and 1917.[23] These incidents occurred in areas where there was much War of Independence activity but few Civil War incidents. There was no geographic correlation between IRA activity during the Civil War on the one hand and previous agrarian trouble on the other in County Sligo. The statement made in 1923 that 'Irregularism and land grabbing go together' finds no support in County Sligo.[24]

Distribution of Civil War Activists

The distribution map of Civil War incidents tells us little about the attitude of the people of the different areas in the county to the warring sides. By definition the map of incidents is a picture of conflict rather than of control or of the sympathies of the population. People in regions controlled by a particular side were not likely to loudly proclaim their allegiance to the opposition. Many, perhaps most, were more interested in their own survival than in which party would triumph in the struggle. MacEoin's remark about the people of Sligo: 'They would be with you one day and against you the next', merely illustrated the concern for survival among the people and the resultant attitude of many of backing whichever side was in the ascendant at the time.[25] 'Sligo county is simply inclined to look on', commented Dr O'Donnell, Medical Officer Sligo, in December 1922 and gave as the reason that the people felt let down by the government forces and consequently would not support them. He added, in apparent contradiction, that 'Carty's column has terrorised the people to such an extent that they will give no information whatever'.[26]

As time went by and the Free State troops gained the upper hand, their reports commonly used such phrases as 'the civilian population is getting friendlier every day',[27] and 'everywhere our troops have gone they have gained the sympathy of the people'.[28] Similarly the report of their penetration of the Dromore West and Skreen district stated that 'with very few exceptions the people hailed the troops as deliverers and were inclined to give all the information they could'.[29] Martin Brennan's remarks on the killing of two 'spies' by Carty's men near Tubbercurry are enlightening, illustrating the point that people were prepared to support the side they perceived as being in the ascendant: 'People began to be hostile in the Gurteen and Moylough area and it looked by their conduct that the people thought we were beaten. Shortly after that we shot two spies.'[30] Such intimidation by the IRA also makes it difficult to decide what the opinions of the people really were. In a Free State report from Boyle at the beginning of May 1923 it was stated that 'the people are all against them [the IRA] but at the same time are afraid to give information. They are threatened with the death penalty if they do so.'[31] This is obviously an overstatement of the facts but it does illustrate the difficulty of interpreting what the people thought, by their actions or lack of action. The death penalty had been used by Carty and it is significant that it was used in the vicinity of the government post at Tubbercurry where there was an overlap of influence and where some people may have been tempted to defy the IRA because of the proximity of the army. Notices had been posted in Tubbercurry warning against speaking to pro-Treaty soldiers in November 1922. [32]

In order to assess the areas of support for each side in County Sligo it is necessary to examine the distribution of activists. This is based on the reasonable premise that an area in which there was widespread support for the pro-Treaty side would be more likely to produce recruits for the army or police than a predominately anti-Treaty area. Likewise more internees should come from areas where anti-Treaty sentiment was greatest. Map 5.6 shows the distribution of internees who gave their address as Sligo and Map 5.7 Free State Army members in December 1922 with Sligo addresses, both arranged according to DED.[33] It may be argued that joining the Free State Army did not necessarily always indicate support for the Free State side. There are, for instance, examples of Free State soldiers deserting and joining the other side.[34] Motives for joining the Free State Army are impossible to certify but it seems probable that many, if not a majority, of those who joined did so for economic reasons rather than reasons of conviction. However, it appears self-evident that persons opposed to the Treaty would not join the Free State Army; so membership of the army can be taken at the very least as indicating a lack of support for the anti-Treaty side. As with the army recruits it is of course impossible to gauge the strength of the support which resulted in a person being interned. All may not have been dedicated anti-Treaty activists. One may have been arrested and interned for doing a favour, carrying a message or hiding a firearm for a friend or relative on the run, while another may have spent months with a guerilla band avoiding, and sometimes engaging, Free State troops. While it may be presumed that most had committed anti-Treaty views, some may have taken part in the war because of friendships, boredom or hope of reward.

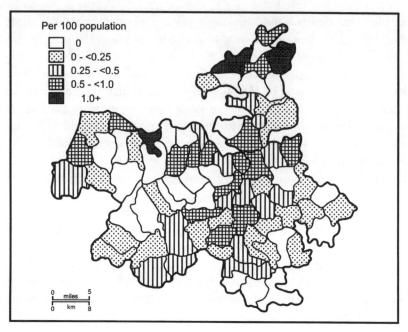

Map 5.6. Distribution of internees from County Sligo

It has often been assumed that internees came from the poorer sections of the community. According to Jack Brennan, 'when the Treaty came, the poor remained republican here but the people with a bit of property went Free State'.[35] This was related to Ernie O'Malley thirty years after the end of the war and may be coloured by simplistic romanticism. An officer of the Free State Army painted a different picture in a report for the Director of Intelligence on the north-western region of County Sligo in December 1922. This is the area then controlled by Frank Carty's IRA group and therefore the same area as that mentioned by Brennan. The officer classified the people there into three groups. Large farmers and shopkeepers of the area would, he said, support strong action against the republicans. The moderate size farming class, however, had everything to gain from lack of order, no rents, no rates, and they supported the IRA. The very poor were suffering great hardship under the IRA and were secretly hostile to them.[36] It should not therefore be taken for granted that the poorer people supported the rebels. Analysis of the distribution of internees in the county should provide sounder evidence.

High rates of internees are recorded for the northern part of the central lowland portion of the county from Sligo town through Ballisodare, Collooney, Ballymote to Bunninadden as well as some few divisions on the coastal lowlands of the north-west. These are areas of better land with low percentages of holdings under £15 valuation. However, the largest concentration of internees came from the areas around Ballisodare Bay from Sligo town to the eastern foothills of the Ox Mountains. The exceptional area north of Sligo town which had high population density as well as a high percentage of small holdings also had a high number of internees. This is the only area in which there appears to be any correlation between poverty and high incidence of internees. Few internees came from the poorer areas on the Ox Mountain slopes and in the extreme south and south-east of the county. These included areas which had been IRA strongholds during the Civil War. Similar areas in the south-west of the county around Tubbercurry had small numbers of internees.

The correlation co-efficient between internees per 100 population and percentage of holdings under £15 valuation is -0.122, an insignificant negative correlation. This confirms what is apparent from Map 5.6, that internees were not more likely to came from areas where the land was poorer or where there was a very high percentage of small holdings.

The distribution map of members of the Free State Army has a similar overall structure as that of the internees. Again, the central lowlands, the coastal lowlands of the north-west and the north Sligo area are strongly represented. However, within each region the area of densest distribution of army members differs from that of internees. In the central area it was the southern portion, from Ballymote to Gurteen, which produced the largest concentration of Free State soldiers. The western edge of the coastal lowlands has the greatest concentration in the north-west coastal region and in north Sligo the eastern portion with lower population density is more strongly represented. These three areas have little in common, population density is different, percentage of holdings under £15 is not similar and land quality is not uniform. The area of high army membership in south Sligo coincides with the area of very high War of Independence activity already discussed. The leadership here supported the Free State and this must have been a factor in determining the number of recruits for the army in this area. The same was not true of the other two areas, both of which were close to regions where the anti-Treaty party was in the ascendant for most of the war. It appears that this did not deter people there from joining the army.

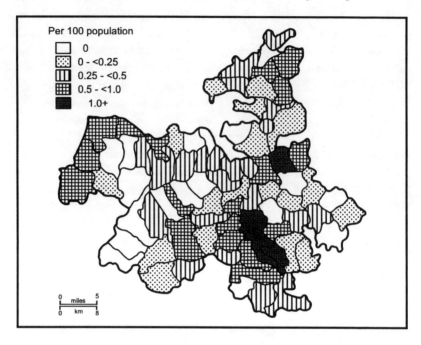

Map 5.7. Distribution of army recruits from County Sligo

The poorer areas on the slopes of the Ox Mountains produced few Free State soldiers or internees while areas on the southern fringe and northern edge produced more. The numbers of each group of activists from the Tubbercurry area are remarkably similar in spite of the fact that this area was regarded as being an IRA stronghold for most of the Civil War. In east Sligo the numbers and distribution of internees and Free State soldiers is also remarkably similar, some divisions registering an equal figure for each. There are 18 divisions which produced no army member and 23 which produced no internee, and of these 13 are common to both. There are therefore no clearly defined areas of the county which produced internees but no Free State Army members or vice versa.

To provide further statistical evidence on the question of whether internees or army members came from poorer areas of the county I compared the DEDs from which there were internees with those for which there were none and I investigated the same comparison for army members. The figures for percentage of holdings of £15 valuation or less is almost identical for each group (Table 5.1) confirming that the internees and army members came from DEDs of similar standards.

In both cases the percentage of smaller holdings was slightly higher in the DEDs which did not produce participants. This is further evidence that poverty as evidenced by holdings of low value did not produce more

Table 5.1. Comparison of DEDs with participants and those without participants

DEDs with:	% Valuation under £15
No Army members	82%
Army members	81%
No internees	83%
Internees	81%

anti-Treaty activists or government army recruits in County Sligo. I examined the set of 39 Sligo district electoral divisions where the percentage of holdings of valuation £15 or less was 80 or greater. This set, comprising the poorest areas in the county, accounted for 47 per cent of the county population. Graph 5.1 shows the number of participants and the number of incidents from this set compared to the rest of the county. The pattern is remarkably similar for each category with the poorer area having fewer participants and fewer incidents than the other. The fact that the participation rate of internees and army members is noticeably lower in the poorer areas is further evidence for the position already outlined.

Confirmation of the fact that even in poorer areas the Civil War division was evenly represented is provided in a strongly pro-republican

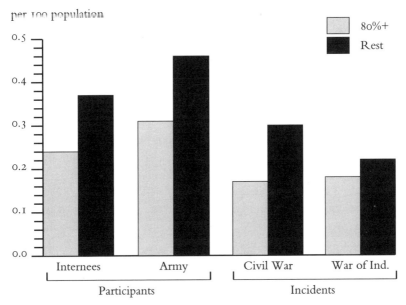

Graph 5.1. Participants and incidents (per 100 population) from areas where the percentage of holdings of £15 valuation or less was 80 per cent or more

memoir of the period. Speaking of his schooldays in the Curry area where over 90 per cent of the holdings were under £15 valuation the author says:

> As all these things were happening, we, little boys, were copying our elders. Our school had between seventy five and eighty boys who were fairly evenly divided between Free Staters and Republicans. We fought each other in the school yard and in the class room . . . We decided to challenge the Free Staters to battle . . . We recruited about twenty boys and there were about twenty Free Staters . . . I wanted to be de Valera but so did Louis Weaver, so I had to be satisfied with being Frank Carty . . . The battle ended with both sides claiming victory.[37]

It would be expected that the distribution of those who joined the new Civic Guard (Map 5.8) would correspond to a large extent with the distribution of those who joined the Free State Army on the understanding that both would have attracted those who supported the legitimacy of the new state. There are similarities in the distributions but there are also major differences. Using the registers from the Garda Archives I have examined the distribution of all those with addresses in County Sligo who joined the Guards between their establishment and the end of the Civil War. Of a total of 172 recruits who gave County Sligo addresses, I have identified to which DED 133 of them belonged. There is a large concentration in the area from Ballymote to Gurteen with just over 30 per cent (52) of the total recruitment coming from this small area. As has already been mentioned this region, where large numbers of the IRA took the pro-Treaty side, was an area that also provided a large number of recruits for the army. Jim Hunt had been appointed recruiting officer for the Civic Guard for Sligo, Leitrim and East Mayo in March 1922 and his assistant was also from the Gurteen area.[38] They naturally appear to have concentrated at least their initial efforts on their native area and it was reported that a large number of recruits presented themselves at Ballymote in early March with the first batch leaving for Dublin in mid-March.[39]

The large expanse in the western half of the county, including the baronies of Tireragh and Leyney, provided in contrast only 30 per cent of the recruits. In particular it is noticeable that DEDs in the north-west coastal lowland area of Tireragh provided very few recruits to the new force. The presence of Carty's anti-Treaty forces nearby did not hinder a large number of men from joining the army from this area but it apparently did from joining the Guards. The reason may have lain in specific intimidation against Guards. In mid-April 1922 Thomas Barrett of Skreen, the father of two Civic Guards from this area, was shot and seriously wounded by an armed gang who demanded to see his sons then at home on leave.[40] It may be that those who joined the Civic Guards had in

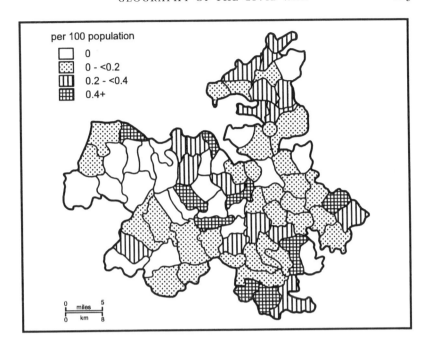

per 100 population

0

0 - <0.2

0.2 - <0.4

0.4+

Map 5.8. Distribution of Garda recruits from County Sligo during the Civil War

the main not been involved in the previous violence of the War of Independence and so were more susceptible to intimidation. Recruits for the army were more likely to have been involved in the earlier struggle and to have been able to withstand such intimidation.

Elsewhere in the county there is an even spread of Garda recruits with only five DEDs in the eastern half of the county without a recruit. Apart from the Gurteen area there are no other pockets of substantial recruitment; typically a DED has one or two recruits. It was not generally the case that the two recruits from the same division joined together. Recruitment, after the initial enrolment, was not a case of groups of locals joining up together because of an ideological determination to assist the stability of the new state. Rather it appears to have been individuals deciding to embrace the opportunity of a new career.

It appears that the position of towns and of road and rail routes were most influential in determining where conflict took place during the Civil War in County Sligo. Once the guerilla phase of the conflict was entered upon, the more remote mountainous regions became the bases of the IRA. In these areas they were for a long time unchallenged and they struck at Free State posts on the edges of their territories. When attempts were made to penetrate their fastnesses, the IRA generally refused to engage the intruders who themselves were unable to round up large numbers of the guerillas. More incidents occurred, therefore, in the areas of better land where the towns with government posts were situated. Because of the altered nature of the conflict there was little correlation between areas of action in the War of Independence and the Civil War. An area of south Sligo, in which political and agrarian activity had been high, had seen much activity during the earlier war but little during the later conflict. It did, however, provide a large number of recruits for the National Army.

Members of the opposing sides came from all areas of the county though in both cases the poorer areas generally provided fewer recruits. Anti-Treaty activists and pro-government recruits came from the same areas with no differentiation on the grounds of poverty. Though I have shown that neither group of the participants came predominantly from areas of poverty, it may be claimed that they themselves came from the poorer sections of the population in the relatively better off regions. Only a detailed study of the individual participants will provide conclusive evidence on which to base answers to questions such as these and the next chapter will examine in detail the backgrounds of the participants from County Sligo.

SIX

_____

COUNTY SLIGO PARTICIPANTS

IN THE PREVIOUS CHAPTER I analysed the geographical origin of over 600 Sligo participants in the Civil War. That analysis showed no pattern of either group of participants coming predominately from particular areas of the county. Participants on both sides came from all areas of the county although the poorer regions generally provided fewer recruits. However, pinpointing what areas participants came from does not tell the full story of their backgrounds. In particular, it does not tell us whether those on either side came largely from a particular social class or strata and examination of individual details of the participants is necessary to investigate this. This chapter will analyse details of the background of the participants on both sides from County Sligo to examine this question. Consideration of fathers' occupations and the valuation of land holdings and houses should provide important evidence as to the social standing of the participants on either side.[1] Were the oft quoted supposed archetypes true? Were anti-Treaty forces composed primarily of the 'men of no property' while the pro-Treaty side consisted mainly of those 'with a stake in the country'?

The Social Dimension of the Civil War Division

The question of the existence and importance of a social dimension to the Civil War division has been touched upon by many commentators on the period. Most, however, deal with supporters of the opposing sides rather than participants in the war. All stress the overriding importance of political, constitutional and military considerations in the split but many consider that social factors played a part also. Michael Hopkinson, in his book on the Civil War, devotes just over a page to 'Social Considerations and the Treaty Response'. He considers that it is difficult to demonstrate any social basis for the divisions on the Treaty yet goes on to state, without adducing anything by way of argument or example, that 'enthusiasm for the Treaty was much greater among prosperous farmers and businessmen than it was among small tenant farmers and farm labourers'. He also claims that 'a remote situation and a backward economy corresponded often with an attitude that was at best lukewarm to the Treaty'.[2] C. Desmond Greaves regards it as logical that 'the tendency was Republican' in Western areas 'with their land-hungry small farmers or large agricultural proletariat based on dairying'.[3] Tom Garvin mentions that there was some correlation between social class and support for the Treaty 'with employers, big farmers and many urban middle and working-class people supporting it, while other workers, small farmers and inhabitants of more remote areas opposed it'. He goes on to say, however, that at the level of the elite there was little correlation between class origin and position on the Treaty.[4] We have already seen that within County Sligo there is no evidence that inhabitants of the more remote areas actively supported the anti-Treaty side to a greater degree that those from other areas. The republicans certainly controlled many of the more remote areas of the county for most of the Civil War period but this did not necessarily reflect the distribution of active participation. As was pointed out in the previous chapter, the inaccessibility and suitability of these areas for guerilla bases, rather than the unforced hospitality of their inhabitants, was the reason for the anti-Treaty strength there.

Erhard Rumpf has made the most detailed study and argument about a possible social basis to the Treaty split. In his consideration of 'The social structure of Irish Nationalism and Republicanism, 1922–23', he stresses that the causes of the Civil War must be sought in Ireland's historical heritage and social structure as well as political manoeuvrings. Dealing with the composition of the opposing forces he claims that it is 'probably true to say that the sons of the larger farmers were to be found on the Free State side, while the sons of small farmers and the landless men were more likely to be Republicans'.[5] To support this theory he analyses public opinion in general. A desire for stability was, according to Rumpf, the reason why prosperous Catholics, the commercial middle class, and those represented by the Farmers' Union supported the Treaty. He goes on to claim that 'it is also true that the growing number of unemployed and the landless sons of small farmers provided an inexhaustible reservoir of recruits for the IRA'.[6] My survey of the course of the Civil War in County Sligo shows that this supply was indeed exhaustible and that numbers involved in active service on the republican side dwindled as hope of victory evaporated. Whether the sons of small farmers were more likely to be active on the anti-Treaty side will be investigated later in this chapter.

Rumpf argues that the division between the pragmatism of the Free Staters and the romantic idealism of the republicans coincided with certain lines of social division within the population. According to him, the small farmers of the west were 'sheltered from the worldly pressures which inclined other parts of the country to take a more practical view'.[7] The argument that the Sligo small farmer was in some way less practical than his counterpart elsewhere in the country seems very tenuous and the persistence of agrarian agitation among the same small farmers suggests the contrary. Paul Bew's view seems to be that the small farmers of Connacht were very practical indeed in their attitude to the struggle for independence: 'Connaught's fairly restrained contribution to the War of Independence had its roots in agrarian disappointments'.[8] According to Rumpf their remoteness and the primitive subsistence farming they practised were among the reasons for the rigid adherence of these small farmers to the ideal of a republic. Rumpf bases his discussion of support for the republicans, not on any analysis of activists, but on maps of IRA divisional attitudes to the Treaty and voting patterns of constituencies in 1922 and 1923.[9] These are very crude indices of support. Much of Rumpf's analysis is based on the idea of the whole of County Sligo as a remote and backward place. A prosperous businessman from Sligo town, or a well-off farmer with a large farm in the relatively rich centre of the county, would hardly have seen things in that light.

In his discussion of the social foundation of the Civil War, Charles Townshend claims that support for the anti-Treaty side among certain social groups was based on support for a different struggle from that of the middle classes for 'nation' or 'freedom' (his quotation marks). This struggle, he claims, was the struggle of the lower classes against the 'bourgeois regime inheriting and operating the apparatus of the English state'.[10] Others, with even less justification, claim a strict social or class division in the Civil War split. A recent polemic work on the Civil War asserts: 'Certainly there was an economic root to the struggle. Most of the republicans came from the rural and urban poorer class levels.'[11] The author lists categories of Treaty supporters as follows: Southern unionists, landed gentry, the vested interests of big business, Academics and intellectuals, the press, the clergy and the middle classes leaving very few groups to oppose the Treaty except the lower classes.[12] In general it appears that all of the above commentators believe that to some extent there was a class basis to the Civil War divisions, though none except Rumpf attempted to provide evidence for it.

Many commentators hold the view that while the proletariat did not actually join or even support the anti-Treaty side they were its natural ally. While admitting that the anti-Treaty side 'were without the slightest concern for class politics'[13] they deduce that since the vociferous propertied and commercial classes obviously supported the Provisional and Free

State Governments the lower classes, whose voice was less likely to be heard, were supporters of the other side. The notes written by Liam Mellows while in Mountjoy Jail in 1922 indicate a recognition that the proletariat did not take the republican side and marks an effort at encouraging the development of policies which might have attracted their support: 'In our efforts now to win back public support to the Republic we are forced to recognise . . . that the commercial interest, so called, money and gombeen men are on the side of the Treaty . . . We are back to Tone – and it is just as well – relying on that great body 'the men of no property'. The 'stake in the country' people were never with the Republic'.[14] Mellows and many like him considered that but for inadequate policy development the proletariat would have been the natural partner of the anti-Treaty side.[15]

Only detailed examination of the profiles of participants can establish the validity of such assertions and little such research has been carried out on Civil War activists. There is, however, some evidence from the War of Independence period as to the profile of volunteers. David Fitzpatrick found that during the final period of the War of Independence in County Clare: 'more of the new officers were . . . sons of labourers rather than of shopkeepers, from medium-sized rather than large holdings'.[16] Joost Augusteijn has analysed the social background of individual members of the IRA in the War of Independence and, while his analysis is confined to the pre-Civil War period, his appendix on 'Social Composition of the IRA' has some relevance. In the two areas of County Mayo which he examined he finds that farmers of holdings just below and just above average size were most likely to join the IRA. He found that 'IRA membership appealed to all sections of society apart from the most well-to-do, and disproportionately little to the lowest social strata'. Farmers were twice as likely as labourers to join the IRA. Augusteijn, like Fitzpatrick, notes a clear if small change in social composition over time which shows that poorer farmers and labourers were more likely to join the IRA in the final more active period of the War of Independence: 'Poorer farmers were less inclined to join when membership was considered a luxury, while they were less inhibited to join when life and possessions were at stake'.[17]

Peter Hart has analysed figures for IRA composition and membership for the periods 1920-1 and 1922-3 in County Cork. According to him 'During 1922 and 1923, as membership and the prospect of victory rapidly receded, farmers and white-collar workers among the rank and file dropped out in large numbers, as did many city officers who worked in shops and offices. Some manual labourers also left the movement but a greater proportion stayed: as a result the army became more proletarian.'[18]

He found that the changes in percentages in occupations of IRA members for the periods 1920–1 and 1922–3 were: farmers or son from 31 per cent to 18 per cent; farm labourers from 12 per cent to 21 per cent; un/semi-skilled workers from 19 per cent to 27 per cent.[19] While these may not be dramatic changes they do represent the only clear evidence for a more proletarian IRA during the Civil War but it is clear that in the case of Cork it is caused by the dropping off of volunteers of higher social standing rather than an influx of the anti-Treaty proletariat. The numbers involved in Hart's samples for instance fell from 878 in 1920–1 to 460 in 1922–3.

Occupations of Fathers of Participants

To investigate the background of the participants from County Sligo I examined the occupations of the fathers (and where no father was at home on census night in 1911, mothers) of those I have identified on both sides. These occupations have been taken from the 1911 census records. Parents' occupations give us an opportunity to see and compare the social and economic background of the two sets of participants. Because of the difference in time between the Army Census and Internment Books on the one hand and the 1911 census on the other hand, it is likely that some occupations are under-represented. Farmers' sons are likely to be over-represented while sons of those whose occupations entailed frequent movement of domicile are likely to be under-represented. Those with a firm stake in the community who owned their own home and property should be easier to trace while labourers and unskilled workmen living in rented accommodation or housing supplied by their employer are more likely to have moved in the period 1911–22.

Those whose families moved into the county after 1911 are also under represented for obvious reasons. In many cases such outsiders had a disproportionately large impact on political and military activity in their adopted area. For instance the Geoghegan family, originally from Limerick, who came to Coolaney Station House sometime around 1916, had a large influence on the IRA in that area. The three active sons took the anti-Treaty side in the Civil War and one was killed in a skirmish in County Sligo in 1923.[20] They appear in the Internment Books but I have been unable to trace them in the 1911 census. In all probability they were not in County Sligo then. Likewise the very influential figure of R.G. Bradshaw does not appear in the 1911 census in Sligo.

It is clear that in County Sligo both sets of participants in the Civil War were made up of a broad range of backgrounds but that farmers' sons provided the majority in both camps: the percentage of farmer's sons on

Table 6.1. Occupations of fathers of Sligo participants

Class	Army	Internees
Farmers and Fishermen	63%	61%
Labourers	12%	14%
Un/Semi-Skilled Workers	9%	5%
Skilled Workers	10%	11%
Clerical Workers	3%	3%
Merchants	3%	5%
Professionals	0%	1%
Sample	*201*	*168*

each side is almost identical. Skilled and clerical workers were also almost equally represented on each side. The group comprising sons of labourers, unskilled and semi-skilled workers provided more army members than internees. On the other hand the sons of shopkeepers, merchants and professionals represented six per cent of the internees but only three per cent of the army members. In the 1911 census the figures for farmers and labourers in Sligo represent 41 per cent and 15 per cent respectively of the total males 'of specified occupation in the county'.[21] This suggests that farmers' sons were greatly over-represented both among internees and army members while labourers' sons were slightly under-represented in each group.

The results of Peter Hart's investigations of the occupations of fathers of Cork rank and file IRA members during the Civil War contrast sharply with my figures for Sligo. His show a much lower percentage, 40 per cent, of farmers' sons involved, but a higher percentage, 26 per cent, of sons of skilled workers, and sons of merchants, 11 per cent, active on the anti-Treaty side.[22] In the case of Cork, 'artisans and tradesmen provided a solid core of support for the movement', but this was not the case in Sligo.[23] This may reflect the fact that the economy of County Sligo was much more rural based and had fewer urban centres of population than did Cork, where 'most Volunteers had non-agricultural occupations, and lived and worked in urban rather than in rural settings'.[24] This was not true of the Sligo IRA where a larger proportion had a rural background.

In Cork, National Army recruits mostly came from Cork city and the East Riding and 'almost none described themselves as farmers' sons'.[25] They were mostly urban and unskilled. This is again in contrast with the Sligo recruits where a majority came from the country areas and almost two-thirds described themselves as farmers' sons.[26]

The large percentage of farmers' sons among the sample from Sligo may hide real differences between occupations of those parents who were not farmers and this may be especially evident in the Sligo urban area. To investigate this I did a separate analysis of the parents' occupations of participants from in this area.

There is a clear difference in the two groups in Sligo town, although the small numbers involved in the sample mean the results must be treated with caution. Of the army members in Sligo urban area whose parents' occupations are known, 64 per cent were labourers or un/semi-skilled workers, while only 34 per cent of internees belonged to the same classes. Skilled workers were the biggest single group of anti-Treaty activists in Sligo town at almost 40 per cent. No army members were sons of merchants or professionals while 12 per cent of internees came from these groupings. This is clear evidence that in the Sligo urban area more army members came from the poorer classes and internees were more likely to come from the better-off sections of the community. In contrast, Hart's figures for activists' backgrounds in Cork city show significantly higher percentages of the sons of the skilled workers and merchants and fewer sons of labourers and un/semi-skilled workers among the Cork city anti-Treaty IRA: 'Nearly half of the men who remained in the city IRA for the Civil War had tradesmen for their fathers'. [27]

Table 6.2. Occupations of fathers of participants from Sligo urban area

Class	Army	Internees
Farmers and Fishermen	0%	0%
Labourers	48%	23%
Un/Semi-Skilled Workers	16%	11%
Skilled Workers	32%	39%
Clerical Workers	4%	15%
Merchants	0%	4%
Professionals	0%	8%
Sample	25	26

Land Valuation

While over 60 per cent of participants from each side were farmers' sons this may still hide a real social division in that one or other of the sides could predominately come from poorer or richer farmers. To investigate this further I examined the valuation figures for land occupied where the participant was the son of a farmer. Because of the varying quality of land held, these valuation figures, which come from the regularly updated Valuation Books, should be a truer assessment of the farm quality and income than acreage. A percentage of those found did not occupy any land of course, and the greater number of these occurred in the urban area of Sligo where obviously extent and quality of land owned was not the principal indicator of wealth.

Table 6.3. Valuation of land holdings of families of Sligo participants whose parents were farmers

Valuation	Army	Internees	County
£4 and under	25%	19%	21%
£4–£10	35%	45%	39%
£10–£15	26%	13%	14%
£15–£20	4%	8%	7%
£20–£30	5%	11%	6%
£30+	4%	2%	13%
Sample	*110*	*88*	—

The evidence from these figures is clear. Of those who were sons of farmers, more army members than internees came from very small holdings, while more internees than army members came from substantial holdings. In all, the classes under £15 produced ten per cent more army members than internees, and while 21 per cent of internees came from holdings of over £15 valuation, only 12 per cent of army members came from the same size of holdings. These findings confirm those from other figures. Certainly there is no evidence here to support statements that large farmers supported the Free State side rather than the republican side. If they did, their sons did not show this by flocking into the army. Likewise the perception that poorer farmers overwhelmingly supported the republican side is not borne out. If they were supporters, they did not show this by rallying to the hills to join the flying columns. Rumpf's assertion that the sons of small farmers were more likely to be active on the anti-Treaty side is not borne out by these figures. More probably these sons were serving in the Free State army.

House Class and Valuation

Another reliable indicator of poverty or wealth is house class and valuation. I first examined the house class of the individuals on both sides from the 1911 census. There were four possible house classes:

4 – one-roomed cottages built of mud or other perishable material,

3 – A better house with one to four rooms,

2 – A good farm house having from five to seven rooms, and

1 – Houses of better quality.

Table 6.4. Family house class (1911 Census) of Sligo participants

Class	Army	Internees
1	1%	4%
2	64%	73%
3	34%	23%
4	1%	0%
Sample	*201*	*177*

There are significant differences here. More internees than army members came from the better class 1 houses. Almost three-quarters of the republicans came from houses of class 2 while 65 per cent of army members came from similar class houses. Ten per cent more army members than internees came from 3rd class houses. This adds strong evidence that army members were more likely to come from the poorer sections of the community than were the internees.

To investigate this question further I used the Valuation Books to examine the valuation of the buildings of both sets of individuals.[n] These were their parents' houses in general though some of these individuals themselves would have come into possession of them after 1911. This confirms the evidence from the house class investigation. Significantly more army members than internees came from buildings of ten shillings valuation or less. Internees were more likely than army members to come from buildings of valuation between ten shillings and two pounds. Each category above £5 valuation had a higher percentage of internees than army members.

I also investigated the valuations of the buildings owned by the families of participants on both sides from Sligo urban area. The pattern here is similar to that for the county at large but much more pronounced. No internee from my sample for Sligo Urban area came from a house of less than £1 valuation, while 20 per cent of army members came from this category. Almost the same percentage from both sides came from houses of valuation £1 to £4. The percentage of internees coming from the categories over £4 is twice that of army members. The picture then of participants from Sligo town is of republicans coming from homes of higher valuation than army members. The urban poor seem to

Table 6.5. Family house valuations of Sligo participants

Valuation	Army	Internees
Under 5s	20%	12%
5s–10s	24%	18%
10s–15s	13%	15%
15s–£1	7%	11%
£1–£2	16%	21%
£2–£3	5%	8%
£3–£4	7%	5%
£4–£5	3%	1%
£5–£10	3%	4%
£10–£20	2%	3%
£20–£40	0%	2%
Sample	*180*	*144*

Table 6.6. Family house valuations of Sligo urban participants

Valuation	Army	Internees
£1 and under	21%	0%
£1–£4	55%	52%
Over £4	24%	48%
Sample	*29*	*21*

have joined the Free State Army rather than the IRA. In my sample there were ten army members and no internees from Holborn Street in Sligo's North Ward which was the epitome of working-class Sligo. The perception would be that it was this same class and the same area in Sligo town which contributed most numbers to the British Army. J.M. Wilson, visiting Sligo in February 1916, was told by W. Russell Fenton, clerk of the Crown and Peace, that 'Sligo town has done magnificently. Those of the lower classes who have joined [the British Army] have done it as a matter of business . . . The labour classes all through the county have done well.' Mr Nelson, a Sligo jeweller told him, 'All the corner-boy class has gone'.[29] Did these same people also join the Free State Army 'as a matter of business'?

While many of these who joined the Free State Army may have done so for economic reasons rather than reasons of conviction it surely can be presumed that at the very least they were not anti-Treaty supporters. Those from the poorer sections of society would have had less to lose in terms of status or employment and so would be expected to join the republicans in greater numbers if they had supported that side. In this regard the figures for Sligo town are most suggestive that the urban poor did not fight on the anti-Treaty side, and so it may be assumed that they did not support that cause in any significant numbers.

The Army Census does not contain any information about previous service in the British Army and it is impossible to gauge the number of Free State soldiers who were ex-British Army members. However, there are individual instances that we know of. The Free State soldier killed in the IRA attack on Sligo Town Hall in December 1922, James Skeffington, a native of Sligo, had served in the Connaught Rangers during the Great War.[30] Likewise Free State Army Volunteer Henry Conlon of Holborn Street, Sligo, accidentally killed in March 1923, had served in the Connaught Rangers during the war.[31] Sergeant John Carter of the Free State Army, a native of Strandhill, County Sligo, was killed in November 1922. He had also served in the British Army during the war.[32] On the republican side the only activist known to have served in the British Army was Thomas Goff who was shot dead by Free State forces while trying to escape at Beltra in February 1923. He had served in the Royal Flying Corps in the Great War.[33]

Sons of policemen appear on both sides, two on the internees' side, both from Sligo town, and one on the army side.[34] Other sons of policemen not in the lists include Harold McBrien, IRA Commandant in the east Sligo area in both the War of Independence and Civil War, who was the son of an RIC constable. Two of his brothers were also members of the RIC.[35] On the other side Jim Hunt, the War of Independence commandant of the Gurteen battalion, had been an RIC member before deserting in 1916. His brother, also an RIC member, remained in the force until its disbandment.[36]

Ages of Participants

Another interesting area of comparison is the ages of participants in 1922, given the common perception of those who fought on the anti-Treaty side as being younger men – 'the young irresponsibles' in Collins's phrase.[37] The most remarkable feature of these figures for County Sligo is surely the fact that one-quarter of the army recruits were under twenty years of age on joining and 65 per cent were under 25. This confirms the impression that the Free State Army was an army of youths, many of whom were inexperienced and poorly trained because of the lack of time between recruitment and active service. Figures compiled by Peter Hart for National Army recruits in Cork are very similar to the Sligo figures, showing the same large 'percentage of the very youthful'.[38]

Secondly, the comparative age patterns of the two groups of participants are interesting and informative. As might be expected the 15–29 age
range dominated both samples with the largest percentage of participants
on both sides in the 20–24 age group. The dominance of this age range
is most marked among the army members with 40 per cent of their
membership coming from this category as against 31 per cent of the
internees. The distribution shows that in general the internees tend to be
older than the army members. Forty-five per cent of internees were 25
years of age or over as against 34 per cent of army members. Figures from
County Cork used by Hart show the same pattern of older anti-Treaty
activists. The percentage of IRA rank and file under 20 in Cork dropped
from 25 per cent in 1920–21 to 20 per cent in 1922–23 with a corresponding rise in the 20–29 age group from 58 per cent to 64 per cent.[39]

Table 6.7. Ages of Sligo participants[40]

Age	Army	Internees
Under 15	1%	0%
15–19	25%	22%
20–24	40%	33%
25–29	22%	29%
30–34	6%	11%
35–39	4%	3%
40–49	1%	1%
50+	1%	1%
Sample	*332*	*173*

National figures for IRA Civil War rank and file members contrast with
the figures for Sligo. The national figures show a greater concentration of
ages between 20 and 30 (75 per cent), than in Sligo (61 per cent). The
Sligo figures show a greater spread of ages with 22 per cent under twenty
as against a national figure of 17 per cent and 16 per cent over 30 as
against 8.1 per cent.[41]

None of the Sligo internees whose age I have found was under 15 years
of age. There is, however, the case of Jack Fowley, whose name does not
appear in the Internment Books, which was raised in the Dáil by Darrell
Figgis in February 1923. Fowley had been arrested and interned the previous October when, according to Figgis, he was only 14 and a half years
old. After investigation Mulcahy replied that Fowley had given his age as
16 when arrested and had also given a false surname, first calling himself
Foley.[42] I have found two army members who, on the basis of the 1911
census, were under 15. They had claimed to be 19 and 20 when joining
the army.

The figures show that younger men joined the army rather than the anti-Treaty forces. As we have seen, many of these were farmers' sons and members of the labouring and semi-skilled classes who are likely to have joined for economic reasons. They may have been people who would have used the avenue of emigration had it been available at the time. On the other hand, the membership of the republican side in the Civil War was older and therefore more likely to consist of those who had been pre-truce IRA fighters. The figures also suggest that few younger people joined the anti-Treaty side after the split and demonstrate the fallacy of the statement: 'Those too young to have fought against Britain followed their elders into the Republican ranks'.[43] These figures, as has been stressed, refer only to activists and so do not necessarily contradict Tom Garvin's finding with reference to TDs that there was 'a slight tendency for older leaders to favour the settlement'.[44] The only IRA pre-Truce commandant in County Sligo to take the pro-Treaty side, Jim Hunt, was also the oldest at thirty and prominent Sligo politicians who took the pro-Treaty side, such as Alec McCabe, Martin Roddy and John Hennigan were significantly older than the anti-Treaty military leaders including William Pilkington and Frank Carty.[45]

Were eldest sons less likely to be active on the anti-Treaty side because doing so might jeopardise their inheritances? Were their younger brothers, Rumpf's 'landless sons of small farmers', more likely to be involved on that side?[46] Were they on the other hand more likely to be army recruits having seizing an opportunity for regular employment? Joost Augusteijn found no evidence of reluctance to participate on the part of first born sons in the pre-Truce IRA in his research on participants in four Irish counties.[47]

Table 6.8. Position of Sligo participants in family[48]

Position	Army	Internees
Eldest son	24%	22%
Not eldest	39%	34%
Not known	37%	44%
Sample	*214*	*171*

In my figures from Sligo the eldest sons among the participants amounted to almost the same percentage of each group suggesting that there was no factor which operated to a greater extent on one side rather than on the other. It has been suggested that farmers' eldest sons may have been reluctant to take part in the Civil War on the republican side for fear of jeopardising their succession rights, but a separate analysis of farmer's sons shows they participated in similar proportions on both sides. The rate of participation of the eldest sons of farmers was similar to that of eldest sons of all classes.

Officers and Rank and File

Another area of interest is the profile of the officers as against the rank and file among the Free State Army. I compared those who were described as Volunteer or Private with those who had other ranks, commissioned or otherwise, and investigated this with reference to age, land valuation and fathers' occupations.

Table 6.9. Ages of rank and file and officers of the Free State Army from Sligo

Age	Rank and File	Officers
Under 15	0%	0%
15–19	30%	4%
20–24	31%	36%
25–29	25%	40%
30–34	13%	6%
35–39	0%	10%
40–49	1%	2%
50+	0%	2%
Sample	*121*	*52*

Comparing the ages one finds as expected that the officers were generally older than the rank and file with most coming from the 25–29 age group. Few officers were under 20 though over a quarter of the rank and file were. Nearly 20 per cent of officers were 30 or over as against 14 per cent of the rank and file.

Table 6.10 Occupations of rank and file and officers of the Free State Army from Sligo

Class	Rank and File	Officers
Farmers and Fishermen	60%	75%
Labourers	13%	9%
Un/Semi-Skilled Workers	10%	4%
Skilled Workers	11%	4%
Clerical Workers	5%	0%
Merchants	1%	8%
Professionals	0%	0%
Sample	*201*	*168*

Almost three-quarters of the officers were sons of farmers compared to only 59 per cent of the rank and file. The only other occupation class that had a larger percentage of officers than rank and file was that of merchants. The percentage of labourers' sons and the sons of un- and semi-skilled workers among the rank and file was twice as high as among officers.

Table 6.11. Valuation of land holdings of rank and file and officers of the Free State Army from Sligo

Valuation	Rank and File	Officers
£0	21%	18%
£4 and under	30%	27%
£4–£10	28%	17%
£10–£15	15%	20%
£15–£20	3%	0%
£20–£30	2%	9%
£30	1%	9%
Sample	*136*	*45*

More officers came from larger holdings than did rank and file. This is as would be expected and shows that the officers in general came from higher strata of society than the rank and file. Free State Army officers from County Sligo then tended to be older than rank and file, less likely to be sons of labourers or unskilled workers and, if sons of land holders, to come from landholdings of higher valuation than the rank and file.

The figures which I have analysed demonstrate that simplistic statements on the social basis for the Civil War split have no basis in fact with regard to County Sligo. Though it is important to stress again that my conclusions refer to activists only, it is clear that the three criteria I have used to determine relative wealth and social standing – occupation, house class and valuation, and land holding valuation – all point to the same conclusions. As far as activists were concerned, the Civil War division in County Sligo was not based on social standing or relative wealth. Not only is there is no evidence that those who served in the Free State Army came from better off backgrounds, there is clear evidence that they tended to come in greater proportions from lower strata of society than the anti-Treaty internees. While this pattern is evident in the county at large it is more marked in the Sligo urban area.

The small village of Coolaney, on the southern slopes of the Ox Mountains, may have little claim to be regarded as a microcosm of Sligo at large but it is interesting to consider the five participants from there whose names appear in the two sources used. Coolaney had three internees and two members of the Free State Army. The three internees were sons of substantial shopkeepers or publicans while the two army members included the son of a farmer of six acres living in a third-class house and the son of a man who described himself as having 'no trade or calling'. Other republican activists in Coolaney included the Geoghegan brothers already mentioned, sons of the local stationmaster.[49]

Having examined individual participants the next chapter will look at the broader picture and consider the impact of the Civil War on daily life.

SEVEN

DAILY LIFE IN COUNTY SLIGO DURING THE CIVIL WAR

THIS CHAPTER WILL CONSIDER the effect of the Civil War on the everyday life of County Sligo under a number of headings and an attempt will be made to judge the degree to which daily life was disrupted by the war. It will also investigate if such disruption changed through time as the character of the war changed. An effort will also be made to ascertain if the interruption of the patterns of ordinary life was more marked in the areas which saw more conflict. It would be expected that the lawlessness of the times and the efforts of the republicans to hamper the mobility of the national army would have had an effect on the communication systems, roads and railways, the number of social functions held, the general economic life including farming and even on school attendance. All of these aspects will be looked at.

Communications

In the latter stages of the War of Independence, when the mobility of the Auxiliaries was putting pressure on the Volunteers, the Volunteers in response began blocking roads and damaging bridges. This meant that by July 1921 there was widespread inconvenience as regards communications in County Sligo. In March 1922 the County Surveyor listed seven major bridges which had been damaged during the War of Independence and needed repair or reconstruction, which he estimated would cost £1,540. A number of smaller bridges would, he considered, cost £400 to repair.[1] During the Truce period the policy of the IRA was that bridges should remain unrepaired because of the possibility of a resumption of hostilities: the County Surveyor for instance had been prevented from repairing Curry bridge in September 1921 by the local IRA.[2] Maintenance work on main roads had resumed in December 1921 but the County Surveyor reported in June 1922 that 'fair progress' only had been made. He said that contractors were in many cases trying to evade the terms of their contracts and there were particular problems in north Sligo where anti-Treaty forces were obstructing the work on the Sligo to Bundoran road.[3] Thus by the time the Civil War started, the road infrastructure of the county had not been repaired.

During the very early days of the conflict 'the attempts to interrupt communication with Sligo by road and rail were persistent and successful'. Rails were torn up on the Sligo to Dublin railway line and a railway bridge near Sligo was damaged by explosives. The strategically important road bridges at Ballisodare and Drumcliff, the former on the main road south from Sligo, the latter on the main road north, were blown up.[4] As the first phase of the war ended and the republicans withdrew from, or were driven out of, the towns, they continued their policy of destroying lines of communications. The pro-Treaty forces on the other hand effected immediate temporary repairs as far as possible in order to facilitate their own mobility and lessen disruption to the populace. By the end of July 1922 the railway line to Dublin was clear, trains were running regularly and the bridges at Drumcliff and Ballisodare had been temporarily repaired.[5] The County Surveyor reported at the end of August that damage to the amount of about £6,000 had been done to bridges in the county since the outbreak of the Civil War.[6] This, in contrast to the cost of about £2,000 for similar War of Independence damage, suggests the more disruptive nature of the Civil War as far as communications were concerned.

Communications continued to be badly disrupted for the rest of the Civil War. In the coastal area north of the Ox Mountains all the roads except one were stated to have been held by the anti-Treaty forces in August 1922 and were 'more or less impassable', communication between Sligo and Ballina being possible only through circuitous routes and by-roads.[7] In January 1923 the IRA, operating in the same area, reported that food supplies in the local country villages had become exhausted. All the principal roads in the area were kept continually blockaded making it more difficult to get 'anything like a decent supply'.[8] Tubbercurry, lying as it did close to the stronghold of the most active republican guerilla group, came in for much attention. In early September all public roads leading to the town were made impassable by broken bridges, felled trees and stone barricades. This caused anxiety: 'Something in the nature of a wild panic prevails there [in Tubbercurry] at the moment. Merchants cannot know how provisions etc. will be procured or from where.' Goods were, however, being taken to Tubbercurry by motor lorry from Sligo and by cart from Ballymote and 'so long as these lines of communications remain open there is no danger of a shortage'. It was said that the horses pulling the Ballymote to Tubbercurry mail car became so accustomed to hold-ups that whenever they saw two or more men on the roadside they stopped of their own accord.[9] After the Provisional Government troops had dispersed the republican concentration in north Sligo in September 1922, bridges in that area were temporarily repaired. However, the County Surveyor reported in October that two of these bridges had again been damaged and he had ordered all work on the Sligo to Bundoran road suspended. He had, he said, good reason to believe that some of the men actually employed on this road had taken part in the destruction. The men denied any involvement.[10]

Sometimes road and bridge repairs were carried out by local civilians in the usually vain hope that this would impress the republicans and dissuade them from further disruption. During October 1922 temporary repairs to Drumcliff bridge were undone and violence was threatened against anyone who again repaired it. On the following Sunday the local parish priest led a group of parishioners who made the bridge passable but these repairs were again undone on the Monday night.[11] In November 1922, at the request of the parish priest of Collooney, civilians helped clear roads in the Skreen and Beltra areas under the protection of Government troops. At Templeboy, roads which had been blocked were cleared in early November but were immediately blocked again. [12]

Railway lines were also a target for the anti-Treaty forces. Of the three lines which ran through the county, two were particularly vulnerable. The Collooney to Claremorris section of the GSWR line ran through countryside along the Ox Mountains controlled by Carty's guerillas and was closed at the outbreak of the conflict. In November 1922 a party of 50 Government troops cleared the line as far as Coolaney but the anti-Treaty forces retaliated by inflicting further damage and this line was not reopened until the cessation of armed opposition.[13]

The Sligo–Leitrim and Northern Railway line from Collooney to Manorhamilton ran through remote territory and was frequently the target of republican sabotage. In early July 1922 the trains on the line were prevented from running and even after normal service had been resumed later in the month trains were frequently stopped and passengers and goods searched. The Chief of Staff reported to the Minister for Defence in November that arrangements had been made for added protection of this line, which was to consist of 'sudden swoops' by National forces on villages in the area.[14]

The third line, the Midland Great Western from Sligo to Dublin, was a vital artery and ran through territory which, after the fall of Collooney in July, was not under anti-Treaty control. Attacks were infrequent and consisted of attempts to disrupt the line or to destroy railway buildings. None of these attacks caused any significant interference with services.

An attempt to burn Ballymote signal cabin in October was foiled by Government troops. Signal cabins were burned in November and March. Unsuccessful attempts were made to cause destruction in September, December, January and March by sending driverless trains careering down the track.[15] The Field Inspecting Engineer, Western Command, anti-Treaty forces, ordered the issuing of instructions to each company O/C through whose area a railway line ran to carry out specified destruction work on the line. In a major operation which may have been a response to this order, Sligo railway station was practically destroyed by anti-Treaty forces on 29 January 1923.[16]

Captured republican diaries of activities in January/February 1923 give an idea of the disruptive activities then being engaged in: 'Our principal activity during this period consisted of demolishing bridges, cutting trenches and felling trees on all roads used by the enemy.'[17] By April the Free State army was reporting that 'Irregular activity is confined to attacking railways, Post Office raids, looting, road blocking, cutting telegraph wires and sniping but it is very little.'[18]

Republican activity was not the only reason for the deterioration of the Sligo roads. Maintenance of the roads depended on direct labour and on contractors who undertook to maintain a fixed stretch of road. At the end of January 1923 it was announced that the County Council had suspended all direct labour on roads because of non-payment of rates and that the main roads, all under direct labour, were in a bad way. As in the Truce period, the contracting scheme had not been successful with contractors unable, unwilling or afraid to carry out maintenance. Because of the absence of a functioning police force or court system in the county there were no means of enforcing the contracts and in a report on the state of the roads for the period ended 30 September, 1922, the Sligo County Surveyor said that few contractors had got their work done during that time. Tom O'Donnell, TD, said that South Sligo was particularly bad, 'some parties do nothing but sit down and earn their money'.[19]

In April the County Surveyor reported that over 40 bridges had been broken since the commencement of hostilities and no work on permanently repairing them or revitalising the road maintenance system in the county began before the end of the Civil War.[20] This emphasised the fact that while the government forces increasingly took control of the county it was still possible for small bands of republicans to cause disruption to the road system. Road maintenance was impossible while this disruption could be repeated and while the absence of a police or legal system allowed those charged with maintenance to escape accountability. Because of this, the road infrastructure of County Sligo deteriorated greatly during the war.

Social and Sporting Events

The disruption of the transport network coupled with the general lawlessness of the times would be expected to affect social and sporting events most of all. Non-essential journeys, it might be thought, would be the first casualties. The farmer would still travel to the fair to sell his cattle but might decide not to venture to the parish hall to view the dramatic society's latest offering. Evidence from local newspapers confirms that there was a huge drop in the number of social and sporting functions in the county during the war period. The outbreak of the Civil War had an immediate effect on events with numerous cancellations announced. The Sligo branch of the Catholic Institute cancelled its annual excursion across the Leitrim border to Dromahair on Sunday 9 July. The annual retreat for ladies due to be held in Banada Abbey near Tubbercurry on 31 July was postponed. Beltra Industries Show fixed for September was not held because 'the abnormal times are altogether against progressive fixtures of this sort'. Sligo Cattle and Horse Show was also abandoned in 1922 as was the Achonry Vegetable and Home Industries Show. Several flapper race meetings due to be held early in August were also cancelled.[21] For the first time in nearly a quarter of a century the annual Sligo Feis Ceoil was not held in 1923, it being decided early in the year to abandon it 'owing chiefly to the impossibility of getting suitable premises under existing circumstances'.[22]

In order to examine the effect of the Civil War on social and sporting events in the county systematically, I recorded the number of such events mentioned in the three newspapers published in Sligo and two published in neighbouring counties which circulated in Sligo for the period August 1921 to July 1923.[23]

The graph of total number of events per month for the period August 1921 to June 1923 shows a very high level of activity from August 1921 to January 1922 followed by a steep decline from then to July 1922, reflecting the growing unrest between the signing of the Treaty and the attack on the Four Courts. The period from July to November 1922 shows a very low level of reported social activity coinciding with the period of the greatest Civil War activity. From then to the end of the war there is a small increase in activity but the level remains far below that of the Truce period.

There was, of course, a seasonal pattern to these social and sporting events, race meetings and athletic meetings being usually held in late summer and early autumn, while dramas and concerts were especially popular during spring, particularly during the period of Lent. To allow for this and to compare like period with like I divided the period into

Number of events

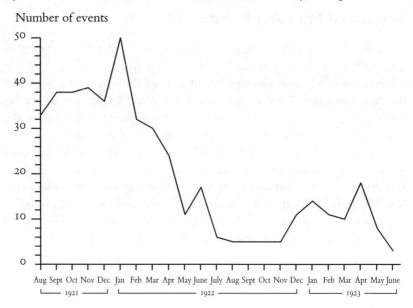

Graph 7.1. Social and sporting events in County Sligo, August 1921–June 1923

four sections: July to December 1921, January to June 1922, July to December 1922 and January to June 1923.

A comparison of the July to December period in 1921 with the same period in 1922 shows a drop of 80 per cent in the number of recorded events. This represents a major decrease in activity in all spheres of social activity. We are, of course, comparing two periods of vastly different moods, the euphoric Truce period and the miserable opening months of the Civil War. During the former period, the IRA were able to flaunt themselves openly and arranged or had arranged many opportunities for parading, for speech-making and for fund-raising. During August and September 1921 there were 30 reported or advertised aeraíochtaí in County Sligo, many of them including Gaelic Football matches featuring teams representing IRA companies.[24] There were also two waves of functions to mark the homecoming of some of those who had been imprisoned or interned, one in autumn 1921 when TDs were released, and another early in 1922 when the rest of the prisoners were freed. Added to these events were fund-raising dances held in various parts of the county, usually in aid of the local company IRA or Cumann na mBan. Indeed the reason given in the local press for the 'disappointing attendance' at a Céilí Mór in Sligo in September 1921 was that 'many such functions have taken place recently'.[25] Twelve dances or concerts in the period September to December 1921 were specifically advertised as

Table 7.1. Comparison of the number of social and sporting events held in County Sligo during four periods 1921–23.

	January–June	July–December
1921	—	184
1922	164	37
1923	64	—
% drop	61%	80%

being in aid of the IRA, Cumann na mBan or Republican Prisoners and some of the other dances and concerts may also have been IRA functions. Even if we disregard such exceptional events the percentage drop is still 74 per cent.

Comparing the period January to June 1922 with the same period in 1923, we find a similarly substantial though smaller drop in volume of activity. The largest drop was in the number of dances held, 94 dances as against 17, a drop of 82 per cent. In the period January to June 1922 there were 28 dances, concerts or dramatic presentations in aid of the IRA, Sinn Féin or in honour of released prisoners, but even when these events are omitted the drop is still remarkable at 53 per cent. A minor influence which might account for a part of the drop in the number of events was the attitude of the Bishop of Elphin who, in December 1921, expressed his disapproval of fund-raising for ecclesiastical purposes by means of 'whist drives, dances and entertainments of a like nature'. This was with reference in particular to fund-raising for the new Strandhill church and for which some functions 'of a like nature' had been advertised.[26]

During the winter and spring of 1921–22 there seems to have been a flowering of dramatic talent in the county, judging from the number of plays produced and advertised. Thirteen different dramatic societies in the county produced plays which were given one or two performances. Many titles suggested patriotic and political themes: *On the Run* was produced by two different societies; *The Smashing of the Van* concerning the Manchester Martyrs, *Lord Edward Fitzgerald*, *The Dawn of Freedom* and *For Ireland's Sake* were among others produced. A bilingual play, *An t-Athrú Mór* by Sligo-born William Partridge, was produced by two Sligo societies.[27] In contrast, only four dramatic societies are recorded as having performed plays during the following winter/spring.[28]

Christmas and the New Year were, of course, times traditionally characterised by a multitude of festive events. The curfew, which had been imposed on Sligo town from 13 December 1922 following the anti-Treaty raid on the Town Hall post, threatened to dampen the holiday spirit and limit holiday spending.[29] The local army authorities were approached by Sligo business people and asked to relax this curfew in order that business might not be adversely affected. It was accordingly only enforced between midnight and 7 a.m.[30] In spite of this, Christmas 1922 was, according to newspaper accounts, a very quiet time in County Sligo. 'Quietest Festival in History Perhaps' and 'Season Barren of Social Functions' were two of the sub-headings used by the Sligo Independent over an account which stressed the lack of public events. Apart from a football match in the Showgrounds and a dance at Rosses Point 'the entire Christmas season was practically barren of any social functions, which, up to recently, were popular events at Christmastide, especially on St Stephen's Night'. The cinemas in Sligo, however, were stated to be full each night during the season.[31] The *Roscommon Herald* noted that there was nothing in Sligo to show 'that the great festival had come except the extra bustle of the shops and the gaily dressed windows'. The same paper noted that the 'festive season was very tame and dull in Ballymote' and that social functions were conspicuous by their absence. A sodality dance in Gurteen was the only event of note held in south Sligo during the Christmas week. Similarly 'there was no demonstration of any kind in Ballymote to mark the arrival of the new year'. According to the *Sligo Champion* '1923 was ushered in in complete quietness in Sligo, no bells, no steamers' sirens. The cathedral's chimes did not play on this occasion.' It was reported that the Bishop of Achonry had asked that no dances 'or similar gatherings' be held in his diocese, which included much of south Sligo, during the Christmas holidays owing to the disturbed conditions prevailing.[32]

During the period from Christmas Eve to 6 January inclusive there were 29 social functions at Christmas 1921 while there were only nine such functions at Christmas 1922. St Patrick's Day 1923 was also reported very quiet in Sligo, 'compared to old days'.[33] Easter 1923 in Ballymote was likewise quiet, 'social functions, which were a feature of the Eastertides of the past were conspicuous by their absence'.[34]

Of interest is a comparison between the number of events in Sligo town as against the rest of the county. The ratios of events in Sligo town as against Sligo county for each of the four periods (July–December 1921, January–June 1922, July–December 1921 and January to June 1923) were 1:3, 1:2.2, 1:3 and 1:0.8. Only in the last period is there a significant difference in the ratio suggesting that Sligo town had begun to recover from the darkness of the troubles quicker than the rural areas of the county. The damage to routes of communications was more significant and disruptive in the countryside than in Sligo town and the hold of the Free State was stronger in the town with its garrison, ineffective though it was at times, than in the countryside where IRA bands had greater freedom and constituted a greater threat for a longer period of time.

Visiting dramatic and variety groups performed in Sligo town on an regular basis during the winter months of 1921–22, entertaining either in the Town Hall or in one of the picture theatres.[35] This type of show did not visit Sligo again for almost a year missing all the first half of the 1922–23 season. A vocal and comedy speciality act, *The Assassins of Sorrow* played for six nights at the end of February 1923 and in March the Harry O'Dempsey Popular Operatic and Variety Company performed extracts from *Il Trovatore* and *Barney McGee Matchmaker*.[36] The return of such shows to Sligo in early 1923 were a signal that the town was returning to normal after the worst of the Civil War disturbances.

All of this evidence points to a remarkable decrease in social activity in the county at large during the period of the Civil War. The decrease in activity was most marked during 1922 with a slight recovery during 1923. Sligo town, however, began to recover earlier than the rest of the county and the recovery there was more marked. This is corroborated by evidence from organised sporting activity, with GAA activity, traditionally stronger in the country areas, ceasing completely during the Civil War, while soccer, which was Sligo-town based, flourished throughout the period.

Sporting Activity

The GAA had been strong in County Sligo in the years leading up to the War of Independence with flourishing regional leagues as well as county football championships, which attracted an average of ten senior teams and ten junior teams each year between 1917 and 1920. The War of Independence had caused a severe drop in these activities with the 1920 championship having to be abandoned and no activity took place on the playing fields during the first half of 1921. As conditions returned to normal in the latter half of the year a number of local competitions resumed. Six teams contested a Sligo and District league competition which was completed in September 1921.[37] Further competitions involving six senior teams and seven junior teams were started in November 1921, but by the following February only eight matches had been played and it appears that these leagues had not been finished by the time the Civil War broke out and were then abandoned.[38] A Ballymote District GAA league comprising eight teams and a North Sligo league comprising seven teams started in late 1921, both being completed by May 1922.[39] Football matches and tournaments were common in the second half of 1921 in the Tireragh area of the county and a league competition involving six teams was begun in March 1922 and was completed sometime in May.[40]

In April 1922 a seven-a-side tournament was being played among the clubs of the Sligo and District League but there is no record of this having been finished.[41] A notice in the local press in mid-October 1922 announced that all matches under the auspices of the Sligo and District GAA League were suspended.[42] A Tireragh league championship had started on the first Sunday in June but there is no other mention of this league until September 1922 when a meeting was called of representatives from the clubs. [43] No report of this meeting or of any subsequent fixtures appeared in the local press and it appears that this league, as with the others, came to a complete standstill during the Civil War.

In spite of all the local league activity Sligo County Board did not organise a county championship until the county convention of March 1922, which decided to abandon the 1920 and 1921 championships and to make fixtures for the 1922 championships. Eight teams were entered in the senior championship and nine in the junior championship.[44] Some championship matches were fixed for June but there is no report of these matches having been played, and the 1922 championship was eventually abandoned at the outbreak of the Civil War.[45]

At the inter-county level there were high hopes that Sligo would do well in the 1922 Connacht championship as a result of good performances in the 1920 Connacht championship and the 1921 Railway Cup Final. A series of preparatory inter-league challenge matches, culminating in a test match between North Sligo and South Sligo selections, was arranged for June 1922, but no reports of these matches appeared in the local press and it seems likely that in the light of increasing tension and unrest they were never played.[46] Sligo were drawn to play Roscommon in the first round of the 1922 Connacht championship on 2 July but again the match was not played owing to the disturbed conditions.[47] GAA activity came to a halt in July 1922 with the outbreak of the Civil War and nothing happened on the Gaelic playing fields of Sligo until early 1923, when tentative steps towards a revival were undertaken.

The first reawakenings of GAA activity in 1923 came from south Sligo, the area least involved in the Civil War. A GAA tournament was held in Knockalassa near Ballymote in March and a Knockalassa/Keash selection played Collooney in two matches in April and May. A match was played between south Sligo teams Curry and Killaville at Tubbercurry in April and the *Sligo Champion* hoped 'that Gaels will show by their presence there that football is not yet dead in the county'. A South Sligo league was organised during May with five teams from the area taking part.[48] It was decided that the 1922 Connacht championship should be finished and the game originally fixed for July 1922 was now played in early May 1923 with Sligo defeating Roscommon. Sligo went on to win the Connacht final and qualify for the All Ireland Final by defeating Tipperary but an objection by defeated Connacht finalists, Galway, resulted in the Connacht final being replayed with Sligo losing the second time.[49]

In May 1923 the Sligo County Board made plans to finish the 1922 championship and the semi-finals of the 1922 County Championship were fixed for July 1923. The attendance at these matches was very small.[50] Twelve teams signified their intention of contesting the 1923 county championship, which was started during the summer of 1923 but eventually was abandoned because of numerous objections and disputes.[51]

With GAA clubs spread all over the county, the pattern of their activity reflects well the general situation in County Sligo over the period of the Civil War. As the tension heightened and erupted into war in mid-1922 Gaelic football activity waned and expired. There was no reawakening until clubs in south Sligo, the area least affected by the conflict, began to reorganise in early 1923 during the final months of the war. Once the war was over matters very soon began to return to normal.

The pattern of activity on the soccer scene in Sligo during this period was different. Soccer was at this time exclusively a Sligo town preserve and those who participated were working class rather than the middle class or farmers who were identified with the GAA. Soccer was not identified with any political persuasion though the presence of a British garrison certainly had been an influence in its development and popularity in Sligo. When a soccer league was eventually organised in Sligo in 1922, the chairman of the meeting and frequent referee of subsequent matches was Michael Conlon who was also a member of the committee of the Sligo Branch of the Legion of Irish Ex-Servicemen. He was one of eight Conlon brothers who fought in the First World War, four of whom were killed in action.[52]

By the end of the War of Independence soccer seems to have been in a similarly disorganised state to Gaelic football in the county. In September 1921 a *Sligo Independent* correspondent, 'Spectator', lamented the state of the game in Sligo. He appealed for the organisation of a local league mentioning the 'partly dismantled clubs' and the 'talent that is lying dormant among the manhood of Sligo'.[53] In a subsequent article the same correspondent asked, 'What is wrong with Sligo?' lamenting that no move towards organising a league had yet taken place in the town.[54] This appeal seems to have fallen on deaf ears and it was not until the end of May 1922 that a meeting of the Sligo Association Football League was held in the Town Hall. A competition involving nine teams from the town was organised and continued until October with good attendances being reported.[55] In spite of the state of war then raging, soccer matches were played in Sligo on the weekends of 1 and 8 July.[56]

This competition was succeeded by the *Sligo Independent* challenge cup, seven teams again participating, which continued during the winter and was finished in April 1923.[57] Thus, unlike the situation in the GAA, there was continuous activity among the soccer fraternity of Sligo during the course of the Civil War and that conflict seems not to have had any detrimental effect on the sport in the town.

There are very few reports of minority sporting activities during this period and those that do appear offer little evidence as to how they were affected by the war. Hunting was revived in the Sligo district with the reorganisation of the Sligo Harriers in October 1921. This club had regular meetings during the winter 1921-22 and 1922-23.[58] The other group of harriers in the county was that run by Major O'Hara which hunted the lands to the south of Collooney on Tuesday and Friday of each week during the season. These harriers also hunted for all of the 1921-22 and 1922-23 seasons.[59] There were no attempts to interfere with either of these groups during the Civil War – though a meeting of North Mayo Hunt Club was stopped by armed men near Enniscrone on St Patrick's Day 1923 and ordered to clear out of the district at once.[60] A tennis club was opened in Ballymote on Easter Monday 1922 and a new tennis court was under construction there in June 1923.[61] Sligo Coursing Club held meetings in November 1921 and in January 1922, but there are no reports of any subsequent meetings during the winter 1922-23.[62] Bunninadden coursing club did not hold any meetings during the same period and at the end of 1922 the committee was said to have 'expressed the hope that conditions will be such in the new year as to admit of a fixture being brought off'.[63]

School Attendance

It seems likely that the extent to which everyday life was disrupted during the Civil War should be reflected in the attendance levels at schools. This should be especially apparent in schools in areas where conflict was common. Evidence from three national schools in County Sligo shows that while there was a drop in attendance figures close to areas of activity this drop was small, suggesting that disruption of ordinary day to day life was not of large proportions. However, it should also be considered that sending a child to school may not have been seen as putting the child at risk even in time of war. Most children would have had a very short walk to and from their nearest school. The parents would have been sure that the children were being supervised which might not have been the case if they were kept at home and allowed out with their peers. There are no figures for the initial intense period of action of the war since this coincided with school holidays, which in 1922 were extended to allow primary teachers attend courses in Irish.

The sparse national figures for school attendance for these years provide little evidence of any adverse effect of the war on attendance at school. The national figures for calendar years (not school years) were: 1920 – 69.7 per cent; 1921 – 73.3 per cent; 1922 – 71.8 per cent; 1923 – 74.3 per cent; and 1924 – 73.5 per cent. No figures are available for 1922 attendance at Sligo schools but the average attendance in County Sligo primary schools was 69.9 per cent for the year ending 31 December 1923 and 70 per cent for the following year.[64] The usefulness of these figures is limited since they do not fit neatly into Civil War chronology but they do suggest that no large decrease in attendance occurred during the conflict.

To investigate school attendance for the period I examined the attendance records for three schools from areas of the county which saw different degrees and patterns of activity during the war, Culleens Boys N.S. (Roll No. 12140), Mullaghmore N.S. (Roll No. 14723) and Moylough Boys N.S. (Roll No. 13831).[65] I looked at the weekly and termly attendance for each school for the period September 1921 to July 1923.

Table 7.2. Percentage attendance at three County Sligo schools for the period September 1921 to July 1923

	Culleens		Mullaghmore		Moylough	
Term 1: Sept.–Dec.	1921	1922	1921	1922	1921	1922
Attendance	46%	46%	72%	67%	71%	65%
Term 2: Jan.–Apr.	1921	1922	1921	1922	1921	1922
Attendance	47%	48%	55%	69%	73%	69%
Term 3: Apr.–July	1921	1922	1921	1922	1921	1922
Attendance	43%	49%	66%	69%	76%	74%

Culleens, on the northern slopes of the Ox Mountains, was in an area where the writ of the Free State did not run until towards the end of the Civil War. Relative calm reigned here with few incidents reported while the anti-Treaty forces were in control. It was the week ending 21 April 1923 before a large-scale sweep was made by Free State troops in the area. Culleens Boys National School was closed for Easter holidays during that week, and during the following term the attendance increased only marginally. The average attendance for September to December 1922, the first period of the war, was exactly the same as it had been for the Truce period, and attendance remained higher during the rest of the war

period than for the corresponding pre-war periods. This is strong
evidence that the events of the Civil War had no obvious effect on school
attendance in this area. The average attendance at Culleens was significantly and uniformly lower than at the other two schools for the whole
period from September 1921 to July 1923, but this apparently had nothing
to do with the Civil War and may have been the result of local factors.

Mullaghmore, a seaside village in north Sligo, saw little action during
the war though it was under the control of the republican forces until the
major attack on north Sligo in September 1922. This school was closed
for four weeks in March 1922, apparently due to an influenza epidemic
which was reported as having closed schools in Sligo town at this time.[66]
The attendance was low during the weeks before and after this, contri-
buting to a very low average attendance for that term. Attendance during
the first period of the war, September to December 1922, was almost
four per cent lower than during the corresponding period in 1921, but
the attendance, like that of Culleens, progressively increased over the
following two terms of wartime. This reflects the lessening in intensity of
the war during this period resulting in a lack of incidents in the area.

Moylough is just off the main Tubbercurry–Ballymote road, close to
the former, and was in an area which saw much action during the war.
Attendance here was lower in each term during the war than in the
previous year's corresponding term. The early period of the war, September
to December 1922, saw the greater difference, five per cent, over the same
months in 1921. As with the other two schools the average attendance
increased each term of the Civil War. Two local men were shot as 'spies'
at Moylough early on the morning of Sunday 5 November. Later that day
a civilian car driver and a local republican were shot dead by Provisional
Government soldiers in the area. Moylough Boys' school opened as usual
on the following day when 52 out of 113 pupils attended, a 46 per cent
attendance rate, well below the term average of 65 per cent. The following
day the school remained closed 'by order of manager'.[67] This was presumably because of fear and apprehension after the events of the weekend.
On Wednesday the school was again open and it operated normally from
then on. Attendance on Wednesday was 50 per cent and on Thursday 63
per cent, close to the term average. The attendance for the remaining
weeks of the term was high at 75 per cent. If the low attendance was due
to the troubles then fear quickly evaporated and children were sent to
school without apprehension. A major ambush occurred at Powellsboro
near Moylough on 30 November 1922 in which republicans killed two
Free State soldiers. This had no effect on attendance at Moylough school
which operated normally the following week recording an attendance of
80 per cent, well above the term average.

The evidence from the three schools suggests that to a large degree they operated normally during the Civil War but that the disturbed times caused a marginal lowering of average attendance. This lowering was more marked during the first term of the 1922/23 school year when the Civil War in Sligo was being waged most actively. Moylough school was the only one where the attendance for each of the three relevant terms was lower than for the corresponding terms of the previous year. This was undoubtedly due to the greater number of incidents in the area, an area where neither side in the conflict was comfortably in control.

Food Prices

To what extent were food prices in County Sligo affected by the disruption and unrest of the period July 1922 to June 1923? Since communications by road and rail were subject to constant interruptions it seems reasonable to suppose that prices would be higher in those parts most affected by the disruption. Consideration must also be given to contemporary national patterns in prices. Food price trends in the UK show a fall from autumn 1921 until June 1922. A sharp rise took place in July followed by an immediate fall during autumn leading to another lower peak in December. From then until mid-1923 prices continued to fall.[68]

There are small collections of price statistics from the Irish Free State area and a price index using July 1914 prices as a base of 100.[69] These are only available from March 1922 at four monthly intervals. These figures, while sparse, do suggest that as in the UK as a whole, food prices rose after June 1922. In Ireland's case the rise continued until January 1923 and subsequently dropped to summer 1923. The difference in pattern is presumably due to the effect of the Civil War.

I have found records of actual prices charged in the village of Coolaney, County Sligo, for this period.[70] Coolaney was served by the Midland Great Western railway line, which was closed for most of the Civil War, and goods had to be transported either from the nearest Great Southern & Western railway station, six miles distant at Collooney, or from the town of Sligo. It might be expected that this extra cartage would mean that prices of foodstuffs would be increased. I have looked at a series of prices for this period for four items – oatmeal, sugar, Indian meal and tea.

The price of oatmeal at Coolaney over the period saw a rise from 30 pence per stone in the pre-Civil War period to 39 pence during August 1922, a rise of 30 per cent, but a drop during December to pre-Civil War levels. The pattern of average Irish oatmeal prices seems to be different with no similar large rise in prices at the same time. The price of sugar at Coolaney shows a similar pattern to that of oatmeal. There was a rise of eight per cent in the price in early August 1922, which was maintained until November when the price returned to its previous level and remained so until February 1923 when it rose sharply and maintained a high level until the end of the period in question. The price of Indian meal at Coolaney, for which there are no comparable national figures, shows the same pattern as the other two commodities. Prices began to rise at the end of July, reached a high at the end of October and by January had fallen to pre-Civil War values.

The price of tea at Coolaney, however, did not follow the same pattern. Tea remained steady at 5 shillings per lb. from May 1922 to the end of July 1922, began to come down then and reached its lowest price of 4s 2d in December 1922. It fluctuated between that and 4s 6d for the rest of the period. The price rises which occurred in three of these commodities are strong evidence of a price rise in food at Coolaney starting in July/August 1922 and lasting for three to four months. If so it would seem sensible to attribute this to the effects of the Civil War disruption. The fact that tea prices do not correspond to this trend suggests the need for caution, however, and the possibility that other factors were at work to a larger degree. The disruption, of course, continued and the later downward adjustment of prices may reflect a coming to terms with economic conditions and the making of alternative arrangements.

I have also found some prices for the Civil War period from Tubbercurry.[71] Like Coolaney, Tubbercurry was on the Midland Great Western railway system and so was without a rail link for most of the period. The nearest operational railway station was ten miles away at Ballymote and in the earlier part of the period the Tubbercurry–Ballymote road was subject to blocking and bridge-damaging operations. A series of Indian meal prices for the period in Tubbercurry show a 27 per cent increase in price between 3 July and 7 August 1922, from 16.5 pence to 21 pence. The price had dropped to 18 pence by December 1922 and remained at this level for the rest of the period. This pattern is similar to that for Indian meal prices at Coolaney. A comparison of the price of flour in Coolaney and Tubbercurry shows that while the price in both places was the same in May 1922, by December 1922/January 1923 there was a 12 per cent differential, flour being more expensive at Tubbercurry than at Coolaney. Tubbercurry's distance from a rail link was presumably the reason for this.

All this suggests that the disruption caused by the Civil War had an effect, though not a major one, on prices of foodstuffs in shops and it appears, though the information is not abundant, that distance from railway connections meant higher prices. This effect was most marked during the early period of the war but by early 1923 the effect was wearing off.

Table 7.3. Business figures for Meehan Bros, Drapers, Sligo

Half-year	Sales	% credit	Profits
1920	£8272	25%	
1920	£7093	26%	£3784
1921	£6780	28%	
1921	£6319	28%	£1339
1922	£6274	33%	
1922	£6660	38%	£3189
1923	£5702	28%	
1923	£4795	26%	£2405

The business accounts of a large drapery store in Sligo town, Meehan Brothers, demonstrate no great detrimental effect of the war, their half yearly sales figures showing no marked decrease during the period of the Civil War.[72] In fact the figures for the second half of 1922, when it might be expected that their business would be most adversely affected, were better than those for the second halves of 1921 and of 1923. Sales for the first half of 1922, which included July, though lower than the corresponding period in 1921 were higher than the same period in 1923.[73] It may be significant, however, that the percentage of sales accounted for by credit as against cash is higher in 1922 than either 1921 or 1923. Normally this percentage lay within the range 25–28 per cent but the 1922 figures were 33 per cent for the first half and 38 per cent for the second half. This is presumably a reflection of the poor prices being paid for farm produce and the fall in employment at the time. A comment by the Tubbercurry correspondent of the *Western People* in November 1922 may be relevant: 'Merchants are complaining of the scarcity of cash but country people while anxious to discharge their liabilities are unable to do so owing to bad fairs and low prices for agricultural matters.'[74]

Industrial Unrest

Moves to reduce wages were common in Britain and Ireland as a result of the general depression which followed the First World War. Bakers in Tighe's Bakery, Sligo, refused to accept a reduction of five shillings per week in their wages in November 1921 and gave a week's strike notice. There is no subsequent mention of this in any of the local papers, which suggests that a compromise settlement was arrived at.[75] According to the Dublin-based *Voice of Labour*, 'a short sharp fight' by builders' labourers in Sligo resulted in the dropping of a planned reduction of twopence per hour in their wages.[76] A tailors' strike in Sligo in early January 1922 against a similar twopence per hour wage reduction eventually resulted in an amicable settlement. In the same month a proposal to reduce the wages of cabinetmakers in Sligo by two pence per hour had to be postponed until the following May.[77] No report of such an attempt at wage reduction appeared in local newspapers later in the year so it is reasonable to assume that it did not take place. At the AGM of the Trades Council in March 1923 the newly elected president, Henry DePew, warned that he expected a big move in Sligo in the near future to reduce wages, suggesting that such a move had not yet taken place on a large scale.[78] At a Labour Day demonstration in Sligo on Sunday 6 May 1923, four resolutions were put, none concerning wage reductions which provides evidence, admittedly circumstantial, that such reductions had not been widely proposed in Sligo.[79]

There are few other indications of industrial unrest in the period. The general depression, the threat of wage reductions and the division in the forces of labour in Sligo were responsible for this. In mid-March 1922, what the *Sligo Independent* called a 'brief strike' took place in the mills in Ballisodare. According to the *Voice of Labour* this was caused when two labourers were dismissed when they refused to perform a 'muck and watery' job. The strike resulted in their reinstatement.[80] In May 1922 labourers who were employed at Rosses Point in direct labour went on strike. 'They are too lazy to work and they don't want anyone else to work either', the County Surveyor told a County Council meeting.[81] Mahon's sawmills and the Sligo Garage both closed during the last week in October 1922, sufficient work not being available.[82] In September 1922 two business premises in Sligo town, McCarrick's Coach Factory and Messrs Cooke and McNeilly's Bacon Factory, were burned to the ground. There was no suggestion in the local press that either fire was malicious, 'more or less a mystery and points to being accidental', the *Sligo Independent* commented on the second fire. It was estimated that 50 to 60 workers were thrown out of employment as a result.[83]

Pollexfen's flour mills, Ballisodare, announced in November 1922 that because of the 'poor demand for flour at the present time' the mills were to be put on half time. The workers brought their case to the Trades Council and asked that the 'dumping' of foreign flour be condemned. The Council called on Dáil Éireann to impose a duty on foreign manufacture and called on organised workers to refuse to handle foreign flour.[84] A letter from Josslyn Gore-Booth the following week pointed out that Pollexfen's 'Avena' flour was in fact made from foreign grain. 'People who live in glass houses should not throw stones', he quoted, pointing out that the mill run by Drumcliff Co-operative Society was again in operation and suggesting that 'if any consumers want meal which is really

Irish let them support the products of this mill'.[85] The *Voice of Labour* had earlier called Gore-Booth 'Jossie the Lissadell Lollipop', claiming that his labourers received only 23 shillings per week and were ready to strike for an increase.[86] In March 1923 Sligo Trades and Labour Council congratulated Sligo workers for refusing to handle a consignment of meal imported from Derry by a Sligo merchant, 'they being of the opinion that a superior article is being manufactured in the mills in Sligo'.[87]

Agricultural Prices

The years 1921–23 saw a general depression in agricultural prices in Ireland. The ending of the war and the gradual return to normal trading conditions resulted in a fall in agricultural prices:

> Between 1920 and 1921 the Sauerbeck–Statist index registered falls of 37% for arable products and 17% for animal products. Thereafter the decline continued. By 1923 the price of arable products was 57% below the level of 1920; that of animal produce – of more concern to Irish farmers – had fallen by 38%. Store cattle prices declined by over 40%, approximately 10% more than the cost of living.[88]

An editorial in *The Irish Farmer*, the organ of the the Irish Farmers' Union, in October 1921 stated that 'the outlook for agriculture as a whole this winter can only be described as one of the blackest and look in what direction one will there is hardly a prospect which can be considered as encouraging.'[89] The column 'Recent Irish Fairs' in the same publication continually reported the downward tendency in livestock prices during the winter of 1921 and spring and early summer of the following year.[90] The organiser of the Sligo Farmers' Association was quoted as saying in October 1922 that 'the price of everything which the farmer has to sell is at its lowest'.[91] Presumably in response to a collapse in demand because of poor agricultural income, the merchants, Woods of Sligo, announced sweeping reductions in the prices of manures in spring 1922.[92]

A study of a series of average prices for six items (young calves, Store cattle 1–2 years old, Lambs under 12 months, Young pigs 8–10 months, Springers, and Store sheep 1–2 years) for Connacht and for Ireland shows that the Connacht prices were similar to the national pattern.[93] Livestock prices were at their lowest in the period December 1921 to June 1922, when they were in the region of 70 per cent of the June 1921 prices. From then there was a very gradual recovery until March 1923 to be followed by a drop by June 1923.

With livestock prices in Connacht rising, albeit very gradually, from June 1922, it appears that the Civil War disturbances had little effect on prices generally. Nevertheless, all the evidence from County Sligo for

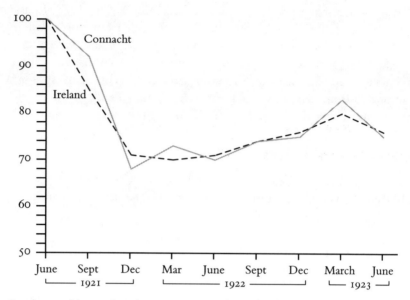

Graph 7.2. Livestock prices per quarter in Ireland and in Connacht, June 1921–June 1923

the period suggests that contemporary commentators considered that the war was a major factor in what they regarded as the continuing collapse of prices in the county. The *Sligo Independent* in its editorial of 6 January 1923 looked forward to the prospects for commerce and agriculture in Ireland. It listed the reasons why both had suffered and put the Civil War as the last of three reasons, citing 'a falling market, a reduced demand, and the disturbed conditions of the country' as the causes. It contrasted the condition of England, which it claimed was well on the way to prosperity, with that of Ireland which was 'committing national suicide'.[94] An article by Michael Nerney, County Secretary Sligo Farmers' Association, which appeared in the local press in early October 1922, considered that the crisis in agricultural prices had its causes both in internal and external influences laying stress on the the former. Among these he named the fact that, even in County Sligo, some fairs could not be held and where they were held, buyers were unwilling to travel because of dislocation of roads and railways.[95]

This pessimism as regards agricultural prices was reflected in reports of prices at fairs in County Sligo during this period, although there is a disappointingly meagre amount of actual figures. Fairs in the second half of 1921 in Gurteen and Ballymote were said to be very poor and each month prices were stated to be worse than those of the previous month. The Gurteen fair of October 1921 was said to be 'the worst held there in the experience of local people'. At the December fair in the same place, though the quantity and quality was good, demand was slow and prices lower than the previous fair with very little business being done.[96] Pig prices at Ballymote October fair 1921 were said to be on average 50 per cent those of the previous year while cattle were said to be down £5 per head since the previous September.[97] In early 1922 similar comments were common: 'Bad prices showing a huge decrease compared to a few months ago'; 'Cattle supply over average . . . demand slowest for a considerable time . . . very few sales'; 'Prices were not satisfactory and showed a big drop on recent weeks'; 'Nice well fed stores found a fairly brisk market at prices slightly below those prevailing at the last fair but inferior beasts were difficult to dispose of'.[98] What reports there are for early 1923 show that the small transient rise already noticed nationally was reflected in the county. Ballymote January and February fairs reported an 'upward tendency' in prices but the March prices 'compared very unfavourably with those of two months ago'. Gurteen February fair was 'one of the briskest held for some time' but the March fair was 'one of the dullest for some considerable time'.[99]

There is some evidence that in the early stages of the war the republicans deliberately targeted fairs with the intention of disrupting them. According to a Free State report in November 1922, 'a threat was made by Irregulars to stop two fairs in Collooney and Ballymote but this was frustrated by a column under Commandant Mitchell from Markree Castle'. Three bridges in the area had been damaged but the troops had repaired them thus allowing people to take cattle to Ballymote November fair.[100] Irregulars broke up the Sligo–Leitrim and Northern Line track and prevented 80 wagons of stock on their way from the September 1922 Collooney fair from reaching their destination. Such actions 'seriously injured future prospects' according to the *Sligo Independent* correspondent.[101]

Tubbercurry appears to have been especially badly affected since it was the largest town in the county whose previously functioning railway link was not operational. During the Tubbercurry fair at the beginning of August an outbreak of firing cleared the streets very quickly.[102] The pig market in Tubbercurry in August 1922 was reported as being 'fairly good', thanks to a number of enterprising Sligo dealers, 'who attended in spite of the stoppage of the railway to Tubbercurry and had the bonhams brought to be railed at Ballymote'.[103] A report in October painted a different picture, 'The absence of railway facilities is playing havoc with the fairs here [Tubbercurry] more especially as regards the pigs but people can only live on in hope that better times will soon prevail.'[104] By December the Tubbercurry correspondent of the *Western People* was even more despairing: 'The monthly fairs held here have been diminishing to a great extent, many preferring to do business in other towns served by railway. Prices have gone down for all classes of stock and the cost of having them taken to other towns has increased.'[105] It appears, if this mainly anecdotal evidence is to be believed, that livestock prices in County Sligo did not follow the upward trend apparent in national and provincial figures for this period and if this is the case then the intensity of the war in the county must be to blame.

In spite of the problems with holding fairs and the poor prices available, there seems to have been no reduction in the numbers of stock raised and sold. Comments on fairs quoted above suggest large numbers of cattle being offered for sale. This is corroborated by figures for the number of animals exported from the port of Sligo during the period. Numbers exported for the three months ended 30 September 1922, when the troubles would be expected to have had the greatest effect, were not significantly lower than previously, either in absolute numbers or as a percentage of the total national exports. The figures for the following two quarters show increases in the livestock numbers exported from Sligo as compared with corresponding periods in the preceding years.[106] The Civil War disturbance did not then effect the volume of animals which were available for export nor did it disrupt the export business.

Co-operative Creamery Societies

There were ten co-operative creamery societies in existence in County Sligo in this period operating a total of 21 creameries. A comparison between turnover figures, where available, for these societies for 1921 to 1923 should provide evidence on the effect of the war on this business.

Total turnover figures available for seven co-operative creamery societies in the county show a 13 per cent increase in 1922 over the 1921 figures and an eight per cent decrease in total turnover in 1923. All societies except one showed a drop in total turnover from 1922 to 1923. Figures for gallons of milk received are available for a smaller number of societies but the pattern is similar. The average increase for 1922 over 1921 was 18 per cent while the figure for 1923 as against 1922 was a decrease of five per cent. The average price per gallon paid for milk by the Sligo societies was 7.11 pence in 1921, 7.17 pence in 1922 and 6.4 pence in 1923 while the average price received for butter per pound for the three years was 21.42 pence, 20.38 pence and 17.49 pence.[107] Relating these figures to the Civil War and establishing cause and effect is not easy. The Civil War was at its most intense during the latter half of 1922, while the second half of 1923 was a period of peace. It is clear from the figures that while 1921 and 1922 were broadly similar years for

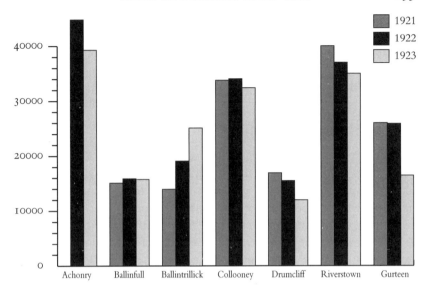

Graph 7.3. Turnover of seven co-operative creamery societies in County Sligo for 1921–23.

turnover, milk production and prices, 1923 was a much less successful year. This was due as much to the general depression in farming as to any specific effect the Civil War had on the operation of the co-operative creameries in the county.

An examination of the files for various societies in the county for this period reveals that most societies had troubles of some kind, none of which stemmed directly from Civil War disruption or splits. Many of these disputes were concerned with the performances of creamery managers. The Irish Agriculture Organisation Society (IAOS) secretary, R.A. Anderson, had a poor opinion of managers in the area: 'There does not seem to be a single creamery in Connacht at present that is not at the beck and call of the manager . . . The manager seems to be able to entrench himself behind relatives and various forms of intrigue and to defy the better judgment of the people whom they are supposed to serve.'[108]

Ballymote creamery had been destroyed by crown forces in September 1920 and it was mid-1923 before the creamery was again operational. There were difficulties about the reappointment of some staff and the secretary of the IAOS had a very low opinion of the manager's abilities, commenting that 'it would be better for Ballymote to rest in its ashes than to be raised again for the gratification of [the manager] for I am afraid he will only spoil it'.[109] A special meeting summoned by a group of dissident shareholders in June 1923, though declared illegal by the manager, went ahead and decided that the committee should be replaced. 'It is believed that the failure of the committee to reinstate some of the old staff is at the root of the trouble', a local newspaper commented.[110]

A dispute in Kilmactranny society between the manager and a section of shareholders resulted in his resignation in April 1921. Very soon afterwards the creamery was burned down, apparently accidentally. Rebuilding did not start until February 1922 and the creamery did not reopen until April 1923.[111] Ballintrillick creamery had been completely destroyed by crown forces after the Moneygold ambush in October 1920. Unlike the others in the county similarly destroyed, Ballintrillick was rebuilt at once and was operational again by June 1921. A dispute concerning an employee who had been laid off had started in January 1920 and dragged on until the end of August 1921 when it 'fizzled out'. By various stratagems he had himself re-employed twice before being finally dismissed. Some incidents of sabotage took place at the creamery culminating in a 'hand to hand fight between partisans of the principal aggrieved person and a number of young men on the other side who took up the cudgels against him'.[112] A long-running dispute at Sooey caused by dissatisfaction among a large number of shareholders and suppliers with the manager, resulted in him being suspended for mismanagement in November 1921 but reinstated in April 1922. 'By reinstating the manager after his record of the last eighteen months I firmly believe the Society has signed its own death warrant', reported the senior IAOS Connacht organiser. Various subsequent attempts to settle the internal difficulties were unsuccessful and by 1925 the creamery was practically in ruins.[113]

In all this sorry catalogue of petty internal disputes and financial mismanagement there is little evidence of any detrimental effect of Civil War disturbances, nor any evidence that any of the disputes paralleled the Civil War divisions. Achonry creamery had suffered some damage by crown forces in November 1920 but it was able to continue operations. The manager wrote to the IAOS in September 1922 concerning difficulties experienced as a result of the Civil War, reporting 'no great difficulty in getting our work done'. He reported some difficulties with blocked roads, especially at the commencement of the trouble, and said that many byroads used to transport milk were in 'awful conditions'. The nearest railway station, being on the Sligo–Claremorris line, was closed and so they used Collooney station on the MGWR instead. They purchased a Ford lorry and used it for transport to and from this station. Anti-Treaty forces had inquired at the creamery on one occasion for the lorry but it was not there. The creamery store had been raided four times and about 110 pounds' worth taken. Bicycles belonging to workers had also been taken and these workers had now to walk to work. The manager commented that they had probably lost more by interrupted telephone services than the value of goods stolen.[114]

Achonry also had its local dispute. This featured James Gilligan, the local politician who had been chairman of the County Council and was a member of the Achonry committee. Since his joining the committee he had 'blossomed out into a shopkeeper' and, in October 1921, the committee used an IAOS rule to have Gilligan removed. This dispute seems to have been purely an economic one with Gilligan 'a trade competitor' of the Society.[115] There is no mention of any similar trouble in the society until the 1923 AGM, when 'a clique including an ex-shopkeeper and his following', presumably Gilligan, was stated to have caused some trouble.[116]

Tubbercurry creamery had been destroyed by Auxiliaries in November 1920. The manager, Thomas Murricane, who had been elected a Sinn Féin County Councillor in 1920 went to Scotland after the burning and did not return. There were, according to an IAOS official, 'rumours to his discredit in circulation concerning his management of the society'. No attempt at rebuilding had been undertaken by July 1921. At that time some members of the Tubbercurry IRA, including officers Charles Gildea and Jack Brennan, began to take an interest in the affairs of the society: 'The young people of the district who have taken matters into their own hands have called to their aid the forces of the Republic and the Republican police are going to see the society through.' Their main concern seems to have been the financial standing of the society and it appears that the republican police got money from the bank in May 1921 to pay some suppliers who had been waiting for their payments. The old committee did not take kindly to being replaced and accused the IAOS of engaging in 'a certain amount of wire pulling'.[117] The disagreements continued through 1922 and 1923 with very little work being done to rebuild the creamery beyond drawing up plans and clearing the site: 'There is very little real enthusiasm about the revival of the creamery and I am afraid that so called politics are still allowed to play too great a part in influencing the actions of those connected with the creamery.'[118]

The evidence from this consideration of daily life during the Civil War is clear in many respects. The road infrastructure of the county deteriorated considerably during the period with many roads and bridges becoming impassable. One railway line did not function at all during the war and the other two were subject to occasional interruption. Destruction by the anti-Treaty forces and lack of maintenance due to war conditions were responsible for this state of affairs. It caused major inconvenience in the everyday life of the people which lasted for the duration of the war. The disruption in communications together with the general lawlessness led to a major decline in the social and sporting life of the county, with a dramatic drop in the number of functions during most of the Civil War period with a slow recovery only apparent from early 1923. Gaelic games came to a halt in the county for almost all of the war period. Rural areas dependent on road and rail transport were affected to a greater degree than the town of Sligo and the recovery was quicker to manifest itself in the urban area. In many respects, such as school attendance, life went on much as before with only a small drop in attendance in areas close to trouble spots.

It is difficult to gauge the extent to which the war impacted on livestock prices and on food prices because of the paucity of evidence and of the difficulty of deciding to what extent price changes were merely reflections of general trends in the British Isles at the time. What is clear is that the Civil War increased to some degree the problems which were already being caused farmers by the general depression in livestock prices, though it appears to have had little effect on output. The drop in the total turnover of most co-operative creamery societies in 1923 and the rise in the prices of some foodstuffs in the immediate aftermath of the outbreak of war suggest the direct influence of the disruption. For most ordinary people the Civil War had an impact in many and varied ways, making what was already an economically difficult period worse and adding many inconveniences to daily life. What must have caused added hardship was the absence of a fully functioning system of law and order. The next chapter will consider the extent if any to which court and police systems operated in Sligo during the period in question.

EIGHT

LAW AND ORDER

ONE OF THE MAIN aims of the independence movement in the pre-Truce period was the disabling of the existing forces of law and order and the replacing of these by structures loyal to Dáil Éireann. This was achieved to a large extent in much of the country and by mid-1921 the British police and courts had ceased to function normally in most of County Sligo. The attempts at replacing these by police and courts answerable to the Dáil or to the IRA had been only partially successful, with the result that there had been 'a long background of non-application of the law in many areas'.[1] With the confusion of the pre- and post-Treaty period and the state of war which followed there was a danger that law and order in particular would suffer and that the county might slide into a state of lawlessness. This chapter examines the relative strength and effectiveness of the competing systems of police and courts during each of the periods in question. It also seeks to determine the extent to which the county did slide into a state of lawlessness and the effectiveness of the attempts by the Free State government to re-establish the rule of law and order by the end of the Civil War.

The Truce Period

When the Truce came into effect the RIC found themselves with no more than a token presence outside Sligo town. They occupied six other barracks in the county, Ballymote, Tubbercurry, Collooney, Cliffony, Dromore West and Easkey, but they appear not to have exercised any power here in the period after the Truce. A *Sligo Champion* editorial said: 'For a couple of years past the Royal Irish Constabulary discharged little or no police duties and since the Truce they have confined themselves more or less to the onerous task of drawing their pay.'[2] The RIC County Inspector continually complained about the widespread operation of IRA training camps and the public sittings of Dáil courts during the Truce period, but no serious effort was made by the British authorities to curtail these activities.[3]

A scheme of republican police had been initiated at the time of the Truce, which envisaged a police officer being appointed for each brigade area, each battalion area and each company area. Each company area was also to have four policemen.[4] To what extent this was implemented in County Sligo is uncertain, but there are few references to such in the period between the Truce and Treaty, and reports of the application of republican policing in County Sligo do not often specifically refer to republican police. More often the reference is to the IRA or Volunteers having carried out police duties. For instance, IRA members in Skreen and Dromard were said to have captured a person who had robbed a public house in early September.[5] In October 1921, 'Volunteer police' were said to have arrested a man in Sligo for disorderly conduct. He was made pay the cost of a broken window.[6] It is clear that while a rudimentary republican police system may have operated in Sligo it was hardly distinguishable from the IRA proper. Alec McCabe's dissatisfaction with the scheme as it operated in the county centred on this point:

> Organisation of police force in this and all areas I have come in contact with leaves a lot to be desired. At a time like this when our administration is on trial it is very important I think . . . that we should give some indication of what our administration will be in peace time . . . I feel that if something is not done the results if we have ever to appeal to the country again will be disastrous. The common expression I hear is that if the Republican law is to be anything like this give us back the old system again as soon as possible.

He blamed this on the 'the mix up of volunteers and police'. The police were under the control of the IRA, he said, the Chief of Police in County Sligo being described as the Brigade Police Officer.[7]

Newspaper reports indicate no great increase in crime in County Sligo in the second half of 1921. The *Sligo Champion* in December 1921 did complain about the scenes of disorderly conduct and drunkenness which, it claimed, regularly occurred at weekends in Sligo: 'The RIC do not appear to be able to act. It is high time the Republican police took the matter in hand.' The following week the paper reported a great improvement: 'Republican police exercised a salutary control over the rowdy element in Sligo on Christmas Eve and that night there was a marked absence of the disgraceful scenes of drunkenness and disorderly conduct which occurred in the town during recent weekends.'[8] The same newspaper devoted an editorial in early January 1922 to 'IR police in Sligo' reporting that this body was doing 'excellent work' in the town and it had 'the sympathy of the public', though its problem was punishment for minor offences. Neither of the two examples of good work done by the body quoted was conclusive evidence of a well-organised efficient force, one being the finding of a British officer's lost terrier and the other the finding of a lady's stolen bicycle.[9]

In the rural parts of County Sligo Petty Sessions courts had not functioned since mid-1920, the majority of courthouses having been burned or damaged by the IRA. This situation continued during the Truce period. Only one report of a Petty Sessions court functioning outside Sligo town appeared in the local press for the period after June 1921 and that was Collooney Petty Sessions which in September 1921 heard over one hundred cases. A large part of this business consisted of signing publicans' certificates for the whole south Sligo area and it appears likely that this court was held specifically for this purpose.[10] When the resignation of the clerk of Collooney Petty Sessions was reported in December of the same year it was stated that very little business had been transacted recently, with the exception of poteen cases, unlicensed dogs and unlighted vehicles.[11]

Sligo Borough Court, which had remained in operation during the latter stages of the War of Independence, sat regularly during the Truce period with the Mayor, John Jinks, usually taking the chair. Cases dealt with were the usual fare of such courts – drunk and disorderly, petty larceny, riotous behaviour and unlighted vehicles.[12] Transfer of publicans' licences were also common business and, because such matters were not within the jurisdiction of the Dáil Courts, Michael Nevin, soon to be anti-Treaty Mayor of Sligo, applied for one at the Sligo Borough Court at the end of October. The only reference to the volume of business transacted occurred in a report of the sitting of 19 December where it was stated that 'the business of the court was of an exceptionally light character comprising a couple of cases'.[13]

The vacuum due to the non-operation of the Petty Session courts should have been filled by the Dáil Courts, but in County Sligo as elsewhere these had to a large extent been driven out of existence during the latter stages of the War of Independence. The Dáil ministry under Austin Stack decided that the republican court system should be developed and that there should be no return to the British system, but it took some months before the alternative system was operational in Sligo.[14] The south Sligo area in particular caused great trouble owing to the inefficiency of the officials and justices but also because of Stack's attitude. He was, according to Mary Kotsonouris, 'self-important, bullying and pedantic' and his Department dealt very unsympathetically with the District Registrars who were charged with responsibility for the operation of the courts. 'The reports and the financial returns – either the lack or infrequency of them – were the subject of an endless stream of corrective correspondence from headquarters, which insisted that its own rigid and unreal demands be met'.[15]

In early August Stack circularised all registrars with details of the new scheme of organisation and the following month sought the assistance of each TD in summoning a meeting of court officials.[16] Such a meeting appears not to have taken place in south Sligo until 14 November. In the meantime Stack had complained repeatedly that he had received no reports on courts from the district and had had no reply to correspondence. He again asked Tom O'Donnell, TD, to have a convention summoned to appoint district and parish justices for the south Sligo area and had sent an organiser to the district by November.[17] Eventually in early October 1921 the registrar of the South Sligo District Court, P.J. O'Brien, wrote lamely that he had been unable to report during the War of Independence because he had not received a covering address for the Ministry. There appears not to have been very much to report. He said that South Sligo District Court had been formed in September 1920 but that there had been only one sitting before 26 September 1921. The position was now much improved, he said, as a result of his efforts, together with those of O'Donnell and M.J. Marren: 'There is not a constituency in Ireland with fewer cases in the British courts', he claimed. 'The Parish and District Courts are now in full working order in South Sligo and are functioning in accordance with your instructions', he said, adding that sub-district courts had been established at Riverstown, Gurteen and Tubbercurry.[18] A court styled Tubbercurry Sinn Féin District Court appears to have been held monthly from September 1921.[19] Only five sittings of the South Sligo District Court were recorded in the court register, though O'Donnell later claimed to have attended 50 sittings of this court in the immediate post-Truce period.[20] Either he was confusing Parish, sub-District and District Courts or the whole system of courts in South Sligo was in a state of disorganisation. The latter appears to have been the interpretation favoured by Stack, and the organiser for the area seems to have agreed, reporting in November 1921, 'I can't say that I am satisfied that things were done properly in the past . . . Things seem to have been conducted in a very slip shod fashion'.[21]

The situation as regards district justices in south Sligo was, to say the least, complicated. Two were local TDs, one was a Catholic curate and one a medical doctor. Of the five originally elected, one had died, one had been imprisoned for much of the period, and the priest, though given permission by his Bishop, had been forbidden by some Parish Priests from officiating in their parishes. Two substitute justices had been selected at a Sinn Féin Comhairle Ceantair meeting but after the Truce one of the substituted justices wanted to become active again.[22]

P.J. O'Brien reported to the Minister that the first public sitting of the South Sligo District Court after the Truce had been held in

Ballymote on 26 September, though in a later report he gave the date as 1 October. TDs McCabe and O'Donnell, Fr Thomas Henry and Edward J. Boles were the justices at this sitting which lasted two days.[23]

Stack placed O'Brien on a month's probation in November 1921 as a result of his continued dissatisfaction. O'Brien's postponement of a meeting of justices and court officials early in that month without the permission of the local court organiser seems to have been the last straw as far as Stack was concerned.[24] This meeting of parish justices, clerks and district justices, which the organiser attended, was eventually held on 14 November and it was decided that the District Court should sit on the first Friday of each month. Every parish in South Sligo was represented at this meeting and all but two were said to be properly organised. It also decided to grant O'Brien a salary of £3 per week retrospective to the date of the Truce.[25] Stack was pleased with the work of the reorganisation meeting and looked forward to the proper functioning of the courts in the area. However, he refused to sanction the award of salary to O'Brien, saying, 'I am quite in the dark as to what work has been done in your district since the truce came into operation'. He complained again of lack of reports from south Sligo: 'I have not received a single monthly report sheet from him', and wondered where the October report was.[26] Stack's action, it must be said, was carried out with the agreement of the court organiser who had reported: 'There seems to have been a great looseness about the conduct of the courts in the past and though the registrar must be blamed for much of it, still I think the justices must bear equal blame. The registrar will, I think, if handled firmly, make good and the probationary period given him may have the desired effect. He is not a bad type of individual and appears willing enough to make good.'[27]

Things got worse, however. O'Brien's first attempt at a report in early December was pathetic. He reported that the first of the post-reorganisation District Courts, that of 2 December, fell through because only one justice was present and all the cases were adjourned to the January sitting. The justices' excuses included being unable to get transport, being absent on Volunteer duties, the clergyman unable to get permission from the parish priest to officiate in his parish, and the doctor engaged on medical work. O'Brien said that he had no reports from Parish Courts to send in because although he had received 'a good many' they were not suitable to send on and he had asked those responsible to rewrite them.[28] Stack wrote to each of the justices asking for an explanation of the 'fiasco' of 2 December, stating 'The courts in your district are in a most unsatisfactory condition'.[29] To O'Brien himself Stack wrote a blistering attack on his inefficiency and on the whole courts system in south Sligo. He pointed out that in spite of the fact that a scheme of organisation had been issued by the Department shortly before the Truce, no District Court had been held in the area until 1 October. No details of any Parish Court in the area had ever been sent to the Ministry and no monthly report sheets had been returned. He pointed out that the debacle of December need not have occurred since one district justice could have disposed of the business of the court with the help of at least two parish justices. O'Brien seems to have decided that silence was the only possible defence, and in early January Stack wrote to O'Brien asking why there had been no reply to his December broadside, threatening that unless he received a reply by 14 January he would suspend him and appoint a more efficient registrar.[30] Two justices, McCabe and Boles, wrote on O'Brien's behalf to Stack with regard to the salary question. 'Taking into consideration all the useful work carried out by Mr O'Brien during the war he was entitled to a fair consideration', Boles said.[31] By this time the Treaty had been signed and its approval by the Dáil had resulted in Stack's resignation from the ministry.

In contrast with its counterpart in the south, North Sligo Republican District Court generated much less correspondence and much less anger on the part of Stack. It had been established in 1920 and sat for the first time after the Truce on 15 August 1921 and fortnightly after that. Minister Stack expressed his approval of the operation of the north Sligo courts and asked only that they be regularly constituted at a convention which would elect five justices.[32] This was held on 5 November. The court functioned regularly between then and the outbreak of the Civil War and appears to have attracted business from all sides of the political divide, including some of the Protestant-owned businesses of Sligo town. For instance, it adjudicated in favour of the Western Wholesale Ltd, Sligo, presumably for debts, in November 1921.[33] Monthly reports of the type so desired by Stack appear not to have been sent in by this District Court either, but this did not lead to the bitter correspondence the South Sligo court engendered. One reason appears to be that while both Sligo District Courts were in the same inspection area which included Mayo and Roscommon, north Sligo was very much on the periphery and appeared to receive little attention from the inspector.[34]

There are few reports of the operation of republican Parish Courts in Sligo during the Truce period, suggesting that, like the District Courts, they were slow to reorganise. It does appear that such courts were almost unknown in north Sligo while sittings are reported sporadically in south Sligo. There is, for instance, no mention of a Parish Court in Sligo town for the Truce period. Ballymote Parish Court sat on 4 August 1921 and, according to the *Sligo Independent,* the Dáil Courts were functioning in the Ballymote area and doing good work in mid-October 1921: 'these courts seem to be winning the confidence of the people', it commented.[35]

The *Connachtman* held up Tourlestrane Parish Court in south Sligo as an example to neighbouring districts. It was sitting regularly during August and September 1921 and a 'considerable number of cases [were] dealt with to the satisfaction of all'.[36] The absence of references may also reflect the official policy of giving these courts no publicity since they were often the subject of complaints from the British side during the Treaty negotiations, Stack's advice being that 'the work should go on quietly and unostentatiously'.[37] The absence of references to court proceedings in accounts of the apprehending of criminals by IRA, Volunteers or republican police during this period, however, also points to the absence of such court infrastructure at the time.[38]

The overall impression gained from this consideration of the Dáil courts in County Sligo during the Truce period is of slow and uneven progress rather than a great immediate resurgence. James Casey says 'it was in the period between the Truce and the Treaty that the courts reached the highest point of their effectiveness'.[39] If this is true then that high point for Sligo was not a signal achievement.

From Treaty to Civil War

Towards the end of 1921 there had been a nation-wide increase in lawlessness, which took advantage of and exposed the lack of an efficient police system. This was made worse by the RIC's evacuation of the remaining occupied barracks in early 1922. In February 1922 Chief of Republican Police mentioned the 'wave of crime which began about three months ago and which has been caused by numerous armed bands operating all over Ireland'.[40] Sligo also suffered. The figures for malicious injury claims in the Sligo Crown and Peace Records show a rise from no claim based on an October incident to five for November and twelve for December.[41]

An incident involving a group of four men, at least two of whom were IRA members, apparently from Ballina, illustrates the attitudes and conditions of the time. One stated at his subsequent trial, 'I met ———— on Friday evening 23 December 1921 and he asked me was I game to go on a stunt with him. I said I did not care.' They collected two others, one of whom had a car, and visited three pubs before starting the 'stunt'. Two were armed with revolvers. They decided against raiding in the town, believing this to be too dangerous, and instead visited three premises in the neighbouring countryside, one in County Mayo and two in County Sligo. In the first they stole 14 shillings and some watches at gunpoint. In the second they announced they were raiding for poteen, took the poteen they found on the premises and drank it. They also imposed a fine of £10 but accepted £5 10s 0d. On being refused entry to a third house they broke windows and fired a shot.[42] In the financial appeal in February 1922 by the 3rd Western Division IRA, the disturbed state of the area was adverted to: 'evilly disposed persons are taking advantage of the unsettled conditions and it is our duty to trace and bring to justice such individuals'.[43]

In recognition of its failure to cope with this outbreak of lawlessness, the republican police system was changed towards the end of 1921. Company police officers were instructed to rejoin their military units, and battalion and brigade officers, where competent, were to act in co-operation with the army in policing the country. The split in the army over the Treaty made the situation worse. The anti-Treaty side established their own republican police force and it appears this operated in those areas of the country controlled by them, including most of County Sligo. In February 1922 it was reported that anti-Treaty IRA police were restoring law and order in the Ballymote district. According to the *Roscommon Herald* the Ballymote IRA were discharging their duty of preserving law and order in the town 'right well', mounting patrols on the streets, meeting all the trains and guarding all the local banks.[44]

Reports in the local newspapers reflect the increase in crime in the county in the early months of 1922. Armed robberies became common. In January 1922 a north Sligo man was robbed by armed men of the proceeds of a sale of cattle. Robbers entered a house at Rosses Point in late January/early February 1922 and stole £25 from the housewife, threatening to shoot her and her baby. In February 1922 two masked men impersonating members of the IRA raided the house of a person who happened to be a member of the 1st Battalion, 4th Brigade IRA. Money was handed over but the IRA investigated and the guilty parties were arrested and returned for trial to Tubbercurry District Court. One hundred pounds was stolen from the offices of Messrs Pollexfen in Wine St., Sligo in February 1922.[45]

The high point of this lawlessness occurred on the afternoon of 13 February when the offices of the Bank of Ireland and of the Provincial Bank in Sligo town, both in Stephen St, were raided and over £10,000 taken. There were eight to ten raiders, described as young men with country accents, only the leader being disguised. The Sligo IRA were notified and chased the raiders in the direction of Northern Ireland. Sligo IRA had to deny that they were involved and no one was ever brought to justice for the raids. As a result of these bank raids Sligo Corporation held a special meeting to discuss the lawless state of the area and it was agreed that the matter should be put in the hands of the local IRA. The 'competent military authority' was asked to afford all the protection possible to citizens and a request was sent to the Minister for

Defence to have a police force set up for Sligo Borough. It was stated that the IRA police had been disbanded only a few days previous to the raids and that in any case there had been only six members of the force in Sligo.[46]

The local newspapers continued to report criminal activities during March to June 1922. These included raids on houses, business premises and mail cars. Such incidents were reported from all parts of the county including Sligo town.[47] It is impossible to distinguish between the incidents which were the work of the anti-Treaty IRA securing funds and transport, and those which were the work of common criminals taking advantage of the unsettled state of the county. Among the malicious injuries claims recorded in the Crown and Peace Records there were seven claims each for January and February, five for March, twelve for April and thirteen for May. These claims were for injuries suffered for a variety of reasons. The twelve April claims included four incidents related to Griffith's meeting in Sligo, four agrarian attacks, three cases of stealing or damaging motor cars and one house burning. The thirteen May claims included nine agrarian incidents, three incidents of stolen cars and one of a stolen bicycle. [48]

There were other series of incidents which increased the amount of crime. Immediately after disbandment there was a campaign of intimidation against ex-members of the RIC in County Sligo as elsewhere in the country. Most of the disbanded RIC appear not to have returned to or settled in the county. Those who did were usually given 24 hours to leave. Most left the county, though one or two fled to Sligo town and remained there. These incidents were reported from all parts of the county.[49] In mid-May 1922 the *Roscommon Herald* reported that houses owned or occupied by ex-RIC had been fired into in the Castlebaldwin district in south Sligo and reported rumours to the effect that ex-RIC in the area had since left.[50] Shots were fired into the houses of ex-RIC at Gurteen and a notice was posted on the gate of the chapel warning all such personnel to leave the area.[51] In two cases intimidation escalated to killing. On 17 June 1922 the brother of an ex-RIC man was shot dead by masked raiders near Ballymote. The disguised raiders apparently wanted to question the ex-RIC man about his involvement with IRA cases where he had been stationed and panicked when recognised by the ex-RIC man's brother.[52] In August 1922 another ex-RIC man was shot dead near Bunninadden.[53]

Incidents of intimidation of Protestants had occurred in County Sligo from late 1921 but increased dramatically in April and May 1922 just after the departure of the RIC.[54] Already feeling isolated, abandoned and threatened by political developments, small wonder that they considered that there was a deliberate campaign 'of loyalist extermination'.[55] There is, however, little evidence that this widespread intimidation was a co-ordinated campaign. Instead it appears to have consisted of numerous settlings of real or imagined old scores in the absence of law and order.

The Provisional Government had established the Civic Guard on 21 February 1922. Jim Hunt of Gurteen was appointed recruiting officer for Sligo, Leitrim and East Mayo and a large number of recruits presented themselves at Ballymote in early March with the first batch leaving for Dublin in mid-March.[56] Hunt was in Sligo town on 27 March to attest suitable men and it was reported that 16 out of 40 candidates examined at Sligo courthouse were successful.[57] This initial scheme of establishment of the Civic Guard was not successful because of internal divisions over the number of ex-RIC recruited, mutinies and indiscipline. It was disbanded by the Provisional Government on 18 August 1922 and was reconstituted in September.[58]

With the approval of the Treaty the position as regards the courts became more confused that ever. Garvin says 'in early 1922 the Dáil and Provisional Government found themselves in charge of two mutually exclusive court systems, the British and the Dáil courts'.[59] The courts previously called 'British courts' had been taken over by the Provisional Government and were operating side by side with the former Dáil Courts. Some still considered these latter courts under Dáil control; others considered that they now operated under the Provisional Government.[60] On 16 January 1922 a proclamation was issued by the Provisional Government which, among other things, directed that all law courts which had acted under authority of the British Government were to continue to operate until the establishment of the Free State. On 20 January the Provisional Government decided that the Dáil Courts were also to remain in operation. The dual system of courts was therefore to continue.

The post-Treaty period was an 'era of uninterrupted expansion' for the Dáil courts according to Kotsonouris.[61] Conor Brady, on the other hand, says that 'once the unifying influence of the common struggle against the British had passed, the Sinn Féin courts would lose much of their acceptability throughout the community' and says that the courts in the post-Treaty period became 'disorganised and ineffective as a result of the split over the Treaty'.[62] The evidence suggests that as far as Sligo was concerned the former view is correct. Both North and South Sligo District Courts continued to function until just before the outbreak of Civil War and there are many reports of Parish Court sittings, especially in south Sligo. The North Sligo District Court sat monthly until May 1922. At the sitting of 2 March 24 new cases and two appeals were to be heard and some cases had to be adjourned. All except one of the justices of this court were anti-Treaty activists but they appear not to have let this disrupt the business. The pro-Treaty member John Hennigan, who was to stand as an independent candidate in the June election, continued to sit as a justice at least until April.[63]

P.J. O'Brien was still the registrar of South Sligo District Court at the sitting of the court held at Riverstown in early February 1922. Cases included land disputes, shop goods claims and some cases referred by Parish Courts.[64] Organiser D.H. O'Donnell was still working in the area and he reported in March that the several Parish Courts in south Sligo which he visited were working satisfactorily and held up the Ballymote Parish Court sitting of 9 March as 'a model one from every standpoint'. However, a District Court sitting fixed for Tubbercurry later the same month fell through.[65] A convention of all the district and parish justices plus registrars was fixed for 10 April 1922 in Tubbercurry 'to put the whole thing on a business-like basis' reflecting continued dissatisfaction with the system.[66] Some time later O'Brien resigned or was dismissed and an advertisement appeared on 1 July under the heading of Saorstát na hÉireann advertising the position of District Registrar for South Sligo District Court.[67] The meeting for the election of the new registrar was not held and the office was still vacant in September.[68]

As in the pre-Treaty period reports and references to sittings of Parish Courts in County Sligo in the January to July 1922 period are confined almost exclusively to the south Sligo area and there are no references to any Parish Court being held in the area north of Sligo town. It may be the case that a Parish Court system was not developed in this area with only the District Court and Sligo town Parish Court functioning. It may also reflect the fact that most of the IRA in this area took the anti-Treaty side and had little time to spend on non-military matters. However, at Collooney Parish Court held on 31 May 1922 the three judges were prominent anti-Treaty leaders from the local area.[69] It may also suggest that south Sligo had become well organised as a result of Stack's 'encouragement' and that north Sligo, neglected by the organiser, never developed a viable system of Parish Courts. Sittings of Sligo Parish Court were, nevertheless, regularly mentioned in the local newspapers during January, February and March 1922.[70]

An examination of the files of cases dealt with by the Winding Up Commission shows that 31 of the 36 Sligo cases referred to were held in the period from October 1921 to May 1922. This confirms that the court system took some time after the Truce to be properly reorganised and suggests that it ceased to function with the outbreak of the war. The sittings categorised by area show that 11 of the 36 were sittings of the North Sligo District Court, with only three sittings of north Sligo Parish Courts. On the other hand, there were only three sittings of the South

Sligo District Court yet eight sittings of south Sligo Parish Courts, the majority sitting only once, although nine Kilmacteige sittings were mentioned. Of 41 cases where the subject matter is identified 16 were cases of non-payment for goods purchased, five were for possession of property and three each were for assault, illegal fishing and trespass.

There is little evidence of differences arising because of the split over the Treaty. As we have seen pro- and anti-Treaty personnel sat together on the North Sligo District Court in the post-Treaty period. A long letter from Enniscrone to Michael Collins in March 1922 by a self-proclaimed Free State supporter complained of her being persecuted by the local Dáil Parish Court in Kilglass because of her allegiance. She said that her son had been imprisoned during the War of Independence and she described the clerk of the court as 'a young truce bird'. However, this case appears to have resulted from a local dispute rather than from conflicting political allegiance.[71]

The main problem faced by the courts was the inability to enforce decrees as a result of the absence of an effective police force. This problem was exacerbated after the Treaty split when many of the police, also members of the IRA, took the anti-Treaty side and were not likely to assist courts they regarded as under the Provisional Government. A report on Kilmacteige Parish Court in September 1922 said that it had been in existence for about a year and that it had continued to sit fortnightly during the first half of the year. The work of the court was 'fairly satisfactory', it said, were it not for the failure of certain sections of the republican police. Obstruction and prejudice were blamed especially on the part of the chief of police in the area who later took the anti-Treaty side in the civil war. There was a long list of writs waiting to be enforced with no means available for so doing. For instance, in January 1922 four men were fined for poaching in a local river, writs for collection were issued to the chief of police but the fines were not collected.[72]

There was some concern that Parish Courts were overstepping their jurisdiction. Rev M.J. Connellan, CC Sooey, Riverstown, wrote to the Minister for Home Affairs in late June 1922 asking if these courts had the power to grant new public house licences. This was because a local court had just granted a new licence in spite of the fact that there was a public house about 200 yards away. 'This new licence will dump down a public house on each side of our church here', he claimed, adding that it was a 'big set-back to public good order especially when here as elsewhere, theft, plunder, land hunger, threatening letters are the order of the day.' The reply on 13 July from the Minister was that the Parish Courts had not been granted jurisdiction in licensing matters. The *Roscommon Herald's* report on what was probably the same case praised the applicant's 'pluck in taking advantage of Irish law which allows any man to get a living as he pleases'.[73] A Keash correspondent wrote to the Minister in August 1922 asking if Parish and District Courts were to continue to grant new publicans' licences. He said that he had seen several granted in places and he knew of people building houses beside existing public houses in the expectation of getting licences.[74]

The former British courts continued to operate as they had during the Truce period although the reports in the local newspapers suggest a falling off in the volume of business of Sligo Borough Court. At the sitting of 6 February 1922 only one case was heard and a sitting on 6 March 1922 had no business before it.[75] With the disbandment of the RIC in April there was no police force to summon petty criminals to the court. The *Roscommon Herald* commented in March 1922 that the Sligo Borough Court had lost its biggest patrons with the departure of the RIC. The IRA police were having all cases dealt with at the Parish Court, it said.[76] However, the Borough Court continued to function in parallel with the Dáil Parish Court. A report for the month of May 1922 by Sligo Resident Magistrate William Murphy says there were no cases for hearing at the Petty Sessions courts outside the town of Sligo during May.[77] None of the county Petty Sessions courts reopened and there is no reference to Collooney Court having sat during this time.

The Quarter Sessions Courts continued to sit in Sligo during 1922 and 1923, those for Sligo, Ballymote, Easkey and Tubbercurry all being held in Sligo. Business transacted was usually confined to applications for transfer of publicans' licences and claims for compensation for malicious injuries.[78] There appears to have been no attempt by republicans to interfere with the workings of this court after the September/October 1921 Sessions when many jurors had been kidnapped.[79] During the May 1922 Sligo Quarter Sessions, however, three anti-Treaty IRA officers walked in and ordered the judge to cease operating crown proceedings. The judge immediately went to the IRA barracks where he reported the matter to IRA adjutant Brian MacNeill who said that the order to cease was given without any authorisation and that the court had been functioning with the approval of the republican authorities.[80] The numbers of cases taken before these courts appears to have varied enormously. Few cases were reported as having been heard at the January 1922 Sessions. On the other hand 150 civil bills, almost all undefended, were dealt with and decrees given in March 1922.[81]

The Civil War Period

The outbreak of the Civil War and the intensity of the conflict in the Sligo area during July 1922 overshadowed all else and during the initial stages of the war there were few reports of ordinary crime in the county. One significant incident occurred in the Riverstown area. A Provisional Government post had been taken by republicans here on the outbreak of the war, but had been retaken when Collooney was attacked and captured by Seán MacEoin on 13 July. Eleven days later, on the night of 24 July, Mrs Nellie McDonagh, Riverstown, was shot dead by one of a gang of armed and masked youths who broke into her house. Her husband had reported persistent larceny of goods and turf and had accosted one of the youths the previous day about the incidents. After a roadside dance the group drank a bottle of whiskey and decided to break into the McDonagh house, beat up the husband and 'raid for a gun'. When they entered the house they found that McDonagh was not at home and instead were confronted by his wife. A shotgun was discharged and she was shot dead. The youth who discharged the shot claimed at the inquest 'I got a stagger and fell up against the jamb of the door. When I was trying to balance myself the gun went off and Mrs McDonagh was shot.' Six local youths, four of whom were aged 15, 16, 18 and 19, were arrested and charged with the killing.[82]

As the conflict settled down some people began to find the situation conducive to lawbreaking. This was especially so in those areas where no significant anti-Treaty forces operated. Areas such as the country part of south Sligo were nominally under pro-Treaty control but in fact were without any law-enforcing element of any kind. Crimes occurring in these places included robberies by criminals and vandalism by youths unfettered by authority. The Gurteen area seems to have been particularly prone to crime of this nature towards the end of 1922: 'From many parts of the Ballymote and Gurteen districts reports reached us . . . of a lot of wanton destruction of property which included the scattering of oats, hay, turf etc.' This state of affairs was attributed to the fact that 'boys want to do damage'. 'Mysterious occurrences' were reported there including the burning of a dozen cocks of hay belonging to a widow and the breaking of windows in a house belonging to the Gurteen postmaster at the end of September. In October 1922 there were reports that gangs of youths were still causing wanton damage to property in the area at night. A Protestant farmer had his apple trees cut down and his house stoned. An old man had been pulled from his house one night, had his hands tied and was thrown into an outhouse while a rick of his hay was burned.[83]

Public houses and business premises were targeted. All public houses in the Mullaghroe district were raided in early November and tobacco, drink and cigarettes taken. One licensed premises near Gurteen was raided in mid-November and money and spirits taken while another was visited twice by raiders towards the end of 1922 but on both occasions the raiders were beaten off. The co-operative store at Seefin was robbed of twenty pounds worth of goods and tobacco and cigarettes in November. Gurteen post office was raided at the end of December and the old age pension money was demanded, but when the postmaster said this money had not been received, the raiders went away empty handed. The same day Kilfree post office was also raided and a small quantity of stamps taken. Other parts of the county were also affected with reports of similar though less numerous occurrences from Sligo town, Bunninadden, Easkey and Collooney from the same period.[84]

It was difficult to differentiate between crimes committed by the IRA and those committed by ordinary criminals especially as the latter often masqueraded as the former. Three men were charged with robbery near Strandhill in October 1922. 'We are Bolsheviks from the Ox Mountains and are starving', they were reported as having told their victims. One was a showman and the others natives of Strandhill. They sampled the justice systems of both Civil War protagonists having been originally apprehended by anti-Treaty forces and tied to church railings at Strandhill. They were then arrested by pro-Treaty army police and removed to Sligo jail.[85]

In the meantime the country was still without a properly organised police force. As the Provisional Government forces regained control of the towns in the county they appear to have set up an army police force. By the end of July such a police force had been organised in Ballymote under the command of Boles, 'a gentleman to his fingertips . . . bound to command respect'.[86] In August 1922 the *Roscommon Herald* reported that the army authorities had set up a police force whose members wore armbands inscribed IAP (Irish Army Police). This was said to have been a great relief to the inhabitants generally, who according to the paper 'had to endure things which with the presence of police forces would not be permissible'. In October 1922 it was mentioned that the troops were efficiently carrying out police duties.[87]

Members of the new Civic Guard force began to take up duties in September 1922 and a Superintendent was sent to Sligo–Leitrim division in October with a complement of men to arrange for accommodation of barracks at Sligo, Ballymote and Manorhamilton. Eighteen members took up duty at Wine St ex-RIC Barracks in Sligo town on 19 October 1922 and seven members of the Civic Guard took up duty in Ballymote at the same time. The following week's issue of the *Sligo Independent* contained the following description of the new police: 'They are a splendid type of Irish manhood indeed, and Sligo is very fortunate in securing such a fine band of young men as protectors of the general public'.[88] The original proposed strength of the Sligo–Leitrim division of the Civic Guards was one Chief Superintendent stationed at Sligo, three Superintendents at Sligo, Carrick on Shannon and Ballymote, four Inspectors at Sligo, Mohill, Manorhamilton and Collooney, 30 sergeants and 209 constables. The Sligo–Leitrim division was to have 43 stations, in two sub-divisions with headquarters at Sligo and Carrick on Shannon. The Sligo sub-division was to have four districts, Sligo, Easkey, Ballymote and Manorhamilton, each with an inspector in charge. There were to be 24 stations in County Sligo.[89]

The Civic Guard report for January 1923 stated that the Guards then still occupied only two stations in County Sligo– Sligo and Ballymote. 'The Guard is not effective here and are merely in occupation of posts', it commented. At this time Sligo, with two stations, had the lowest number of occupied Garda stations of all the counties of the Irish Free State. Leitrim had three stations, Mayo four, Roscommon six and Galway 14.[90] There was no increase in Civic Guard numbers in the county until the following April when Civic Guards took up duty in Tubbercurry. Sligo then had one sergeant and 15 guards, Ballymote one sergeant and six guards and Tubbercurry one sergeant and five guards.[91]

Thus the Civic Guards played no significant role in the Civil War in County Sligo. They were, of course, intended to be an unarmed body with a purely policing role and in Sligo they were deployed only in those areas where the Free State was more or less in complete control. This resulted in very few incidents involving Guards being reported in the county during the early part of 1923. In an attack on a patrol in Sligo on 6 January 1923, two Guards were held up and deprived of their waterproof coats, batons and handcuffs and three days later a Sergeant and a Guard were held for over three hours by republicans.[92]

Lawlessness continued and again the south Sligo area seems to have been badly affected. Numerous arrests of robbers who had been posing as irregulars were made in the Ballymote area in January 1923. 'It goes without saying that there are men and boys who are taking advantage of the disturbed times to prey on the people and take whatever comes their way in the matter of ready cash, goods and valuables', the *Roscommon Herald* said. The newspaper reported two such raids in the Ballymote district during the last week of January.[93] The Bunninadden area of south Sligo was particularly subject to lawlessness during early 1923. This area had been a centre of agrarian trouble during the whole 1921–23 period with two landowners in the area, Charles Phibbs and J. Ormsby Cooke, subject to particular attention. Woods there were totally destroyed during January with the timber being 'cut down and carried away openly by anyone and everyone. It certainly illustrates the strange times that we are passing through when a man can scarcely call his soul his own', said the report in the *Roscommon Herald*.[94] In early February the same newspaper reported that armed and disguised men had raided several houses in the area between Bunninadden and Gurteen stealing guns, cash and goods: 'That the raiding spirit is abroad there can be no doubt and it is certainly not confined to any particular district', the newspaper commented, adding that for each incident reported there were probably at least two others not spoken about, 'many people preferring to suffer in silence rather than let the public know of their victimisation'. The *Sligo Champion* reported that 'armed raiders have been operating in the Bunninadden district for some time past giving the people of that district a lively and by no means a pleasant time'.[95]

It appears to have been mid-1923 before this area was taken in hand. In June 1923 Alec McCabe suggested the sending down to the Bunninadden area of some Oriel House men to try to curb the 'gang of armed marauders'. This was done and Doddy, a native of the Ballymote area, was sent with a group who arrested three or four men thought to have been involved. A request from McCabe to allow the Oriel House men further time in the Bunninadden area was turned down.[96]

Statistics on raids on post offices, mail cars and postmen for the period February 1922 to June 1923 show that the big increase in numbers of raids coincided with the Civil War period, July 1922 to March 1923. There was an average of 21 such raids per month during this period, with December 1922 recording the greatest number of raids per month with 47 raids in the county. Raids per month for the immediate pre-Civil War period averaged little over three per month and March 1923 was the last month with a significant number of such raids. These figures show very little overspill of post office raids after the end of the Civil War.[97] How many of these raids were carried out by IRA members acting officially collecting money or searching mails for incriminating correspondence is not known. Many must have been the work of IRA members acting independently in their own interest and others were the actions of criminals taking advantage of the unsettled times.

Another death was recorded as a result of lawlessness towards the end of the war. On 2 April 1923, 77-year-old Catherine McGuinness of Cairns, Culleens was shot dead by armed men. It appears that a group of armed anti-Treaty IRA visited the house late at night and were entertained by two sons of Mrs McGuinness, a quantity of poteen being consumed. After some time a row developed about an earlier incident and about spies. One IRA man and a son started to fight and the IRA man was thrown out. Stones were thrown at him and he was called names. In reply he fired shots at the house from the road and Mrs McGuinness was fatally injured and a son dangerously injured. The IRA man remained at large until February 1924 when he was arrested and charged with the murder. When the case was brought to trial both McGuinness sons refused to implicate the suspect and he was set free.[98]

The outbreak of the Civil War affected the operation of the courts in different ways in different areas. In most cases courts did not function in the immediate aftermath of the outbreak. Sligo Borough Court and Sligo Parish Court resumed operations in mid-August after having been out of action in July and early August. Both Sligo Borough and Parish Courts were held on 14 August 1922 and Joseph Graham who attended at the Borough Court as a magistrate went on to attend the Parish Court as a witness in a case where two men were charged with having assaulted him.[99] At the end of September Sligo Parish Court heard the case of a row in Holborn Hill in which a Free State soldier home on leave was told: 'You shouldn't come up here, we are all republicans'. His retort: 'I was never with a British soldier anyway', led to a fracas resulting in the court case.[100] These two courts appear to have functioned side by side as in the pre-war days.

The North Sligo District Court on the other hand appears to have ceased operation with the outbreak of war, almost all its justices being anti-Treaty activists. A letter referring to this court said: 'Unfortunately every official attached to the court . . . is in opposition to the established government . . . The former officials are either in jail or on the run.'[101] In July 1922 the registrar of the court had been arrested by the Provisional Government forces. D.A. Mulcahy, presiding chairman of the court, wrote a letter to Pilkington and sent a copy to the local newspapers in which he said that courts were very necessary at that time 'when evil minded persons are almost bound to take advantage of the situation and the property of others is likely to be regarded as fair spoil by the criminally inclined'.[102]

In south Sligo, whatever advance in the court organisation had been achieved before the outbreak of war was set aside as many courts ceased to function. This seems to have been the case in particular in those areas where the anti-Treaty forces were stronger. Kilmacteige Parish Court, which had been held regularly before the war, 'owing to local political disturbance . . . ceased to function'.[103] Likewise the Tubbercurry area saw the cessation of the Dáil Courts: 'The work in South Sligo but particularly in the sub-district of Tubbercurry has ceased to be carried out'.[104] No sitting of the District Court is recorded for the period after the outbreak of war though a court organiser was still operating in south Sligo.[105] A meeting to elect a replacement for Registrar P.J. O'Brien had not been held. Some Parish Courts did continue to function during the war especially those in the Ballymote and Gurteen areas. Sittings of Ballymote Parish Court, which had been suspended during the summer of 1922, resumed in mid-August 1922 and Mullaghroe Parish Court was regularly held each month from June until December 1922.[106] Gurteen Parish Court was held at the end of September 1922, one defamation of character case involved a person calling another 'A Black and Tan'. Quarter Sessions continued to be held in Sligo, Superintendent Neary of the Civic Guard attended the January 1923 Sessions and in May 1923 Judge Wakely presided under an Irish tricolour.[107]

In mid-1922 the Provisional Government moved to regularise the court system. The Supreme Court and the Dublin area Dáil Courts were closed down in early July and the remainder of the Dáil Courts, including Parish Courts, were closed down by decree in October. A new simplified District Court system, presided over by 27 District Justices with powers of summary jurisdiction, was announced on 31 August 1922.[108] No court was held in Sligo from October 1922 pending official notification regarding the new courts.[109] A District Justice appointed for Leitrim and North Roscommon held his first sitting in Boyle in early November and at the end of December 1922 the *Roscommon Herald* reported an expectation that courts would be functioning in Sligo at an early date in the new year, commenting that 'it is now some months since a court of any kind has been held in Sligo'. Finally a notice signed by District Justice Charles A. Flattery appeared in the *Sligo Champion* of 3 February 1923 announcing the first sitting of District Court No. 3 area at the Courthouse, Sligo on 8 February. A short report of this court mentioned that five men had been charged and convicted of breaches of the licensing laws.[110] Ballymote District Court under District Justice Flattery was held on 13 February 1923 in the Hibernian Hall, Ballymote and a small amount of business transacted.[111] Sligo District Court under Justice Flattery was held during the last week in February and Sligo and Ballymote District Courts continued to be held monthly for the remainder of the Civil War period.[112] The coming of the new court system signalled the replacement of a chaotic and inefficient system, which seems not to have been unduly lamented by the people of County Sligo. It also signalled the effective end of the Civil War and the beginning of the return to normal conditions with the gradual re-establishment of the rule of law.

No generally accepted or effective police force or court system had operated in County Sligo since early 1920. This situation continued for most of the succeeding period with competing parallel systems adding to the confusion. The Truce and Treaty periods had seen a slow reorganisation of the Dáil Courts without a concomitant development of an effective police force. Lacking such an enforcement agency the courts were powerless to prevent a rise in lawlessness in early 1922. Agrarian unrest, intimidation of Protestants, robbery, petty crime and hooliganism became widespread. With the outbreak of the war things became worse as official and unofficial actions by anti-Treaty forces added to the chaos. Large areas of the county were without any semblance of police force and here lawless element had free rein. As the Free State forces slowly gained control, courts began to function again and the new Civic Guards were introduced. By July 1923 the Civic Guards could report that 'this county is on the whole in a satisfactory condition and is rapidly recovering from the lawlessness which some ago prevailed. The county is in a peaceful condition as regards ordinary crime.'[113] Sligo county appeared to be well on its way back to normality. One group, the non-Catholics, might have been particularly vulnerable during such a period and the degree to which they suffered is the subject of the next chapter.

NINE

===

SLIGO PROTESTANTS AFTER
THE REVOLUTION

DURING THE REVOLUTIONARY period republican definitions of Irishness were often expressed in narrow terms which excluded non-Catholics. The *Connachtman* listed those it claimed would not vote republican in the 1922 election as follows: shoneen, Unionist, British subject, recruiting sergeant, Loyalist, Castle hack, place hunter. 'Who is there left?' it asked, answering, 'The Irish People and the Irish People will stand by the Republic'.[1] In response to a query from headquarters, Sligo IRA reported that three prominent Sligo Protestant loyalists were 'all Unionist of the bitter type and men of considerable means', and also Freemasons, they reported, saying that they would have their correspondence watched and reported on.[2] Sligo town was treated as a special case in a report to IRA Headquarters probably dating from the Truce period:

> The town of Sligo presents a special problem . . . If the enemy were once demoralised in and around Sligo he would suffer a really severe blow as far as Connacht was concerned . . . The Belfast Boycott should be vigorously enforced because Sligo is an important trading centre. Telegraph and telephone wires should be cut regularly. As regards the outlying Unionists who are fairly numerous they should be subject to comprehensive requisitions of every kind – food, implements, clothing, billets if thought suitable, fuel, bedding, animals and vehicles. It must be brought home to them unmistakably that the English are helpless to protect them . . . In all respects Sligo can be treated as mainly a hostile town and an enemy area of influence.[3]

This group, variously called non-Catholic, Protestant, Unionist or Loyalist, which made up 8.8 per cent of Sligo's population in 1911 might have been expected to suffer more than a little during the period of national unrest and lawlessness. As one commentator said, 'The Anglo-Irish, by reason of their past, their politics, their religion, and their larger stake in the country, had most to fear from the growth of lawlessness, and they suffered their fair share of outrage.'[4] This chapter will investigate the extent to which Sligo non-Catholics suffered during the period of the Truce and Civil War.

The Decline in the Protestant Population

There was a large drop in the non-Catholic population of county Sligo between 1911 and 1926. The census returns for 1926 show this fall to have been 26.6 per cent as against a fall of eight per cent in the Catholic population. The comparable figures for Saorstát Éireann were 32.5 per cent and 2.2 per cent while the figures for Connacht were 36.3 per cent and 8.5 per cent. Of the five Connacht counties, Sligo, with the largest percentage of non-Catholics in 1911, had the smallest percentage drop in non-Catholic population during this period. Leitrim with the next largest percentage non-Catholic population had the second smallest population drop in the province. 5

Table 9.1. Decrease in the non-Catholic population of each of the counties of Connacht, 1911–26

Connacht Counties	% non-Catholic 1911 Census	Non-Catholic % drop 1911–26
Galway	2.32	53.1
Mayo	2.10	39.7
Roscommon	2.35	39.5
Leitrim	8.47	31.6
Sligo	8.73	26.7

Figures for ten Connacht towns show the same general pattern, the larger the percentage of non-Catholics, the smaller the percentage drop in their numbers during the period 1911–26.[6] In Sligo town the non-Catholic population decreased by 35.6 per cent while Galway town non-Catholics who represented only 2.7 per cent of the population dropped by almost 52 per cent during the same period.[7] This may have been owing to the impact of violence during the troubled times but it is just as likely to be owing to lack of social amenities and pressure from mixed marriages.

While the drop in question in County Sligo was large, it was part of a pattern already well established. The rate of non-Catholic population decline had been falling in Ireland since 1881 but in Sligo the rate of percentage decrease had been increasing since 1871. The non-Catholic percentage of the population of Ireland had been increasing since 1861 but this was not the case in county Sligo where the pattern was the reverse. A trend was therefore already evident well before the outbreak of

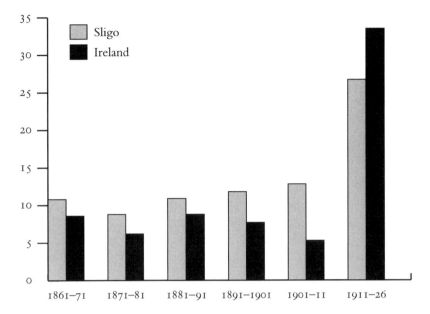

Graph 9.1. Percentage decline in the non-Catholic population in Sligo and in
Ireland, 1861–1926

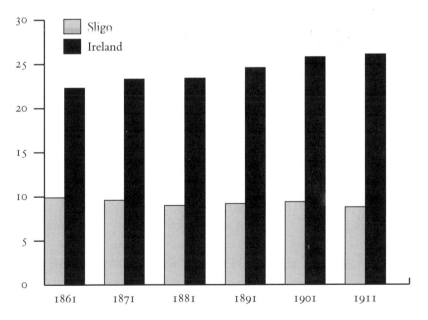

Graph 9.2. Non-Catholics as a percentage of total population of Sligo and of
Ireland, 1861–1911

the War of Independence of increasing fall in the non-Catholic population of County Sligo. The outbreak of hostilities and the effect of these hostilities on a community which was perceived and which largely regarded itself as out of tune with the expressed aims of the majority, could only be expected to accelerate this decrease.

The emigration of non-Irish Protestants in response to the setting up of the Free State may account for some of the population drop. According to the 1911 Census there were 1,022 residents of County Sligo who had been born in England, Scotland or Wales. Their religion is not given but it is fair to assume that many, probably most, were Protestant. In addition, 611 residents had been born in the six counties of Northern Ireland. The departure of a sizeable number of these would have had an influence on the figures. Likewise, there were 22 non-Catholic army members and 22 non-Catholic navy members in County Sligo when the census was taken. There were also 45 non-Catholic civil servants and 31 non-Catholic policemen in the county.[8] This makes a total of 120 non-Catholics who possibly would have left. If we allow half of these to be married with an average of three children each, we are dealing with a maximum of about 400 persons whose departure would have also made an impact on the population figures.

Of the five Connacht counties, Sligo had the highest percentage of non-Catholics, 8.8 per cent, in 1911. This non-Catholic population was not evenly distributed, the highest percentages being found in the areas in the north and centre of the county, from Calry and Drumcliff in the north to Collooney and Ballymote in the centre, as far east as Riverstown and as far west as Skreen and Dromard. The areas on the periphery of the county especially in the south-west had few non-Catholics.[9]

The decline in the population of the various denominations of non-Catholics in the county over the period 1911 to 1926 was not uniform. Protestant Episcopalian numbers fell by almost 23 per cent, Methodist numbers fell by 31 per cent but the fall in the number of Presbyterians was dramatic, a decline of 55 per cent. To examine why this should have happened it is first necessary to look at the differing distribution patterns for each denomination. Protestant Episcopalians were the most numerous, with seven per cent of the population, and most evenly distributed of the Protestant groups with members in every parish of the county. A comparison of the distribution of this denomination over three different areas of the county in 1911 and in 1926 shows that it suffered an almost uniform drop all over the county.

The minutes of the Select Vestry of St John's Church of Ireland Parish in Sligo town provide no evidence that there was a crisis in numbers at the specific 1921–23 period. The parochial finances were in a poor state in early 1921 but the treasurer put this down to difficulty in securing subscriptions with many members in arrears. A general meeting of the congregation was then called and the financial position outlined. By October of the same year the treasurer could report a great improvement in the finances as a result of increased subscriptions from old members and a substantial sum, £55 15s 0d, from new subscribers. In March 1922 the list of registered vestrymen and women was revised and the names of all those who had left and who had died were removed. When the names of new members were added there were then 200 names as against 118 for the previous year. When the list was revised in 1923, 22 persons who had left or died were removed but the same number of new names were added. In February 1924 Vestryman J.J. Nelson did suggest, however, 'that an effort should be made by the present generation to secure the continuance of the Church work for all time because with the present continuous falling away of the Church population, a day might come when the congregation of St John's may not have sufficient funds to carry on the good work'.[10]

The distribution of the Presbyterian faithful, which numbered 0.9 per cent of the population in 1911, was dispersed with 59 per cent, just over 400, living either in Sligo town or in its immediate hinterland. The remainder was widely scattered, 99 living in the Barony of Tireragh from Ballisodare all along the coast to Ballina while 177 lived in south-east Sligo from Collooney towards Boyle. The south-western area was almost devoid of Presbyterians. The intercensal drop in population was widespread but the dispersed country areas suffered most. While 59 per cent of the Presbyterian population lived in Sligo and its environs in 1911, this had risen to 72 per cent in 1926. The population of the Tireragh area fell by 74 per cent and that of the south-east Sligo area by 59 per cent. The population of the Sligo town area fell by a lower figure, 45 per cent. The population drop was greater in the more remote areas.

Records from the three Presbyterian congregations in County Sligo, Ballymote, Dromore West and Sligo, for the period in question show that there was in all cases a large drop in the number of families in each in the period 1921–23.[11] This drop is most marked in the case of the smallest rural congregation in Dromore West, where the republicans held sway for most of the Civil War. This suggests that the more dispersed distribution of the Presbyterians made them prone to more pressure whether this was from hostile elements within the independence movement or from the greater necessity or possibility of intermarriage with other denominations. It also suggests that the drop in the Presbyterian population during the 1911 to 1926 period was more marked in the turbulent Civil War period.

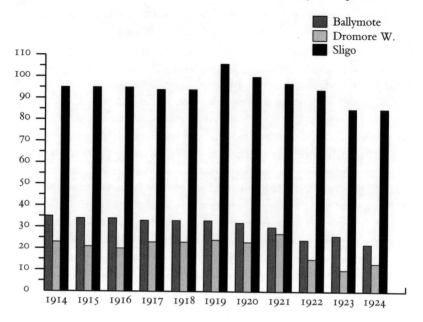

Graph 9.3. Number of families in each of the three Presbyterian congregations in Sligo, 1914–24

Methodists, only 0.6 per cent of the population, formed more concentrated communities with almost the entire rural population in 1926 concentrated in twelve contiguous district electoral divisions in the Collooney – Ballymote – Riverstown area of south-east Sligo. There were also concentrations in the Sligo town area and in Drumcliff parish north of Sligo. They were almost completely absent from the western half of the county. The fact that they appear to have had tightly knit communities must account to a great degree for the relatively low percentage drop in population. In fact their percentage population drop in the rural areas between 1911 and 1926 was only 19 per cent while that in the Sligo town area was 36 per cent.

Actual membership figures for the five Methodist church areas in the county for the period 1914–24 show a marked decline during the 1921–3 period in the case of the Sligo town and north Sligo congregations but no such decline in the case of the more rural communities in south and east Sligo.[12] These latter communities were in areas of relative peace during the Civil War where there were no concentrations of anti-Treaty forces. The general picture here is of a gradual decline in population during the whole period.

The three main Protestant denominations then show different patterns of decline and these patterns seem to be heavily influenced by the

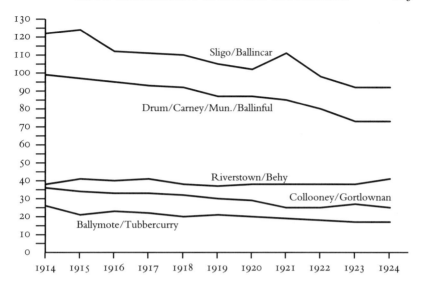

Graph 9.4. Population changes in each of five Methodist church areas in Sligo, 1914–24

distribution of each denomination. This information, taken with the information on non-Catholic population decline in the counties of Connacht, strongly suggest that the decline was general and gradual and affected denominations who were a small minority, especially if they were also dispersed and did not form concentrated local groups. A small, widely dispersed group, such as the Presbyterians, appear to have been especially affected during the period of the independence struggle and the subsequent Civil War.

The Protestants of County Sligo

Although they amounted to less than ten per cent of the population, the Protestants of Sligo were making a significant contribution to the life of the county. Mary O'Dowd mentioned 'the rather claustrophobic and inward-looking atmosphere of the Protestant merchant families in the town [Sligo]. Looked down on, socially, by local Protestant landed families, such as the Gore-Booths in Lissadell or the Coopers in Markree, the Sligo merchant families felt increasingly under threat from the Catholics of the town.'[13] There is little hint of this from the newspapers of the time; rather the feeling is of the strength of the Sligo business families having being augmented by the arrival of fresh blood from the north of Ireland during the previous decades and by renewed interest in and impact on the political life of the town through the Ratepayers

Association and the use of proportional representation in elections. There is also a sense of a community with close contacts, business and social, through a variety of clubs and societies. The following description of a typical Sligo loyalist gives an idea of the profile of such in this period:

> Prior to the Truce applicant was a leading figure in the commercial, official and social life of Sligo . . . J.P., Grand Juror, Member of Sligo Harbour Commissioners, Member Sligo Chamber of Commerce, hon sec of the Select Vestry of St John's Church, Sligo, Vice-President Sligo Tennis Club, member of Sligo Constitutional Club, the members of which were all loyalists, and acted as agent for conservative party at local elections, owner of considerable house property in Sligo . . . Ancestors always staunch supporters of the crown. He himself was brought up in a strong atmosphere of loyalty where the supremacy of the Empire was ever in the forefront of his education.[14]

The Protestant community in Sligo produced powerful figures in the commercial and political life of the county and beyond. One of the more prominent of these was Belfast-born Arthur Jackson, who married into the Pollexfen family and was brought to Sligo to rescue the ailing businesses of that family. He managed the Sligo Steam Navigation Company and joined Sligo Harbour Commissioners of which he served as chairman for 14 years. He was elected a Ratepayers Association member of Sligo Corporation in 1919 and was nominated by the President to the Senate of the Irish Free State in 1922. Another leading businessman was Harper Campbell Perry who came to Sligo in the 1880s to join his grandfather's company, the large provision and curing business of Harper Campbell, of which he later became chairman. He too was elected to Sligo Corporation in 1919. He was also a director of the Sligo Steam Navigation Company and a Harbour Commissioner. Both were prominent Freemasons, Jackson becoming Deputy Provincial Grand Master and Perry Provincial Grand Secretary.[15] A measure of the confidence of the Sligo Protestant business community was the fact that, in spite of the troubles, they were to the fore in setting up Sligo Chamber of Commerce in early 1923, the idea having been originally floated at a meeting of the Harbour Commissioners in late 1922 – hardly a time when one would expect Protestant businessmen in the Free State to be sanguine about the future. Its first president was Harper Campbell Perry, one of the seven Freemasons on the original committee of eleven, only two being Catholic.

Politically the Protestant businessmen had also been to the fore. Many of the business concerns in Sligo had been complaining for years of mismanagement in the affairs of Sligo Corporation, claiming that one of the reasons for this was their lack of representation on that body. They formed a Ratepayers Association; a government enquiry agreeing with their assessment, proposed that the Proportional Representation system of voting be introduced at Sligo Corporation elections to ensure a more equitable representation. This was accepted and this system was used for the first time in Britain or Ireland at the Sligo Corporation election of January 1919. The Ratepayers Association secured 37 per cent of the vote and eight seats.[16] Sinn Féin got seven seats and Labour got five. The Ratepayers Association members became the effective and vocal opposition over the next four years, voting against the non-recognition of the British Local Government Board by the Corporation. At a meeting in December 1920 in the absence of many Sinn Féin–Labour councillors they passed a motion that the Corporation should contest malicious injury claims and answer a letter from the British Board which was tantamount to recognising it. This was rescinded at the next meeting when there was a large muster of Sinn Féin and Labour members.[17] The Ratepayers councillors inflicted a severe blow to the morale of the Sinn Féin–Labour group on the Corporation when in January 1921 they assisted in the defeat of the republican nominee and the election of an independent as Mayor of Sligo.[18] This appears to be the end of the activities of this group and there are no references to the Ratepayers Association as an active political group during the years 1922–23.

In the county, non-Catholic farmers in general had bigger farms than their Catholic counterparts. According to the 1926 Census, 37.5 per cent of Protestant farmers and 6.5 per cent of Catholic farmers had farms of 50 acres or more, 49 per cent of Protestant farmers and 54 per cent of Catholic farmers had farms of between 15 and 50 acres and 12 per cent of Protestant farmers and 39 per cent of Catholic farmers had farms of less than 15 acres. There were only 91 non-Catholic owned farms in the whole county of less than 15 acres, an average of just over one per district electoral division.[19]

The Protestants of County Sligo were almost entirely loyalist and made no effort to hide this even in the troubled times of 1921–23. During October 1921 memorials to the dead of the Great War were dedicated in Calry Church and in Sligo Grammar School. A Memorial service was held in Calry church on Armistice Day 1921, attended by the band of the Bedfordshire and Hertfordshire regiment.[20] There was no reticence in commemorating the departure of the British military from Sligo, which was marked by Protestant church services and functions under the auspices of the two Sligo Protestant parishes. 'A big loss to Sligo' was the heading of a short editorial in the *Sligo Independent* in which it stated that the military's departure was a loss to Sligo from the social, musical and business point of view. The same paper's editorial comments during these times reinforce the impression of a people who, if fearful for their future, were still proud, sure of their stance and self-confident.[21] This loyalty was not translated in action during the War of Independence and only three Protestant claimants to the Irish Grants Committee claimed to have helped the RIC by passing on information. John Russell, District Inspector, who had also been the County Sligo RIC Intelligence Officer provided references for two and was cited as a referee by the other.[22] The loyalty of the other Protestants claimants did not apparently extend to rendering any special assistance to the crown forces in their struggle against the IRA, although in the context of the Grants Committee it would have been in their interest so to claim. This was the common experience elsewhere in the country.[23]

Few non-Catholic Sinn Féiners were active in County Sligo during the period. Countess Markievicz, formerly Constance Gore-Booth of Lissadell, was the best known but her activities in County Sligo were confined to receiving the Freedom of Sligo in 1917 and some appearances at public meetings during the War of Independence. The political development of R.G. Bradshaw from anti-Sinn Féin letter writer in 1916 to anti-Treaty publicist in 1922 has already been dealt with. Another non-Catholic republican was Robert Basil Anderson of Calry who, on returning home from the continent at the outbreak of war, joined the Volunteers instead of the British army as had been his original intention. He became a prominent speaker at Volunteer and Sinn Féin meetings in the county and was arrested in early 1919. He took the anti-Treaty side in the Civil War and was imprisoned in Sligo jail.[24] The only other non-Catholic mentioned as having played any part was Presbyterian Jim Heuston of Ballymote. He was originally from Belfast and took the anti-Treaty side in the Civil War.[25] None of these four republican non-Catholics could be regarded as typical of Sligo Protestants and it is interesting that all took the anti-Treaty side. Tom Garvin in his analysis of the vote on the Treaty mentions that 'Protestants and the foreign-born were more inclined to fundamentalism', suggesting that those marginal to an ethnic group who join it take collective values more seriously.[26]

Protestant Social Organisations

The Protestants of Sligo had a vibrant network of social outlets where they could meet like-minded people and which reinforced their sense of community. The County Club was described in 1907 as 'the rendezvous of the aristocracy of the county'. Its committee at that time, however, contained none of the members of the old landed families of Sligo but did include relative newcomers like Jackson and Campbell Perry. The Constitutional Club formed some years after the County Club was described as 'the headquarters of conservatism in Sligo'. Its committee in 1907 showed a leaning towards the large businessmen of the town, men such as Lyons, Nelson and Pollexfen.[27] By the time of the Civil War it appears that the Constitutional Club was more politically active and it called the meeting of Sligo Protestants in 1922 to express their abhorrence at the attacks on Catholics in Northern Ireland. There was considerable overlap in membership of the various clubs. In 1907 nine of the twelve Constitutional Club committee members were Masons.[28] Of 125 persons who applied for membership between 1907 and 1917, 49 were members of a Masonic Lodge in Sligo. Of the 59 who proposed or seconded these applicants 32 were Masons.[29]

In July 1921 Sligo Brigade IRA listed 'Enemy Social Institutions' as follows: 'County Club, Sligo – Aristocratic enemy club; Constitutional Club – Businessmen, shopkeepers etc.; Town and County Club – Dangerous mixed club frequented by sub sheriff, DI, so called republicans and enemy agents. Rosses Point Golf Club'.[30] Other clubs in Sligo town frequented and run by loyalists were Sligo United YMCA, Sligo Boating and Rowing Club, County Sligo Cricket Club and the County Sligo Hockey Club. The County Sligo lawn tennis tournament held in July 1921 was described as 'almost a typical pre-war local Society gathering' with the list of those attending including many names from the former landed families – O'Haras, Percevals and Wynnes together with business-men such as Jackson and Campbell Perry. [31]

There were two Freemason lodges in operation in Sligo town at this time. Lodge 20, the Light of the West Lodge, had been in existence since the early part of the previous century and Lodge 165 had been founded in 1895 and had grown in popularity so that by the middle of the twentieth century it had become the largest lodge in the province of Connacht.[32] Lodge 20 appears to have attracted the upper echelons of Sligo Protestants. The 17 merchants who were members included Pollexfens, Jackson, Campbell, Nelson and Lyons. Only seven merchants were members of Lodge 165. On the other hand, 20 clerks were members of Lodge 20 but only three members of 165. All shop assistants who joined the Freemasons joined Lodge 165. Notable by their absence from the lodges' membership lists were members of Sligo's older landlord families. There were no Coopers, O'Haras or Croftons among the members. H.R. Wood-Martin was a member of Lodge 20 but he was prominent in Sligo business circles as well as being a member of a landed family.

Freemasons did not dominate public positions in the town and county. Of 19 Borough of Sligo magistrates in 1907 only five were Freemasons and in 1916 none of the 16 Deputy Lieutenants in the County were Masons. Only ten of the 107 magistrates in the County were Masons.[33]

No member of the RIC joined the Masons in Sligo between 1902 and 1920. Only eleven clergymen are recorded as members for the period surveyed.[34] An analysis of the numbers of new entrants to the lodges each year from 1910 to 1923 shows a steady decline in new enrolments from 1910 until 1916 when there was a levelling off. The war years, 1914 to 1918, were the years with the lowest new membership. The three troubled years from 1919 to 1921 saw very large enrolments while 1922 and 1923 saw a return to more normal levels. This growth in membership during the years after the 1918 election may be explained by a gathering together of a group which felt threatened by the rising tide of Sinn Féin and sought safety in the comradeship and the companionship of fellow loyalists.

There is little information on the operation and numbers of Orange lodges in County Sligo during this time and no references to Orange lodges or Orange functions in the county appear in the local newspapers of the period. In 1901 six Orange warrants had been cancelled in the county, indicating the closure of that number of lodges. The official reports of the Grand Lodge suggest that at least three Orange lodges were operating in 1921, in Sligo town, Ballymote and Riverstown. There was also one chapter of the Royal Arch Purple connected with the Orange lodge at Riverstown in 1911.[35] After 1921 there are no further references to County Sligo in the reports of the Grand Lodge and the last meeting involving the county in the proceedings of the Grand Orange Lodge of Ireland was held on 14 December 1921.[36] It appears that the importance

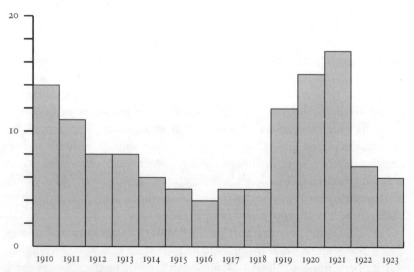

Graph 9.5. New members of Masonic lodges in Sligo each year 1910–23

of the Orange Order had declined considerably in the county during the early years of the century. Robert Beattie of Keash told the Irish Grants Committee that he was 'still an Orangeman of the old school' and Rev. Algernon Harris of Ballymote wrote that the Murrays, coach-builders, of that town 'were out and out Orangemen and were hated for being so'.[37] However, it may be that 'Orangeman' was being used here as a synonym for 'Protestant loyalist' and may not necessarily indicate membership of an Orange lodge.

1916–22: A Succession of Disappointments

While their public tone was self confident and proud, it is clear that, by the time of the Civil War, loyalists in Sligo as elsewhere in the south had been subject to a succession of disappointments. They felt they had been let down by the British government, by their co-religionists in the north, by the British administration in Ireland and even by the Dáil government. In early 1916 there were signs of dissatisfaction with the reaction of the British government to the growth of Sinn Féin. Sligo Unionist landowner Sir Malby Crofton wrote, 'I suppose there is no use in trying to wake up the authorities to the state of things in parts of the country . . . I do not know how the government can go on urging us to use every means to get recruits, while they do nothing to put down a movement which is directed against recruiting.'[38] J.M. Wilson's interviews with Sligo Unionists in 1916 revealed their poor opinion of government policy and of Chief Secretary Birrell: 'He does not represent loyalists of Ireland'.[39] Wilson's general comment on Sligo loyalists was that 'People seem to drift from day to day not knowing either what to expect, or what to hope for'.[40] With the growth of Sinn Féin, the worst fears of the loyalists seemed to be realised. Charles O'Hara wrote in 1918 'Home Rule in any form would be absolutely unthinkable under the existing state of affairs, it would mean handing over this country to Sinn Féiners'.[41] In 1920 he wrote to District Inspector Russell asking him to withdraw a poteen prosecution which was to come up at the local Petty Sessions in case the courthouse, his property, would be burned: 'I know it is useless to look to the Government to protect it, even if it were given, the place would suffer as the Barracks and Market House did as soon as the police were withdrawn'.[42] After the Truce he frequently wrote to local IRA leaders recognising their de facto positions of authority.[43] In the absence of an effective response by the government, the attempts by Sinn Féin to impose order through courts and policing was a straw to grasp at:

> Slowly realisation is coming, and side by side with the realisation that the government is either unable or unwilling to protect them is coming the yet

more startling discovery that on the whole Sinn Féin is trying to prevent anarchy and maintain order . . . This had made a considerable impression on the Unionist mind . . . There is a growing tendency among those whose main desire is a quiet life to say, 'The government can't protect us or govern the country. Sinn Féin is doing the latter and seems disposed to do the former. Won't it suit my book to make friends with Sinn Féin?'[44]

When the Treaty was signed, Sligo unionists, recognising the inevitability of some form of self-government and weary of the disruption caused by the War of Independence, were strongly on the side of ratification. Sir Malby Crofton said that he supported the Treaty because it promised peace: 'They, as farmers, depended entirely on peace and law and order and they hadn't those things for a long time past'.[45] At the December 1921 corporation meeting Ratepayers councillors supported ratification of the Treaty: 'It was a decision either for peace or war and they had suffered enough from war', said Wood-Martin. Perry said, 'While a lifelong unionist I am convinced that the march of time brings certain changes. We are, I believe, on the threshold of a happy destiny for this country. I welcome this opportunity, while not approving of the necessity which led up to it, of joining with the majority for the ratification which I hope will bring lasting peace. Let us all work together to make this country what it can be – one of the best in the world.'[46]

With the ratification of the Treaty and the immediate departure of the British military, loyalist nervousness grew. The *Sligo Independent* decided to start printing leading articles from 21 January 1922 saying that with the establishment of the Free State 'there will be an entire new order of things' and 'its readers may have no opportunity of voicing their opinions through any other source except the medium of this newspaper'.[47] The foreboding here expressed is that the new state would not be generous to members of the minority churches and minority political outlook. The publicity given to the sectarian outrages in Northern Ireland by local newspapers was calculated to add to the feeling of unease on the part of loyalists and a meeting of Sligo Protestants of all denominations at the end of March passed a resolution condemning the northern violence. The chairman, Arthur Jackson, spoke at length mentioning the fact that they represented a small minority among a people who differed from them in religion and politics:

It was agreed that during perhaps the greatest political upheaval that had ever occurred in Ireland no Protestant member of the community had been injured and certainly no one had lost his life. He did not know if that could be said of any other town of over 10,000 inhabitants in the south and west. (hear, hear and applause) It was not often they got a public opportunity of expressing what he felt sure they all felt that they could not be living in a community which had shown itself to be more liberal to the many and various opinions which they held.

Dr MacDowell said that he had been a surgeon in Sligo for over 45 years and though he had strong opinions of the unionist type he had received extraordinary kindness and sympathy from his fellow countrymen of all classes and creeds in Sligo.[48] These fulsome expressions of fellow feeling with Catholics betray a nervous desire for acceptance. No Protestant had indeed been murdered in Sligo town but not far north of the town a Protestant process server had been killed by the IRA. His death was not mentioned now when it was more politic to forget it.[49] While the reaction of the non-Catholic communities was to support the Treaty, they did not take any part in public pro-Treaty meetings nor did they take any part in the election campaign of 1922. This aloofness from politics was to be a hallmark of ex-unionists in the Free State.

There were other events which increased the foreboding of the Protestants. In February 1922 a number of prominent Protestants in the north-west were kidnapped and held as hostages until death sentences on three Derry republican prisoners had been commuted. The *Sligo Independent* denounced this 'outrage' in a strongly worded editorial:

> It is the grossest insult ever committed perhaps against the rights and liberties of the subject and common citizenship, and a very bad omen for the future of Ireland for such things can only add to the flames of bitterness and turmoil in the country to the detriment of everybody no matter to what creed or class or political party they may belong . . . This is certainly a poor response to the willingness with which the minority in the South and West of Ireland agree to work with their fellow-countrymen in the interests of peace and progress and prosperity for the whole of Ireland . . . and at the very first opportunity of the slightest pretext the very men who shouted most about freedom from England denied the simplest exercise of freedom to their own citizens.[50]

Tom Scanlon said that Freemasons were especially targeted, 'We had heard of all the Masons in Sligo town and county for we had raided them in the Tan war and we had all their names . . . We arrested 50–60 and we brought them into different barracks in our area'. Those arrested in County Sligo included representatives from many of the major business houses of Sligo but only one representative of the landed gentry. A rumour in circulation to the effect that Freemasons had passed a resolution or signed a memorial petitioning for the execution of the Derry prisoners was denied by both the *Sligo Independent* and the *Connachtman*.[51]

With the departure of the RIC in April 1922 and the realisation that no new efficient force was to replace them for some time, the pressure on the Protestants of County Sligo, especially those who lived in the countryside, was increased. Neighbouring counties were badly affected. A letter from Ballina to Arthur Griffith in May 1922 asked for immediate steps to prevent the expulsion of 'prominent Protestant merchants and businessmen', saying that notices to that effect were being printed in the town by the IRA. Protestant refugees from North Leitrim were reported arriving in Enniskillen in June 1922.[52] In County Sligo there were numerous incidents of intimidation and petty crime directed against Protestants including the commandeering and burning of vehicles.[53] In May 1922 Gurteen Sinn Féin Cumann condemned raids on private houses of 'well to do Protestants' for 'mere loot'. The *Roscommon Herald* reported in June 1922 that several Protestants in the Riverstown area had been warned to clear out but it considered the threat as 'something in the nature of a stupid joke', suggesting that it had no effect since 'notices and warnings are of such common occurrences nowadays'. Some Protestant jurors were kidnapped to prevent their attendance at Sligo Assizes in July 1922.[54]

Having compromised by expressing their acceptance of the Treaty, the Protestants now found that it did not result in the much-desired peace. A *Sligo Independent* editorial in July 1922 lamented that 'Civilisation is practically gone. Life is not worth living, and all are asking when will it all end, and praying for Peace, Perfect Peace, so that Ireland might be glorious and free.'[55] In spite of public pronouncements of support for the Treaty, many loyalists must have been bitterly disappointed at the settlement and the outbreak of the Civil War served only to confirm this opinion. H.R. Wood-Martin confided to a correspondent: 'I only wish that some of the late politicians who handed over this country were in this town last Wednesday night. A band of irregulars came in, burned the station to the ground and sent six engines down the line . . . The rest of the night was made hideous by gunfire.'[56] It was difficult enough to accept self-government but now they found that it had not prevented further violence and disorder and that in many areas they were at the mercy of the anti-Treaty extremists.

Protestants as Victims

How badly were the Protestants of County Sligo treated during the period 1921–23? Peter Hart has shown how, in particular, between the Treaty and the outbreak of the Civil War non-Catholics in County Cork were subject to murder and persecution. During the revolution, the IRA shot at least 202 civilians in Cork, the vast majority of whom were alleged to be spies or informers. Of these, 36 per cent were Protestant.[57] This contrasts with Sligo where the IRA shot one civilian 'spy', a

Protestant, during the War of Independence and two, both Catholics, during the Civil War. Few incidents of Protestant victimisation were reported from Sligo during the War of Independence. Peter Hart's statement that 'At least two [Protestant churches] in Sligo were burned before the truce' lacks evidence. The two reports he cites refer to the same incident, an unsuccessful attempt to burn Tubbercurry Protestant Church and school. Three men were apprehended for this crime by Volunteers, convicted at a Sinn Féin court and were ordered to pay fines to the local Protestant clergyman.[58]

A 'campaign of loyalist extermination' was mentioned at least three times in claims put forward by Sligo non-Catholics to the Irish Grants Committee, but there is little evidence that a campaign to drive out Protestants was waged in the county during the Truce and Civil War period.[59] Of a total number of 69 Sligo persons who claimed compensation from the Irish Grants Committee at least 36 were Protestant. Of these, six were refused awards.[60] To a large extent the distribution of the thirty successful claimants mirrors closely the distribution of the non-Catholic population in the county with concentrations to the north of the town of Sligo and south through Collooney, Riverstown, Ballymote and Bunninadden. Applicants came from areas where the non-Catholic population was significant, not from areas where there were few isolated non-Catholics. Apart from the town of Tubbercurry the whole western half of the county where Protestants were thinly scattered was free of applicants. The Barony of Tireragh, which contained a large non Catholic population and had been under the control of the anti-Treaty forces until May 1923, had no applicant. The Bunninadden area, already mentioned as having been particularly disturbed, had a group of four claimants of which three obtained grants. There was also a concentration of claimants in the Riverstown area though only three of the six claimants here obtained awards.

Consideration of the occupations of the claimants shows that the majority – 14 – were farmers or landowners, 11 were shopkeepers, traders or in one case a hotelier and three others described themselves as farmers and shopkeepers. Many of these claims were for goods looted and for boycotting. When goods were to be commandeered it made sense for the IRA to take those goods from one who was perceived as 'the enemy', and so a Protestant shopkeeper was often targeted rather than a Catholic one. Of the Protestant claimants from County Sligo there were nine which I have classified as very serious cases, that is they involved serious and prolonged loss of earnings and physical hardship and/or serious destruction of property. Five of these were farmers or landowners where the damage and agitation was of an agrarian nature and three were cases of shopkeepers being boycotted and/or being raided and looted more than once. One was both a farmer and a shopkeeper and suffered on both accounts.[61] Their distribution reflect the general distribution of the claimants, two came from Sligo town, two from Kilturra, two from Riverstown and the other two from elsewhere in south Sligo.

Of the 36 Protestant claimants from County Sligo, ten included a claim for loss as a result of agrarian trouble. This usually took the form of the forcible taking over of lands for grazing by locals often under the banner of the local Sinn Féin club. Some agrarian disturbances had been reported in County Sligo in early 1921 but it was not until early 1922 that more widespread and serious cases occurred. On the one hand the absence of an efficient police force meant that these acts could be engaged in with little danger of the perpetrators being brought to justice. On the other hand it appears there was a widespread belief that the new Irish government would make it a priority to distribute the ranches among the smaller farmers. Keash Sinn Féin Club echoed this feeling when it passed a resolution that 'all ranch lands in the parish should be left for the accommodation of the small landholders for grazing until the new government takes it over to divide it among them'.[62] In all of these agrarian cases there had been a history of trouble in the years previous to the Civil War. The following statement made on behalf of Richard Bell to the Irish Grants Committee describes the situation well:

> In 1920 the Sinn Féin organisation demanded these lands from the applicant. He was able to hold out until the Imperial forces were withdrawn in 1922. Bereft of all protection he was then completely at the mercy of the lawless element and his attitude as a British supporter coupled with his steadfast refusal to recognise or submit to the revolutionary faction was not long without a sequel . . . He had no-one to appeal to for protection and living in the midst of a rebel community who hated and would not hesitate to shoot any loyalist who showed courage enough to oppose them he had to yield to outrage threats and intimidation.[63]

Bell was a loyalist from the vicinity of Ballymote whose lands had been confiscated and ploughed during the Sinn Féin conacre campaign of 1918. In December 1922 he had been physically attacked, dragged out of his house and assaulted, his hay burned and his cattle driven. His attempt to sell the farm at public auction in 1922 failed because of boycott and he eventually had to dispose of his lands on the terms set by the IRA.

Palmer J. McCloughrey, a farmer, veterinary surgeon and a self-styled 'strong supporter of British rule in Ireland', claimed that he had been constantly victimised and eventually driven from his farm of 133 acres in the Riverstown area. This agitation dated at least from 1920. In 1921, when his tenants conspired not to pay the rents, he obtained civil bills for non-payment of rents, but in April 1922 he was dragged from his house, beaten and kicked and had to promise at gunpoint not to execute the decrees. From that time until April 1923 he slept either outdoors or in the house of a neighbouring loyalist and he left the area in April 1923 to live in Sligo town.[64] John Lougheed farmed about 350 acres in the Riverstown area. He had been the subject of agrarian trouble since at least 1920. Some of his lands had been forcibly entered and grazed, hay and outoffices burned and meadows cut. This action became worse after July 1921 and the lands were especially subject to overstocking and overgrazing. Lougheed's enquiries about a British soldier who had been shot as a spy in the vicinity in 1920 also raised suspicions among the local IRA. A group of armed men visited his house and, not finding Lougheed, told his wife that he would be shot because 'he was an Orangeman and a spy'. For a long time afterwards he did not dare to sleep at home.[66]

There had been almost continuous agitation against Charles Phibbs of Doobeg, Bunninadden since the family acquired a large farm there in 1877. In the early months of 1922 this agitation reached a new level when hay and a barn were destroyed by fire. There was some speculation in the local newspapers as to the cause of the fire; the *Western People* was convinced that it was accidental, insisting against all the evidence that 'Mr Phibbs is exceedingly popular in the district'.[66] The agitation continued, gates and fences were stolen or damaged, cattle driven, shots fired, and his workers had received threatening notices signed 'The Irish Tenants Organisation' and 'The Red Hand Murder Gang'. By May 1922 his house had been vandalised, his farm was derelict and stock belonging to neighbours grazed the lands. Eventually Phibbs sold his land at Bunninadden and settled on his other property in Wales.[67]

Miss Jessie Hunter, a Protestant of Ardagh House, Riverstown, owned a farm of 175 acres. There had been a history of agrarian unrest on the farm since the conacre campaign of 1918 and it was taken over by local smallholders in May 1921. She eventually sold the farm, which she claimed was worth around £2,000, to the occupiers in March 1923 for just over £1,000 because a free sale was impossible. This holding was only part of Hunter's total holdings of 300 acres in the area and she retained possession of the rest, continuing to live and farm in the area after the Civil War.[68]

Charles Graham, Knockalassa, was a Protestant shopkeeper and farmer, owner of over 200 acres. He had been the victim of continual persecution from 1920 and his business was boycotted from October 1921. His shop was looted by masked and armed men on at least four occasions in 1922 and twice in early 1923. He closed down his premises in December 1922. In October 1921 he was arrested by the IRA and taken to a camp where he was 'court-martialled' and charged with refusing to resign his commission of the peace, of having spoken against Home Rule ten years previously and of having brought civil proceedings in a British court for debts due. He was held for three days until a fine of £200 was paid. He remained in the area and reopened his shop after the Civil War.[69] The remaining cases of agrarian trouble were less serious, consisting of cattle driving and taking over of parts of farms usually some distance from the residence of the owner and without personal attack or serious destruction of property.[70]

In spite of all this agitation only one loyalist was killed during the period. Edwin Williams, aged 23, son of Essex Williams of Skreen, was shot dead on the night of 15 April 1923 as a result, it was believed, of a long-running agrarian dispute. In December 1920 and March 1921 there had been incidents involving Williams's land including the burning of a farmhouse, stable and contents.[71] Four others reported having been shot at but these all appear to have been cases of intimidation rather than serious attempts on their lives.

This was not an exclusively anti-Protestant agrarian campaign. A Catholic neighbour of Charles Phibbs, J. Ormsby Cooke, Kilturra, Bunninadden, suffered similarly. He tried to let his land for grazing at auction in May 1922 but was seized by armed men and held blindfolded for more than twelve hours, during which time he was thrown into an open grave, threatened with shooting, and robbed of money and personal belongings.[72] Cooke appears to have been an atypical Catholic who was chosen for attention partly because he was a large landowner but also because he was seen as aping the Protestant gentry:

> He was a small fussy little man . . . He had a leaning for the aristocracy who shunned him; and he would not fraternise with the tenantry . . . He sold his lands to what was known as the Parish Committee of Bunninadden, who had set up for to acquire lands from the landlords of the neighbourhood. These were the 1918–1922 days when persuasion was not always done by the tongue. Cooke vacated Kilterra in the year '21 . . . Cooke came back again to Kilterra in 1922 but his stay this time was very short . . . Let me tell you that the reception he got then left him in such a way that he never wanted to revisit Kilterra again. Nor did he.[73]

Protestant shopkeepers and businessmen also suffered during this period and fourteen of them made claims for losses to the Irish Grants Commission.[74] Of these one said that he had had to give up his business in Tubbercurry and leave the area in September 1922.[75] Another two claimed that the trouble resulted in their businesses being ruined.[76] Seven of those who claimed did so because they had been fined for stocking Belfast goods. Six reported that goods had been taken from their shops, generally more than once. Five shopkeepers reported damage to premises consisting of two cases of a store being burned, two cases of windows being broken by shots and one case of a bomb being thrown at a shop wall – the extent of the damage seems to have been slight. There was no case where the complete shop premises were destroyed. Those shop-keepers who suffered most appear to have been those most prominent in supporting the police during the War of Independence. These include Jonathan Walpole-Boyers of Rosses Point who was, according to ex-RIC District Inspector John Russell, 'of the greatest possible assistance to the RIC in rounding up parties wanted for serious crime including the murder of crown forces'. After the RIC station at Rosses Point was closed he was subject to intimidation and threats. His storehouse was burned down, he was fined for dealing in Belfast goods and his shop was looted.[77]

Joseph Graham carried on a business as ironmonger and gunsmith in Sligo town. He was 'a remarkable loyalist', a Justice of the Peace, a member of the Unionist Alliance, indefatigable in getting recruits for the army and very outspoken in 1916; 'during the years 1919, 1920 and up to the Truce in 1921 when murder and anarchy were rampant applicant did not content himself with denunciation but took a very active part in bringing to justice the perpetrators of crime and assisting the police'. 'When the Truce left the republicans a free hand' his business was severely boycotted and he was forced into debt. In 1924 he had to go out of business.[78] Though he blamed his treatment by republicans for this he was unable to produce any accounts for the Grants Committee. George R. Williams was a prosperous Sligo flour merchant who was 'a leading figure in the commercial, official and social life of Sligo'. He claimed to have given a considerable amount of information to the police during the War of Independence period, including information leading to the arrest of Frank Carty in 1920 and the arrest of members of the IRA in November 1920 when conveying the arms captured at Cliffony ambush to south Sligo.[79] He claimed that because of this activity he was boycotted and his business was badly damaged. However, the figures he produced for the Irish Grants Committee show that his income from the flour agency was actually greater in 1922 and 1923 than in previous or subsequent years. He claimed £15,000 and was awarded £7,000.

Catholic shopkeepers also suffered, in some case as badly as Protestants. Five Sligo Catholic shopkeepers submitted claims to the Irish Grants Commission because of serious disruption of business. All were targeted because they had been friendly with Crown forces during the War of Independence and/or were active in recruiting during the Great War. At least three, John P. Jordan, John O'Dowd, former Nationalist MP for South Sligo, and P.J. McDermott, suffered because of their anti-Sinn Féin political activities. One of those worst affected was John R. Keating, a

Catholic hardware merchant from Sligo town, who was awarded £2,050. He had been friendly with the RIC and had been suspected of having given information which had led to the arrest of Alec McCabe in 1915. He also claimed to have rendered other assistance to the RIC, evidence of which he refused to commit to paper. His business, which had been boycotted since 1920, declined and he had to sell it in early 1923.[80] John P. Jordan had supplied the RIC with goods and had been suspected of giving information to them. He had been election agent for Tom Scanlan MP in 1918 and for the independent candidates in the June 1922 election. He had to close his premises after they had been looted and boycotted.[81] A Tubbercurry shopkeeper who had supplied the Auxiliaries with goods was boycotted after their departure and shots were fired into her premises.[82]

Another campaign which affected Protestants disproportionately was the Belfast Boycott. This boycott appears to have been strictly enforced by the IRA in the Ballymote area particularly in October 1921. Those who had their accounts in the Ulster Bank were especially targeted. Robert Beattie told the Irish Grants Committee 'I always kept my account at the Ulster Bank with my brother Orangemen which being the Orangeman's bank was definitely marked out for reprisals through the troubled times'.[83] On the day of the October fair in Ballymote the IRA visited a number of traders and presented them with a printed order demanding that they paid a fine for trading with the Ulster Bank. Amounts demanded ranged from £25 to £100. On their refusal to pay, the IRA put an armed guard on each premises, refusing entry to customers. After some negotiation a reduced fine was paid in each case and the premises was allowed to reopen. According to one of the affected traders, 'the very moment that the notices were received every single trader immediately withdrew their accounts from this bank but that had no effect as was evident afterwards it was the cash that was wanted'.[84]

Of the 69 Irish Grants Committee claimants, eleven included a claim for losses due to or fines paid for the Belfast Boycott.[85] Of these eleven, seven were Protestant, one was Catholic and the religion of the other three has not been determined. All except one were shopkeepers or dealers. The names of 22 business persons from the Ballymote area are included in claims made to the Department of Finance arising from Belfast Boycott fines.[86] There is some overlap between this and the Irish Grants Committee list. In total there were 28 claimants. Of these eight were Protestant, nine were Catholic and the religion of the other eleven is not known.[87] Richard Gorman, Templevanney, with reference to a £50 fine which he paid for having his account in the Ulster Bank, said 'that fine was inflicted as the simplest way to get at supporters of the

Government and at the same time to fill the Irregulars' depleted coffers'.[88] There is no evidence of the Belfast Boycott campaign having the same effect in other parts of the county or being activated in the Ballymote area at a later date during the Truce or Civil War periods.

Many statements by loyalists to the Irish Grants Committee stress the isolation and terror felt by individual Protestants during this period: 'There is no getting away from the fact that from 1920 to the end of 1923 isolated loyalists were made a shuttlecock for the worst and most desperate of the revolutionary element and that our client (Miss Jessie Hunter) received a liberal share of their attention . . . her treatment was due entirely to her support of and unswerving loyalty to British rule in Ireland previous to 11 July 1921'. Jessie Hunter herself said, 'I was a well known Protestant loyalist living in a very disaffected locality. Because I was alone and unprotected and a supporter of British rule in Ireland these persistent outrages were committed on me and my property with impunity and as part of a campaign of loyalist extermination.'[89]

While this terror and feeling of isolation was real there is no evidence of a campaign of loyalist extermination in County Sligo. If we allow that each of the 36 Protestant claimants represents a family of five persons this still represents less than three per cent of the Protestant population of the county. Many Catholics also suffered. Isolated Protestants were not targeted to a greater extent, most claims coming from areas where Protestants were relatively numerous. Shopkeeper H.T. Evans described himself as 'the only loyalist, the only Protestant' in the remote village of Aclare, and said that his shop had been raided four times during 1920 and 1921, the last raid taking place on 14 June 1921 when he was fined £10 for not resigning his Commission of the Peace. No award was recommended in his case since he could claim no damages during the Civil War period, even though his area was under the control of the anti-Treaty forces for most of the period.[90] Thomas J. Ewing, hotelkeeper at Rosses Point, claimed to have received many threatening letters warning him to 'give up my business and to clear out of Rosses Point but still held on'. However, the only claim he could make was for his Ford car and garage which were destroyed by fire in June 1922. He seems not to have been interfered with in any other way during the subsequent period.[91]

H.R. Wood-Martin was involved in collecting rents for many of the absentee landlords of unpurchased lands in the county. According to John Russell, 'Mr Wood-Martin being a well known loyalist in this county was selected for exceptionally bad treatment' as part of 'the campaign of loyalist extermination which was being intensely carried out by the revolutionary element at the time'. In fact all Wood-Martin was able to claim for was deprivation of use of a grazing farm near

Keash, seized in 1920 by Sinn Féiners and held during the War of Independence and Civil War.[92] In other cases referees did not agree with the claimants assessment of the damages. A Bunninadden Protestant claimed that his house had been raided on three occasions during the period and that one raid, not the last, resulted in the 'total destruction of the dwelling house'. The local Protestant clergyman, however, said that material damage done during the raids was slight.[93] There was no attempt to target the numerous Protestant former landlords such as the Coopers, the O'Haras and the Gore-Booths.[94] The absence of claims from any of the larger Protestant businesses in Sligo town indicates that there were no attempts to target them. The statement in the claim of Joseph Graham of Sligo town to the effect that 'every loyalist who had rendered active assistance to the crown was being victimised and arrangements were being made to clear them out of the country' suggests that those Protestants (and Catholics) who were seriously victimised were attacked not because of their religion but because in the eyes of their attackers they had done something to deserve attack. Graham's case, indeed, was said to have been 'a very rare one'.[95] All Protestants may have been regarded as enemies but relatively few suffered seriously. Only three Protestant claimants said that they had to leave the county permanently and one had to move residence within the county.[96]

I have found no references to Protestant refugees fleeing from Sligo during this period. If refugees were to leave the county it would be logical to suggest that they fled to the nearest part of Northern Ireland, County Fermanagh, with which there was a rail link. A census dated 1925 of 2,117 Protestants who had left what became the Free State during the preceding five years and who were then living in Fermanagh contains only 51 Protestants from County Sligo. The figures for the other Connacht counties are Leitrim – 292, Galway – 55, Mayo – 34 and Roscommon – 6.[97] The figures for Sligo suggest that there was no exodus of refugees from the county to the nearest place of refuge, unlike, for instance, from Leitrim or indeed from Monaghan from which 454 Protestants had fled to Fermanagh.[98]

The evidence points to an acceleration of the already increasing decline in the non-Catholic population in County Sligo over the 1911–26 period. There is some evidence that this decline was more marked in the Truce and Civil War period. Small, dispersed communities of non-Catholics, especially those in areas where the anti-Treaty forces held sway for long periods, were most affected. On the other hand there is little evidence that this decline resulted from specific violence against these people. The area where the greatest decline in Presbyterian numbers occurred, the barony of Tireragh, had no claimant to the Irish Grants Committee. These claims demonstrate a large amount of fear and intimidation but they did not constitute a concerted anti-Protestant campaign. Rather, it was a mixture of continued agrarian agitation and the seizing of opportunities for 'inflicting injuries on obnoxious persons, for paying off old scores and for widespread looting'.[99] Protestants were often targeted in County Sligo over this period but seldom because of their religion alone.

The accumulation of disappointments and dashed hopes during the whole second decade of the century, the feeling that the nadir had been reached only to find that further depths were still to be plumbed, caused many Protestant loyalists at various times during the period to give up and leave County Sligo. Most stayed, however, and looked for security and comfort in increased membership of fraternal organisations and business organisations.

CONCLUSION

THE CESSATION OF Civil War violence in mid-1923 was greeted in County Sligo with no elation, no pronouncements welcoming victory and no flags. Instead the tone was a weary air of acceptance. This was in marked contrast to the rapturous welcome which had greeted the Truce of 1921. Sligo had experienced little hardship and just enough violent activity during 1919–21 to be able to claim, no matter what others said, that it had played an important part in the glorious revolution of those years. In the immediate aftermath of the revolution, however, Sligo experienced the growth and proliferation of dissention and division which resulted in a degree of violence and disruption greater than that of the War of Independence. Small wonder then that the ending of the Civil War was greeted with an attitude close to indifference by a war-weary populace. In a sense there were no winners. The county had suffered in many ways – infrastructure had been badly damaged, the economy had been injured, social and sporting activity had been seriously curtailed and many relationships had been poisoned. The republicans had survived in Sligo, some of their leaders had not been captured and they were still able to carry out small-scale nuisance operations. The previous year had seen much military action by both side but few glorious victories. Indeed both sides had committed shameful deeds which were destined to be recalled for years by the other side. This book has investigated the whole period 1921 to 1923 with a view to answering the questions posed in the introduction.

I have endeavoured in the first place to investigate how County Sligo, the epitome of nationalist orthodoxy during the first two decades of the century, became a thorn in the side of the new post-Treaty regime and how a county so lacking in warlike activities during the Anglo-Irish conflict could become such a centre of conflict during the Civil War. It is clear that what headquarters claimed of the county concerning the War of Independence was to a great extent true; Sligo's level of activity during that struggle was low. This was owing to a range of interdependent factors: the level of political orthodoxy; the lack of early radical organisation and activity; the lack of experience of the IRA leaders; the poor armament of the IRA and the slow pace of the escalation of violence. Criticism by headquarters in the period just before the Truce stung the Sligo leadership and no doubt engendered a desire to prove themselves.

The Truce period, then, came at an opportune moment for the Sligo IRA giving them the time to re-organise, arm and train their members, the impotence of the RIC giving them almost a free rein. The Sligo IRA leaders, soon to be elevated to divisional officerships, seemed determined to establish themselves as the dominant force in the county with scant regard for any dissenting voices including those of Sinn Féin representatives. In local government in particular there were bitter divisions which reflected the resentment of vested local interests at any attempt at effective and reforming central control. Those IRA councillors again at liberty to attend meetings allied themselves with these local interests and attempted to control Sligo's local authorities, expressing their belief in the supremecy of the 'men of action' over the 'men of words'. They opposed the Dáil Local Government Department amalgamation scheme and fought tooth and nail to thwart its implementation. Eventually they failed. This split in the local authorities especially in Sligo County Council mirrored to a large degree the Treaty split. At the outbreak of the Civil War the active anti-Treaty IRA members once again found themselves unable to attend council meetings. Thus the pro-Treaty councillors were given ample time to develop local government under the amalgamation scheme and by the time anti-Treaty members were again able to attend in numbers the new order of local democracy had been well established.

The power and independence which the Sligo IRA claimed and enjoyed during the Truce period was fundamentally threatened by the signing of the Treaty and it was natural that a majority of that group would oppose it. At the same time, events caught them typically unprepared and they failed to formulate a quick and coherent opposition, allowing the pro-Treaty side to take the initiative. The popular verdict in favour of the Treaty was clear and the leading Sligo newspaper, the *Sligo Champion*, was to the fore in expressing this. Many of those who had been at the receiving end of the IRA's vituperation during the Truce period delighted in combining against them now. The bitterness of the divisions in the county suggested that it would be very difficult to heal the split, and the long drawn out nature of the events of the following six months with postponements of the Sinn Féin Árd-Fheis and of the election, the numerous incidents within the county, and the involvement of the Sligo IRA in such actions as the Limerick crisis and the guerilla warfare along the border all helped to reinforce the Sligo IRA's opposition to the new regime and their confidence in their own righteousness.

I have shown that the fact that a majority of voters gave their first preferences to anti-Treaty candidates in Sligo–Mayo East constituency in the Pact election of June was a factor of the geographical distribution of the candidates rather than a reflection of the voters' opinion of the Treaty. The pro-Treaty candidates were unfavourably clustered in south Sligo, while their opponents were strategically placed in east Mayo and north and south Sligo. In spite of this there is no doubt but that the results in the constituency gave a great boost to the anti-Treaty side.

' The outbreak of Civil War found the Sligo IRA strong in resolve but weak in ideas. Old animosities and lack of offensive planning and co-ordinated action combined to deprive the anti-Treaty side of the fruits of the numerical advantage they enjoyed at the start of hostilities. They waited for the enemy to advance against them and then abandoned or were driven out of their posts to resume the more familiar guerilla war. The Free State troops established positions in towns and only very slowly increased their hold on the country areas. The anti-Treaty forces proved hardest to defeat in the mountainous areas especially in the north-west and east of the county. As the war progressed, the government forces utilised large-scale sweeps to break up anti-Treaty concentrations. These sweeps gradually diminished the areas under the control of the anti-Treaty forces and, coupled with arrests and deaths, reduced their numbers and influence. Because of problems of poor organisation and morale, and difficulties with supplies, transport and numbers, the government forces were not at any time strong enough to inflict a decisive defeat on their opponents. On the other hand, the IRA seemed content to survive and inflict irregular severe blows such as the burning of Sligo Railway Station. Because of the IRA's lack of co-operation and lack of realistic offensive strategy it was inevitable that the government troops would eventually wear them down and clear republican strongholds, allowing normality to return to most of the county while at the same time being unable to finish them off completely. That most of the IRA leadership in the county were apparently against the ceasefire, believing that they could survive indefinitely, is a tribute both to their capacity for survival and the inability of the Free State army to deliver the coup de grace.

While the strongholds of the anti-Treaty forces were in the remote mountainous regions, most incidents occurred in the areas of better land near towns where government posts were situated. Attacks on lines of communications also ensured that such areas as the central north–south corridor of communication saw plenty of action.

My analysis of the background of those Sligo people who participated on each side in the Civil War demonstrates clearly the absence of a social basis for the Civil War in County Sligo. While fewer recruits for both sides came from the poorer areas of the county the distribution of anti-Treaty internees and pro-government army recruits is similar over the whole county. My examination of the personal backgrounds of the participants, parents' occupation, valuation of house and land holding shows that neither group of activists came predominantly from a clearly defined social stratum. In particular there is no evidence to support the notion that the republican activists were overwhelmingly from the 'men of no property' or that the Free State army members came from the propertied classes. In fact there is clear evidence that the latter were more likely to come from the lower strata of society than the anti-Treaty activists and this pattern is more marked in the Sligo urban area. While these conclusions refer only to activists, my analysis shows the danger in ascribing a simplistic class basis for the divisions which occurred in Ireland in 1921–23.

To what extent did the Civil War disrupt daily life in Sligo? The volume of military activity during the war was much greater than during the War of Independence and so the conflict was much more likely to impinge on everyday life. Estimates and statistics suggest that at its height the war involved over 800 armed men in County Sligo, about 500 on the government side and over 300 on the anti-Treaty side. Thus the likelihood of being affected by the war was much greater and disruption and destruction were much more widespread. The evidence which I have collated demonstrates clearly the hardship which was inflicted on the populace during the period. The dramatic fall in the numbers of social and sporting functions testifies to a period in which normal daily life was circumscribed with non-essential journeys and outings severely curtailed. The country areas, more dependent on road and rail transport and less likely to be protected by a government post, suffered to a greater degree than did the town of Sligo, and a recovery in early 1923 manifested itself earlier in the urban area. In particular the deterioration of the transport infrastructure, through destruction by the anti-Treaty forces and the lack of any repairs or maintenance, imposed considerable hardship.

The extent to which livestock prices and food prices were affected is difficult to ascertain but the figures I have considered certainly suggest that the general depression in livestock prices at that time was worsened by the effect of the war. The apparent rise in the cost of some foodstuffs in the period after the outbreak of war and the drop in the turnover of most of Sligo's co-operative creamery societies in 1923 are evidence of difficulties caused by the war. On the other hand the evidence, admittedly scant, from the business house of Meehan Brothers in Sligo town suggests that the conflict made little impact on its turnover but some on the ability of its customers to pay cash.

The lack of a functioning system of justice caused considerable hardship and disruption. No widely recognised or effective system of police or courts had been in operation in the county since early 1920 and while the Dáil Courts were slowly reorganised during the Truce period and after, the lack of an effective police force meant that they were ultimately powerless. The confusion of the post-Treaty period as regards law and order and the rise of factional strife led to a rise in lawlessness in early 1922. Petty crime, hooliganism and robbery intermingled with and were often indistinguishable from agrarian agitation, intimidation of Protestants, attacks on ex-RIC and politically motivated crime. For most of the Civil War period large areas of the county were without effective law. If anything the areas nominally under control by the government forces seem to have been subject to lawlessness more than those areas under strong republican control. Towards the end of the war as the threat from anti-Treaty forces dwindled the newly established Civic Guard began to occupy barracks and courts began to function again. As the Civil War ended the county was still in a state of disturbance and unrest but appears to have settled down remarkably quickly afterwards.

What of the vulnerable non-Catholic population in this period? There is no doubt that over the 1911–26 period there was an acceleration in the decline of the non-Catholic population in County Sligo. All Protestant denominations were affected but to a varying extent and in relation to the dispersal patterns of each in the county. The small, widely dispersed Presbyterian community in the country areas seems especially to have declined, while more concentrated Methodist communities seem to have suffered less. There is some inconclusive evidence that this decline was more marked during the Truce and Civil War period. The evidence I have presented suggests that this decline was due to the accumulation of disappointments and dashed hopes during the whole second decade of the century which caused many Protestant loyalists at various times during the period to give up and leave County Sligo. There was also an amount of violence directed against the non-Catholic population in unco-ordinated campaigns such as agarrarianism, the Belfast Boycott, looting, requisitioning of materials by the IRA, and some settling of old scores. That these did not constitute a co-ordinated campaign of intimidation with the aim of removing the Protestants from County Sligo is clear. Most Protestants remained in Sligo and looked for security and comfort in increased membership of fraternal and business organisations. In particular, urban Protestant businessmen while understandably apprehensive about their future in the new state still appeared confident that they had an important role to play in that state.

They, like most others in the county, were delighted when the confusion, the unpredictability and the personal danger of the post-revolution era finished with the dumping of arms by the remaining anti-Treaty forces. Sligo, as elsewhere in the country, could begin to come to terms with the havoc and destruction wreaked over the previous two years. The years of revolution with their vision of an imminent golden age of freedom had been years of hope and glorious anticipation, but the Civil War shattered that vision and provided a bitter aftermath of division, violence and hardship.

NOTES

INTRODUCTION

1 David Fitzpatrick, *Politics and Irish Life, 1913–1921* (Dublin, 1977), p. 231.
2 S.J. Connolly (ed.), *The Oxford Companion to Irish History* (Oxford, 1998), p. 265.
3 Michael Hopkinson, *Green Against Green: The Irish Civil War* (Dublin, 1988), p. xii.
4 Maryann Gialanella Valiulis, *General Richard Mulcahy: Portrait of a Revolutionary* (Dublin, 1992), p. 57; Hopkinson, *Green Against Green*, p. 10; Calton Younger, *Ireland's Civil War* (London, 1968), p. 263.
5 *Daily Mail*, 28 Nov. 1917.
6 Tadhg Kilgannon, *Sligo and its Surroundings* (Sligo, 1926), p. 313.
7 Peter Hart, *The IRA and its Enemies* (Oxford, 1998), p. 47.
8 David Fitzpatrick, 'The Geography of Irish Nationalism, 1910–1921', in *Past and Present*, lxxvii (1978), Statistical Appendix, pp 432–3.
9 See Ciarán Ó Duibhir, *Sinn Féin, The First Election 1908* (Manorhamilton, 1993).
10 John Jinks (1873–1934) was born in north Sligo but settled in Sligo town where he established his own business as a publican, auctioneer and undertaker. He was a member of Sligo Corporation from 1898 and presided over the inaugural meeting of Sligo branch of the Volunteers. He was generally a loyal follower of Redmond though he had supported a rival local candidate in 1909 when Thomas Scanlan was imposed by the party as North Sligo MP. See Michael Farry, *Sligo 1914–1921: A Chronicle of Conflict* (Trim, 1992), p. 2.
11 *S.C.*, 7 Feb. 1914.
12 Alec McCabe (1886–1972) was born at Keash near Ballymote, and was educated at Summerhill College and St Patrick's Training College, Dublin where he trained as a primary teacher. He became principal of Drumnagranchy N.S., Keash but lost his job because of his political activities. He was a member of Supreme Council of the IRB in 1914 and an early supporter and organiser of Sinn Féin and the Volunteers in Sligo. He served several terms of imprisonment 1917–21. He was elected Sinn Féin TD for South Sligo in December 1918 and returned as TD for Sligo from then until 1923. A letter bemoaning the 'lack of enthusiasm shown in Ballymote' appeared in *S.C.*, 23 May 1914.

13 See Sligo Co. Inspector RIC (SCI RIC) May 1914 Monthly Report, PRO, CO 904/93.

14 SCI RIC, Sept. 1914 Monthly Report, PRO, CO 904/94.

15 This was Major W.R. Hillas of Donnecoy, Templeboy. Letters to and from Hillas, and other Sligo material relevant to the Volunteers, are in National Library, Dublin, Maurice Moore Papers, Ms 10544.

16 This disturbance was reported in the pro-unionist *S.I.* 26 Sept. 1914 though not in the nationalist *S.C.*

17 SCI RIC, Sept. 1915 Monthly Report, PRO, CO 904/98.

18 Reports on 1916, PRO, CO 904/120.

19 *S.C.*, 15 Apr. 1916.

20 Sir Malby Crofton to Irish Unionist Alliance, 11 Mar. 1916 (PRONI, J.N. Wilson Papers D989A/8/6).

21 J.N. Wilson notes on interviews with Sligo loyalists, 24 Feb. 1916 (PRONI, J.N. Wilson Papers, D989A/9/7).

22 Editorial in *S.C.*, 20 May 1916.

23 For example Jinks's welcome for released Cliffony man McGarrigle, reported in *S.I.*, 10 June 1916.

24 SCI RIC, June–Dec. 1916 Monthly Reports, PRO, CO 904/99–101.

25 Hanley, a native of west Sligo, was a businessman and had been Jinks' opponent in the 1916 mayoral election. (*S.C.*, 27 Jan. 1917).

26 *S.C.*, 20 Oct. 1917.

27 Joost Augusteijn, *From Public Defiance to Guerilla Warfare* (PhD thesis Amsterdam, 1994), pp 24–5.

28 Fitzpatrick, 'The Geography of Irish Nationalism', pp 432–3. Sligo was third best organised in Connacht behind Leitrim and Roscommon. PRO, UIL files, CO 904/20.

29 *S.C.*, Feb. 1918; Interview with Alec McCabe, *The Irish Times*, 6–7 May 1970; SCI RIC Feb. 1918 Monthly Report, CO 904/105.

30 SCI RIC, Jan.–Feb. 1918 Monthly Reports, PRO, CO 904/105.

31 In particular the trial of McCabe and his associates in Feb. 1918 when the defendants smoked and sang songs during the hearing (*S.C.*, 2 Mar. 1918).

32 SCI RIC, May 1918 Monthly Report, CO 904/106.

33 *S.C.*, 20 and 27 April 1918.

34 SCI RIC, Nov. 1918 Monthly Report, CO 904/107.

35 Election results in *S.C.*, 4 Jan. 1919.

36 This was the only local government election to be held at this time and Proportional Representation was used because of the complaints of Sligo ratepayers that their under-representation previously had led to mismanagement of Sligo Corporation. See Farry, *Sligo 1914–1921*, pp 154 ff.

37 Almost half the independent vote was accounted for by John Jinks. The number of seats obtained by each party was as follows: Ratepayers – 8, Sinn Féin – 7, Labour – 5, Independents – 4. Results from *S.C.*, 25 Jan. and 1 Feb. 1919.

38 Nominations in *S.C.*, 1 May 1920; Results in *S.C.*, 5 and 12 June 1920; Intimidation reported in *S.I.*, 15 May 1920.

39 Sligo Co. Council Minute Book, 21 June 1920. Sligo Co. Library.

40 See report: 'To be or not to be' in *S.C.*, 8 Jan. 1921.

41 Michael Nevin statement, Sligo Co. Library; Report in *S.C.* and *CM*, 5 Feb. 1921.

42 Chief of Inspection to Local Government Inspector Sligo, 13 May 1921 and 8 July 1921, NA, Dáil Éireann Local Government files, Sligo Co. Council – Miscellaneous Papers, 8 Oct. 1921–7 April 1922, DE LG 26/9.

43 Frank Carty statement, NLI, Collins Papers, P914. Charles Gildea mentions that he had organised branches of the Hibernian Rifles in the same places. This group was created by the Irish-American Alliance faction of the AOH. No mention of the Hibernian Rifles or the Irish-American Alliance AOH is made by the RIC County Inspector during this period. (Charles Gildea material in Fr O'Kane Papers, Archdiocese of Armagh, Records Centre, Armagh: Augusteijn, *From Public Defiance to Guerilla Warfare*, pp 40 ff.).

44 SCI RIC, May 1915 Monthly Report, PRO, CO 904/97. On St. Patrick's Day 1916, there were three Volunteer parades in the county. In Cliffoney, 50 Volunteers paraded, 69 paraded in Ballymote and 52 marched at a sports meeting in Mullinabreena. (Reports on St Patrick's Day 1916, Sinn Féin Material, PRO, CO 904/23).

45 Frank Carty statement, NLI, Collins Papers P914; Interview with Alec McCabe, *The Irish Times*, 6–7 May, 1970; Batt Keaney statement in author's possession; Patrick McCannon statement in author's possession; Thomas Kilcoyne interview 14 August 1986; Thady McGowan and Tom Brehony, 'Keash/Culfadda Volunteer movement' in *Corran Herald* (July 1987), p. 6; Farry, *Sligo 1914–1921*, pp 76 ff.

46 *S.C.*, 20 May 1916.

47 Augusteijn, *From Public Defiance to Guerilla Warfare*, table 1.5, p. 19. Sligo figures from SCI RIC, Jan. 1918 Monthly Report, CO904/105 and Nov. 1918, Monthly Report, CO/904/107.

48 Irish Volunteers, Return of Arms, 28 Feb. 1917. PRO, CO 904/29.

49 Augusteijn, *From Public Defiance to Guerilla Warfare*, p. 27.

50 Batt Keaney statement in author's possession; Interview with Alec McCabe, *The Irish Times*, 6–7 May 1970.

51 Illegal Drillings Midland and Connacht District, 1917, PRO, CO 904/122.

52 Augusteijn, *From Public Defiance to Guerilla Warfare*, p. 7.

53 Peter Hart, *The IRA and its Enemies*, pp 62 and 71.

54 Reports in *S.C.* and *S.I.*, March–July 1919.

55 Report in *S.C.*, 22 Nov. 1919; Jim Hunt statement, Sligo Co. Library; Jim Hunt, AD UCD, O'Malley Notebooks, P17b/133; P.S. O'Hegarty, AD UCD, O'Malley Notebooks, P17b/137.

56 Sligo Brigade material, NLI, Collins Papers, P 914,

57 SCI RIC, Dec. 1919 Monthly Report, PRO, CO 904/110.

58 SCI RIC, Oct. 1919 Monthly Report, PRO, CO 904/110.

59 Farry, *Sligo 1914–1921*, pp 190–1.

60 Volunteer GHQ issued an official order to enforce a boycott of police on 4 June 1920.

61 Farry, *Sligo 1914–1921*, pp 193 ff.

62 Outrages against police, PRO, CO 904/148.

63 Cecil King's father was stationed at Collooney during this period, (C.A. King, *Memorabilia*, Donegal ?, 1989), pp 22–24.

64 SCI RIC, June 1920 Monthly Report, PRO, CO 904/112. See also *Irish Bulletin*, 17 June 1920.
65 Dáil Courts files, NA, Correspondence re. Sligo cases, DE6; North Sligo, DE10/57; South Sligo, DE10/58.
66 Farry, *Sligo 1914–1921*, p. 291.
67 Mentioned in a letter C/S to M/D, 11 June 121, AD UCD, Mulcahy Papers, P7/A/20.
68 Augusteijn, *From Public Defiance to Guerilla Warfare*, p. 159.
69 Hart, *The IRA and its Enemies*, p. 72.
70 Farry, *Sligo 1914–1921*, p. 191.
71 Augusteijn, *From Public Defiance to Guerilla Warfare*, Table 1.9, p. 33.
72 SCI RIC, June. 1920 Monthly Report, PRO, CO 904/112.
73 Tom Scanlon, AD UCD, O'Malley Notebooks, P17b/133.
74 Tom Deignan, AD UCD, O'Malley Notebooks, P17b/133.
75 Matt Kilcawley, AD UCD, O'Malley Notebooks, P17b/136.
76 Jim Hunt statement, Sligo Co. Library; Jim Hunt, AD UCD, O'Malley Notebooks, P17b/133.
77 Tom Scanlon, AD UCD, O'Malley Notebooks, P17b/133; Jack Brennan, AD UCD, O'Malley Notebooks, P17b/137. Frank Carty (1897–1942) was born at Clooncunny, Ballymote, the son of a small farmer. He joined the Volunteers in 1914 and became prominent in organisation in the Tubbercurry area. He was arrested for his involvement in the raid for arms on Perceval's at Templehouse but was rescued from Sligo jail in May 1920.
78 Frank Carty statement, NLI, Collins Papers, P914; Martin Brennan, AD UCD, O'Malley Notebooks, P 17b/133; Jack Brennan, AD UCD, O'Malley Notebooks, P17b/137.
79 Eugene Gilbride, AD UCD, O'Malley Notebooks, P17b/137; Bernard Conway, AD UCD, O'Malley Notebooks, P17b/133; Patrick McCannon statement in private possession.
80 Fitzpatrick, *Politics and Irish Life 1913–1921*, p. 216.
81 See map of British reprisals in E. Rumpf and A.C. Hepburn, *Nationalism and Socialism in Twentieth-Century Ireland* (Liverpool, 1977), p. 39. Nine are given for Sligo, none caused death or serious injury and some were very minor.
82 Tom Scanlon blamed Linda Kearns for the capture. Tom Scanlon, AD UCD, O'Malley Notebooks, P17b/133; Linda Kearns statement in private possession; Eugene Gilbride, AD UCD, O'Malley Notebooks, P17b/137.
83 SCI RIC, Jan. 1921 Monthly Report, PRO, CO 904/114.
84 Jim Hunt statement, Sligo Co. Library; Jim Hunt, AD UCD, O'Malley Notebooks, P17b/133.
85 Sligo Co. Council claimed over £1000 for eight major bridges and 'about twenty smaller ones' damaged or destroyed during April and May 1921. Claims Registers, Co. Sligo. PRO, CO 905/10.
86 AD UCD, O'Malley Notebooks, P17b/127, cited in Augusteijn, *From Public Defiance to Guerilla Warfare*, p.101.
87 Eugene Gilbride, AD UCD, O'Malley Notebooks, P17b/137.
88 Paddy Dwyer interview 28 Nov. 1987; Charles Gildea material in Fr O'Kane Papers, Archdiocese of Armagh, Records Centre, Armagh.

89 Tom Scanlon, AD UCD, O'Malley Notebooks, P17b/133.

90 Jack Brennan, AD UCD, O'Malley Notebooks, P17b/137; Martin Brennan, AD UCD, O'Malley Notebooks, P 17b/133; Matt Kilcawley, AD UCD, O'Malley Notebooks, P17b/136.

91 Jim Hunt statement, Sligo Co. Library; Jim Hunt, AD UCD, O'Malley Notebooks, P17b/133.

92 Jack Brennan, AD UCD, O'Malley Notebooks, P17b/137.

93 This number is an estimate based on the sources mentioned in the previous paragraph, twenty on the Ox Mountains, ten each in Sligo town, Ballymote and Tubbercurry areas.

94 Augusteijn, *From Public Defiance to Guerilla Warfare*, Table 1.9, p. 33.

95 Michael Coleman, AD UCD, O'Malley Notebooks, P17b/137.

96 Patrick McCannon statement in private possession; Joe McGowan, *In the Shadow of Benbulben* (Manorhamilton, 1993), pp 113-24 and 126.

97 Martin Brennan, AD UCD, O'Malley Notebooks, P17b/133: Matt Kilcawley, AD UCD, O'Malley Notebooks, P17b/136; SCI RIC, July 1921 Monthly Report, CO 904/116.

98 *S.C.* and *S.I.*, 23 Apr. 1921; Daniel Waters statement; SCI RIC, Apr. 1921 Monthly Report, PRO, CO 914/115.

99 Linda Kearns statement in private possession.

100 Martin Brennan, AD UCD, O'Malley Notebooks, P17b/133.

101 Statement of munitions, undated, probably late 1921, AD UCD, Mulcahy Papers, P7/A/28.

102 William (Billy) Pilkington was a native of Sligo town and worked in Wehrly watchmakers. He had been a member of the Volunteers since 1913. He became O/C Sligo Brigade in 1917 when J.J. O'Connell joined Volunteers headquarters. Michael Collins (1890-1922), IRA leader and Minister of Finance in the first Dáil Éireann, was a member of the Treay delegation in December 1921. He was Commander in Chief of the Free State forces in the Civil War. Shot and killed, 22 Aug. 1922.

103 Tom Deignan, AD UCD, O'Malley Notebooks, P17b/133; Thady McGowan and Tom Brehony, 'Keash/Culfadda Volunteer movement' in *Corran Herald*, (July 1987), p. 8.

104 The Information Officer was R.G. Bradshaw. A series of correspondence between the I/O. Sligo and the I/O, GHQ is in MA, Collins Papers, IRA Sligo Brigade, A/0747.

105 Sligo Brigade Report for March 1921, 5 Apr. 1921, AD UCD, Mulcahy Papers, P17/A/22.

106 A/G to C/S, 13 April 1921, AD UCD, Mulcahy Papers, P7/A/22.

107 Sligo O/C to C/S, 2 July 1921, AD UCD, Mulcahy Papers, P7/A/22.

108 C/S to Sligo O/C, 6 June 1921, AD UCD, Mulcahy Papers, P7/A/19.

109 O/Cs Sligo Battalions to C/S, 24 May 1921, AD UCD, Mulcahy Papers, P7/A/19.

110 C/S to Sligo O/C, 6 June 1921, AD UCD, Mulcahy Papers, P7/A/19.

111 Sligo O/C to C/S, 2 July 1921, AD UCD, Mulcahy Papers, P7/A/22.

112 There is a reference to 'the promise of the QMG to send on weekly consignments here from far side [Liverpool]' in a letter from the Brigade

Commandant to C/S, 2 July 1921, and references to these consignments in QMG to C/S, 25 June 1921 and C/S to Brigade Commandant, 29 June 1921, AD UCD, Mulcahy Papers, P7/A/22.

113 These figures include the casualties at Ratra, just across the Roscommon border where the South Sligo IRA ambushed a police patrol. The lone IRA death occurred here.

114 Augusteijn, *From Public Defiance to Guerilla Warfare*, Table 1.9, p. 33.

115 Fitzpatrick, *Politics and Irish Life 1913–1921*, p. 226.

116 Hart, *The IRA and its Enemies*, table 7, p. 87.

117 Augusteijn, *From Public Defiance to Guerilla Warfare*, pp 317–18; Tom Garvin, *The Evolution of Irish Nationalist Politics* (Dublin, 1981), p. 124; Fitzpatrick, 'The Geography of Irish Nationalism', p. 431.

118 Augusteijn, *From Public Defiance to Guerilla Warfare*, p. 317.

119 Garvin, *The Evolution of Irish Nationalist Politics*, p. 126; Charles Townshend, 'The Irish Republican Army and the Development of Guerilla Warfare, 1916–1921', in *English Historical Review*, xciv (April 1979), pp 324–5.

1 THE TRUCE PERIOD

1 SCI RIC, July 1921 Monthly Report, PRO, CO 904/116.

2 *S.C.*, 8 Oct. 1921. O'Domhnalláin, a native of Galway, had been one of the pioneers of the Volunteers and of Sinn Féin in Sligo but had been unsuccessful in an attempt to gain a nomination for South Sligo constituency in the 1918 election. About this time he accepted a teaching post in Dublin and left Sligo.

3 *S.C.*, 1 Oct. 1921.

4 At Enniscrone aeraíocht (*S.C.*, 1 Oct. 1921).

5 Address by Tireragh Sinn Féin Executive to Seamus Devins (*S.C.*, 17 Sept. 1921).

6 *S.C.*, 20 Aug. 1921 – Ballymote; *S.C.*, 27 Aug. 1921 – Gurteen and Maugherow.

7 *S.C.*, 27 Oct. 1921.

8 *S.C.*, 30 July 1921.

9 C.S. Andrews, *Dublin Made Me: An Autobiography* (Cork, 1979), p. 208.

10 At Cloonacool aeraíocht 4 Sept. 1921 (*S.C.*, 10 Sept. 1921).

11 *S.C.*, 1 Oct. 1921.

12 He had of course not been elected having been selected as a candidate by the IRA Commandants and returned unopposed.

13 *S.C.*, 22 Oct. 1921.

14 Minutes of meetings 21 Mar., 4 and 11 Apr. 1920, North Sligo Comhairle Ceantair Sinn Féin Minute Book, Sligo Co. Library. Where clubs could not agree the Comhairle Ceantair made the selection. *S.I.*, 15 May 1920; *S.I.* and *S.C.*, 5 June 1920.

15 *S.C.*, 12 June 1920.

16 O/C of Collooney Battalion.

17 Minutes of meeting 13 June 1920, North Sligo Comhairle Ceantair Sinn Féin Minute Book, Sligo Co. Library.

18 Minutes of meeting 21 June 1920, Sligo Co. Council Minute Book, Sligo Co. Library.
19 Minutes of meetings 24 Aug. and 16 Oct. 1920, Sligo Co. Council Minute Book, Sligo Co. Library.
20 EC to Chief of Inspection, 23 Nov. 1921, NA, DELG 26/9.
21 Inspector to Chief of Inspection, 23 Oct. 1921, NA, DELG 26/9
22 C/S to Sligo Brigade Commandant, 16 June 1921, AD UCD, Mulcahy Papers, P7/A/19.
23 Cosgrave to Carty and Devins, 1 Nov. 1921, NA, DELG 26/9; Dáil Éireann Loc. Gov. report for 1921, 28 Apr. 1922, AD UCD, Mulcahy Papers, P7/A/63.
24 *CM.*, 2 Apr. 1921.
25 Inspector to Chief of Inspection, 16 Nov. 1921, NA, DELG 26/9.
26 *S.C.*, 28 Sept. 1918. The new five seat constituency of Sligo and Mayo East was created for the 1921 election.
27 *S.C.*, 14 May 1921.
28 Councillors on the run who attended this meeting included Jim Hunt, M.J. Marren, Tom O'Donnell, Jack Brennan and Frank O'Beirne (*S.C.* and *CM.*, 5 Mar. 1921).
29 This term was actually used by the Local Government Inspector. (Inspector to Chief of Inspection, 23 Oct. 1921, NA, DELG 26/9). A solution of sorts to enforced absenteeism was attempted in July 1921 when instructions were received from councillors who were unable to attend naming persons to be their substitutes (Minutes of meeting 9 July 1921, Sligo Co. Council Minute Book, Sligo Co. Library; *S.I.*, 16 July 1921).
30 Minutes of meeting 9 July 1921, Sligo Co. Council Minute Book, Sligo Co. Library; *CM.*, 23 July 1921.
31 Inspector to Chief of Inspection, 23 Oct. 1921, NA DELG 26/9; Minutes of meeting 22 Feb. 1919, Sligo Co. Council Minute Book, Sligo Co. Library.
32 *CM.*, 22 Oct. 1920.
33 Minutes of meeting 16 Oct. 1920, Sligo Co. Council Minute Book, Sligo Co. Library.
34 *CM.*, 9 July 1921.
35 *CM.*, 16 and 23 July 1921.
36 Inspector to Chief of Inspection, 23 Oct. 1921, NA DELG 26/9.
37 Minutes of meeting 27 Aug.1921, Sligo Co. Council Minute Book, Sligo Co. Library; Martin Roddy was born in Breeogue near Sligo town in 1887 and spent some years in the British Civil Service in London. He returned to Sligo and was elected a member of Sligo RDC in 1920. He became a Cumann na nGaedheal TD in 1925 and a Parliamentary Secretary in 1928. He became managing director and editor of the *Sligo Champion* and died in 1948. (John C. McTernan, *Worthies of Sligo* (Sligo, 1994), pp 401–5).
38 *CM.*, 3 Sept. 1921.
39 *S.C.*, 1 Apr. 1922.
40 Reports from Bradshaw to Collins in A/0747, Collins Papers, Military Archives; Sligo material in Liaison File, Military Archives, LE 4/16A.

41 *S.C.*, 22 Oct. 1921. This committee never functioned (Arthur Mitchell, *Revolutionary Government in Ireland* (Dublin, 1995), p. 309).

42 Inspector to Chief of Inspection, 23 Oct. 1921, NA DELG 26/9.

43 Report on Union Amalgamation, NA DELG 26/9.

44 Tom Garvin, *1922: The Birth of Irish Democracy* (Dublin, 1996), pp 78–82.

45 *CM.*, 9 April 1921.

46 *CM.*, 23 and 30 July 1921.

47 Eamon Coogan was described by Tom Garvin as the 'roving Dáil Department of Local Government trouble-shooter in the west' (Garvin, *1922*, p. 79).

48 *S.C.*, 3 Sept. 1921.

49 Mins. Local Gov. to Sec. County Council, 26 Sept. 1921, NA, DELG 26/9.

50 *S.C.*, 13 Aug. 1921; *S.I.*, 17 Sept. 1921.

51 *S.C.*, 13 Aug. and 3 Sept. 1921: *S.I.*, 24 Sept. 1921.

52 *S.I.*, 17 Sept. 1921; *S.I.*, 22 Oct. 1921; *S.C.* 19 Nov. 1921.

53 *S.I.*, 17 and 24 Sept. 1921; Report to Chief of Inspection, 26 Sept. 1921, NA, DELG 26/9.

54 *S.C.* and *S.I.*, 15 Oct. 1921.

55 Circular letter, Local Gov. Dept., 17 Nov. 1921, NA, DELG 26/9.

56 O/C 5th Batt. Nt. Mayo Bde, IRA to Local Gov. Dept., 2 Nov. 1921, NA, DELG 26/9.

57 Mins. Loc. Gov. to clerk Dromore West, 8 Dec. 1921, NA, DELG 26/9; *S.I.*, 10 Dec. 1921.

58 *S.C.*, 17 Dec. 1921; Inspector O'Ceallaigh to Chief of Inspection, 13 Dec. 1921, NA, DELG 26/9.

59 Inspector McGrath to Chief of Inspection, 6 Feb. 1922, NA, DELG 26/9.

60 *S.I.*, 21 Jan. 1922.

61 *S.C.* and *S.I.*, 3 Dec. 1921; *S.C.*, 10 Dec.1921.

62 Inspector O'Ceallaigh to Chief of Inspection, 13 Dec. 1921, NA, DELG 26/9; Supplementary report on Union Amalgamation by inspector, 13 Feb. 1922, NA, DELG 26/9.

63 *S.C.*, 6 Aug. 1921.

64 Extracts from 8 Aug. Tubbercurry RDC meeting, NA DELG 26/7.

65 Inspector's report on 8 Aug. Tubbercurry RDC meeting, NA DELG 26/7.

66 O/C Sligo Brigade to A/G, 14 Sept. 1921, NA DELG 26/7.

67 Inspector's report, 12 Oct. 1921, NA DELG 26/7.

68 *S.C.* and *S.I.*, 1 Oct. 1921; Minutes of meeting 24 Sept. 1921, Sligo Co. Council Minute Book, Sligo Co. Library.

69 Inspector to Chief of Inspection, 26 Sept. 1921, NA DELG 26/9.

70 A/G to Mins. Loc. Gov., 14 Oct. 1921, NA, DELG 26/9.

71 *S.I.* and *S.C.*, 15 Oct. 1921.

72 Gilligan to Cosgrave, 14 Oct. 1921, NA DELG 26/9.

73 Inspector to Chief of Inspection, 23 Oct. 1921, NA DELG 26/9.

74 Mitchell, *Revolutionary Government in Ireland*, p. 306.

75 Inspection report, 17 Oct. 1921, MA, Collins Papers, A/0747.

76 These were at Cloonamahon Sanatorium, Tubbercurry Workhouse, Dromore West Workhouse, Rahilly House, Loughill Lodge, Cabra Lodge, Keogh's

Lodge, Kilfree, Rathcarrick, Moneygold, Cooga, Mullaghmore, Culfadda, Enniscrone, Beltra, Bloomfield.

77 All these camps are mentioned in the file entitled 'Alleged Truce Breaches by the IRA' in PRO, CO 904/155. There was no mention of IRA training camps in any contemporary Sligo newspaper. Information on training camp at Geevagh from interview with Michael Burgess, 15 Aug. 1991.

78 Report on Officers' Training Camp 22 Aug. 1921 to 27 Aug. 1921, MA, Collins Papers, A/0747.

79 Brian MacNeill was a son of Eoin MacNeill the former Chief of Staff of the Volunteers and minister in the first Dáil, Provisional Government and Free State Government.

80 Inspection Report T. Burke to GHQ, 17 Oct. 1921, MA, Collins Papers A/0747.

81 Frank Carty statement, NLI, Collins Papers, P914.

82 Report 19 Oct. 1921, Alleged Truce Breaches by the IRA, PRO, CO 904/155. The same or similar incident is mentioned by the RIC County Inspector in his September report (PRO, CO 904/116).

83 S.C., 29 Oct. 1921.

84 The White Cross was set up in Feb. 1921 to assist republicans and their families who were suffering hardship because of their involvement in the War of Independence. The Sligo branch was established on 9 Aug. 1921 and its chairman was Michael Nevin (S.C., 13 Aug. 1921).

85 CM., 27 Aug. 1921.

86 S.C. and CM., 3 Sept. 1921.

87 CM., 8 Oct. 1921. (Two persons who claimed to have contributed under duress were named in the report).

88 The IRA liaison officer reported that the Marines believed that Bofin was responsible for the killing of a Marine near Rosses Point during the War of Independence. (Statements from Marines and reply from IRA Liaison Officer, Alleged Truce Breaches, PRO, CO904/155).

89 Report by Russell, 3 Oct. 1921, Alleged Truce Breaches, PRO, CO 904/155.

90 Report by Russell, 13 Sept. 1921, Alleged Truce Breaches, PRO, CO 904/155.

91 Weekly Reports 545 and 522, Outrages against police, PRO, CO 904/150.

92 These are contained in the files of the Irish Grants Committee (IGC) in the Public Record Office, London, CO 762. These have been used extensively as a source for Chapter 9.

93 The premises were those of Richard T. Kerr-Taylor (IGC, PRO, CO 762/48), raided twice, Thomas Hunt (/202) also raided twice and Charles Graham (/90).

94 Mary Feeney (IGC, PRO, CO 762/20), John Scanlon (/20), Gilbert J. Hanly (/50), John Barlow (/54), Palmer McCloughrey (/63), Bartholomew Sweeney (/84), George R. Williams (/197).

95 S.C., 19 Nov. 1921.

96 S.C., 20 Aug. 1921.

97 S.C., 20 Aug. 1921.

98 M/D to C/S 18 Nov. and C/S to A/G 19 Oct. 1921, AD UCD, Mulcahy Papers, P7/A/33; Report on the affair by Gurteen Battalion, 27 Oct. 1921 in Sligo Brigade HQRS to A/G, 29 Oct. 1921, AD UCD, Mulcahy Papers, P7/A/33.

99 Report from HQRS Gurteen Battalion 21 Nov. 1921 in Sligo Brigade HQRS to A/G, 22 Nov. 1921, AD UCD, Mulcahy Papers, P7/A/33.

100 A/G to O/C Sligo Brigade, 8 Nov. 1921, AD UCD, Mulcahy Papers, P7/A/33.

101 Letter to the editor by Seaghan Mac Murchadha, Irish teacher, *CM.*, 3 Dec. 1921.

102 *S.C.*, 8 Apr. 1922.

103 Dorothy Macardle, *The Irish Republic* (Dublin, 1968 paperback edition), p. 492.

2 THE TREATY

1 *S.C.*, 10 Dec. 1921.

2 *S.I.*, 27 Aug. 1921.

3 *S.I.*, 10 Dec. 1921.

4 *CM.*, 10 Dec. 1921.

5 *CM.*, 17 Dec. 1921.

6 *CM.*, 24 Dec. 1921.

7 Michael Hopkinson, *Green Against Green: The Irish Civil War* (Dublin, 1988), p. 41.

8 Dept of Organisation to C/S, 7 Dec. 1921, AD UCD, Mulcahy Papers, P7/A/33.

9 J.J. (Ginger) O'Connell (1887–1944) served in the US army 1912–14 and joined the Volunteers when he returned to Ireland. He was interned after the rising and after his release lived in Sligo where his father was a schools inspector. He became O/C Sligo Brigade before joining GHQ as Director of Training in late 1919. He later became Deputy Chief of Staff of the Free State Army.

10 Tom Scanlon, AD UCD, OMN, P17b/133.

11 Martin Brennan, AD UCD, OMN, P17b/133.

12 *R.H.*, 21 Jan. 1922.

13 *CM.*, 25 Feb. 1922.

14 Pilkington was described by O'Malley thus 'fair-haired, thin faced, ruddy cheeks, straight, a pair of flashing blue eyes and an insistent directness of speech. He was very much loved by his men; very religious, a fighting saint' (Ernie O'Malley, *The Singing Flame* (Dublin 1978), p. 50).

15 O'Malley, *The Singing Flame*, pp 51–2.

16 Joseph M. Curran, *The Birth of the Irish Free State 1921–1923* (Alabama, 1980), p. 170.

17 O'Malley, *The Singing Flame*, p. 52.

18 Eamon de Valera (1882–1975), President of the first Dáil Éireann, elected President of Irish Republic, August 1921, resigning on 9 January 1922 after ratification of the Treaty in the Dáil. Formed the anti-Treaty party Cumann

na Poblachta and was adjutant to anti-Treaty IRA Director of Operations during the Civil War.

19 Arthur Griffith (1871–1922), founder of Sinn Féin. Headed the Irish delegation in the Treaty negotiations and was elected President of the Dáil in 1922 after de Valera's resignation.

20 *CM.*, 10 Dec. 1921.

21 Oliver Coogan. *Politics and War in County Meath 1913–23* (Dublin, 1983), pp 265–6

22 *S.C., S.I.* and *CM.*, 31 Dec. 1921.

23 *CM.*, 31 Dec. 1921.

24 *R.H., CM.* and *S.C.*, 7 Jan. 1922.

25 Hopkinson, *Green Against Green*, p. 35.

26 *S.C.* and *S.I.*, 7 Jan. 1922; Minutes of meeting 31 Dec. 1921, Sligo Co. Council Minute Book, Sligo Co. Library.

27 *S.C.*, 7 Jan. 1922.

28 *S.C.* and *S.I.*, 7 Jan. 1922.

29 *S.C.*, 7 Jan. 1922.

30 *S.C.* and *R.H.*, 14 Jan. 1922.

31 *S.I., W.P.* and *R.H.*, 7 Jan. 1922.

32 *W.P.*, 14 Jan. 1922; *R.H.*, 7 Jan. 1922.

33 *R.H.*, 7 and 14 Jan. 1922.

34 *W.P.*, 7 Jan. 1922.

35 David W. Miller, *Church, State and Nation in Ireland 1898–1921* (Dublin, 1921), p. 491.

36 *S.C.*, 24 and 31 Dec. 1921.

37 *S.C.* and *CM.*, 7 Jan. 1922.

38 *W.P.*, 14 Nov. 1921.

39 *R.H.*, 14 Jan. 1922.

40 *S.C.*, 14 Jan. 1922.

41 *S.C.*, 14 Jan. 1922.

42 *CM.*, 14 Jan. 1922.

43 *CM.*, 4 Feb. 1922.

44 *S.I.*, 21 Jan. 1922.

45 *S.I.*, 18 Feb. 1922.

46 Henry DePew was a tradesman from Sligo town. He had been one of the pioneers of Sinn Féin in Sligo and had been a member of the Corporation since January 1913 when he had been elected as a Labour candidate. *S.C.* and *S.I.*, 4 Feb. 1922.

47 Hopkinson, *Green Against Green*, pp 36–9; Tom Garvin, 'Unenthusiastic Democrats: The Emergence of Irish Democracy' in Ronald J. Hill and Michael Marsh (eds), *Modern Irish Democracy – Essays in Honour of Basil Chubb* (Dublin, 1993), pp 9–23.

48 Editorial, *S.C.*, 10 Jan. 1922.

49 *CM.*, 21 Jan. 1922.

50 *CM.*, 17 Dec. 1921.

51 *CM.*, 14 Jan. 1922.

52 *CM.*, 4 Feb. 1922.

53 Carty's speech at the Tubbercurry meeting was reported in *CM.*, 25 Feb. 1922 and repeated in the following week's issue.

54 *CM.*, 21 Jan. 1922.

55 John M. Regan, 'The politics of reaction: the dynamics of treatyite government and policy, 1922–33', *I.H.S.*, xxx, no. 120 (Nov. 1997), p. 544.

56 *S.I.*, 7 Jan. 1922.

57 *R.H.*, 21 Jan. 1922. During the Treaty debates McCabe had said, 'I vote for this Treaty but I will be a Republican and will continue to pursue the ideals of the Republic as long as I am in public life' (Dáil Éireann private sessions, p. 206 [16 Dec. 1921]).

58 *S.C.*, 24 Dec. 1921.

59 *R.H.*, 18 Feb. 1922.

60 At Jim Hunt's homecoming to Gurteen (*R.H.*, 21 Jan. 1922).

61 *S.I.*, 31 Dec. 1921.

62 *S.C.*, 10 Dec. 1921.

63 *CM.*, 14 Jan. 1922.

64 *CM.*, 28 Jan. 1922.

65 McDonagh was killed while ambushing a police cycling party just outside the county boundary at Ratra in North Roscommon. (Michael Farry, *Sligo 1914–1921: A Chronicle of Conflict* (Trim, 1992), pp 241–2).

66 *S.C.*, *S.I.* and *CM.*, 31 Dec. 1921.

67 *CM.*, 25 Feb. 1922 repeated in the following week's issue.

68 *S.I.*, 7 Jan. 1922.

69 At Jim Hunt's homecoming. *R.H.*, 21 Jan. 1922. O'Donnell, a friend of de Valera's since their teaching days at Rockwell College and reputedly the first person to call him Dev, voted in favour of de Valera in the contest for President immediately after the Treaty vote.

70 *S.C.*, 24 and 31 Dec. 1921.

71 *CM.*, 31 Dec. 1921.

72 *CM.*, 28 Jan. 1922.

73 *CM.*, 14 Jan. 1922.

74 At the Corporation meeting reported in *S.C.*, 31 Jan. 1921.

75 *CM.*, 14 Jan. 1922.

76 Editorial, *S.C.*, 31 Dec. 1921.

77 *S.C.*, 7 Jan. 1922.

78 Garvin, 'Unenthusiastic Democrats', p. 13.

79 *S.I.*, 4 Feb. 1922.

80 At Cliffony on 25 Oct. 1920. (Farry, *Sligo 1914–1921*, pp 253–6).

81 A copy of Nevin's statement to the Bureau of Military History dated 29 Mar. 1956 is in Sligo Co. Library.

82 GHQ to and from 'P' in Liverpool, May 1921, AD UCD, Mulcahy Papers, P7/A/5.

3 THE DRIFT TO CIVIL WAR

1 *R.H.*, 25 Feb. 1922.
2 *R.H.*, 4 Mar. 1922.
3 *S.C.*, 18 Feb. 1922.
4 *CM.*, 4 Feb. 1922. A similar editorial was printed in its issue of 18 Feb. as a result of the postponement of the Árd-Fheis.
5 *Irish Independent*, 28 Jan. 1922.
6 Newspaper cuttings, Sinn Féin Árd Comhairle Jan. 1922, NA, Dáil Éireann files. DE 2/486.
7 *CM.*, 4 Feb. 1922.
8 Michael Hopkinson, *Green Against Green: The Irish Civil War* (Dublin, 1988), p. 56.
9 *CM.*, 25 Feb. 1922.
10 *S.C.*, 25 Feb. 1922.
11 Most of the 270 strong garrison of the Bedfordshire and Hertfordshire Regiment left Sligo by train on Wednesday 1 Feb. and the remainder left the following morning. That barracks was then occupied by the IRA under William Pilkington (*S.C.* and *S.I.*, 4 Feb. 1922). On 9 Mar. both police stations in Sligo were evacuated and taken over by the IRA (*S.C.* and *CM.*, 11 Mar. 1922).
12 Hopkinson, *Green Against Green*, p. 58.
13 *R.H.*, 28 Jan. and 25 Feb. 1922.
14 Hopkinson, *Green Against Green*, p. 79 ff.; Tim Pat Coogan, *Michael Collins* (London 1990), pp 343 ff.
15 Not Coolaney as read by Hopkinson, *Green Against Green*, p. 80.
16 *S.C.*, 11 Feb. 1922.
17 *The Times*, 21 March 1922, quoted in Hopkinson, *Green Against Green*, p. 81.
18 Tom Scanlon, AD UCD, O'Malley Notebooks, P17b/133. The Ulster Special Constabulary (the B Specials), recruited from the Protestant Ulster Volunteer Force, was established in 1921 to reinforce the RIC in Northern Ireland and took a leading role in containing IRA attacks on the North in 1922.
19 Hopkinson, *Green Against Green*, p. 82.
20 According to Hopkinson 'Evidence for the joint IRA policy is sketchy and heavily dependent on oral evidence', *Green Against Green*, p. 83.
21 *R.H.*, 3 June 1922.
22 Florence O'Donoghue, *No Other Law* (Dublin, 1986), pp 250, 252; Maryann Gialanella Valiulis, *Portrait of a Revolutionary: General Richard Mulcahy* (Dublin, 1992), p 141; Hopkinson, *Green Against Green*, pp 83–84.
23 Tom Scanlon, AD UCD, O'Malley Notebooks, P17b/133.
24 Matt Kilcawley, AD UCD, O'Malley Notebooks, P17b/137.
25 *R.H.*, 11 Mar. 1922; S.C., 18 Mar. 1922. Tom Scanlon, AD UCD, O'Malley Notebooks, P17b/133; Charles Gildea List of Activities, Fr O'Kane Papers, Archdiocese of Armagh Record Centre. The *R.H.* report said that included in the Sligo contingent were four each from Ballymote and Collooney and eight from Tubbercurry. Scanlon said that 150 men were sent from the division, Gildea said 60.

26 Hopkinson, *Green Against Green*, pp 62–6.

27 This diocese includes the Barony of Tireragh between Ballina and Ballisodare north of the Ox Mountains.

28 *S.C., CM., R.H.* and *W.P.*, 4 Mar. 1922.

29 See draft of letter to the Bishop by Count Plunkett attacking his statement after the Tubbercurry burnings during War of Independence (NLI, Plunkett Papers, Ms 11408).

30 O'Donoghue, *No Other Law*, p. 220. The figures from the other Western Divisions were: 1st – 13, 2nd – 17, 4th – 20.

31 Twomey Papers, AD UCD, P69/144, 179; O'Donoghue, *No Other Law*, p. 224.

32 Hopkinson, *Green Against Green*, p. 68.

33 Hopkinson, *Green Against Green*, p. 73.

34 Macardle, *The Irish Republic* (Dublin, 1968 paperback edition), p. 612.

35 Tom Scanlon called him 'a skunk named Fallon' (Tom Scanlon, AD UCD, O'Malley Notebooks, P17b/133).

36 Interview with anti-Treaty Divisional Adjutant Brian MacNeill in *R.H.*, 8 April 1922; Letter from Martin Fallon, *R.H.*, 3 May 1922; Tom Scanlon, AD UCD, O'Malley Notebooks, P17b/133.

37 *W.P.*, 18 Mar. 1922.

38 Interviews with one of the organisers of the dance, and with Tubbercurry Commandant in *R.H.*, 8 Apr. 1922.

39 Reports on raids on railways, 25 Apr. 1922, AD UCD, Mulcahy Papers. P7/A/63.

40 *S.C.*, 1 and 15 Apr. 1922.

41 Hopkinson, *Green Against Green*, p. 90.

42 *S.C.*, 6 May 1922.

43 Tom Scanlon, AD UCD, O'Malley Notebooks, P17b/137; Charles Gildea List of Activities, Fr O'Kane Papers, Archdiocese of Armagh Record Centre.

44 *S.C.* and *S.I.*, 11 Mar. 1922. The Dáil refused to sanction this IRA rate.

45 *S.C.*, 1 Apr. 1922; Minutes of meeting 25 Mar. 1922, Sligo Co. Council Minute Book, Sligo Co. Library.

46 *S.C.*, 25 Mar. 1922.

47 Martin Roddy was the Director of Elections and P.J. O'Brien, District Court Clerk of the Sinn Féin courts in South Sligo, was appointed sub-director.

48 Ben Ryan, a native of Bundoran Co. Donegal, who had been interned after 1916, was appointed for North Sligo and J.S. O'Donnell, a journalist from Gurteen, for South Sligo (*W.P.* and *R.H.*, 18 Mar. 1922; *S.I.*, 25 Mar. 1922).

49 *W.P.* and *S.I.*, 25 Mar. 1922.

50 *S.I.* and *W.P.*, 25 Mar. 1922; *S.C.*, 1 Apr. 1922.

51 *CM.*, 25 Mar. 1922; *S.I.*, 1 Apr. 1922.

52 *S.I.*, 1 Apr. 1922.

53 John Cunningham, *Labour in the West of Ireland* (Belfast, 1995), p.160.

54 *The Voice of Labour*, 25 Feb. 1922; Arthur Mitchell, *Labour in Irish Politics* (Dublin, 1974), pp 153–5.

55 *S.C.* and *CM.*, 4 Mar. 1922.

56 Cunningham, *Labour in the West of Ireland*, p. 105.

57 *CM.*, 25 Mar. 1922 and 1 Apr. 1922.

58 *S.C.* and *CM.*, 1 Apr. 1922; *The Voice of Labour*, 1 May 1922.

59 *CM.*, 27 May 1922; *The Voice of Labour*, April–June 1922.

60 Hopkinson, *Green Against Green*, pp 76–7.

61 *R.H.*, *S.C.* and *S.I.*, 8 Apr. 1922.

62 *S.C.*, 29 Apr. 1922.

63 *W.P.*, *S.I.* and *S.C.*, 8 Apr. 1922.

64 *S.I.*, 1 Apr. 1922.

65 *R.H.* and *CM.*, 8 Apr. 1922; *S.I.*, 15 Apr. 1922.

66 *S.C.*, 8 Apr. 1922; *R.H.* and *S.I.*, 15 Apr. 1922.

67 *S.I.*, 15 Apr. 1922.

68 *S.C.*, *S.I.* and *R.H.*, 15 Apr. 1922.

69 *S.I.*, 15 Apr. 1922.

70 Batt Keaney interviews 8 Oct. 1988 and 30 Aug. 1990. They had to climb over the jail wall using a rope ladder and find a known pro-Treaty warder who opened the gates and allowed the troops in.

71 Tom Scanlon, AD UCD, O'Malley Notebooks, P17b/133.

72 *S.I.*, 15 Apr. 1922.

73 Padraig Hegarty, AD UCD, O'Malley Notebooks, P17b/137; *S.I.*, 15 Apr. 1922.

74 Tom Scanlon, AD UCD, O'Malley Notebooks, P17b/133.

75 Liam Mellows, Some events leading up to the Civil War, M.A. Collins Papers, A 0790.

76 Tom Deignan, AD UCD, O'Malley Notebooks, P17b/133.

77 Tom Scanlon, AD UCD, O'Malley Notebooks, P17b/137.

78 Padraig Hegarty, AD UCD, O'Malley Notebooks, P17b/137.

79 Tom Scanlon, AD UCD, O'Malley Notebooks, P17b/133.

80 Tom Scanlon, AD UCD, O'Malley Notebooks, P17b/137.

81 Jack Brennan, AD UCD, O'Malley Notebooks, P17b/137.

82 *S.I.*, 22 Apr. 1922.

83 *S.I.*, 22 Apr. 1922. A colourful account of the Sligo meeting appears in Calton Younger, *Ireland's Civil War* (London, 1968), pp 260 ff. A long editorial in *Free State*, 22 Apr.1922 gloated over this 'striking and remarkable victory'.

84 *S.C.*, 29 Apr. 1922. The issue of the *Connachtman* for 22 April 1922 is also missing from the file in Sligo Library.

85 *S.I.* and *R.H.*, 22 Apr. 1922; *S.I.*, 29 Apr. 1922.

86 Padraig Hegarty, AD UCD, O'Malley Notebooks, P17b/137.

87 Martin Brennan, AD UCD, O'Malley Notebooks, P17b/133.

88 Tom Scanlon, AD UCD, O'Malley Notebooks, P17b/137.

89 Frank Carty Statement, 1935 (NLI, Collins Papers, P914).

90 For comments on Sligo's poor performance during War of Independence see Valiulis, *General Richard Mulcahy*, p. 57; Hopkinson, *Green Against Green*, p. 10; Younger, *Ireland's Civil War*, p. 263.

91 These were the Custom House, the Bond stores and the Bank of Ireland (*R.H.*, 6 May 1922).

92 *R.H.* and *S.C.*, 13 May 1922.

93 *W.P.*, 10 June 1922.

94 What appears to have been an anti-Treaty press statement on the matter was printed verbatim in three newspapers, *S.C.*, *W.P.* and *R.H.*, without comment on 10 June 1922.

95 *R.H.*, 10 June 1922. Markree Castle was the residence of Bryan Cooper but at the time he was residing in Dublin.

96 An interview with Jim Hunt was reported in *W.P.*, 13 May 1922 and a letter from Adj. Nealon, the anti-Treaty officer involved was printed in *R.H.*, 20 May, 1922. A short report was published in *CM.*, 29 April 1922.

97 This party numbered 20 claimed Hunt, seven said Nealon. The latter also claimed that no shots were fired.

98 *R.H.*, 13 and 20 May 1922; *W.P.*, 20 May 1922.

99 Godfrey O'Donnell to Mins H/A, 19 Apr. 1922, NA, Dept of Justice, H6/15.

100 J. McLoughlin to Mins H/A/, 1 May 1922 and acknowledgement by secretary, 15 May 1922, NA. Dept of Justice. H6/15.

101 At Calry, Cliffony, Coolera and Maugherow in north Sligo, Culfadda and Keash in south Sligo.

102 *S.C.*, 29 May 1922.

103 *S.C.*, 29 Apr. 1922.

104 *W.P.*, 6 May 1922.

105 *R.H.*, 29 Apr. 1922.

106 *S.C.* and *R.H.*, 6 May 1922.

107 *S.C.* and *R.H.*, 13 May 1922.

108 Hopkinson, *Green Against Green*, pp 97 ff.

109 *CM.*, 27 May 1922.

110 *S.C.*, 27 May 1922.

111 *S.C.*, 3 June 1922.

112 *S.C.*, *W.P.* and *R.H.*, 3 June 1922.

113 *S.C.*, *S.I.* and *R.H.*, 10 June 1922.

114 *R.H.*, 10 June 1922.

115 *CM.*, 10 June 1922.

116 *CM.*, 10 June 1922.

117 *CM.*, 14 June 1922.

118 *R.H.*, 29 Apr. 1922.

119 *R.H.*, 10 June 1922.

120 Described in those terms by the local press it may or may not have been a Farmers' Union meeting.

121 *R.H.*, 10 June 1922.

122 *W.P.*, 10 June 1922; *Connacht Telegraph*, 10 June 1922.

123 Gallagher, 'The Pact General Election of 1922' in *I.H.S.*, xxi, no. 84 (Sept. 1979), p. 159. The candidate was T.J. O'Connell, General Secretary of the Irish National Teachers' Organisation.

124 *S.I.*, 2 June 1922; *S.C.*, 10 June 1922.

125 *CM.*, *S.C.* and *S.I.*, 10 June 1922.

126 *CM.*, 14 June 1922; *S.I.*, 17 June 1922.

127 *CM.*, 14 June 1922; *S.C.*, 17 June 1922. Speakers included Mayor Michael Nevin, Lynch, Devins, Bradshaw and Mulcahy.

128 *R.H.*, 17 June 1922.
129 *S.I.*, 10 June 1922.
130 *R.H.*, 17 June 1922.
131 *S.C.*, 10 June 1922.
132 *S.C.*, 17 June 1922.
133 *S.C.*, 17 June 1922.
134 *S.C.*, *S.I.* and *CM.*, 17 June 1922.
135 Sean P. Farragher, *Dev and his Alma Mater* (Dublin, 1984), p. 74.
136 *S.C.*, *S.I.* and *R.H.*, 17 June 1922.
137 Cliffony, Ballintrillick, Maugherow, Grange, Calry and Ransboro.
138 *CM.*, 14 June 1922; *S.C.*, 17 June 1922.
139 Raids on Post Offices etc., NA, Dept of Justice, H5/67B.
140 *S.I.* and *S.C*, 24 June 1922.
141 *S.C.*, 17 June 1922.
142 *S.I.*, 10 June 1922.
143 *CM.*, 14 June 1922.
144 *W.P.*, 24 June 1922.
145 Ballymote Notes, *S.C.*, 24 June 1922.
146 *R.H.*, 24 June 1922.
147 *S.C.*, 17 June 1922; *R.H.*, 24 June 1922; *S.C.*, 1 July 1922.
148 *R.H.*, 24 June 1922.
149 Letter to the *Irish Independent*, 22 June, reprinted in *S.C.*, 24 June 1922.
150 *Irish Independent*, 21 June 1922; *R.H.*, 24 June 1922.
151 *S.C.* and *R.H.*, 24 June 1922.
152 Election figures from Michael Gallagher (ed.), *Irish Elections 1922–44: Results and Analysis* (Limerick, 1993); Gallagher, 'The Pact General Election of 1922', pp 404–21 and from local Sligo newspapers, June 1922.
153 The 1922 election was the only one fought using the Sligo–Mayo East constituency.
154 *CM.*, 24 June 1922.
155 *S.C.*, 24 June 1922.
156 Minutes of meeting 21 July 1922, Sligo Co. Council Minute Book, Sligo Co. Library.

4 THE COURSE OF THE CIVIL WAR

1 Martin Brennan, AD UCD, O'Malley Notebooks, P17b/133; Tom Scanlon, AD UCD, O'Malley Notebooks, P17b/133; Frank Carty Statement, NLI, Collins Papers, P914.
2 Michael Hopkinson, *Green Against Green: The Irish Civil War* (Dublin, 1988), p. 142.
3 Martin Brennan, AD UCD, O'Malley Notebooks, P17b/133. Tom Carney was O/C 5th (East Mayo) Brigade, 3rd Western Division.
4 4th Brigade 3rd Western Division diary of activities from opening of hostilities to 30 Nov. 1922, AD UCD, Twomey Papers, Western Command Material, P69/33(17).

5 *S.C.*, *S.I.* and *CM.*, 8 July 1922; Report by Commandant McCann on the attack and capture of Collooney Market House, July 1922, Institute of Celtic Studies and Historical Research, Killiney, Co. Dublin, MacEoin Papers, CSD/76; Martin Brennan, AD UCD, O'Malley Notebooks, P17b/133; Frank Carty Statement, NLI, Collins Papers, P914; 4th Brigade Diary of activities, AD UCD, Twomey Papers, Western Command Material, P69/33(17); Joe Baker, *My Stand for Freedom* (Westport, 1988), pp 42–3.

6 4th Brigade Diary of activities, AD UCD, Twomey Papers, Western Command Material, P69/33(17).

7 Baker, *My Stand for Freedom*, pp 43–4.

8 1st Brigade Diary, AD UCD, Twomey Papers, Western Command Material, P69/33(27); *CM*, 15 July 1922.

9 Tom Scanlon, AD UCD, O'Malley Notebooks, P17b/133; *S.C.*, *S.I.* and *CM.*, 8 July 1922; Western Command Report 6 July 1922, AD UCD, Mulcahy Papers, P7/B/106; Western Command Reports 6 July 1922, MA, Radio and Phone Reports, CW/R/1; Diary of activities 1st Brigade 3rd Western Division from 30 June, 1922, AD UCD, Twomey Papers, Western Command Material, P69/33(27).

10 MacNeill to O/C 4th Western Division, 2 July 1922, AD UCD, Twomey Papers, Western Command Material, P69/33(50).

11 *S.C.*, *S.I.* and *CM.*, 8 July 1922; Western Command Reports 4 and 5 July 1922, MA, Radio and Phone Reports, CW/R/1; 1st Brigade Diary, AD UCD, Twomey Papers, Western Command Material, P69/33(27).

12 *S.I.*, *S.C.* and *CM.*, 8 July 1922. The Ballinalee was so named after the birthplace and scene of the greatest military success of General Séan MacEoin. The car was renamed the Lough Gill by some republicans after its capture in Sligo though most apparently referred to it by its original name.

13 This ambush is often referred to as the Dooney Rock ambush. *S.C.*, *S.I.* and *CM.*, 15 July 1922; War News Western Command, 14 July 1922, MacEoin Papers C/60; Tom Scanlon, AD UCD, O'Malley Notebooks, P17b/133; Report by MacEoin, 15 July 1922, AD UCD, Mulcahy Papers, P7/B/106; Martin Brennan, AD UCD, O'Malley Notebooks, P17b/133; Frank Carty Statement, NLI, Collins Papers, P914; 4th Brigade Diary of activities, AD UCD, Twomey Papers, Western Command Material, P69/33(17); 1st Brigade Diary, AD UCD, Twomey Papers, Western Command Material, P69/33(27).

14 *S.C.*, *S.I.* and *CM.*, 22 July 1922; Tom Scanlon, AD UCD, O'Malley Notebooks, P17b/133; *Poblacht na hÉireann War News*, 25 July 1922, NLI Microfilm Reel 52; 1st Brigade Diary. AD UCD, Twomey Papers, Western Command Material, P69/33(27). The republicans privately dubbed the bishop 'a sandbag'. A similar incident occurred some days later when the 1st Brigade attacked Manorhamilton pro-Treaty post. The local curate took up position at the barrack door and the attackers decided to withdraw.

15 MacEoin was O/C Western Command based at Athlone. *S.C.*, *S.I.* and *CM.*, 22 July 1922; Report by MacEoin, 15 July 1922. AD UCD, Mulcahy Papers, P7/B/106; Martin Brennan, AD UCD, O'Malley Notebooks, P17b/133; 4th Brigade Diary of activities, AD UCD, Twomey Papers, Western Command Material, P69/33(17); Frank Carty Statement, NLI,

Collins Papers, P914. The republican who was killed was P. Mullan. *CM*, 30 Aug. 1924.

16 Letter Lillie Martin, Rathrippon, Collooney, in private possession.

17 4th Brigade Diary of activities, AD UCD, Twomey Papers, Western Command Material, P69/33(17); Martin Brennan, AD UCD, O'Malley Notebooks, P17b/133; Frank Carty Statement, NLI, Collins Papers, P914. Martin Brennan was O/C 4th Brigade ASU and opposed Carty unsuccessfully as an independent candidate in Sligo in 1927 and 1937 before joining Fianna Fail in 1938 and becoming a TD in the same year.

18 *S.C.*, *S.I.* and *CM.*, 29 July and 5 Aug. 1922.

19 Western Command, Office of C/S, July 1922, AD UCD, Mulcahy Papers, P7/B/73.

20 Hopkinson, *Green Against Green*, p. 173.

21 Reports Western Command I/O to D/I, 8 and 22 Aug. 1922, MA, Western Command Papers, CW/Ops/7(c); Tom Scanlon, AD UCD, O'Malley Notebooks, P17b/133; *S.C.*, 5 Aug. 1922.

22 1st Brigade Diary. AD UCD, Twomey Papers, Western Command Material, P69/33(27); Report Western Command I/O to D/I, 5 Aug. 1922. MA, Western Command Papers, CW/Ops/7(c); *S.C.*, 5 Aug. 1922. The republicans held the post at the Ulster Bank for only a short time.

23 Reports Western Command I/O to D/I, 4 Aug. 1922, MA, Western Command Papers, CW/Ops/7(c).

24 *S.C.* and *S.I.*, 29 July 1922; Report by McCabe, 22 July 1922, AD UCD, Mulcahy Papers, P7/B/73; SS Tartar, General file of correspondence, MA, Dept Defence Files, A7438; 1st Brigade Diary, AD UCD, Twomey Papers, Western Command Material, P69/33(27); *Poblacht na hÉireann* (Scottish Edition), 2 Sept. 1922, NLI, Microfilm Reel 51. The Tartar belonged to the Sligo Steam Navigation Company and plied regularly between Sligo and Belmullet, Co. Mayo.

25 MacNeill to Liam Lynch, 2 Aug. 1922, AD UCD, Twomey Papers, Western Command Material, P69/33(49).

26 1st Brigade Diary of activities, AD UCD, Twomey Papers, Western Command Material, P69/33(27).

27 4th Brigade Diary of activities, AD UCD, Twomey Papers, Western Command Material, P69/33(17); Frank Carty Statement, NLI, Collins Papers, P914.

28 *S.C.* and *S.I.*, 12 Aug. 1922; Report Divisional Adj. to Command Adj., 26 Aug. 1922, MA, Western Command Papers, CW/Ops/7(c); Martin Brennan, AD UCD, O'Malley Notebooks, P17b/133; Frank Carty Statement, NLI, Collins Papers, P914; 4th Brigade Diary of activities, AD UCD, Twomey Papers, Western Command Material, P69/33(17).

29 4th Brigade Diary of activities, AD UCD, Twomey Papers, Western Command Material, P69/33(17).

30 *S.C.* and *S.I.*, 2 Sept. 1922; Telegrams from manager Sligo, Leitrim and Northern Counties Railway to M/D 27 and 28 July 1922, and reply from Assistant QM Western Command to C/S 31 July 1922, AD UCD, Mulcahy Papers, P7/B/73; Protection and Compensation: Sligo, Leitrim and Northern Counties Railway, MA, Dept Defence Files, A7160.

31 Daily Reports 10 and 21 Aug. 1922, MA, Western Command Papers, CW/Ops/7(c); I/O W/C to D/I, 10 Aug. 1922, AD UCD, Mulcahy Papers, P7/B/4.

32 Reports Western Command I/O to D/I, 4, 11, 21 and 22 Aug. 1922, MA, Western Command Papers, CW/Ops/7(c).

33 Report to C/S, 11 July 1922, AD UCD, Mulcahy Papers, P/7B/106. Tom Maguire was O/C 2nd Western Division.

34 MacEoin to Army Comms, 15 Sept. 1922, AD UCD, Mulcahy Papers, P/7B/73.

35 Report Thomas Henry, Reports Officer, 3rd Western Division to O/C 3rd Western Division, 17 Nov. 1922, MA, Western Command Papers, CW/Ops/7(b).

36 Report Henry to O/C 3rd Western Division, 17 Nov. 1922, MA, Western Command Papers, CW/Ops/7(b); Carty had descended on Templehouse, home of the landed Perceval family, and ordered a dinner for 25 column members at a half hour's notice (Report on Irregulars, 4 Aug. 1922, MA, Western Command Papers, CW/Ops/7(c)).

37 C/S to MacEoin, 7 Aug. 1922, AD UCD, Mulcahy Papers, P/7B/74; General position of the army, Aug. 1922, AD UCD, Mulcahy Papers, P/7B/29; MacEoin to C/S, 10 Aug. 1922 and reply 14 Aug. 1922, AD UCD, Mulcahy Papers, P7/B/73.

38 On 4 September Dromahair Army Barracks was captured by eight republicans. Forty-six prisoners were taken. (1st Brigade Diary, AD UCD, Twomey Papers, Western Command Material, P69/33(27); Report, 4 Sept. 1922, MA, Western Command Papers, CW/Ops/7(c); MacEoin to C/S and C-in-C to MacEoin, 4 Sept. 1922, AD UCD, Mulcahy Papers, P/7B/73).

39 MacEoin to C-in-C, 12 Sept. 1922, AD UCD, Mulcahy Papers, P/7B/74, Lawlor to MacEoin, 12 Sept. 1922, AD UCD, Mulcahy Papers, P7/B/74; Farrelly to MacEoin, 11 Sept. 1922, AD UCD, Mulcahy Papers, P7/B/74.

40 Statement by Vol. James Carr, undated, MA, Western Command Papers, CW/Ops/7(c); Report from Tubbercurry Adj., 14 Sept. 1922, MA, Western Command Papers, CW/Ops/7(c); S.C., S.I. and CM., 16 Sept. 1922.

41 Report from Ballymote I/O, 13 Sept. 1922, MA, Western Command Papers, CW/Ops/7(c).

42 S.C., S.I. and CM., 16 Sept. 1922; Patrick Rutledge, AD UCD, O'Malley Notebooks, P17b/90; Martin Brennan, AD UCD, O'Malley Notebooks, P17b/133; Frank Carty Statement, NLI, Collins Papers, P914. Anthony Lawlor had been appointed Adjutant, Western Command.

43 S.C., S.I. and CM., 23 Sept. 1922; Martin Brennan, AD UCD, O'Malley Notebooks, P17b/133; Frank Carty Statement, NLI, Collins Papers, P914; 4th Brigade Diary of activities, AD UCD, Twomey Papers, Western Command Material, P69/33(17).

44 Western Command Operation Order No. 1, undated, MacEoin Papers, C/57/1; S.C. and S.I., 23 Sept. 1922; Tom Scanlon, AD UCD, O'Malley Notebooks, P17b/133.

45 Hopkinson, *Green Against Green*, p. 215; In MacEoin's account to Younger he makes no mention of the Ballinalee having been put out of action. (Calton Younger, *Ireland's Civil War* (London, 1968), p. 461).

46 Told in later years to Bernard McDonagh, Sligo.

47 *S.C.* and *S.I.* 23 Sept. 1922; Report I/O 3rd Western Division., to D/I, 20 Sept. 1922, MA, Western Command Papers, CW/Ops/7(c). This armoured car had first seen service in Egypt in 1918. It was apparently not used again during the Civil War but was reported as having been in service during the Emergency. Information supplied by Bernard McDonagh, Sligo.

48 The others were Vol. Joseph Banks, Vol. Tommy Langan, Lieut. Paddy Carroll and Capt. Harry Benson. Usually referred to as 'Sligo's Noble Six', pilgrimages to the place of their death were common in the years after the Civil War. Four versions of the event were recorded by primary school children as part of the national folklore collection in 1937–8. (Lug na nGall, Rossinver school, Co. Sligo, UCD Folklore Collection, S157).

49 Joe McGowan, *In the Shadow of Benbulben* (Sligo, 1993), p. 134; Reports Conroy I/O, Western Command to D/I, 21 Sept. 1922, MA, Western Command Papers, CW/Ops/7(c); *S.C.*, *S.I.* and *CM.*, 23 and 30 Sept. 1922; 'Murder will out' in *Daily Bulletin* 100, 26 Jan. 1923, MacEoin Papers, C/14; Wireless message Athlone to C-in-C, 18 Sept. 1922 and Message from O'Doherty Ballyshannon, 20 Sept. 1922, AD UCD, Mulcahy Papers, P7/B/73; Report on the deaths of Divisional Adjutant MacNeill and Brigadier Devins with four others, O/C 3rd Western Division to C/S IRA, 8 Dec. 1922, AD UCD, Twomey Papers, Western Command Material, P69/33(43); 1st Brigade Diary, AD UCD, Twomey Papers, Western Command Material, P69/33(27); *Poblacht na hÉireann War News*, 22 and 27 Jan. 1923, NLI Microfilm Reel 52; *Poblacht na hÉireann* (Scottish Edition), 30 Sept. and 7 Oct. 1922, NLI Microfilm Reel 51. MacEoin account states erroneously that the six casualties were 'the crew of the armoured car [Ballinalee]'. This was not the case. (Younger, *Ireland's Civil War*, p. 462).

50 *S.I.*, 23 Sept. 1922.

51 1st Brigade Diary, AD UCD, Twomey Papers, Western Command Material, P69/33(27); O/C 3rd Western Division to C/S IRA, 28 Nov. 1922, AD UCD, Twomey Papers, Western Command Material, P69/33(45).

52 Report from Conroy, 6 Oct. 1922, MA, Western Command Papers, CW/Ops/7(c).

53 *S.C.* and *S.I.*, 21 Oct. 1922.

54 Report from Boyle, 4 Nov. 1922, MA, Western Command Papers, CW/Ops/7(b).

55 Report on The Enemy, 4 Nov. 1922, MA, Western Command Papers, CW/Ops/7(b); Weekly Appreciation of Situation, 6 Nov. 1922, MA, Western Command Papers, CW/Ops/7(b).

56 *S.I.* and *S.C.*, 14 Oct. 1922; Martin Brennan, O'MN, P17b/133; MP, P7/B/114.

57 4th Brigade Diary of activities, AD UCD, Twomey Papers, Western Command Material, P69/33(17).

58 Daily Operations Report, 20 Nov. 1922, MA, Western Command Papers, CW/Ops/7(b); *S.C.*, 18 Nov. 1922; 1st Brigade Diary, AD UCD, Twomey Papers, Western Command Material, P69/33(27).

59 Phone message from MacEoin, 24 Oct. 1922, AD UCD, Mulcahy Papers, P7/B/74.

60 Reports Officer 3rd Western Division to Reports Officer Western Command, 7 Nov. 1922, MacEoin Papers, C57/9; Also in AD UCD, Mulcahy Papers, P7/B/114.

61 Report Capt. Henry to O/C 3rd Western Division, 17 Nov. 1922, MA, Western Command Papers, CW/Ops/7(b).

62 C-in-C to MacEoin, 19 Oct. 1922, AD UCD, Mulcahy Papers, P7/B/74.

63 Appreciation of situation up to 31 Dec. 1922, MA, Radio and Phone Reports, CW/R/4.

64 Interview with MO Garrison, Sligo, 21 Dec. 1922, AD UCD, Mulcahy Papers, P7/B/75.

65 List of successful activities, 21 Oct.–1 Nov. 1922, MA, Western Command Papers, CW/Ops/7(b); *S.C., S.I.* and *CM.*, 11 Nov. 1922; 4th Brigade Diary of activities. AD UCD, Twomey Papers, Western Command Material, P69/33(17); Report by McCabe, 5 Nov. 1922, MA, Western Command Papers, CW/Ops/7(b); Report by McCabe, 7 Nov. 1922, AD UCD, Mulcahy Papers, P7/B/114; Report by Reports Officer, 3rd Western Division, 7 Nov. 1922, MacEoin Papers, C57/18A.

66 C/S IRA to O/C 3rd Western Division, 9 Nov. 1922, AD UCD, Twomey Papers, Western Command Material, P69/33(48).

67 It was superseded by General Order No. 12 re. spies on 24 November 1922. Instead of having to be ratified by GHQ the sentence had now to be ratified by the Divisional Commandant (AD UCD, Twomey Papers, P69/1 (7) and (16)).

68 Daily Operations Report, 17 Nov. 1922, MA, Western Command Papers, CW/Ops/7(b); Report by McCabe, 7 Nov. 1922, AD UCD, Mulcahy Papers, P7/B/114.

69 4th Brigade Diary of activities, AD UCD, Twomey Papers, Western Command Material, P69/33(17); Telephone message from Conroy, 30 Nov. 1922, MA, Western Command Papers, CW/Ops/7(b); Report by I/O Sligo, 30 Nov. 1922, MA, Donegal Command Papers, CW/Ops/6.

70 4th Brigade Diary of Activities for Dec. 1922, MA, Western Command Papers, CW/Ops/7(a); Report from I/O Boyle, 15 Dec. 1922, MA, Western Command Papers, CW/Ops/7(c); Frank Carty Statement, NLI, Collins Papers, P914.

71 Report from I/O Sligo, 15 Dec. 1922, MA, Western Command Papers, CW/Ops/7(c); Report from HQRS Western Command, 18 Dec. 1922, MA, Western Command Papers, CW/Ops/7(c); Daily Operations Report, 27 Dec. 1922, MA, Western Command Papers, CW/Ops/7(b).

72 *S.C.* and *S.I.*, 16 Dec. 1922; Report O/C 1st Brigade to O/C 3rd Western Division, 10 Dec. 1922, AD UCD, Twomey Papers, Western Command Material, P69/33(3); Report by Divisional I/O, Sligo, 11 Dec. 1922, MacEoin Papers, C57/18A; Letter to prisoner J. Quinn, 17 Dec. 1922, AD UCD, Mulcahy Papers, P7/B/75; Report Adj. Sligo to Adj. 3rd Western Division, 14 Dec. 1922, MA, Western Command Papers, CW/Ops/7(c); Report on attack on Sligo Town Hall, 18 Dec. 1922, MacEoin Papers, C60/4.

73 *S.C.* and *S.I.*, 13 and 20 Jan. 1923; 1st Brigade 3rd Western Division Diary of Activities for fortnight ended 15 Jan. 1923, AD UCD, Mulcahy Papers, P7/B/91; Report Adj. 3rd Western Division to Western Command, 27 Feb. 1923, MA, Western Command Papers, CW/Ops/7(a); Daily Operations Report, 12 Jan. 1923, MA, Western Command Papers, CW/Ops/7(b); Burning of Sligo Railway Station, MA, Dept Defence Files, A8125; *Poblacht na hÉireann War News*, 26 Jan. 1923, NLI Microfilm Reel 52.

74 Report on north west Sligo area, 29 Dec. 1922, AD UCD, Mulcahy Papers, P7/B/75.

75 Report by Sligo I/O, 1 Dec. 1922, MA, Donegal Command Files, CW/Ops/6; 3rd Western Division strengths, Nov. 1922, MA, Western Command Papers, CW/Ops/7(b).

76 C/S IRA to O/C 3rd Western Division, 9 Nov. 1922, AD UCD, Twomey Papers, Western Command Material, P69/33(46). Liam Lynch appears to be introducing the idea to Pilkington in November 1922.

77 Report from Adj. Western Command to C/S IRA, 25 Jan.1923, AD UCD, Twomey Papers, Western Command Material, P69/31; Letter to D/E GHQ, 16 Dec. 1922, MA, Captured Documents, Lot No. 232. Four officers from the 3rd Western Division attended this meeting.

78 Report from Adj. Western Command to C/S IRA, and reply 17 Jan.1923, AD UCD, Twomey Papers, Western Command Material, P69/31. Michael Kilroy was captured at Newport, Co. Mayo on 24 November 1922.

79 C/S to O/C 3rd Western Division, 9 Nov. 1922, AD UCD, Twomey Papers, Western Command Material, P69/33(46); O/C 3rd Western Division to C/S, 28 Nov. 1922, AD UCD, Twomey Papers, Western Command Material, P69/33(45).

80 O/C 3rd Western Division to C/S, 10 Dec.1922, AD UCD, Twomey Papers, Western Command Material, P69/33(39).

81 Report on food supplies to O/C 4th Western Division, 20 Jan. 1923, MA, Captured Documents, Lot No. 11.

82 Hopkinson, *Green Against Green*, p. 228 and 242-3.

83 Army Orders, General Routine Orders No. 4, Reorganisation of Commands, MA. This reorganisation came into effect on 20 Jan. 1923.

84 Report, 26 Mar. 1923, AD UCD, Mulcahy Papers, P7/B/130; Martin Brennan, O'MN, P17b/133; Report 25 Mar. 1923, MA, Donegal Command Papers, CW/Ops/6(o); Operation Reports, 17 Feb. and 26 Mar. 1923, MA, Claremorris Command Papers, CW/Ops/4(d); *S.C.*, 7 Apr. 1923. These included Coleman, Ballymote, Brennan and Ginty, Tubbercurry and Bofin, Arigna who were captured, and Brehony and Geoghegan, Collooney who were killed.

85 *S.C.*, 3 Feb. 1923; 4th Brigade Diary of Activities for fortnight ended 15 Feb. 1923, MA, Western Command Papers, CW/Ops/7(a).

86 1st Brigade Diary of Activities for fortnight ended 31 Jan. 1923, MA, Western Command Papers, CW/Ops/7(a); Letter Adj. 4th Brigade to O/C 3rd Battalion, 21 Mar. 1923, MA, Captured documents, Lot No. 30/2a.

87 Particulars of Residences destroyed in Area, 1st Jan. to 28 Feb. 1923, AD UCD, Twomey Papers, 3rd Western Division Material, P69/33; Diary of

Activities for fortnight ended 28 Feb. 1923, 4th Brigade 3rd Western Division, MA, Western Command Papers, CW/Ops/7(a); *S.C.*, 3 and 10 Mar. 1923; *Éire*, 7 July 1923; Interview with Willie Frizzelle, 14 Aug. 1987; Diary of Activities for fortnight ended 15 March 1923, 1st Brigade, 3rd Western Division, AD UCD, Twomey Papers, Western Command Material, P69/30.
88 Reports, 19 and 27 Mar. 1923, MA, Donegal Command Papers, CW/Ops/6(o); *S.C.*, 27 Jan., 3 Feb. and 31 Mar. 1923.
89 *S.C.*, 17 Mar. 1923.
90 Report on Western Command, 17 Mar. 1923, AD UCD, Twomey Papers, Western Command Material, P69/30.
91 C/S IRA to Adj. Western Command, 12 Mar. 1923, 3 May 1923, AD UCD, Twomey Papers, Western Command Material, P69/30.
92 C/S IRA to O/C Western Command, 23 Mar. 1923, AD UCD, Twomey Papers, Western Command Material, P69/30.
93 C/S IRA to O/C Western Command, 3 May 1923, AD UCD, Twomey Papers, Western Command Material, P69/30.
94 Report, 26 Mar. 1923, AD UCD, Mulcahy Papers, P7/B/130; Report 25 Mar. 1923, MA, Donegal Command Papers, CW/Ops/6(o).
95 Operation Order No. 2, Operation in Dromore West area, undated but refers to Easter Sunday, MA, Donegal Command Papers, CW/Ops/6; Report on Operations in Dromore West area, 14 Apr. 1923, Donegal Command Papers, CW/Ops/6; Operation Report, 14 Apr. 1923, MA, Claremorris Command Papers, CW/Ops/4(d); Report 21 Apr. 1923, MA, Dept Defence Files, A/8083.
96 Report Adj. 3rd Western Division to O/C Western Command, 16 Apr. 1923, AD UCD, Twomey Papers, Western Command Material, P69/30. The report includes the following statement: 'With 4 exceptions not a single volunteer was captured.'
97 Operation Report, 14 Apr. 1923, MA, Claremorris Command Papers, CW/Ops/4(d); The new posts were Aclare with *c.* 80 government troops, Enniscrone 60 and Dromore West 73. (Inspection Reports, 9 and 25 May 1923, MA, LA/10; *Éire*, 7 July 1923).
98 Operation Report, 14 Apr. 1923, MA, Claremorris Command Papers, CW/Ops/4(d); Report, 27 Apr. 1923, MA, Donegal Command Papers, CW/Ops/6(n).
99 Report MacEoin to C/S, 19 Apr. 1923, MacEoin Papers, C57/9; Report on Irregular Activities, 24 Apr. 1923, MacEoin Papers, C57/9.
100 Report, 1 May 1923, MA, Donegal Command Papers, CW/Ops/6(n); Fortnightly Report, 2 June 1923, MA, Dept Defence Files, A8079.
101 Thomas Scanlon, O'MN, P17B/133.
102 Pilkington to C/S IRA, 15 June 1923, AD UCD, Twomey Papers, Western Command Material, P69/30(7).
103 Report, 21 Apr. 1923, MA, Dept Defence Files, A/8083.
104 General Weekly Survey, 26 May 1923, MA, Dept Defence Files, A8083.
105 Fortnightly Report, 2 June 1923, MA, Dept Defence Files, A8079.
106 Weekly Report Donegal Command, 16 June 1923, MA, Dept Defence Files, A8083.

107 Civic Guards Monthly Report July 1923, MA, Dept Defence Files, A8454.
108 Casualty figures were compiled from reports in local newspapers, 3rd Western Division reports in Twomey Papers, Western Command correspondence in Mulcahy Papers, Operation and Intelligence files in the Military Archives as well as the incomplete but useful Roll of Deceased Personnel in the latter archive.

5 THE GEOGRAPHY OF THE CIVIL WAR IN COUNTY SLIGO

1 Royal Irish Academy, *Atlas of Ireland* (Dublin, 1979), p. 28.
2 T.W. Freeman, 'Population Distribution in County Sligo' in *Irish Geography*, 17 (1943–4), pp 254–68.
3 Census of Ireland, 1911, Table VI.
4 Second appendix to the seventh report, Co. Sligo, tables I, Royal Commission on Congestion in Ireland (Dublin, 1907).
5 *S.C.* and *S.I.*, 16 Dec. 1922; Report O/C 1st Brigade to O/C 3rd Western Division, 10 Dec. 1922, AD UCD, Twomey Papers, Western Command Material, P69/33; Report by Divisional I/O, Sligo, 11 Dec. 1922, MacEoin Papers, C57/18A; Letter to prisoner J. Quinn, 17 Dec. 1922, AD UCD, Mulcahy Papers, P7/B/75; Report Adj. Sligo to Adj. 3rd Western Division, 14 Dec. 1922, MA, Western Command Papers, CW/Ops/7(c).
6 Intelligence Reports for August to December 1922 give details of each group and estimate of numbers involved in each. (MA, Western Command Papers, CW/Ops/7(c)).
7 Report on Irregulars, 8 Aug. 1922, MA, Western Command Papers, CW/Ops/7(c); Report on north west Sligo area, 29 Dec. 1922, AD UCD, Mulcahy Papers, P7/B/75; Report for week ending 21 Apr. 1923, MA, Dept Defence Files, A8083, Operations – Donegal Command.
8 General Manager Sligo Leitrim and Northern Counties Railway to M/D, 27 July 1922 and Asst. QM Western Command to C/S, 31 July 1922, AD UCD, Mulcahy Papers, P7/B/73; A Dept of Defence file, A7160, in the Military Archives deals with attacks on this railway line; A Sept. 1922 report says that Bofin's column frequented the Geevagh and Highwood area nearly every Sunday evening 'meeting lady friends' (Report I/O Boyle, 15 Sept. 1922, MA, Western Command Papers, CW/Ops/7(c)).
9 Report on military situation, 21 Nov. 1922, AD UCD, Mulcahy Papers, P7/B/111. This column did, however, carry out some attacks on the Leitrim and Roscommon sides of the border (Tom Scanlon, AD UCD, O'Malley Notebooks, P17b/133).
10 Intelligence reports, 4, 8, 22 Aug., 5 and 11 Sept. 1922, MA, Western Command Papers, CW/Ops/7(c).
11 Reports in *S.C.* and *S.I.*, 23 Sept. 1922.
12 4th Brigade Diary of Activities for fortnight ended 15 Feb. 1923, MA, Western Command Papers, CW/Ops/7(a).
13 4th Brigade Diary of Activities for fortnight beginning 6 Dec. 1922, MA, Western Command Papers, CW/Ops/7(a). Carty was named as leader of

the attack on the train at Culfadda by the Boyle I/O. (Report I/O Boyle, 15 Dec. 1922, MA, Western Command Papers, CW/Ops/7(c)).

14 Reports in *S.C.*, *S.I.* and *CM.*, 8 and 15 July 1922.

15 There are lists of Sligo pro-Treaty garrisons with their strengths in AD UCD, Mulcahy Papers, P7/B/22, P7/B/74 and P7/B/75.

16 *S.C.*, *S.I.* and *CM.*, July 1922: Frank Carty Statement, NLI, Collins Papers, P914.

17 O'Donnell to MacEoin, 30 Nov. 1923, MacEoin Papers, C11/3.

18 Martin Brennan, AD UCD, O'Malley Notebooks, P17b/133; Intelligence reports, 4 and 8 Aug. 1922, MA, Western Command Papers, CW/Ops/7(c).

19 Thomas Henry to O/C 3rd Western Division, 17 Nov. 1922, MA, Western Command Papers, CW/Ops/7(b).

20 These were compiled from local newspaper reports and from Agrarian Outrages, PRO, CO 904/121.

21 SCI RIC June 1920 Monthly Report, PRO, CO 904/112; *Irish Bulletin*, 17 June 1920.

22 SCI RIC Mar. 1916 and Dec. 1917 Monthly Reports, PRO, CO 904/100 and 104.

23 These included Keash (Feb. 1915), Ballymote area (May–June 1915, Mar 1916 and Nov. 1917), Ballintogher (Dec. 1915–Feb. 1916), Castlebaldwin (Mar. 1916) and Ballintogher (Mar–Dec 1916) (SCI RIC Feb. 1915–Nov.1917 Monthly Reports, PRO, CO 904/96–104).

24 *Manchester Guardian*, 15 Mar. 1923. Quoted in E. Rumpf and A.C. Hepburn, *Nationalism and Socialism in Twentieth-Century Ireland* (Liverpool, 1977), p. 61.

25 Padraig O'Farrell, *The Séan MacEoin Story* (Cork, 1981), p. 89.

26 Interview with Dr O'Donnell MO Garrison, Sligo, 21 Dec. 1922, AD UCD, Mulcahy Papers, P7/B/75.

27 O/C Athlone to C/S, 9 May 1923, McEoin Papers C 57/1.

28 Report Boyle, 4 Nov. 1922, MA, Western Command Papers, CW/Ops/7(b).

29 Report for week ending 21 Apr. 1923, MA, Dept Defence Files, A8083, Operations – Donegal Command.

30 Martin Brennan, AD UCD, O'Malley Notebooks, P17b/133.

31 General Report, Boyle, 1 May 1923, MacEoin Papers, C57/18c.

32 Newspaper cutting, 30 Nov. 1922, AD UCD, Mulcahy Papers, P7/B/74.

33 Internment Prisoner Location Books, MA; Free State Army Census Dec. 1922, MA.

34 The re-arrest of deserters is mentioned in Claremorris Radio Reports, Military Archives, Report from Claremorris, 20 June and 31 July 1923, MA, Radio and Phone Reports, CW/R/2.

35 Jack Brennan, AD UCD, O'Malley Notebooks, P17b/137.

36 Report on north west Sligo area, 29 Dec. 1922, AD UCD, Mulcahy Papers, P7/B/75.

37 J.J. Jennings, *The Big Stone* (Athlone, 1989), pp 48–9.

38 *R.H.*, 11 Mar. 1922.

39 *R.H.*, 18 Mar. 1922.

40 *W.P.*, 22 Apr. 1922; *S.I.*, 7 Oct. 1922.

6 COUNTY SLIGO PARTICIPANTS

1 Army Census, Military Archives; Internment Location Books, Military Archives; Valuation Books for Co. Sligo, Irish Valuation Office; Census returns for Co. Sligo, 1911, NA. I located just over 60 per cent of participants on each list in either the Census returns or Valuation Books or both and used the details to build up a picture of each side. The Internment Books in particular provided very little information beyond name and address, and this made searching difficult. The Army Census gave ages and (in most cases) a parent's Christian name which made them easier to trace.

2 Michael Hopkinson, *Green Against Green: The Irish Civil War* (Dublin, 1988), pp 45–6.

3 C. Desmond Greaves, *Liam Mellows and the Irish Revolution* (London, 1971), p. 302.

4 Tom Garvin, *Nationalist Revolutionaries in Ireland* (Oxford, 1987), p. 142.

5 E. Rumpf and A.C. Hepburn, *Nationalism and Socialism in Twentieth-Century Ireland* (Liverpool, 1977), p. 36.

6 Rumpf and Hepburn, *Nationalism and Socialism*, p. 37.

7 ibid., pp 61–2.

8 Paul Bew, 'Sinn Féin and Agrarian Radicalism, 1919–1921' in D.G. Boyce (ed.), *The Revolution in Ireland 1879–1923* (Basingstoke, 1988), p. 233.

9 Rumpf and Hepburn, *Nationalism and Socialism*, maps 13, 14 and 15, pp 58–60.

10 Charles Townshend, *Political Violence in Ireland* (Oxford, 1983), pp 370–1.

11 Frances M. Blake, *The Irish Civil War and what it still means to the Irish people* (London, 1986), p. 17.

12 ibid., pp 16–17.

13 Conor Kostick, *Revolution in Ireland* (London, 1996), p. 182.

14 Greaves, *Liam Mellows and the Irish Revolution*, p. 365.

15 See section on The Civil War and the Emergence of Social Republicanism in Henry Patterson, *The Politics of Illusion* (London, 1997), pp 22–31. See also Richard English, *Radicals and the Republic* (Oxford, 1994), pp 52–65.

16 David Fitzpatrick, *Politics and Irish Life 1913–1921* (Dublin, 1977), p. 224.

17 Joost Augusteijn, *From Public Defiance to Guerilla Warfare* (Amsterdam, 1994), p. 325–40.

18 Peter Hart, *The IRA and its Enemies* (Oxford, 1998), p. 160.

19 ibid., table 18, p. 155. These figures refer to the occupations of Volunteer rank and file (not officers) in Co. Cork.

20 Information from Séan Lee, Coolaney, Co. Sligo.

21 Census of Ireland 1911, County of Sligo, Table XX, Occupations of the People, pp 50, 52.

22 Hart, *The IRA and its Enemies*, table 21, p. 156.

23 ibid., p. 155.

24 ibid., p. 159.

25 ibid., p. 163.

26 Hart's figures for National Army recruits refer to the occupations of the recruits themselves not those of their fathers. Many of the farm labourers and

un/semi-skilled workers who made up 70 per cent of the recruits may have been sons of farmers.

27 Hart, *The IRA and its Enemies*, p. 156.

28 The valuation books include the valuation of the buildings occupied by the person. These obviously include dwelling houses, out offices and business premises and are thus probably a better index of wealth than the house class from the census returns.

29 J.M. Wilson's notes on his tour of Ireland, Co. Sligo, 24 Feb. 1916, PRONI D989A/9/7.

30 *S.C.*, 16 Dec. 1922.

31 *S.I.*, 24 Mar. 1923.

32 *S.C.*, 9 Dec. 1922.

33 *S.C.*, 24 Feb. 1923. The Information Officer at the Volunteers HQR had asked the Sligo I.O. for information about Goff in Nov. 1921 claiming that he had been heard using 'very unfriendly terms about the republican movement and its leaders' while in Dublin en route to an army hospital at Henley for treatment for war wounds (Intelligence Dublin to I.O. Sligo, 30 Nov. 1921, MA, Collins Papers, A 0747).

34 On the republican side were J. Doocey and G. Glynn, while the army member was J. Barry from Cliffony.

35 Copy of statement by Harold McBrien to the Bureau of Military History and additional information from his daughter, Margaret McBrien, Ballygawley, Co. Sligo.

36 Statement by Jim Hunt in Sligo Co. Library; Additional information supplied by Jim Hunt's widow and sons, Gurteen, Co. Sligo and Mullingar, Co. Westmeath.

37 Quoted in Hart, *The IRA and its Enemies*, p. 170.

38 Hart, *The IRA and its Enemies*, table 31, p. 173.

39 Hart, *The IRA and its Enemies*, table 29, p. 171.

40 The Army Census provides the ages of almost all the army members while the internment books provides no such information. Therefore the sample size for the Army Census is much larger. For those I found in the 1911 census, both army members and internees, I added eleven to their stated age in the census. This age did not always coincide with the age given in the Army Census but I have used the 1911 census age where both are available on the basis that the age given there was more likely to be correct. The person was in general a young child then, and there was no incentive to add to the age as there might have been when joining the army.

41 Hart, *The IRA and its Enemies*, table 30, p. 172.

42 Request for information from Sligo, Feb. 1923, Dept Defence Files, MA, A8332; Dáil question by Darghal Figes and written answer by General Mulcahy, 27 Feb. 1923, *Dáil Éireann Parliamentary Debates*, Vol. 2, 6 Jan. 1922–27 Mar. 1923, p. 1728.

43 Frances M. Blake, *The Irish Civil War*, p. 18.

44 Garvin, *Nationalist Revolutionaries in Ireland*, p. 147.

45 McCabe was 35, Roddy 34, Hennigan 45, Carty 24 and Pilkington 27 in 1921.

46 Rumpf and Hepburn, *Nationalism and Socialism in Twentieth-Century Ireland*, p. 37.
47 Augusteijn, *From Public Defiance to Guerilla Warfare*, table A.8, p. 338.
48 I used information from the 1911 census returns though it was not always possible to tell if a son was the eldest in cases where the total number of surviving children was more than those returned on the census form. I recorded those who were obviously the eldest sons and those who clearly were not from both groups of participants.
49 The army members were H. Monaghan and P. Kane; the internees R. Heffernan, W. Conlon and M. Coleman.

7 DAILY LIFE IN COUNTY SLIGO DURING THE CIVIL WAR

1 Minutes of meeting, 25 Mar. 1922, Sligo Co. Council Minute Book, Sligo Co. Library.
2 *S.C.*, 21 Sept. 1921.
3 Minutes of meeting, 21 June 1922, Sligo Co. Council Minute Book, Sligo Co. Library.
4 *S.C.*, 8 July 1922.
5 *S.C.*, 22 July 1922.
6 Minutes of meeting, 2 Sept. 1922, Sligo Co. Council Minute Book, Sligo Co. Library; *S.C.*, 26 Aug. 1922.
7 Reports on Irregulars, 8 and 22 Aug. 1922, MA, Western Command Papers, CW/Ops/7(c); *S.C.*, 2 Sept. 1922. The pro-Treaty side believed that an assistant County Surveyor from the area was responsible for destroying the bridges.
8 Report on Food Supplies, O/C 2nd Brigade to O/C 4th Western Division, 20 Jan. 1923, MA, Captured Documents, Lot No. 11.
9 *W.P.*, 19 Aug, 2 Sept. 30 Sept. and 4 Nov. 1922.
10 Minutes of meeting, 28 Oct. 1922, Sligo Co. Council Minute Book, Sligo Co. Library; *S.I.*, 4 Nov. 1922; *S.C.*, 2 Dec. 1922.
11 *S.C.* and *S.I.*, 4 Nov. 1922.
12 Western Command Daily Operations Reports, 3 and 7 Nov. 1922, AD UCD, Mulcahy Papers, P7/B/114.
13 *S.C.*, 11 Nov. 1922; Daily Operations Reports, 13 Nov. and 20 Nov. 1922, MA, Western Command Files, CW/Ops/7(b); Communications Report, 22 May 1923, MA, Donegal Command Files, CW/Ops/6(j).
14 Manager SL and NC line to M/D, 28 July 1922 and Ass Q/M Western Command to C/S, 31 July 1922, AD UCD, Mulcahy Papers, P7/B/73; Manager SL and NC line to Government and C/S to M/D, Nov. 1922, MA, Dept. Defence, A7160.
15 Intelligence Report, 12 Oct. 1922, MA, Western Command Files, CW/Ops/7(c); *R.H.*, 18 Nov. 1922; Radio Report, 19 March 1923, MA, Donegal Command Files, CW/Ops/6(o); *S.C.*, 2 Sept. and 16 Dec. 1922, 27 Jan. and 31 Mar. 1923.

16 Letter to O/C 5th Brigade, 3rd Western Division from Field Inspecting Engineer Western Command, 24 Jan. 1923, MA, Captured Documents, Lot No. 11; Correspondence on reply to Dáil Question by Darrell Figgis on the burning of Sligo station, Jan. 1923, MA, Dept. Defence, A8125.

17 1st Brigade Diary of Activities for fortnight ending Wednesday 31 Jan. 1923 and 4th Brigade Diary of Operations for fortnight 1–15 Feb. 1923, MA, Western Command Files, CW/Ops/7(a).

18 Report from Seán MacEoin to C/S, 19 Apr. 1923, MacEoin Papers, C 57/9.

19 S.C., 2 Dec. 1922 and 27 Jan. 1923.

20 Minutes of meeting, 28 Apr. 1923, Sligo Co. Council Minute Book, Sligo Co. Library.

21 R.H. and S.C., 1 and July 1922; S.C., 8 and 22 July 1922; S.I., 19 and 26 Aug, 16 Sept. 1922.

22 S.I. and R.H., 7 Apr. 1923.

23 S.C., S.I. and C.M., R.H. and W.P. The W.P. for 1923 was not available.

24 As at Ballymote sports on 28 Aug. (S.C., 20 Aug. 1921)

25 S.C., 17 Sept. 1921.

26 S.C., 3 Dec. 1921. The money which had been collected in this way, £111 5s 6d, was not put towards the church but was divided between the St Vincent de Paul Society and the Sligo Volunteers. (S.C., 10 Dec. 1921).

27 Partridge had been a member of the Citizen Army, Dublin labour organiser and city councillor, took part in the 1916 Rising, was imprisoned and died after release in 1917.

28 Easkey, Kilmacoen, Knocknarea and Rosses Point Dramatic Clubs. The latter was the most active, producing two plays in September and two more the following January (S.I., 23 Sept. 1922 and S.C., 20 Jan. 1923).

29 Note from C-in-C to M/D, 14 Dec. 1922, MA, Dept. Defence, A7751.

30 S.C., 23 Dec. 1922.

31 S.I., 30 Dec. 1922.

32 R.H., 30 Dec. 1922 and 6 Jan. 1923; S.C., 6 Jan. 1923; S.I., 30 Dec. 1922.

33 R.H., 24 Mar. 1923.

34 R.H., 7 Apr. 1923.

35 S.C., 17 Sept. 1921 and 4 Mar. 1922; S.I., 26 Nov. 1921.

36 S.C., 24 Feb. 1923; S.C., 28 Apr. 1923.

37 John McTernan (ed.), *Sligo GAA: A Centenary History 1884–1984* (Sligo, 1984), pp 52–5; S.C., 1 Oct. 1921. The winners received a cup presented by Seamus Devins, TD, then in Dartmoor prison.

38 S.C., 8 Oct., 5 and 11 Nov. 1921, and 11 Feb. 1922.

39 S.C., 19 and 26 Nov., 3 Dec. 1921; S.C. and R.H., 1 Apr. 1922; S.C., 27 May 1922. Alec McCabe, TD, presented a set of silver medals as prizes for the Ballymote league.

40 S.C., 3, 10 and 17 Sept. 1921, 4, 11 and 18 Feb., and 25 Mar. 1922; W.P., 28 Jan. and 11 Feb. 1922.

41 S.C., 8 Apr. 1922.

42 S.C., 14 Sept. 1922.

43 S.C., 10 June 1922.

44 *S.C.*, 13 and 18 May 1922; *W.P.*, 1 Apr. 1922. Teams from all the local leagues were involved with the exception of Tireragh whose committee had decided that 'to take part in the County Championship this year would be detrimental to the interests of football in Tireragh' (*W.P.*, 22 Apr. 1922).

45 *S.I.*, 17 June 1922; McTernan, *Sligo GAA*, p. 55.

46 *S.C.*, 27 May and 24 June 1922.

47 *R.H.*, 22 July 1922.

48 *R.H.*, 24 and 31 Mar., 29 Apr. 1923; *S.C.*, 21 Apr. 1923; *R.H.*, 26 May and 9 June 1923.

49 *S.C.*, 5 and 12 May 1923 and McTernan, *Sligo GAA*, pp 56–7.

50 *S.C.*, 12 May 1923; *R.H.*, 16 June and 14 July 1923.

51 *R.H.*, 16 June 1923; McTernan, *Sligo GAA*, p. 57.

52 *S.C.*, 6 Jan. 1923; James McGuinn, *Sligo Men in the Great War* (Belturbet, 1994), pp 48–9.

53 *S.I.*, 3 Sept. 1921.

54 *S.I.*, 1 Oct. 1921.

55 *S.I.*, 3 June, 12,19 and 26 July and 12 Aug. 1922.

56 *S.I.*, 1 and 8 July 1922.

57 *S.I.*, 4 Nov. 1922, 3 Mar. and 21 Apr. 1923.

58 *S.I.*, 4 Nov. 1922: *S.C.*, 1 and 28 Oct. 1922.

59 *S.C.*, 30 Dec. 1922, 6 and 13 Jan. and 3 Mar. 1923.

60 *S.C.*, 24 Mar.1923.

61 *S.I.*, 29 Apr. 1922; *R.H.*, 16 July 1923.

62 *S.C.*, 12 Nov. 1921 and 7 Jan. 1922.

63 *W.P.*, 18 Nov. 1922.

64 Statistics relating to National Education in Ireland for the years 1920–1, 1921–2, 1922–3, Saorstát Éireann Government Publications.

65 These Daily Report Books containing the attendance figures are still in the schools named with the exception of those for Mullaghmore School which has been closed. Its records are now being kept in Cliffony Boys NS.

66 Hamilton, teacher, to inspector, 6 Mar. 1922, NA, ED 11, 75/6.

67 Daily Report Book, Moylough Boys' National School, Roll No. 13831.

68 Average Percentage Increase as Compared with July 1914, in Retail Prices etc. in the United Kingdom, 1915–25, *Eighteenth Abstract of Labour Statistics of the United Kingdom*, pp 139–40 [Cmd 2740], HC 1926, v xxix (29). As from January 1923, the figures relate to Great Britain and Northern Ireland.

69 Cost of Living Reports, June and Oct. 1922, Jan., Apr., July and Oct. 1923, Saorstát Éireann Government Publications.

70 Ledger of Michael Coleman, General Merchant, Coolaney, 1904–1930. In private possession.

71 James Mullarkey, Teeling St., Tubbercurry, Business Records, NA, Sligo 3/3.

72 Meehan Bros Sligo, Business Records, NA, Sligo 9/3.

73 For accounting purposes Feb. to July was regarded as the first half year and Aug. to Jan. the second half year.

74 *W.P.*, 4 Nov. 1922.

75 *S.I.*, 19 Nov. 1921.

76 *The Voice of Labour*, 14 and 21 Jan. 1922. The local press did not report this.

77 *S.C.* and *S.I.*, 7 Jan. 1922; *S.I.*, 28 Jan. 1922.
78 *S.C.*, 10 Mar. 1923.
79 *S.I.*, 12 May 1923.
80 *S.I.*, 25 Mar. 1922; *The Voice of Labour*, 18 Mar. 1922.
81 *S.C.*, 6 May 1922.
82 *R.H.*, 4 Nov. 1922.
83 *S.I.*, 16 and 30 Sept. 1922.
84 *S.I.*, 11 Nov. 1922; *S.C.*, 18 Nov. 1922; *The Voice of Labour*, 21 Oct. 1922.
85 *S.I.*, 25 Nov. 1922.
86 *The Voice of Labour*, 11 Mar. 1922.
87 *S.C.*, 17 Mar. 1923.
88 David Johnson, *The Interwar Economy in Ireland* (Dublin, 1985), p. 5.
89 *The Irish Farmer*, 22 Oct. 1921.
90 No issues of *The Irish Farmer* are available for the period after Aug. 1922.
91 *S.C.*, 7 Oct. 1922.
92 *S.C.*, 11 Mar. 1922.
93 Quarterly Average Prices for Each Province and for Ireland of Crops, Livestock, Meat, Provisions etc., Statistical tables, *Journal of the Department of Agriculture and Technical Instruction* (Dublin), vols xxi and xxii.
94 *S.I.*, 6 Jan. 1923.
95 *S.C.*, 7 Oct. 1922.
96 *R.H.*, 20 Oct. and 17 Dec. 1921.
97 *S.I.*, 8 Oct. 1921.
98 *S.I.*, 11 Mar. 1921; *R.H.*, 25 Mar., 9 and 16 Dec. 1922.
99 *R.H.*, 6 Jan., 10 and 24 Feb. and 24 Mar. 1923.
100 Weekly Appreciation of Situation, 6 Nov. 1922. MA, Western Command files, CW/Ops/7(b); *R.H.*, 4 Nov. 1922.
101 *S.I.*, 23 Sept. 1922.
102 *R.H.*, 12 Aug. 1922.
103 *S.I.*, 12 Aug. 1922.
104 *W.P.*, 28 Oct. 1922.
105 *W.P.*, 2 Dec. 1922.
106 Statistical Tables, Tables showing the exports and imports of animals (Quarterly), *Journal of the Department of Agriculture and Technical Instruction* (Dublin), vols xxi, xxii and xxiii.
107 Appendix E, Creamery Statistics, IAOS Annual Reports, 1921, 1922 and 1923.
108 Anderson to James Moore, 25 Mar. 1923, NA, IAOS files, Ballymote, 1088/79/9.
109 Anderson to James Moore, 25 Mar. 1923, NA, IAOS files, Ballymote, 1088/79/9.
110 *R.H.*, 9, 16 and 23 June 1923.
111 Report by Moore, 5 Apr. 1921, NA, IAOS files, Kilmactranny, 1088/567/6; Series of letters and reports, Jan. 1922 to Apr. 1923, NA, IAOS files, Kilmactranny. 1088/567/7.
112 Letter from secretary IAOS, 29 Aug. 1921, NA, IAOS files, Ballintrillick, 1088/42/5.

113 Sec. IAOS to Moore, 11 Aug. 1922, NA, IAOS files, Sooey, 1088/844/5; Report on special meeting at Sooey by Moore, 19 Apr. 1922, NA, IAOS files, Sooey 1088/844/5; Report by Moore on visit to Sooey, 8 Aug. 1922, NA, IAOS files, Sooey, 1088/844/5; Correspondence 1923–25, NA, IAOS files, Sooey, 1088/844/6.
114 Manager to IAOS, 6 Sept. 1922, NA, IAOS files, Achonry, 1088/5/10.
115 Report on AGM, 6 Aug. 1921 and Report on Special General Meeting, 8 Oct. 1921, NA, IAOS files, Achonry, 1088/5/9.
116 Report of AGM, 7 Dec. 1923, NA, IAOS files, Achonry, 1088/5/10.
117 Confidential report by Moore to Assistant Secretary IAOS, 25 Aug. 1921, NA, IAOS files, Tubbercurry, 1088/906/4; Confidential addendum to report by Moore, 24 Nov. 1921, NA, IAOS files, Tubbercurry, 1088/906/4; Cooke to sec. IAOS, 7 Dec. 1921, NA, IAOS files, Tubbercurry, 1088/906/4.
118 Moore to IAOS, 11 July 1923, NA, IAOS files, Tubbercurry, 1088/906/6.

8 LAW AND ORDER

1 Michael Hopkinson, *Green Against Green: The Irish Civil War* (Dublin, 1988), p. 91.
2 *S.C.* editorial 'IR police in Sligo', 7 Jan. 1922.
3 Alleged Truce Breaches by the IRA, PRO, CO 904/155.
4 Payment of Brigade Police Officers, NA, Dept. Justice, H97/3.
5 *S.C.*, 17 Sept. 1921.
6 *S.C.*, 15 Oct.1921. See references to similar cases in *S.C.*, 15 Oct., *S.I.*, 10 Sept. and *S.C.* and *S.I.*, 3 Dec. 1921.
7 Letter McCabe to Stack, 24 Nov. 1921, NA, Dáil Éireann Courts Winding Up Commission (Courts Commission), DE 11/219a.
8 *S.C.*, 24 and 31 Dec. 1921.
9 *S.C.*, 7 Jan. 1922.
10 *S.I.*, 8 Oct. 1921.
11 *S.C.*, 3 Dec. 1921.
12 *S.I.*, 29 Oct. 1921.
13 *S.I.*, 24 Dec. 1921.
14 Arthur Mitchell, *Revolutionary Government in Ireland: Dáil Eireann 1919–22* (Dublin, 1995), pp 305–6; James Casey, 'Republican Courts in Ireland 1919–1922', in *Irish Jurist*, v (1970), pp 210–11, 330–1; Michael Farry, *Sligo 1914–1921: A Chronicle of Conflict* (Trim, 1992), p. 291.
15 Mary Kotsonouris, *Retreat from Revolution* (Dublin, 1994), p. 37.
16 See Kotsonouris, *Retreat from Revolution*, ch. 4; Stack to TDs, 13 Sept., 1921, AD UCD, Mulcahy Papers, P7/A/24.
17 Stack to Registrar, 17 Sept. and 10 Oct. 1921, NA, Courts Commission, DE 10/58.
18 Letter Registrar to Stack, 4 Oct. 1921, NA, Courts Commission, DE 10/58.
19 *S.I.*, 1 Oct. 1921; McAllister *v* McCoy, NA, Courts Commission, DE 6/4136.

20 Claims in respect of services etc., Dáil courts, NA, Dept. Justice, H 189/77.

21 Tom O'Donnell to Stack, 5 Oct. 1921, NA, Courts Commission, DE 10/58; Report to Minister by inspector, 18 Nov. 1921, NA, Courts Commission, DE 11/219a.

22 Tom O'Donnell to Stack, 5 Oct. 1921, NA, Courts Commission, DE 10/58.

23 Reports Registrar to Stack and McCabe to Stack, 15 Nov. 1921 and Report Registrar to Stack, 30 Dec. 1921, NA, Courts Commission, DE 10/58. The next sitting on 25 Nov. was interrupted by the arrival of enemy forces who however left when the court refused to disperse.

24 Correspondence of court organiser for Roscommon, Mayo and Sligo, NA, Courts Commission, DE 11/219a; Stack to Registrar, 16 Nov. 1921, NA, Courts Commission, DE 10/58.

25 Reports Registrar to Stack and McCabe to Stack, 15 Nov. 1921, Report Registrar to Stack, 30 Dec. 1921, NA, Courts Commission, DE 10/58.

26 Stack to Registrar and to McCabe, 18 Nov. 1921, NA, Courts Commission, DE 10/58.

27 D.A. O'Donnell to Stack, 23 Nov. 1921, NA, Courts Commission, DE 11/219a.

28 Report Registrar to Stack, 3 Dec. 1921, NA, Courts Commission, DE 10/58.

29 Stack to Rev Fr. Henry, 8 Dec. 1921, NA, Courts Commission, DE 10/58.

30 Stack to Registrar, 8 Dec. 1921 and 6 Jan. 1922, NA, Courts Commission, DE 10/58.

31 McCabe to Stack, 28 Dec. 1921 and Boles to Stack, 2 Jan. 1922, NA, Courts Commission, DE 10/58.

32 Bradshaw to Stack, 17 Oct.1921 and Stack to Bradshaw, 20 Oct. 1921, NA, Courts Commission, DE 10/57; North Sligo District Court, 10 Jan. 1922, NA, Courts Commission, DE 6/4118.

33 Western Wholesale Co. Ltd *v* Tolan, NA, Courts Commission, DE 6/4161.

34 Correspondence of D.A. O'Donnell, NA, DE 11/219a and b.

35 Scanlan v King, NA, Courts Commission, DE 6/4157; *S.I.*, 29 Oct. 1921.

36 *CM.*, 17 Sept. 1921.

37 Kotsonouris, *Retreat from Revolution*, p. 53; Mitchell, *Revolutionary Government in Ireland*, p. 305.

38 See for example such accounts in *S.C.*, 17 Sept., 15 Oct. and 3 Dec. 1921.

39 Casey, 'Republican Courts in Ireland', p. 332.

40 Reports by Simon Donnelly, Chief of Republican Police, 24 Feb. and 16 Mar. 1922, NA, Dept. Justice, H97/3.

41 Crown and Peace Records, Co. Sligo, Criminal Injuries Papers 1922, NA. Those claims relating to the Belfast Boycott have not been included in these figures.

42 The State *v* Several, NA, Courts Commission, DE 8/68.

43 *CM.*, 25 Feb. 1922.

44 *S.I.*, 11 Feb. 1922; *R.H.*, 4 Mar. 1922. They were under the command of Patrick Coleman, who later fought with the anti-Treaty side.

45 *R.H.*, 13 Jan. and 11 Feb. 1922; *CM.*, 18 and 25 Feb. 1922.

46 *S.C.* and *CM.*, 18 Feb. 1922. In Aug. 1923 sums of money were repaid to the Provincial Bank of Ireland (£802) and the Bank of Ireland (£2,203) part of

the money stolen on 13 Feb. 1922 in Sligo and these were acknowledged in the national newspapers of 3 Aug. 1923. (Daily Press Survey, 3 Aug. 1923, MA, M1/PR/2).

47 *R.H.*, 11 Mar. 1922; *S.C.*, 18 Mar. and20 May 1922; *S.I.*, *S.C.* and *R.H.*, 13 May 1922.
48 Crown and Peace Records, Co. Sligo, Criminal Injuries Papers 1922, NA. Belfast Boycott related claims have not been included in these figures.
49 Simon Grumbleton, Irish Grants Committee (IGC), PRO, CO 762/23; Michael Mullaney, /41; Martin Gilroy, /44; Jeremiah O'Sullivan, /82; Charles Graham, /90; Peter Healy, /118; Charles O'Donnell, /157; Delia McKeon, /172.
50 *R.H.*, 20 May 1922.
51 *R.H.*, *CM.* and *S.C.* 3 June 1922.
52 *W.P.*, 24 June 1922. The victim, John Brehony, was shot by a member of the IRA garrison at Ballymote (confidential information).
53 The man was James Cullen (*W.P.* and *R.H.*, 2 Sept. 1922).
54 *S.C.*, 22 Apr., 6 and 20 May, 17 June 1922; *R.H.*, 29 Apr., 6 May, 3 June 1922.
55 Statement of John Russell ex-RIC, H.R. Wood-Martin, IGC, PRO, CO 762/78.
56 *R.H.*, 11 and 18 Mar. 1922.
57 *S.C.*, 25 Mar. and 1 Apr. 1922; *R.H.*, 8 Apr. 1922.
58 See ch. 3, Conor Brady, *Guardians of the Peace* (Dublin, 1974); Hopkinson, *Green Against Green*, pp 91–2; Tom Garvin, *1922: The Birth of Irish Democracy* (Dublin, 1996), pp 104–15; ch. 3, Liam McNiff, *A History of the Garda Síochána* (Dublin, 1997). Sligo was to the fore as regards the number of recruits it supplied to the Guards. It ranked eighth best county in this regard for the pre-mutiny Feb.–May 1922 period and 6th for 1922–32. McNiff, *A History of the Garda Síochána*, tables 3.3 and 3.4, pp 36 and 38.
59 Garvin, *1922*, p. 171.
60 Casey, 'Republican Courts in Ireland', p. 337.
61 Kotsonouris, *Retreat from Revolution*, pp 61–8.
62 Brady, *Guardians of the Peace*, p. 49.
63 *CM.*, *S.I.* and *S.C.*, 4 Mar 1922; *CM.*, 15 Apr. 1922.
64 *R.H.*, 18 and 25 Feb. 1922; *S.C.*, 25 Feb. 1922.
65 Report by D.A. O'Donnell, 10 Mar. 1922, NA, Courts Commission, DE 11/219b.
66 *R.H.*, 1 Apr. 1922.
67 *S.I.*, 1 July 1922.
68 Quinn to Minister, 5 Sept. 1922, NA, Courts Commission, DE 14/22.
69 *CM.*, 10 June 1922. The three were Michael Coleman, Henry Brehony and Michael O'Beirne.
70 *S.C.*, 4 Feb. 1922; *S.I.*, 28 Jan. 1922; *CM.*, 18 Feb. and 4 Mar. 1922.
71 O'Neill to Collins, 6 Mar. 1922 and to Mins H/A, 5 Mar. 1922, NA, Courts Commission, DE 12/174.
72 Quinn to Minister, 5 Sept. 1922, NA, Courts Commission, DE 14/22; NA, Courts Commission, DE 6/4132, /4140, /4141, /4148, /4149, /4150, /4151 and /4160.

73 Spirit Licenses – Jurisdiction of Parish Courts, NA, Dept. Justice, H47/42; *R.H.*, 12 Aug. 1922.

74 Egan to Minister, 17 Aug. 1922, NA, Courts Commission, DE 14/22.

75 *S.I.*, 11 Feb. and 11 Mar. 1922. Anti-Treaty Mayor Michael Nevin did not sit on the bench.

76 *R.H.*, 18 Mar. 1922.

77 Resident Magistrates' Leave 1922, NA, Dept. Justice, H137/5.

78 *S.I.*, 21 Jan. 1922.

79 *S.C.*, 10 Sept. 1922; *S.I.*, 8, 15 and 22 Oct. 1921.

80 *R.H.*, *W.P.* and *S.C.*, 27 May 1922.

81 *W.P.*, 21 Jan. 1922; *CM.*, 25 Mar. 1922.

82 *W.P.*, 29 July 1922; *R.H.*, 5 Aug. 1922; *S.C.*, 29 July and 5 Aug. 1922.

83 *R.H.*, 14 Oct., 30 Sept. and 21 Oct. 1922.

84 *S.C.* and *W.P.*, 28 Oct.; *S.C.*, 25 Nov.; *R.H.*, 18 Nov., 23 and 30 Dec. 1922.

85 *S.I.* and *S.C.*, 28 Apr. 1923.

86 *S.C.*, 29 July 1922.

87 *R.H.*, 12 Aug., 14 and 28 Oct. 1922.

88 Civic Guard – General Distribution, NA, Dept Justice, H99/29; *R.H.* and *S.I.*, 4 Nov. 1922; *S.I.*, 28 Oct. 1922.

89 Civic Guard Organisation Scheme, NA, Dept. Justice, H99; *Iris an Ghárda*, 7 May 1923.

90 Civic Guards Monthly Reports, Co. Sligo, July 1923, MA, Dept. Defence, A8454; Civic Guard, NA, Dept Justice, H99/125.

91 *S.I.* and *S.C.*, 14 Apr. 1923; *Iris an Ghárda*, 7 May 1923.

92 Attacks on Gárda Siochána, NA, Dept. Justice, H99/109.

93 *R.H.*, 20 Jan. and 3 Feb. 1923.

94 Protection of lands of Charles Phibbs, MA, Dept. Defence, A3642; Damage to property, C. Phibbs, NA, Dept. Justice, H5/215; Charles Phibbs, IGC, PRO, CO 762/70; Robbery and ill treatment of J. Ormsby Cooke at Kilturra, Bunninadden, Co. Sligo, NA, Dept Justice, H5/269; *R.H.*, 10 Feb. 1923.

95 *R.H.*, 10 Feb.; *S.C.*, 24 Feb. 1923.

96 *S.C.*, 23 June 1923; Letter from McCabe, 20 June 1923 and Report CID to Mins H/A, 10 July 1923, Armed Robberies at Bunninadden, Co. Sligo, NA, Dept. Justice, H5/856.

97 Raids on Post Offices etc., NA. Dept. Justice, H5/67 A–H.

98 *S.I.* and *S.C.*, 7 Apr. 1923; Murder of Mrs Catherine McGuinness of Carns, Culleens, Co. Sligo, NA, Dept. Justice, H5/700.

99 *R.H.*, 19 Aug. and 9 Sept. 1922; *S.C.*, 26 Aug. 1922. Joseph Graham was a prominent unionist.

100 *S.I.*, 30 Sept. 1922.

101 O'Reilly to Commission, 13 Oct. 1923, NA, Courts Commission, DE 6/4161.

102 *S.C.*, 15 July 1922.

103 Walsh *v* Noone, NA, Courts Commission, DE 6/4160. Its final sitting may have been the one mentioned as taking place in early September. (*W.P.*, 9 Sept. 1922).

104 Quinn to Minister, 7 Sept. 1922, NA, Courts Commission, DE 14/22.
105 Paul Vignoles was now the organiser.
106 *R.H.*, 19 Aug. 1922; Nerney to Minister, 21 Feb. 1922, NA, Courts Commission, DE 21/15.
107 *S.C., W.P.* and *R.H.*, 30 Sept. and 7 Oct. 1922; *R.H.*, 30 Dec. 1922 and 26 May 1923; *S.C.*, 13 Jan. 1923.
108 Kotsonouris, *Retreat from Revolution*, pp 93–4; Garvin, *1922*, p. 171.
109 *S.I.*, 4 and 11 Nov., 30 Dec. 1922.
110 *R.H.*, 11 Nov. and 30 Dec. 1922; *S.C.*, 3 and 10 Feb. 1923; *Iris an Ghárda*, 26 Feb. 1923.
111 *R.H.*, 17 Feb. 1923; *S.C.* and *S.I.*, 24 Feb. 1923.
112 *Iris an Ghárda*, 7 and 14 May, 11 and 25 June 1923; *S.I.*, 3 Mar. and 7 Apr. 1922.
113 Civic Guards Monthly Reports, Co. Sligo, July 1923, MA, Dept. Defence, A8454.

9 SLIGO PROTESTANTS AFTER THE REVOLUTION

1 *CM.*, 25 Mar. 1922.
2 HQRS I/O to Sligo Brigade I/O, 15 Oct. 1921, and reply 24 Oct. 1921, Sligo Brigade IRA material, MA, Collins Papers, A/747. D. Perceval, landowner, Thomas Brian, auctioneer and land agent and Arthur Jackson, later a Senator, were the three in question.
3 Report on Sligo area, undated, AD UCD, Mulcahy Papers, P7/A/32.
4 Patrick Buckland, *Irish Unionism 1: The Anglo-Irish and the New Ireland 1885 to 1922* (Dublin, 1972), p. 202.
5 Percentage increase or decrease from 1911 to 1926 of persons of each religion in each county in Saorstát Éireann on 18 April 1926, Volume III Table 8B, Saorstát Éireann, Census of Population 1926.
6 Sligo, Tuam, Westport, Boyle, Ballina, Castlebar, Loughrea, Galway, Roscommon, Ballinasloe.
7 Number of persons of each religion in each town of 1500 or more in Saorstát Éireann on 18 April 1926 showing percentage changes from 1911 to 1926, Volume III Table 7, Saorstát Éireann, Census of Population 1926.
8 See discussion in Robert E. Kennedy, *The Irish: Emigration, Marriage and Fertility* (Berkeley, 1973), pp 119–21 and Peter Hart, 'The Protestant Experience of Revolution in Southern Ireland' in Richard English and Graham Walker (eds), *Unionism in Modern Ireland* (Belfast, 1996), p. 83; Table XX, Occupations of Males by Ages, Religious Professions, and Education in the County of Sligo, Census of Ireland 1911, pp 48–52.
9 Summary showing by provinces and counties the Religious Professions of the people, General Report, Census of Ireland, 1911, pp 6–7. Leitrim was closest with 8.5% non-Catholics. The other Connacht counties had non-Catholic populations of between 2.1 and 2.4 per cent; Religious Professions, Table XXIX, County of Sligo, Census of Ireland 1911, p. 69.
10 Minutes of meetings 14 and 28 Apr., 21 May and 27 Oct. 1921, 2 Mar. 1922 and 2 Mar. 1923, 8 Feb. 1924, St John's Vestry Minute Book, Representative Church Body Library, Dublin.

11 Statistics of the Presbyterian Church in Ireland for years ending 1914–1924, Minutes of the Proceedings of the General Assembly of the Presbyterian Church in Ireland, Vols 12 (1911–15), 13 (1916–20) and 14 (1921–24).
12 Information supplied from Sligo Methodist records by Rev. Ian Henderson, Methodist Manse, Ardgowen, Sligo.
13 Mary O'Dowd, 'Sligo' in Anngret Simms and J.H. Andrews (eds), *Irish Country Towns* (Dublin, 1994), p. 152.
14 George R. Williams, Irish Grants Committee (IGC), PRO, CO 762/195.
15 Steven Reid, *Get to the Point at County Sligo Golf Club* (Naas, 1991), pp 82–5.
16 The successful Ratepayers candidates were: Harper Campbell Perry, Merchant; Percy Campbell Kerr, Shipping Agent; Edward J. Tighe, Merchant; James Connolly, Albert Line, Merchant; Young Warren, Tea Merchant; Bernard McDonagh, Draper; Arthur Jackson, Merchant; and H.R. Wood-Martin, House and Land Owner. (*S.C.*, 25 Jan. 1919).
17 Michael Farry, *Sligo 1914–1921: A Chronicle of Conflict* (Trim, 1992), p. 210.
18 Farry, *Sligo 1914–1921*, p. 278. John Jinks became the independent Mayor of Sligo.
19 Table 21, Saorstát Éireann, Census of Population 1926.
20 *S.I.*, 8 Oct. and 12 Nov. 1921.
21 *S.I.*, 14 and 28 Jan., 4 Feb. 1922. See editorials such as 'Opening of a new era in Ireland', *S.I.*, 21 Jan. 1922 and 'We must have True Liberty', *S.I.*, 4 Feb. 1922.
22 George R. Williams, IGC, CO 762/195; J. Walpole-Boyers, IGC, CO 762/202; Joseph Graham, IGC, CO 762/205.
23 See Hart 'The Protestant Experience', pp 84–7.
24 John C. McTernan, *Worthies of Sligo* (Sligo, 1994), pp 318–20.
25 See article by Catherine Finn in *The Corran Herald*, no. 16 (Ballymote, 1988).
26 Tom Garvin, *Nationalist Revolutionaries in Ireland* (Oxford, 1987), p. 147.
27 Kilgannon, *Almanac and Directory of County Sligo 1907*, Sligo Co. Library.
28 Ibid.
29 Sligo Constitutional Club, Register of Candidates, 1907–17, Sligo Co. Library.
30 Report from Sligo Brigade July 1921, AD UCD, Mulcahy Papers, P7/a/15. The Town and County Club had been founded in 1891 as the Catholic and Nationalist equivalent of the Constitutional Club.
31 *S.I.*, 6 Aug. 1921.
32 VW Bro. R.H. Campbell-Perry, 'A Glimpse of Freemasonry in Sligo 1767–1951' in *The Lodge of Research Transactions for Years 1949–57* (Dublin, 1959).
33 These figures are based on an analysis of membership registers of Lodge 165 from 1895 to 1923 and of Lodge 20 from 1872 to 1923, Freemasonry Archives, Dublin. The occupations of 159 members of Lodge 165 and 130 of Lodge 20 are known.
34 The parish of Calry seems to have had a closer relationship with the Freemasons that the other Sligo Church of Ireland parish, St John's. In 1907 the incumbent, both Churchwardens and the organist were all members of Lodge 20.

35 Nos 464, 795 and 1733 respectively. Information on Orange Lodges in Co. Sligo supplied by Cecil Kilpatrick, Archivist, Grand Orange Lodge of Ireland, Belfast.

36 The Grand Master for Co. Sligo in 1921 was John Milliken of Rusheen, Riverstown, the Grand Secretary was John Shannon, 8 Church St., Sligo and the Grand Treasurer John Mullen, Chapel St., Sligo.

37 Robert Beattie, IGC, CO 762/66; Joseph Murray, IGC, CO 762/173.

38 Sir Malby Crofton to Beresford, Hon Sec IUL, 11 Mar. 1916, PRONI, D989A/8/6.

39 J.M. Wilson's notes on his tour of Ireland, Co. Sligo, 24 Feb. 1916, PRONI, D989A/9/7.

40 ibid., 28 June 1917, PRONI, D989A/9/7.

41 O'Hara to Lord Midleton, 8 July 1918, Letter Book of C.K. O'Hara, NLI, Ms 16826.

42 O'Hara to John Russell, DI RIC, 11 Sept. 1920, Letter Book of C.K. O'Hara, NLI, Ms 16827.

43 See letters from O'Hara to Frank O'Beirne, 13 Oct. 1921; to Carty, 27 Mar. 1922; to Carty, 20 and 26 June 1922, Letter Book of C.K. O'Hara, NLI, Ms 16827.

44 B. Cooper, undated statement quoted in Lennox Robinson, *Bryan Cooper* (London, 1931), p. 126.

45 *S.I.* and *S.C.*, 7 Jan. 1922.

46 *S.C.* and *CM.*, 31 Dec. 1921.

47 *S.I.*, 21 Jan. 1922.

48 *S.C.*, 1 Apr. 1922.

49 Seventy-two-year-old Thomas Walker had been killed 14 Apr. 1921 by four members of the local IRA acting on orders. (Farry, *Sligo 1914–1921*, pp 288–9).

50 *S.I.*, 11 Feb. 1922.

51 *S.I.*, *S.C.* and *R.H.*, 11 Feb. 1922; *S.I.* and *CM.*, 25 Feb. 1922; Tom Scanlon, AD UCD, O'Malley Notebooks, P17b/133. Those arrested included Robert Dodd of Lyons and Co.; Alderman Percy Campbell Kerr, manager of the Laird Line Shipping Co.; Chris Bellew, of Bellew Bros.; Tom Brien, Frazier's and Brown auctioneers; George Lewis, of Thornhill, who was reported as holding an important position in Pollexfen's; Josslyn Gore-Booth and Major Eccles.*S.I.* and *CM.*, 25 Feb. 1922.

52 Expulsion of Protestants in Mayo, NA, Department of the Taoiseach, S565; Army Truce 1922, Breaches, NA, Department of the Taoiseach, S572.

53 For Riverstown area see *R.H.*, 3 June 1922; For Ballisodare and Beltra areas see *S.I.*, 22 Apr. 1922 and 17 June 1922. Other incidents are reported in *S.I.*, 6 and 20 May 1922 and *R.H.*, 29 Apr. and 3 June 1922.

54 *R.H.*, 6 and 27 May, 17 June 1922. *S.I.* and *S.C.*, 16 July 1921.

55 *S.I.*, 22 July 1922.

56 Letter H.R. Wood-Martin to Sir Douglas Newton, England, 12 Jan. 1923, Robinson Estate Office Letter Books, Sligo Co. Library.

57 Peter Hart, *The IRA and its Enemies* (Oxford, 1998), table 37, p 304.

58 Hart, 'The Protestant Experience', p. 93; *The Irish Times*, 31 Aug. and 27 Sept. 1921. Almost identical reports appeared in *S.C.* 4 Sept. and 2 Oct. 1921.

59 Jessie Hunter, IGC, PRO, CO 762/51; Richard T. Kerr-Taylor, IGC, CO 762/48; H.R. Wood-Martin, IGC, CO 762/78. The Irish Grants Committee was set up by the British Government to hear claims from loyalists for losses and injuries sustained between the Truce and the end of the Civil War and to recommend awards. (Niamh Brennan, 'A Political Minefield: Southern Loyalists, the Irish Grants Committee and the British Government, 1922–31' in *IHS*, xxx, no. 119 (May 1997), pp 406–20; R.B. McDowell, *Crisis and Decline: The Fate of the Southern Unionists* (Dublin, 1997), pp 137–62).

60 Four of these were refused because the trouble had occurred in the pre-Truce period, one was outside the scope of the committee and one was an ex-RIC member who, it was considered, had already been adequately compensated. The religion of the claimant is sometimes given in the IGC files. The religion of others was found by searching the 1911 Census records for Sligo in NA, Dublin. Thirteen were Catholics and the religion of the other twenty I have been unable to ascertain.

61 Farmers were: Jessie Hunter, IGC, CO 762/51; Richard G. Bell, IGC, CO 762/205; John Lougheed, IGC, CO 762/137; Palmer J. McCloughrey, IGC, CO 762/63 and Charles Phibbs, IGC, CO 762/70. Shopkeepers were: George Williams, IGC, CO 762/195; Joseph Graham, IGC, CO 762/205; Richard Kerr-Taylor, IGC, CO 762/48. Charles Graham was the farmer/shopkeeper.

62 *R.H.*, 18 Feb. 1922.

63 Richard G. Bell, IGC, CO 762/205.

64 Palmer J. McCloughrey, IGC, CO 762/63.

65 Farry, *Sligo 1914–1921*, pp 223–4; John Lougheed, IGC, CO 762/137; Illegal seizure of lands of John Lougheed, Rockbrook, Riverstown, NA, Department of Justice, H5/1091.

66 *W.P.*, 14 Jan. 1922.

67 *R.H.*, 13 and 20 May 1922; Protection of lands at Bunninadden, NA, Dept Defence, A3642; Damage to property of C. Phibbs, Doobeg, Bunninadden, NA, Dept. Justice, H5/215; Charles Phibbs, IGC, CO 762/70.

68 Jessica Hunter, IGC, CO 762/51; Valuation Book no. 26, Riverstown DED, Valuation Office, Dublin. The Valuation Book records the transfer of ownership of Hunter's Ardvarney farm (179 acres) in 1925.

69 Charles Graham, IGC, CO 762/90. During his imprisonment one of his captors produced a newspaper cutting from 1912 which contained a speech of Graham's in support of the Union.

70 See the case of Basil Phibbs (Damage to lands at Ardcumber, Riverstown, Co. Sligo, NA, Dept. Justice, H5/214).

71 *R.H.*, 14 Apr. 1923; *S.I.*, 21 Apr. 1923; Farry, *Sligo 1914–1921*, p. 224.

72 Robbery and ill treatment of J. Ormsby Cooke at Kilturra, Bunninadden, Co. Sligo, NA, Department of Justice, H5/269.

73 Martin Kelleher, Doocastle, *The History of Kilterra and Bunninadden*, Recording made 5 Nov. 1959 by Owen B. Hunt, Transcript in Sligo Co. Library.

74 Including three who described themselves as Farmer and Shopkeeper/Dealer. Only one of the 14 was awarded nothing.

75 Thomas E. Guthrie, IGC, CO762/40.

76 Joseph Graham, IGC, CO762/205; R.S. Allen, IGC, CO 762/134.

77 J. Walpole-Boyers, IGC, CO 762/202.

78 Joseph Graham, IGC, CO 762/205.

79 He also claimed to have recognised Michael Collins disguised as a priest on the Boyle to Sligo train in July 1921. According to Williams, Collins escaped with the help of scouts. (George R. Williams, IGC, CO 762/195).

80 John R. Keating, IGC, CO 762/201.

81 John P. Jordan, IGC, CO 762/20.

82 Annie Brennan, IGC, CO 762/108. Some of the Auxiliaries had left without settling their accounts.

83 Robert Beattie, IGC, CO 762/66.

84 Belfast Boycott, Ballymote claims, NA, Dept Finance, F 311/8–12; S.I., 15 Oct. 1921; M.C. Kevins to John Hennigan, 11 Feb. 1925, Fines imposed by the Republican Army on persons dealing with the Ulster Bank, NA, Dept Finance, F 837/4.

85 The eleven were: Robert Beattie, IGC CO 762/66, John R. McKim, /75, R.S. Allen, /134, Joseph Flanagan, /168, M.C. Kevins, /169, J.R. Gorman, /172, Joseph Murray /173, C. Smith /173, Richard Gorman /174, Thomas Hunt /202 and J. Walpole-Boyers /202.

86 W.J. O'Reilly Solr, Sligo to Dept. Finance 3 Aug. 1923 and M.C. Kevins to John Hennigan 11 Feb. 1925, Fines imposed by the Republican Army on persons dealing with the Ulster Bank, NA, Dept Finance, F 837/4.

87 Religion where not given was found in the 1911 Census records or from conversation with Tom McGettrick, formerly of Ballymote.

88 Letter from Rev. Algernon Harris Ballymote, 7 Jan. 1929, Richard Gorman, IGC, CO 762/172. The IRA involved were not 'Irregulars' since this happened pre-Treaty.

89 Reference from St. G. Robinson solrs, Sligo, 27 Jan. 1927 and Letter from J. Russell ex-DI RIC Sligo, 3 Feb. 1927, Jessie Hunter, IGC, CO 762/51.

90 H.T. Evans, IGC, CO 762/68.

91 Thomas J. Ewing, IGC, PRO, CO 762/172.

92 H.R. Wood-Martin, IGC, CO 762/78

93 Charles J. Allen, IGC, CO 762/54.

94 In March 1923 Bryan Cooper did call for help in dealing with theft of timber from Union Wood on his Sligo estate and with some cattle being illegally grazed on his lands. (Robbery of property near Collooney, Bryan Cooper, NA, Dept. Justice, H5/639). The Cooper residence, Markree Castle, which had emerged unscathed from the War of Independence was occupied by Free State troops and suffered £10,000 worth of 'wanton, mischievous and filthy' damage from the raw and often undisciplined Government troops. (Robinson, *Bryan Cooper*, pp 138–9).

95 Joseph Graham, IGC, CO 762/205.

96 Edith Anderson, IGC, CO 762/62; T.E. Guthrie /40; Joseph Graham /205; P.J. McCloughery /63.

97 Census enclosed with a letter from James Cooper, Solicitor, Enniskillen to the Irish Boundary Commission, 15 May 1925, N.L.I., Boundary Commission Papers, Pos 6515.

98 Terence Dooley, 'Monaghan Protestants in a time of crisis 1919-1922' in R.V. Comerford, Mary Cullen, J.R. Hill, Colm Lennon (eds), *Religion, Conflict and Coexistence in Ireland* (Dublin, 1990), p. 249.
99 McDowell, *Crisis and Decline*, p. 120.

BIBLIOGRAPHY

1. MANUSCRIPT COLLECTIONS

Dublin

University College Dublin, Archives

Richard Mulcahy Papers:
The following contained especially useful material:
P7/A/5: GHQ to and from 'P' in Liverpool, May 1921.
P7/A/18–23: Includes correspondence with and reports from Sligo Brigade
    Commandant.
P7/A/28: Statement of munitions, undated, probably late 1921.
P7/A/32: Report on Sligo area, undated.
P7/A/33: Correspondence dealing with the dispute between Gurteen Battalion
    and Canon O'Connor PP.
P7/A/38: Report by Sligo Brigade Commandant, May 1921.
P7/A/63: Reports on raids on railways, Apr. 1922.
P7/B/22: Correspondence with O/C Western Command, July–Aug 1922.
P7/B/73–75: Correspondence with Western Command July, 1923.
P7/B/106: Correspondence with Western Command, July 1922.
P7/B/114: Reports from Western Command, Oct–Nov 1922.
P7/a/15: Report to GHQ by Sligo Brigade IRA, July 1921.

Ernie O'Malley Notebooks.
P17b/96: Tom Ketterick.
P17b/133: Martin Brennan; Tom Scanlon; Jim Hunt; Tom Duignan; Bernard
    Conway; Thady McGowan; Phelim Collery; James Mulholland.
P17b/136: Matt Kilcawley; Tom Leonard; Tom Scanlon.
P17b/137: Jack Brennan; Michael Coleman; Matt Kilcawley; Paddy Hegarty;
    Eugene Gilbride.

Moss Twomey Papers.
Chief of Staff communication with army units 1922–5.
    P 69/30–31: Western Command.

Chief of Staff communication with army units 1922–5.
    P 69/33: 3rd Western Division.
Adjutant General communication with army units 1922–5.
    P 69/107–109: 3rd Western Division.

Department of Irish Folklore, UCD

Schools manuscripts, County Sligo.

National Library of Ireland

Boundary Commission Papers:
P 6515: Census enclosed with a letter from James Cooper, Solicitor, Enniskillen
    to the Irish Boundary Commission, 15 May 1925.

Collins Papers:
P 914: Sligo Brigade material including Frank Carty statement.

Maurice Moore Papers:
Ms 10544: Sligo Material on Irish National Volunteers.

JJ (Ginger) O'Connell Papers:
Ms 22118: Sligo Brigade, IRA, 1918–20.
Ms 22120: Some letters re. 1916–23 period in Sligo.

O'Hara Papers:
Mss 16826 and 16827: Letter Books of C.K. O'Hara, Annaghmore, County Sligo.

Count Plunkett Papers:
Ms 11408: Includes the draft of a letter to the Bishop of Achonry, 13 Oct. 1920.

The National Archives

Chief Secretary's Office, Registered Papers:
CSORP 2195/1921. Ministry of Labour returns of numbers of ex-servicemen
    employed in various districts in Ireland.
CSORP 22861/1920. Crop and Livestock conditions in Ireland.

Records of the Clerks of the Crown and Peace, County Sligo:
Civil Bill Books, 1920–3.
Criminal Injuries Papers, 1922.

Manuscript Census Returns:
County Sligo, 1901 and 1911.

Dáil Éireann Records:
DE 2/486: Newspaper cuttings, Sinn Féin Árd Comhairle Jan. 1922.
    Files of Dáil Éireann Secretariat 1919–1922.

Records of the Dáil Éireann Courts (Winding Up) Commission:

DE 3/26: Registers of unexecuted decrees and orders in Sligo District and Parish Courts.

DE 6/4094–4161: Files on cases dealt with by the Commission, County Sligo.

DE 8/68: Decrees sent for registration, County Sligo.

DE 10: Correspondence files of Minister of Home Affairs with registrars of Dáil Éireann Courts, 57: North Sligo; 58: South Sligo.

DE 11/219: Correspondence files of Minister of Home Affairs with D.A. O'Donnell, court organiser for Roscommon, Mayo and Sligo.

DE 12/174: Organisation of courts in district of North Sligo.

DE 12/203: Report by B. Farry, registrar, on functioning of work in Ballymote.

DE 14/22: Functioning of courts in County Sligo.

DE 14/63: Correspondence with solicitors relating to registering of unexecuted decrees.

DE 16/32: Monthly reports of court registrars County Sligo to Minister for Home Affairs.

DE 21/15: Mullaghroe alias Gurteen Parish Court, County Sligo.

Dáil Éireann Local Government Records:

DELG 26/1: Boyle Rural District Council No. 2, 16 July–15 Oct. 1921.

DELG 26/2: Dromore West Poor Law Union, 19 Oct. 1920–17 July 1922.

DELG 26/3: Dromore West Rural District Council, 19 Oct. 1920–13 Dec. 1921.

DELG 26/4: Sligo Poor Law Union, 22 Sept. 1920–20 Dec. 1921.

DELG 26/5: Sligo Rural District Council, 19 Mar.–9 Dec. 1921.

DELG 26/6: Tubbercurry Poor Law Union, 20 Nov, 1920–17 July 1922.

DELG 26/7: Tubbercurry Rural District Council, 27 Jun.–20 Dec. 1921.

DELG 26/8: Sligo Rural District Council, 31 Jan. 1921– 6 May 1922.

DELG 26/9: Sligo County Council, 15 Sept. 1920–9 Jan. 1923.

Department of Finance Files:

F 303/14: Victimised loyalists, John Anderson, Cliffony, County Sligo.

F 311/8–12: Belfast boycott, Ballymote claims.

F 700/63: East Mayo–Sligo election account, 1922.

F 837/4: Fines imposed by the Republican Army on persons dealing with the Ulster Bank.

Department of Justice Files:

H 5/67: A–H: Raids on Post Offices etc.

H 5/214: Damage to lands at Ardcumber, Riverstown, County Sligo.

H 5/215: Damage to property, C. Phibbs.

H 5/269: Robbery and ill treatment of J. Ormsby Cooke at Kilturra, County Sligo.

H 5/856: Armed Robberies at Bunninadden, County Sligo.

H 5/700: Murder of Mrs Catherine McGuinness of Carns, Culleens, County Sligo.

H 5/1091: Illegal seizure of lands of John Lougheed, Rockbrook, Riverstown.

H 6/15: Godfrey O'Donnell to Mins H/A, 19 Apr. 1922.

H 8/302: Return of Prisoners sentenced by Republican Courts.
H 47/42: Spirit Licenses–Jurisdiction of Parish Courts.
H 97/3: Payment of Brigade Police Officers.
H 99: Civic Guard Organisation Scheme.
H 99/29: Civic Guard–General Distribution.
H 99/109: Attacks on Gárda Siochána.
H 137/5: Resident Magistrates' Leave 1922.
H 189/77: Claims in respect of services etc, Dáil courts.

Department of the Taoiseach General Files:
S565: Expulsion of Protestants in Mayo.
S572: Army Truce 1922, Breaches.
S1842: Persecution of ex-members of the RIC.

Irish Agricultural Organisation Societies files:
1088/5/9–10: Achonry Co-operative Agricultural and Dairy Society.
1088/34/4–5: Ballinfull Co-operative Agricultural and Dairy Society.
1088/42/5: Ballintrillick Co-operative Agricultural and Dairy Society.
1088/78/9: Ballymote Co-operative Agricultural and Dairy Society.
1088/84/1: Ballyrush Co-operative Agricultural and Dairy Society.
1088/361/8: Drumcliff Co-operative Milling Society.
1088/405/2: Enniscrone Co-operative Agricultural and Dairy Society.
1088/443/1: Geevagh Co-operative Dairy Society.
1088/567/6–8: Kilmactranny Co-operative Agricultural and Dairy Society.
1088/805/3: Riverstown Co-operative Agricultural and Dairy Society.
1088/835/1: Skreen Co-operative Agricultural Society.
1088/844/4–6: Sooey Co-operative Agricultural and Dairy Society.
1088/906/4–6: Tubbercurry Co-operative Agricultural and Dairy Society.

Business Records:
Sligo 3/3: James Mullarkey, Teeling St., Tubbercurry. Records and Sales, 1913–1929.
Sligo 9/2 and 3: Meehan Bros. Sligo. Ledger 1917–1932.

Irish Military Archives

Civil War Operation and Intelligence Files:
CW/Ops/4: Claremorris Command.
    a. Operations Reports.
        1. Daily Operations Reports. 23 Jan.–15 Nov. 1923.
        2. Communications Reports. 23 Jan–10 July 1923.
    b. Irregulars.
        1. Daily Reports. 14 Apr.–16 Nov. 1923.
        2. General Weekly Reports. 15 Jan.–26 Oct. 1923.
    c. Combined File.
        1. Operations Reports. 2 June–3 Oct. 1923.
        2. Irregular Activity. 2 June–3 Oct. 1923.
    d. Radio Reports and Messages. 27 Feb.–7 Nov. 1923.

CW/Ops/6: Donegal Command.
    h. Communications Reports. 27 Dec. 1922–17 Jan. 1923.
    j. Communications Reports. 31 Jan.–31 July 1923.
    k. Intelligence Reports. 2 Sept. 1922–15 Feb. 1924.
    l. Intelligence Reports. 20 Dec. 1922–26 June 1923.
    m. Intelligence Reports. 11 Apr.–28 June 1923.
    n. General Weekly Summary. 6 Apr.–4 Oct. 1923.
    o. Radio Reports and Messages. 27 Feb.–12 Nov 1923.

CW/Ops/7: Western Command.
    a. Operations Reports.
        1. Operations Reports and some Radio Messages. 4 Oct.–
        1 Nov. 1922.
        2. Communications Reports. 1 Dec. 1922–22 Mar. 1923.
    b. Routine Reports on Irregulars. Sept–Dec. 1922.
    c. Combined File.
        1. Operations Reports. 27 Oct.–18 Dec. 1922.
        2. Irregular Activity. 27 Oct.–18 Dec. 1922.
    d. Civil Affairs.
        1. Civil Affairs–Police. 13 Nov. 1922–23 Jan. 1923.

Radio and Phone Reports:
CW/R/1–5: July 1922–July 1923.

Daily Press Survey:
M1/PR/1–3: Nov. 1922–June 1923.

Captured Documents:
Lot No. 11: Claremorris Papers, 2nd, 3rd and 4th Western Division.
Lot No. 30: Papers captured in a dug-out at Skreen, County Sligo.
Lot No. 112: Captured on Commandant Dick Walsh, Claremorris, Nov. 1922.
Lot No. 131: Letter captured on William Pilkington, Aug. 1923.
Lot No. 232: IRA Documents including 3rd. Western Division material.

Department of Defence Files:
A/3642: Protection of lands of Charles Phibbs at Bunninadden.
A/7160: Reports on attacks on the Sligo Leitrim and Northern Counties Railway.
A/7438: SS Tartar: General file of correspondence.
A/7588: Report on interview with Dr O'Donnell about army problems in Sligo.
A/7751: Report on the Sligo Town Hall attack.
A/8079: Operation Reports from Claremorris Command.
A/8083: Operation Reports from Donegal Command.
A/8125: Correspondence on the burning of Sligo Railway station, Jan. 1923.
A/8454: Civic Guards Monthly Reports, County Sligo, July 1923.

Collins Papers:
A/0629: IRA Divisional Organisation, 1921.
A/0747: A large quantity of Sligo Brigade material including Brigade I/O corres-
    pondence with HQRS and Report on Officers' Training Camp, Aug. 1921.

Other Material:
Roll of deceased personnel.
Deceased Members of the Defence Forces.
Special Infantry Corps Material, SIC 1 and 2.
Truce Liason Material.
Internment Prisoner Location Books.
Free State Army Census, Dec. 1922.

Irish Valuation Office

Valuation Books for County Sligo.

Garda Museum and Record Office

Gárda Siochána register of appointments.

Representative Church Body Library

Vestry Minute Book, St John's Parish, Sligo.

Grand Lodge of Freemasons Archive

Membership registers, Lodge 165,1895 to 1923; Lodge 20, 1872 to 1923.

Institute of Celtic Studies and Historical Research, Killiney, County Dublin

McEoin Papers:
C Series:
C57: Reports on Rahilly Irregulars.
      Western Command Intelligence Reports, Sept.–Nov. 1922.
      Report by Reports Officer, 3rd Western Division, 7 Nov. 1922.
      Report of Western Command Council Meeting (IRA) Feb. 1923.
      Report on Irregular Activities, Apr.–May 1923.
C60: War News Western Command, 14 July 1922.
      Lawlor's report of his campaign in the west, Dec. 1922.
      Report on the enquiry into the Sligo Town Hall attack, Dec. 1922.
CSD Series:
CSD76: Report by Commandant McCann on the attack and capture of
      Collooney Market House, July 1922.

Belfast

Public Record Office of Northern Ireland

J.M. Wilson's Papers:
D989A/9/7: J.M. Wilson's notes on his tour of County Sligo, 24 Feb. 1916.

London

Public Record Office

Colonial Office, Dublin Castle Records:
CO 762: Irish Grants Committee Records.
CO 904/20: UIL files.
CO 904/23: Reports on St Patrick's Day 1916, Sinn Féin Material.
CO 904/29: Irish Volunteers, Return of Arms, 28 Feb. 1917.
CO 904/114–6: Monthly RIC Reports, 1921.
CO 904/121: Agrarian Outrages, 1920–1.
CO 904/122: Illegal Drillings Midland and Connacht District, 1917.
CO 904/155: Alleged Truce Breaches by the IRA.
CO 904/157: Daily Railway Situation, 1920–1.
CO 905/10: Claims Registers, County Sligo.

Sligo

County Sligo Library

Sligo County Council Minute Books. 1920–3.
Sligo County Home and Hospital Committee Minute Books. Feb.–June 1923.
Sligo Union Board of Guardians Minute Books. 1920– July 1922.
Dromore West Miscellaneous Records. 1915–22.
North Sligo Comhairle Ceantair Sinn Féin Minute Book. Feb–July 1920.
Hennessy, S. *The Life and Career of John Jinks* (Typescript).
James Hunt, statement concerning his involvement with the Irish Volunteers 1916–1921.
Michael Nevin, statement to the Bureau of Military History dated 29 Mar. 1956.
Robinson Estate Office, Sligo: Letter Books, 1921–23.
Gray family, Ballynalough, statement re republican activities, 1920.
Martin Kelleher, Doocastle, *The History of Kilterra and Bunninadden*, transcript of recording made 5 Nov. 1959 by Owen B. Hunt.
Harlech Masonic Lodge. List of attendance at meetings 1918, 1919.
Sligo Constitutional Club Register of Candidates, 1905–29.

Sligo Town Hall

Sligo Corporation Minute Books, 1920–3.

Sligo Primary Schools

Daily Report Books 1921–3:
St Joseph's N.S., Culleens.
Moylough N.S.
Mullaghmore N.S. in Cliffony BNS.

Armagh

Archdiocese of Armagh, Records Centre

Fr O'Kane Papers:
Charles Gildea material.

In private possession

Batt Keaney statement.
Patrick McCannon statement.
Linda Kearns statement.
Ledger of Michael Coleman, General Merchant, Coolaney, 1904–30.

2. CONTEMPORARY NEWSPAPERS AND PERIODICALS

Daily Bulletin
Éire
Free State
Iris an Ghárda
Poblacht na hÉireann
Poblacht na hÉireann (Scottish Edition)
Poblacht na hÉireann War News
The Connachtman
The Irish Bulletin
The Irish Farmer
The Irish People
The Plain People
The Roscommon Herald
The Sligo Champion
The Sligo Independent
The Voice of Labour
The Western People

3. GOVERNMENT PUBLICATIONS

Eighteenth Abstract of Labour Statistics of the United Kingdom, PP 1926, v xxix (29)
(Cmd 2740)
Journal of the Department of Agriculture and Technical Instruction (Dublin),
vols xxi, xxii and xxiii.
Saorstát Éireann. Statistics relating to National Education in Ireland for the years
1920–21, 1921–22, 1922–23.
Saorstát Éireann. *Cost of Living Reports, June and Oct. 1922, Jan., Apr., July and Oct.
1923.*
Saorstát Éireann. *Report of the Commission on Prices, 1923.*
Saorstát Éireann. *Census of Population 1926.*
Dáil Éireann. *Parliamentary Debates*, Vol. 2, 6 Jan. 1922–27 Mar. 1923.
Dáil Éireann. *Private Sessions of Second Dáil.* 18 Aug.–14 Sept. 1921 and 14 Dec.
1921–6 Jan. 1922.

4. INTERVIEWS WITH SURVIVORS

Michael Burgess	Kathleen Carroll
Jackie Conlon	Paddy Dwyer
Agnes Farry	Willie Frizzelle
Martin Dan Gallagher	Thomas Harrington
Jim Hever	Pat Hunt
Bat Keaney	Thomas Kilcoyne
Mary McGuinn	Andy Marren
Michael O'Beirne	Sis O'Brien
John Sweeney	Michael Walsh.

5. PUBLISHED WORKS: SLIGO

Campbell-Perry, VW Bro. R.H. 'A Glimpse of Freemasonry in Sligo
1767–1951' in *The Lodge of Research Transactions for Years 1949–1957*. Dublin,
1959.
Duffy, P.J. *Killaville and its People*. Ballymote, 1985.
Farry, Michael. *Sligo 1914–1921: A Chronicle of Conflict*. Trim, 1994.
Farry, Neal. 'Ballymote during "the Troubles"', in *Corran Herald*. May, 1986.
Finn, John. *The History of Gurteen*. Boyle, 1981.
Freeman, T.W. 'Population Distribution in County Sligo' in *Irish Geography*, 17
(1943–4).
Jennings, J.J. *The Big Stone*. Athlone, 1989.
Kilgannon, Thady. *Almanac for North Connaught*. Sligo, 1905.
Kilgannon, Thady. *Directory of County Sligo*. Sligo, 1907.
McGowan, Thady and Brehony, Tom. 'Keash/Culfadda Volunteer movement' in
Corran Herald. July, 1987.

MaGowan, Joe. *In the Shadow of Benbulben*. Manorhamilton, 1993.

McCabe, Alec. 'Cradling a Revolution' in *An tÓglach*. Christmas, 1962.

McCabe, Alec. Interview by Dermot Mullane, *The Irish Times*, 6–7 May 1970.

McGuinn, James. *Curry*. Cavan, 1984.

McGuinn, James. *Sligo Men in the Great War*. Belturbet, 1994.

McTernan, John (ed.). *Sligo GAA – A Centenary History 1884–1984*. Sligo, 1984.

McTernan, John C. *Worthies of Sligo*. Sligo, 1994.

McTernan, John C. (ed). *Sligo: Sources of Local History*. Sligo, 1994.

McTernan, John C. *At the Foot of Knocknarea: A Chronicle of Coolera in Bygone Days*. Sligo, 1990.

Murphy, W.M. *The Yeats Family and the Pollexfens of Sligo*. Dublin, 1971.

O'Dowd, Mary. 'Sligo', in Anngret Simms and J.H. Andrews (eds), *Irish Country Towns*. Dublin, 1994.

Reid, Steven. *Get to the Point at County Sligo Golf Club*. Naas, 1991.

Robinson, Lennox. *Bryan Cooper*. London, 1931.

Sligo Champion Centenary Number. Sligo, 1936.

Sligo Champion Sesquicentenary Supplement. Sligo, 1986.

Smithson, A.P. (ed.). *In Times of Peril: Leaves from the diary of Nurse Linda Kearns*. Dublin, 1922.

6. PUBLISHED WORKS: OTHER

Andrews, C.S. *Dublin Made Me, An Autobiography*. Cork, 1979.

Augusteijn, Joost. *From Public Defiance to Guerilla Warfare*. Amsterdam, 1994.

Baker, Joe. *My Stand for Freedom*. Westport, 1988.

Blake, Frances M. *The Irish Civil War and what it still means to the Irish people*. London, 1986.

Boyce D.G. (ed.). *The Revolution in Ireland 1879–1923*. Basingstoke, 1988.

Brennan, Niamh. 'A political minefield: Southern Loyalists, the Irish Grants Committee and the British Government, 1922–31', *I.H.S.*, xxx, no. 119 (May 1997).

Brady, Conor. *Guardians of the Peace*. Dublin, 1974.

Buckland, Patrick. *Irish Unionism 1: The Anglo-Irish and the New Ireland 1885 to 1922*. Dublin, 1972.

de Burca, Padraig and Boyle, John F. *Free State or Republic? Pen Pictures of the historic Treaty session of Dáil Éireann*. Dublin, 1922.

Casey, James. 'Republican Courts in Ireland 1919–1922', *Irish Jurist*, v (1970).

Casey, James. 'The Genesis of the Dáil Courts', *Irish Jurist*, ix (1974).

Cohan, Al. *The Irish Political Elite*. Dublin. 1992.

Comerford, R.V., Cullen, Mary, Hill, J.R., Lennon, Colm (eds). *Religion, Conflict and Coexistence in Ireland*. Dublin, 1990.

Coogan, Tim Pat. *Michael Collins*. London, 1990.

Coogan, Oliver. *Politics and War in County Meath 1913–23*. Dublin, 1983.

Cunningham, John. *Labour in the West of Ireland*. Belfast, 1995.

Curran, Joseph M. *The Birth of the Irish Free State 1921–1923*. Alabama, 1980.

English, Richard. *Radicals and the Republic*. Oxford, 1994.

English, Richard and Walker, Graham (eds). *Unionism in Modern Ireland*. Belfast, 1996.

Farragher, Sean P. *Dev and his Alma Mater*. Dublin, 1984.

Fitzpatrick, David. *Politics and Irish Life 1913–1921: Provincial Experience of War and Revolution*. Dublin, 1977.

Fitzpatrick, David. 'The Geography of Irish Nationalism, 1910–1921', in *Past and Present*, lxxvii (1978).

Gallagher, Michael. 'The Pact General Election of 1922' in *I.H.S.*, xxi, no. 84 (Sept. 1979).

Gallagher, Michael (ed). *Irish Elections 1922–44: Results and Analysis*. Limerick, 1993.

Garvin, Tom. *The Evolution of Irish Nationalist Politics*. Dublin, 1981.

Garvin, Tom. *Nationalist Revolutionaries in Ireland*. Oxford, 1987.

Garvin, Tom. *1922: The Birth of Irish Democracy*. Dublin, 1996.

General Assembly of the Presbyterian Church in Ireland, *Minutes of the Proceedings of*. Vols 12 (1911–1915), 13 (1916–1920) and 14 (1921–1924).

Greaves, C. Desmond. *Liam Mellows and the Irish Revolution*. London, 1971.

Hart, Peter. *The IRA and its Enemies*. Oxford, 1998.

Harte, Frederick E. *The Road I have Travelled: The experiences of an Irish Methodist Minister*. Belfast, n.d.

Hill, Ronald J. and Marsh, Michael (ed.). *Modern Irish Democracy – Essays in Honour of Basil Chubb*. Dublin, 1993.

Hopkinson, Michael. *Green Against Green – The Irish Civil War*. Dublin, 1988.

IAOS Annual Reports, 1921, 1922 and 1923.

Johnson, David. *The Interwar Economy in Ireland*. Dublin, 1985.

Kennedy, Robert E. *The Irish – Emigration, Marriage and Fertility*. Berkeley, 1973.

Kostick, Conor. *Revolution in Ireland*. London, 1996.

King, Cecil A. *Memorabilia*. Donegal ?, 1989.

Kotsonouris, Mary. *Retreat from Revolution*. Dublin, 1994.

Lyons, F.S. *Ireland since the Famine*. London, 1982.

Lawlor, S. *Britain and Ireland, 1914–23*. Dublin, 1983.

Lawlor, S.M. 'Ireland from truce to treaty: war or peace', in *I.H.S.*, xxii, no. 85, (March 1980).

Litton, Helen. *The Irish Civil War: An Illustrated History*. Dublin, 1995.

Macardle, Dorothy. *The Irish Republic*. Dublin, 1968 paperback edn.

McColgan, John. *British Policy and the Irish Administration, 1920–22*. London 1983.

McDowell, R.B. *Crisis and Decline: The Fate of the Southern Unionists*. Dublin, 1997.

MacEoin, Uinseann. *Survivors*. Dublin, 1980.

McNiff, Liam. *A History of the Garda Síochána*. Dublin, 1997.

Miller, David W. *Church, State and Nation in Ireland 1898–1921*. Dublin, 1921.

Mitchell, Arthur. *Labour in Irish Politics*. Dublin, 1974.

Mitchell, Arthur. *Revolutionary Government in Ireland – Dáil Eireann 1919–22*. Dublin, 1995.

Morrison, George. *The Irish Civil War: An Illustrated History*. Dublin, 1981.

Neeson, Eoin. *The Civil War in Ireland 1922–23*. Cork, 1966.

O'Connor, Emmet. *Syndicalism in Ireland 1917–1923*. Cork, 1988.

O'Donoghue, Florence. *No Other Law*. Dublin, 1986.

Ó Duibhir, Ciarán. *Sinn Féin, The First Election 1908*. Manorhamilton, 1993.

O'Farrell, Padraig. *Who's Who in the Irish War of Independence*. Cork, 1980.

O'Farrell, Padraig. *The Séan MacEoin Story*. Cork, 1981.

Ó Gadhra, Nollaig. *Civil War in Connacht 1922–1923*. Cork, 1999.

O'Malley, Ernie. *The Singing Flame*. Dublin, 1978.

Patterson, Henry. *The Politics of Illusion*. London, 1997.

Prager, Jeffrey. *Building Democracy in Ireland*. Cambridge, 1986.

Regan, John M. 'The Politics of Reaction: The Dynamics of Treatyite Government and Policy, 1922–33', in *I.H.S.*, xxx, no. 120 (Nov. 1997).

Royal Irish Academy. *Atlas of Ireland*. Dublin, 1979.

Rumpf, E. and Hepburn, A.C.. *Nationalism and Socialism in Twentieth-Century Ireland*. Liverpool, 1977.

Towey, Thomas 'The Reaction of the British Government to the 1922 Collins–de Valera Pact', *I.H.S.*, xxii, March 1980.

Townshend, Charles. 'The Irish Republican Army and the Development of Guerilla Warfare, 1916–1921', in *English Historical Review*, xciv (April 1979).

Townshend, Charles. *Political Violence in Ireland*. Oxford, 1983.

Valiulis, Maryann Gialanella, *Portrait of a Revolutionary – General Richard Mulcahy*. Dublin, 1992.

Williams, T.D. (ed.). *The Irish Struggle 1916–26*. London, 1966.

Younger, Calton. *Ireland's Civil War*. London, 1968.

INDEX

Bradshaw, Robert George, 19, 20, 23–4,
 28–30, 50, 61, 119, 186
 anti-Treaty, 37
 Treaty election, 68
Brady, Conor, 166
Brehony, Harry, 79
Brennan, Jack, 23, 27–9, 40, 61, 108, 155
Brennan, Martin, 38, 61, 105, 107
 Civil War, 78–9, 86
British army, 15, 18, 41, 50, 124, 125, 186
 departs, 51–2, 185
Brugha, Cathal, 32
Bundoran, Co. Sligo, 80, 132, 133
Bunninadden, Co. Sligo, 109, 142, 165, 200
 agrarian agitation, 195, 196
 crime, 171, 172–3
 Protestants, 193
Burke, Captain T., 31–2
Butler, Revd P.A., 64

Cairns, Co. Sligo, 173–4
Calry, Co. Sligo, 59, 89, 180, 185, 186
Campbell Perry, Harper, 32, 184, 186, 187, 190
Carney, Tom, 76
Carrick-on-Shannon, Co. Leitrim, 55, 60, 172
Carrignagat, Co. Sligo, 91
Carroll, Paddy, 84
Carter, Sergeant John, 125
Carty, Frank, 15, 30, 50, 55, 106, 112, 127
 anti-Treaty, 38, 39, 45, 46–7
 arrest, 12, 197
 Civil War, 75–86, 89, 92, 93
  area of activity, 101, 102–3, 105, 108
  spies shot, 87–8, 107
 jail rescue, 11, 13
 report on, 32
 Sligo County Council, 18, 19, 20, 21, 23,
  27, 29
 Sligo County Home, 25–6
 South Sligo O/C, 32
 Treaty election, 57, 62, 71, 72
Casey, James, 163
Castlebaldwin, Co. Sligo, 165
Castlebar, Co. Mayo, 55, 59, 82
Castleconnor, Co. Sligo, 42
Catholic church, 64
 attitude to IRA, 18, 33–5
 reactions to Treaty, 42, 53–4
Catholic Institute, 135
census, 1911, 119–21
Chaffpool, Co. Sligo, 13
Charlestown, Co. Mayo, 62
Christmas, 137–8
Church of Ireland, 180–1, 206
Civic Guard, 56, 93, 166, 171–2, 175, 206
 distribution of recruits, 112–13
Civil War, 25, 28, 31, see also Civil War, Sligo
 ceasefire, 92–3
 compared with War of Independence,
  104–6
 drift to, 50–74
 food prices, 145

historiography, 1
 social dimension of split, 115–19
 truce rumoured, 81–2
Civil War, Sligo
 casualties, 93
 communications disruption, 103
 course of, 75–94
  August–October 1922, 79–87
  January–June 1923, 90–4
  July 1922, 75–9
  November 1922–January 1923, 87–90
 and daily life, 131–56, 205
  agricultural prices, 149–52
  communications, 131–4
  co-operative creamery societies, 152–5
  food prices, 145–7
  industrial unrest, 147–9
  school attendance, 142–5
  social activities, 135–9
  sports, 135, 136, 139–42
 distribution of activists, 106–14
 distribution of incidents, 98–104
 end of, 202–7
 geography of, 95–114
 Jinks dispute, 23
 law and order, 170–6, 206
 participation, 204–5
  age of, 125–8
  and father's occupation, 119–21
  house class and valuation, 122–5
  and land valuation, 121–2
  officers and rank and file, 128–30
  social background, 115–30
  Protestant victims, 195–201
 reprisals, 91
Clancy, J.J., 7, 20–1, 27
Clare, Co., 15
Claremorris, Co. Mayo, 58, 81, 86, 133, 154
Claremorris Command, Free State army, 90, 93
Cliffony, Co. Sligo, 8, 11, 12, 13, 33, 157
Clonfert, Bishop of, 34
Clonmel, Co. Tipperary, 89
Cloonamahon sanatorium, 31
Cloonloo, Co. Sligo, 41
Collins, Michael, 14, 39, 43, 50, 73, 125, 168
 de Valera pact, 64–70
 Northern policy, 52
 Treaty election, 58, 59
Collooney, Co. Sligo, 11, 13, 34, 41–2, 57,
  145, 154, 180
 barracks, 14
 Civic Guard, 172
 Civil War, 76, 78–80, 82, 85–6, 89, 94,
  103, 109, 170
  crime rates, 171
  fair, 151
  GAA, 139
  incidents, 88, 100
 courts, 159, 167, 169
 cross-border raids, 52
 IRA dispute with priest, 35
 IRA training camp, 31